HOW TO LOOK IT UP
ONLINE

Praise for Alfred Glossbrenner's other books,
The Complete Handbook of Personal Computer
Communications, **Completely Revised and Updated . . .**

"For intelligence and thoroughness, no one else comes close."
—*The Whole Earth Software Review*

"Invaluable—and how! Highly recommended."
—Peter A. McWilliams

"The first truly complete book on 'connecting your computer to the world.'"
—*Esquire*

"Essential . . ."
—*Forbes*

"Definitely required reading . . ."
—*Microcomputing*

"The book's enthusiasm and clarity will never age."
—*The Whole Earth Software Catalog*

"Still considered by many insiders to be the best."
—UPI

"Excellent . . ."
—*Dallas Morning News*

"One of the best . . . a readable, useful consumer's guide to the communications supermarket."
—*Popular Computing*

"One of the best and most complete sources of information. There have probably been more words written about this book than any other serious book in the personal computer field."
—*Personal Computing*

"If any book can be described as 'the bible' on telecomputing, this is it."
—*Link-Up*

... *How to Buy Software* ...

"A tour de force of software and all its possibilities."
—*The New York Times*

"I wouldn't consider, for a moment, buying a piece of computer software until I read this book."
—Peter A. McWilliams

"Glossbrenner has written the most comprehensive software guide in print today."
—Martin B. Schneiderman, director,
Computer Education Programs,
Educational Testing Service (ETS)

"Head, shoulders, and torso above the competition. . . . The definitive text—the book we most strongly recommend."
—*The Whole Earth Software Catalog*

"This book, like the last one, is crammed with information—very solid, sensible information. Recommended."
—*The Philadelphia Inquirer*

"This book contains a wealth of practical, usable material collected for the first time under one cover."
—*Popular Computing*

"The most straightforward and literate introduction to the mysteries of (micro based) computing I've yet come across."
—Russell Jones
Computer Talk

. . . and *How to Get FREE Software*

"Truly has chapter and verse on the subject."
—*The Whole Earth Software Catalog*

"The best buy in computer books is *How to Get FREE Software* by Alfred Glossbrenner."
—*Detroit News*

"Extremely informative and readable. . . . Unlike most other free software guides . . . a fine reference to what's available, a superior treatment of where the programs are and how to obtain them."
—*Popular Computing*

"A marvelous book! Alfred Glossbrenner has put into *How to Get FREE Software* a wealth of tips and information about free software previously available only by word of mouth."
—Andrew T. Williams
author of *Keeping Track of Your Stocks*

"*How to Get FREE Software* is solid gold. The money saved could easily pay for a second computer (or justify the first one). This book would have saved me at least a year of my life."
—Tom Beeston
co-author of *Hooking In*

"One of the few 'must buy' books for every computer owner. Buy this before you start buying software and you won't *need* to buy software! Not only proves that 'the good stuff' is free, but tells exactly how to get it."
—Doug Clapp, *InfoWorld*

"A richly detailed resource book which will keep readers busy exploring its hundreds of sources of free software . . . deserves a place of honor within easy reach of your computer."
—*Wall Street Computer Review*

"The most complete . . ."
—*Money*

"Could pay for itself many times over."
—*Science*

HOW TO LOOK IT UP
ONLINE

*Get the Information Edge
with Your Personal Computer*

Alfred
Glossbrenner

A
Glossbrenner
Guide

St. Martin's Press   New York

The author has made every effort to check information such as shipping
charges, addresses, telephone numbers, and availability of updated products,
but cautions the reader that these are subject to change. Readers should verify
costs and product descriptions with sources before ordering.

Library of Congress Cataloging in Publication Data

Glossbrenner, Alfred.
  How to look it up online.

  Includes index.
  1. On-line data processing.   2. Information
retrieval.   I. Title.
QA76.55.G57   1987   025.5'24   86-27945
ISBN 0-312-00132-0 (paperback)
ISBN 0-312-00133-9 (hardcover)

First Edition

10 9 8 7 6 5 4 3 2 1

Contents

PART I • Essentials

PART II • Profiling the Majors

Contents

PART III • The Information

Contents

HOW TO LOOK IT UP
ONLINE

Part I:

—ESSENTIALS—

Introduction
The Information Edge

This is a book about power. Not political, military, or economic power, but the energizing substratum that lies beneath these and every other form of power: the power of information. Whether you're a politician, a general, a captain of industry—or a corporal on the way up—success almost always depends on having the right information:

- How many times did your opponent vote against a particular issue over the last ten years? What corporations, labor unions, or political action committees have donated money to his campaign? (Chapter 18)

- What's the *real* financial condition of the firm you're negotiating to acquire? Which of its key employees have left or been promoted in the last five years? (Chapter 16)

- Is there an investment play in the consumer electronics field, or would you be better off staying in mutual funds? What *privately* held Midwestern specialty stores have a current ratio of 1.2? (Chapter 16)

- Quick! The vice president has just announced he's having lunch with a prospective client. You have one hour to find out where she went to school, the positions she has held during her career, and the charitable organizations she actively supports. And, oh yes, see if she's ever been quoted in *Time, Business Week, Forbes, Fortune,* or *The Wall Street Journal.* (Chapters 13, 14, and 15)

3

Most people aren't aware of it yet, but all of this information can be obtained instantly—whenever you want it, from wherever you happen to be on the globe. All it takes is a telephone, a communicating personal computer, and access to one or more online electronic databases.

You also need to know *where* to look and *how* to look for the information you seek. And that's what this book will show you. Chapter 1 explains how the book is laid out and how to use it to best advantage. But before moving on to the essential nuts and bolts, it's important to have an idea of the kind of power and the kinds of problems the new "information technology" has delivered to your doorstep.

Riches and Frustrations

There is so much information available electronically today that simply choosing the right database is no small task. For example, in the fall of 1979 there were 400 "machine readable databases" worldwide. There are now over 3,000. And according to Ken Duzy, co-editor of the authoritative *Cuadra Directory of Online Databases*, an average of three new databases become available each business day. ("Cuadra," by the way, is pronounced "Qwah-dra.")

Of course not all of these are heavy-hitting, major-league databases. Single electronic newsletters are included in those figures, as are such non-database features as electronic online clubs and special interest groups. But any way you look at it, it's still an embarrassment of riches. Oddly, this is in itself a problem. Having so much information available can be almost as bad as having none at all, for all the good it will do you. The quantity is simply overwhelming. And it can be enormously frustrating. It's one thing to know that the information you need exists in a library somewhere, buried so deeply within the stacks that no one could ever find it. It is quite another to know that the same information could be scrolling up your PC screen in seconds—if only you knew where to look for it online.

At the Point of the Pyramid

But selecting the right database is only part of the task. Each database offers you access to literally hundreds of magazines and journals or newspapers or research reports and analytical studies or some other type of publication. Indeed, if you own a communicating personal computer and a modem, you're sitting on the point of an information pyramid. Move down one level and you discover 3,000 databases. Move down another level and you discover that a single database can cover hundreds of magazines. Move down once again and you find that a decade's worth of issues of a single magazine can contain hundreds or even thousands of articles.

A final iteration and you're at the base of the pyramid surrounded by the individual pieces of each article. Here paragraphs lie like grains of sand—hundreds of millions of them stretching in every direction as far as the eye can see, with tens of thousands more springing into electronic existence each day as current databases are updated and new ones come online.

And you're supposed to locate just those paragraphs that will tell you, say, how wind power compares to the cost of traditional methods of generating electricity? Good luck. We'll check back with you around, oh about the year 2000 or so to see how you're making out.

Information in an Instant

Actually, though good luck is always welcome when searching online, there's no need to hang a rabbit's foot from your disk drive. Once you know where to look and which commands to key in to get the database computer to do your bidding, you can find the answer to the above question in about 12 minutes. And here it is:

> Cost estimates of wind power range from 3.25c/kwh (cents/kilowatt hour) to 10c/kwh. The installed cost of wind turbines is estimated to be $1,000-2,500/kw as compared to $800/kw for fossil fuel plants and $1,050/kw for a nuclear plant.

This information is from *Chemical Week* (May 13, 1981), one of 660 magazines and journals—everything from *Accounting Review* to *Datamation; Foreign Affairs* and *Fortune* to *Sales & Marketing Management; Wharton Magazine* and *The Yale Law Journal* to *ZIP/Target Marketing*—covered by a single database.

Feeling lucky, we decided to broaden the search and enter a command to look for facts on the largest wind turbine as well as for information about the relative cost of wind power. We searched a second database of 300 trade and industry journals *(Automotive News* to *World Oil)* and a third database covering over 400 general interest magazines *(American Heritage* to *Yachting)*.

From the *Tulsa Business Chronicle* (January 21, 1985) came the information that commercial capacity wind turbine systems cost a minimum of $10,000 and that the industry was feeling the effect of lower energy prices and the end of federal tax credits. But as a result of all three searches we learned that:

• General Electric's Space Division contracted with NASA to build the world's largest wind turbine, the first in the megawatt power range *(Public Utilities Fortnightly*, December 16, 1976).

- The Department of Energy estimated that by the year 2000 wind power will account for roughly 4% of U.S. power requirements *(Chemical Week,* May 13, 1981).

- In 1983 California led the country in wind power production with over 1,400 commercial windfarms in four locations, with a total capacity of 72,000 kilowatts. Most of these were financed through limited partnerships made attractive by federal and state tax credits and rapid depreciation schedules *(Dun's Business Month,* July 1983).

- Most of those tax credits were set to expire at the end of 1985 *(Forbes,* June 3, 1985).

- By 1983, GE had decided to build the above-mentioned "world's largest wind turbine" in Hawaii for the Hawaiian Electric Company *(Solar Age,* August 1983).

- Approximately 39% of captured wind energy can be converted to electricity, according to the DOE's national wind-assessment studies. The largest wind turbine as of 1981 was located in the Bonneville Salt Flats in Utah and began operations early that year *(Electrical World,* May 1981).

Now for the punch line: The total time required to search through every issue of over 1,000 magazines and journals dating back to 1971—a collection of over 2.38 *million* paragraphs—was 25 minutes. And by far the largest component of that was the time required to display the retrieved information on the screen. The total cost: $7.61.

Compare *that* to the cost of sending a $23,000-a-year research assistant to the library for a week and you begin to get some idea of the power that lies at the fingertips of anyone with a communicating personal computer. If that someone happens to be a competitor—in business, in investing, in politics, in school, or in any other arena—he or she will have an information edge that you may not be able to overcome.

The Need for Information Skills

Clearly, a familiarity with information technology—or a high degree of "information literacy," to use an unfortunate but increasingly popular term—is more crucial now than it has ever been. It doesn't matter what you do for a living or where you are in the corporate structure. It doesn't matter whether you plan to conduct your own searches or expect to have them done by an assistant. You've got to know what this new tool can and cannot do if you are ever going to benefit from it.

If you're a manager, you must know what kind of information is available electronically and what you're *not* likely to find online. You have to know the strengths and weaknesses of online databases, when to have a search done by staff personnel (and how to judge the effectiveness of that search), and when it makes sense to call in an information professional.

If you prefer to do your own searches, you've got to have a hands-on familiarity with the technology. The search-and-retrieval process is so fast that, as many managers are discovering, it is often quicker to conduct a search yourself than to explain what you want to someone else. This is especially true when you are not sure exactly what you are after, since when searching on your own you're free to browse. That makes it easy to experiment with "I wonder if . . ." information relationships, much as you might ask "What if . . ." questions involving the figures on an electronic spreadsheet.

You've got to know not only how to choose the right databases, but also how to confect a search strategy, what to do when it produces unexpected results and how to fix it "on the fly," and the various ways the information can be displayed or delivered.

Information technology, in short, is too important to be left to the technicians. Regardless of your field of activity, it is going to become increasingly necessary to develop a set of information *skills* if you want to succeed. Ultimately, those skills may turn out to be as important to your success as any you have yet mastered.

"Le Brigade de Cuisine"

No book can turn you into a *cordon bleu* chef of online information. Only you can do that and only through many hours of practice and study. But that level of skill really isn't necessary. You do not have to be an expert to successfully "look it up online."

Your initial search strategies may not be the most efficient and they may lack a certain intellectual elegance, but they will get the job done. We are not interested in artistry. We're interested in *results*. This book will give you the essential familiarity with the information industry, a working knowledge of the most important tools and techniques, and the major points of access you need to quickly become a top-flight short-order cook. With a little practice, you can easily become a competent member of the "brigade de cuisine."

As noted, Chapter 1 will get you started by explaining how the book is organized and how to use it most effectively. For those who have yet to go online, there is a quick-start guide at the end of that chapter to use in buying a modem and acquiring a free communications program. One thing that may be of special interest are the boxed "Online Tips" you'll find scattered throughout the book. These contain suggestions, ideas, addresses, asides, and other information that is relevant, but not necessarily vital, to the issue at hand.

Some Online Tips are also addressed to the more experienced personal computer user and online communicator and thus make no attempt to explain everything in detail. Consequently, if you are new to personal computer communications, some of this information may not make much sense the first time you read it. Don't let that slow you down. Instead, skip the tip and go back later after you've had a little more experience.

Online Tip: This is a tip for everyone. If you've read this far, there's a good chance that at some point in the future you are going to want to go online and search for information. And more than likely, you'll want to use one of the database vendors profiled in Part II. So instead of waiting until the need or the spirit moves you, do this. *Right now, contact the vendors at the toll-free numbers below and request an information packet and a subscription form.* This will not only help you decide which vendor or vendors to subscribe to, it will put you one step ahead of the game when you're ready to make your decision.

You will find quick snapshots of these systems in Chapter 3 and complete treatments, including phone numbers for non-U.S. residents, of each of them in Part II. For now, we suggest you simply call the toll-free numbers and ask for information on all of the systems offered by a given vendor. In other words, when you call DIALOG, ask for information on DIALOG, the Knowledge Index, and the DIALOG Business Connection. There's no obligation, and you can bet these companies will be glad to hear from you:

- DIALOG, the Knowledge Index (KI), and the DIALOG Business Connection (DBC). Call: 800-334-2564.

- BRS/SEARCH, BRS/BRKTHRU, and BRS/After Dark. Call: 800-227-5277 or 518-783-7251, collect.

- NEXIS from Mead Data Central (MDC). Call: 800-227-4908.

- ORBIT Search Service (SDC). Call: 800-421-7229 or 800-352-6689, in California.

- Dow Jones News/Retrieval Service (DJN/R). Call: 800-257-5114 or 609-452-1511, in New Jersey.

• VU/TEXT. Call: 800-258-8080 or 215-665-3300, in Pennsylvania.

• NewsNet. Call: 800-345-1301 or 215-527-8030, in Pennsylvania.

• Wilsonline. Call: 800-622-4002 or 800-538-3888, in New York.

Online Tip: Because it is likely that many readers will have gotten started online by subscribing to CompuServe, The Source, or Delphi, we have referred to these systems whenever a comparison seemed especially helpful. Each is covered in detail in *The Complete Handbook of Personal Computer Communications* (St. Martin's Press, New York). If you want more information on them please either consult that volume or contact the firms at these addresses:

CompuServe Information Service, Inc.
5000 Arlington Centre Blvd.
Columbus, OH 43220
(800) 848-8990 (contiguous U.S., except Ohio)
(614) 457-8650

The Source
1616 Anderson Road
McLean, VA 22102
(800) 336-3330 (contiguous U.S., except Virginia)
(703) 821-8888

General Videotex Corporation (Delphi)
3 Blackstone Street
Cambridge, MA 02139
(800) 544-4005 (except Massachusetts)
(617) 491-3393

...1...

Joining the Revolution:
How to Use this Book

W e're going to assume that you are familiar with the basics of personal computer communications. (If you don't know about modems and communications software, turn to the end of this chapter for a quick-start guide and some tips on how to get a free communications program.) Regardless of your level of online experience, however, there's a good chance that the first time you connect with a major-league information service, you'll feel like you're entering a foreign country.

The chapters here in *Part I: Essentials* are designed to ease the transition by telling you what you need to know about the information industry to use its resources effectively. Chapter 2 will show you what you can expect from a major-league database. (It's far different from what you may have become accustomed to on CompuServe, The Source, or on a bulletin board system.) You'll learn about bibliographic citations, abstracts, descriptor fields, and all the other elements that go into a database.

Chapter 3 will show you how databases are made available and how information is sold. Some products, for example, are offered by their creators as "single-subject databases." But hundreds of others are available under the same roof, as it were, through a "database vendor." Methods of charging for information vary widely in this largely immature industry. That makes it difficult to compare prices, but Chapter 3 will give you the tools you need to be a smart information consumer.

Database vendors are also known as "supermarket services," "encyclopedic databases," "online services," or "databanks," but to one degree or another all of them offer essentially the same basket of services. To use their systems effectively it is essential to be aware of the resources at your disposal. Chapter 4 outlines and explains those services and suggests ways to best take advantage of them.

Once you've become familiar with the look and feel of online information and how it is offered, you'll be ready to learn how to conduct a search. The commands you must enter to search any database are dictated by the software that governs the database vendor's system. Naturally, they vary considerably in syntax (the actual words or characters you must enter). But the search *concepts* are the same. Once you master the concepts, you can search *any* database on *any* vendor's system with just a few key commands. Chapter 5 will show you how to do it.

Next we'll consider a variety of software packages and other search aids. These "front end" programs are intended to make it easier for non-information professionals to use a database. The programs are not always successful, but every prospective searcher should be aware that they exist. Chapter 6 also discusses how and when to call in a professional searcher or "information broker" instead of attempting a complex search yourself. We'll also look at programs that let you retrieve information stored on a personal computer's hard disk using search commands that are nearly as powerful as those of a commercial online system. This means that you can download (capture) information, store it to disk, and search it again and again anytime you like.

Part II: Profiling the Majors begins with an Introduction that explains how to access the database systems in this book from virtually any country in the world. Then Chapters 7 through 11 profile eight of the major database vendors online today. Each chapter discusses how a given vendor handles subscriptions, billing, documentation and manuals, and the other points outlined in general terms in Chapters 3 and 4. At this writing there are over 454 online services worldwide. Most of the eight vendors profiled in Chapters 7 through 11 were chosen because they are among the largest systems and thus offer a wide variety of information.

Others were chosen because the kind of information they offer is likely to be of interest to most people. VU/TEXT, for example, is not an especially large system, but it is the nation's leading database of regional newspapers. As we'll see in Chapter 14, having access to newspapers from Anchorage to Fort Lauderdale and from Boston to Sacramento offers some very interesting possibilities.

Part III: The Information includes seven chapters that together present approximately 100 leading databases. Chapter 12 shows you how to tap into the Library of Congress and how to use other online resources to find any book, on any subject, anywhere in the world. Chapter 13 puts most of the world's magazines at your fingertips for instant scanning. Chapter 14 shows you how to do the same thing with leading national and regional newspapers, the "MacNeil/Lehrer News-hour," the AP and UPI wire services, and much more. Chapter 15 de-scribes how to search *Who's Who* and other databases to get information on people, as well as how to find out what companies make a particular type of product and where their stores are anywhere in the country. We'll also show you how to use the Electronic Yellow Pages to create instant, customized mailing or telemarketing lists.

Chapter 16 presents all the tools you need to become a super sleuth business and investment intelligence operative. It will show you how to get the balance sheets, income statements, and other information on privately held companies, for example, as well as how to pull up an on-demand TRW credit report on any one of millions of businesses for just $29. A veritable treasure trove of privileged investment information is available online as well. This is the kind of information leading bro-kerage firms and investment banking concerns usually provide to only their best customers, but much of it can be obtained electronically, and Chapter 16 will show you how to get it.

Chapter 17 will show you how to uncover scads of sales opportunities both here and abroad. It will show you how to quickly search through over 11,000 marketing studies and reports to locate one that discusses your products (or those of your competitors). We'll also show you how to call up demographic information for any region of the country and how to check the U.S. Patents and Trademarks Office to see if the prod-uct name you have in mind has been registered by anyone else.

Chapter 18 takes the wraps off the wealth of top-quality information (much of it free) available from the United States Government. We'll show you, for example, how to monitor the activities of any senator or representative, how to find out if a federal agency is about to issue a regulation that will affect your business, and how to quickly locate the one report, study, or other publication out of the tens of thousands is-sued by the government each year that deals with your subject of inter-est. Chapter 18 will also show you how to get Consumer and Producer Price Index figures, data from the Census Bureau, and any other statis-tic issued by the U.S. Government.

Appendix A will show you the easy way to import those statistics and other data into Lotus 1-2-3®, dBASE II® or III, or any other program for further processing. We'll also look at Chart-Master®, a program that will transform that data into virtually any kind of chart or graph you could want.

Appendix B will give you the tools you need to locate *other* online databases. Most of the major printed database directories are online themselves, making it easy to scan for the databases that cover the topic you have in mind. There are other books, magazines, and organizations you should know about as well. All of them are described in this appendix.

A Word About the Databases Selected

The online field is so huge that any book attempting to be comprehensive is destined to quickly devolve into little more than a catalog offering scant coverage of any given database. Such books have a place, to be sure, but while the typical 250-word database write-up found in most catalogs can be a good starting point, it isn't designed to tell you what you need to know to search a database effectively. Consequently, we have opted for selectivity and depth.

The individual databases were chosen because they offer the kind of information most personal computer users are likely to find of greatest value. Since most personal computer users are businesspeople, there is a distinct business orientation to the selection. In virtually every case we have directly contacted the companies who actually produce the databases and, where possible, obtained copies of the printed materials from which many of them are created.

We have tried to go "behind the screens," as it were, to talk to the people who produce the databases and run the online systems. When necessary we have asked where the information comes from, how far back in time the database goes, how often it is updated, what's the lag time between publication date and online availability, and always, what does it cost? This is the kind of information that *should* be in every database brochure and catalog description but isn't. Indeed, in a discouragingly large number of cases, even the people who work for the vendor or database producer did not know.

In at least one instance, an official at a major vendor, in whose information we had every reason to believe, gave us prices that turned out to be completely wrong. Against such incompetence, online searchers have no defense. Nor is there any defense against the inevitable changes that take place between the time a book is written and the time it is published. No book on this field can ever be completely up-to-date for very long. With this in mind, we have deliberately tried to present not only information about databases as they exist today, but also the tools and access points you need to keep up with them tomorrow.

Cultural Conflict and the Death of a Priesthood

There is one more thing you should be aware of before entering the world of online information: Some of its denizens don't think you should be here. The situation is changing, as it must, but it is not uncommon to read articles and opinion pieces in information industry trade journals that cast a baleful eye on the advent of the microcomputer and the Age of the End-User. ("End-user" is what information professionals call people like yourself.)

When the Information Industry Was Young

We in the microworld must never forget that when the information industry was aborning, there was no such thing as a personal computer. DIALOG, the largest of the database supermarket systems, first became available to the public in 1972. In contrast, the first personal computer, the mail-order, assemble-it-yourself MITS Altair 8800 (36 lights, 25 toggle switches, 256 *bytes*, no keyboard), wasn't introduced until 1975. And the personal computer revolution as a whole didn't really get started until 1982, following the introduction of the first IBM/PC in the fall of the previous year. Only recently have personal computers become a major factor in online communications.

During the information industry's formative years, the only way to obtain online information was with a dumb terminal. This was typically little more than a clunky electric typewriter coupled to the telephone with acoustic modem cups. Add to this the fact that most databases were created by and for professional librarians, and you begin to see the problem.

The evidence is everywhere. Even today, the industry's trade journals and publications reveal a consistent and fundamental lack of understanding of personal computers and the needs of the businesspeople who use them. This is one of the reasons why database brochures and promotional materials neglect to include information on cost, frequency of updating, and extent of coverage. A number of database marketers and customer service representatives we spoke with admit that they know virtually nothing about computers, communications software, or how they manage to get online. Says one: "Someone else set it up for me. I just put the disk in and turn on the machine."

The Profession as Priesthood

There is a second problem as well. It might be called the "Profession as Priesthood" approach adopted by some people in the industry. Its badge is the Master of Library Science (MLS) degree. And like every priesthood, it has its own special language, symbols, rituals, and signs.

This distressing attitude can best be characterized as elitist. The individuals who have it tend to think of themselves as gatekeepers to the world's information treasure houses. It is not difficult to find people in the information industry who scoff at the suggestion that a mere layman could locate what he or she was looking for using a major-league database. You don't have the training. You haven't gone to school. You must be joking.

Thankfully this attitude is not typical of the majority of information professionals. Most are bright, dedicated people who enjoy pitting their wits against the challenge of a library patron's or other individual's information request. If they weren't eager to help they wouldn't have gotten into the profession in the first place. Many are perceptive enough to realize that the influx of micro users will only increase the demand for their skills and services.

Online Tip: One especially bright bulb in the library field is Eric S. Anderson, editor of "The Wired Librarian's Newsletter." As its masthead proclaims, this is "a monthly rag with library hardware and software opinions found nowhere else . . . published whenever we feel like it which historically has been once a month." Mr. Anderson's knowledge is deep and his reviews are both pointed and refreshingly frank.

A subscription is $15 a year, making it an ideal and affordable way to say "thank you" with a gift subscription to a librarian who has been of special help, particularly if he or she is interested in computers. For more information contact:

> Mr. Eric S. Anderson
> Wired Librarian's Newsletter
> 20 Congress Avenue
> Sioux City, IA 51104

Nevertheless, the priesthood mentality still exists, just as it does in the mainframe world. And this, combined with an improving but still lagging familiarity with microcomputers, will affect *you*. It may affect your dealings with customer service people at a database or a vendor. Someone who is unfamiliar with communications software isn't likely to be much help if strange characters are inexplicably appearing on your screen whenever you log on to a particular system.

It definitely affects the "user interface" you'll encounter on many information systems. They generally lack the spiffy look and feel of the more consumer-oriented systems. And if you're an experienced Source or CompuServe user, you'll be frustrated by the fact that on many systems there is no way to turn off time-consuming menus or control the screen width or number of lines displayed before the system pauses. In effect, the design of many of these systems has changed little since the days when users had nothing but printing dumb terminals. Though things are definitely getting better.

Perhaps most important of all, this cultural conflict influences what you are offered and what and how you are expected to pay for it. We'll discuss this subject in detail in Chapter 3. For now it is enough to say that most database producers have no idea that they are really in the business of providing services. As a result, they tend to hoard their information, parceling it out on a "the more you pay the more we display" basis.

Conclusion

The online information industry is still very young. Accustomed to serving only a relatively small group of professionally trained searchers, it has yet to make the leap into the age of the microcomputer. Ultimately, however, the conflict must disappear because the two cultures need each other. Micro users need the information only the information industry can provide. And if that industry's enormous investment in hardware and in the labor of data entry and database preparation is ever to pay off, it needs to attract micro users by the millions.

The situation will take a while to sort itself out. In the meantime, remember that you are about to enter the world of the information professional. They *live* here, and you must of necessity speak their language and play by their rules.

Now let's start bilding some bridges.

———————————— **Special Section** ————————————

A Quick-Start Guide to Modems and Communications Software

The Complete Handbook of Personal Computer Communications devotes a total of 113 pages to modems and communications software. Since it is part of the Glossbrenner canon, we naturally suggest that you buy or borrow a copy of it. However, if you want to go online as soon as possible, if you do not need to know how communications works or all the options that are open to you, and if you will accept our advice, it's very simple: Buy a genuine Hayes® or Hayes-compatible modem and contact one of the sources listed below for a copy of a public domain (free for the price of a disk) or user-supported (contribution requested) communications program.

Modems

A modem's job is to sit between your computer and the telephone line and translate (*modulate/dem*odulate) signals from one to the other. We suggest that you get a stand-alone, 1200 bit-per-second (bps) Hayes or Hayes-compatible modem. A stand-alone modem is a separate "box" that can be used with any computer, does not take up an expansion slot, and does not add its heat to the insides of your system. You'll need a communications (RS-232C) port to plug the modem into. If you don't already have such a port, see your computer dealer for details.

A speed of 1200 bps is the accurate way to refer to what is often called "1200 baud." Modems capable of 2400 bps are available, but many database vendors do not offer this speed. Besides, 2400 bps is usually not cost-effective when conducting an online search. A speed of 300 bps, on the other hand, is too slow to be comfortable.

Hayes compatibility is important because most communications software is designed to work with a Hayes modem. Hayes is the IBM of modems. It sets the standards, both in quality and in the command language used for modem control. A Hayes modem is without a doubt the low-risk, hassle-free solution. However, it can be expensive. If you opt for a lower-cost clone, make sure that it is at least "Hayes command language compatible." That means that it will respond to the same commands that a genuine Hayes would. All of these commands begin with an AT (for "attention") and thus are sometimes referred to as "Hayes AT compatible commands."

One word of warning. If you buy a Hayes clone you should plan on paying about $125 for a 1200 bps unit. Prices will probably fall, but at this writing, modems selling in the $65 range may not have all of the capacitors, integrated circuits, and electronic filters needed for clean, largely error-free communications. This may not matter to you if you will be downloading only text, since an error is easily detected. But if you plan to also download computer software or statistical data, an el cheapo modem may be more trouble than it's worth.

Two of the best sources of low-cost and used equipment are *The Computer Shopper* and The Boston Computer Exchange. The first is a monthly publication in which the main feature is the full-page and classified advertising. You may be able to find copies on your local newsstand or at your bookstore. The cost is $2.50 per issue. Subscriptions are $18 a year. Contact:

> *The Computer Shopper*
> 407 S. Washington Avenue
> P.O. Box F

Titusville, FL 32780
(305) 269-3211

Source: TCS575
CompuServe: 70275,1023

The Boston Computer Exchange (BCE) is a matching or brokering service for computer equipment of all kinds. Each week it publishes a list of items for sale by their owners and their owners' asking price. BCE sells its list for $10. If you see something you're interested in, you contact BCE and BCE puts you in touch with the seller. BCE gets its commission from the seller. In mid-1986, used Hayes 1200 bps modems were going for $250. The same unit new, purchased at a discount through the mail, would be $400. You can order the current BCE list over the phone (Visa and MasterCard are accepted) or you can scan it on the Delphi system if you already have a modem and are looking for something else. For more information on BCE, contact:

Boston Computer Exchange
Box 1177
Boston, MA 02103
(617) 542-4414

Communications Software

IBMs and Compatibles
The best-selling communications program for these machines is CrossTalk XVI from Microstuff, Inc. ($95 at a discount through the mail). However, if you want to save some money without giving up features, the program to get is Qmodem ("cue-modem"). Written by John Friel III, this user-supported (contribution requested) software just keeps getting better and better. Starting with Qmodem Version 2.0, Mr. Friel added a script language that lets you program Qmodem to automatically dial the phone, log on to a system, download data and record it to disk, and sign off. It can do this at any time of day you specify. You don't even have to be there.

You can find Qmodem in most user group (computer club) software collections. Ask your computer dealer for the names of user groups in your area or see *How to Get FREE Software* (St. Martin's Press, New York) for information on how to plug into the worldwide free software-user group network. To be assured of obtaining the latest version, however, your best bet is to send $35 ($5 for the disk and postage and $30 for the requested contribution) directly to Mr. Friel. The manual is on the disk. Site licenses for corporations are available. Contact:

> The Forbin Project
> % John Friel III
> 4945 Colfax Avenue
> Minneapolis, MN 55409

Apple Macintosh, //e, //c, and Compatibles
We have been unable to find a public domain program for the Apple II line capable of operating at 1200 bits per second. One of the best 300 bps programs, however, is Disk 169, the Hayes Terminal Program disk, from the Washington Apple Pi users group. The cost is $5 for members, $8 for non-members, plus $1 for postage in both cases. The commercial program many Apple owners use is ASCII Express from Southwestern Data Systems (about $60 at retail).

If you own a Macintosh, one of the best user-supported (contribution requested) programs is Red Ryder Version 9.2. This too is available from Washington Apple Pi. The cost is $6 for members, and $9 for non-members, plus $1 for postage. Contact:

> DISKATERIA
> Washington Apple Pi, Ltd.
> 8227 Woodmont Avenue, Suite 201
> Bethesda, MD 20814
> (301) 654-8060

Commodore Computers
For any Commodore computer (64, 128, Amiga, etc.), the place to contact is the Toronto PET Users Group (TPUG), the largest Commodore group in the world. TPUG has extensive public-domain libraries for all Commodore machines. Prices vary with the disk format but typically run about $10, including postage. The group issues *TPUG* magazine ten times a year, and it's an excellent source of Commodore information. Membership fees vary depending on where you live. If you do not live in the Toronto area, the cost is $25 for U.S. and Canadian members. If you live overseas, the cost is $35 (seamail) or $45 (airmail). Contact:

> TPUG, Inc.
> 101 Duncan Mill Road, Suite G7
> Don Mills, ON
> Canada M3B 1Z3
> (416) 445-4524

...2...

Behind the Screens:
The Flesh, Blood, and Bones of an Online Database

Sometimes, particularly if you're new to the online communications field, electronic information doesn't seem quite real. You start your computer, load a communications program, and dial the phone. Then you tap a few keys, and like magic the latest stock quotes, statistics from the Consumer Price Index, or the full text of every article Peter Drucker ever wrote for the *Harvard Business Review* begins scrolling up your screen.

Where does it come from? Apparently out of the ether itself. For all one can tell, hitting the keys of a communicating computer could be the moral equivalent of spinning a Tibetan prayer wheel, each revolution of which transmits a copy of the paper prayer within to the gods. The difference is that the gods' response to the supplications of the modern personal computer are decidedly more manifest. And a lot quicker. Such is progress.

Arthur C. Clarke has observed that a sufficiently advanced technology is indistinguishable from magic. In reality, however, the system that delivers a complete summary of your major competitor's June advertising outlays to your screen (See Chapter 17) isn't advanced at all. It's just different from what you may have experienced so far. Like all systems, it can be understood, mastered, and manipulated to suit your ends.

The Links of the Chain

Whenever you want to tap into a database, the first step is to establish a communications chain linking you to the database's mainframe computers. The process starts when you load a communications program into your computer and plug the machine into a modem. For its

20

part, the modem plugs into the telephone line. Its job is to translate your computer's electrical impulses into sound so they can be sent over those lines and to translate sounds coming in from a remote computer into electrical impulses so they can be used by your machine.

The next step is to dial a local number that will connect you with Tymnet, Telenet, or some other packet switching network serving the database you wish to access. Once the connection is made, whatever you key in at your PC will be received by the large mainframe or minicomputers that house the database. Software running on those distant computers will interpret your commands and act accordingly.

Specific details will vary, but generally you can think of the computer center of a large database or online service as a huge air-conditioned room with a false floor hiding a rat's nest of cables and a ceiling concealing a grid of pipes capable of flooding the room with fire-asphyxiating gas in seconds at the first hint of flame.

The computers, large refrigerator-sized beasts, are over in the corner next to the rack systems that hold the modems and telephone multiplexors. The modems silently blink as calls come in or disconnect. The computers, each of which is called a "system," are also silent except for the constant hum of their cooling fans.

The real action is taking place in the center of the room, an area filled with row upon row of identical metal boxes. Each box is about the size and height of a top-loading washing machine, and there may be literally hundreds of them lined up cheek-by-jowl. Together they form the heart of the database, for each contains a disk pack holding millions of pieces of information.

In the microworld we would refer to these boxes as "hard disk drives." They are the direct descendants of the so-called "Winchester" drives introduced by IBM in 1973, though today they are usually referred to as DASD ("daz-dee") for Direct Access Storage Device(s). However, to cut down on this book's CAQ (Confusing Acronym Quotient), we'll continue to call them disk packs.

Online Tip: Why "Winchester?" IBM has never been keen on giving potential competitors hints about what it is planning to introduce. So like most high-tech companies it often uses code words to refer to products during the development stage. The original IBM/PC was supposedly code-named "Acorn," for example, and of course the PCjr was supposedly called "Peanut." Though the company specifically denies it, the PC Convertible was widely thought to have been code-named "Clamshell."

The first fixed disk—to use the IBM-approved term for hard

Online Tip (cont.)

disks—developed by the company was initially called the "30-30" because it could store 30 megabytes per side with an access time of 30 milliseconds. That was a bit too revealing, however, so someone decided to call the project "Winchester" after the famous Winchester 30-30 rifle.

A disk pack consists of a stack of large metal platters coated with magnetic film. An inch or less of space separates each platter in the pack from the one beneath it and the one above it. The whole arrangement occupies about as much space as a large layer cake, but it can hold up to two and a half billion letters or "characters." Since one "byte" is required to store one character, the capacity of these disk packs can be expressed as 2.5 "gigabytes." When mounted in a disk drive, the platters spin at speeds in excess of 60 revolutions per second.

Each disk drive in the computer center has an address number, of course, and once you've decided on the information you want, the database software can easily locate the disk pack with the platter containing it. The software also knows exactly where on the platter the information can be found. Thus, when you enter a command at your computer telling the remote system to display an article from *Time* magazine, the database mainframe orders the appropriate disk machine into action.

A device in the disk drive that can be likened to a large comb on a mechanical arm moves out from where it's been hiding in one corner of the machine. On the tip of each "tooth" of the comb is a read/write head similar in function to those found in a tape recorder. The teeth of the comb intersect the spinning disk pack in the spaces between the platters. Approximately 16 one-thousandths of a second after the drive receives its marching orders from the mainframe, the correct magnetic track on the correct platter is located and the appropriate read/write head, floating on a film of air directly above the disk surface, begins shoveling up the data.

The *Time* magazine article, long since reduced to digital form, consists of nothing but a pattern of tens of thousands of magnetic marks on the disk symbolizing either an "on" or an "off" pulse. Using those marks as its guide, the read/write head duplicates that pattern as a series of high- and low-voltage pulses at rates as fast as three megabytes (three million bytes or characters) a second. It pumps those pulses to the database's main computer, which in turn sends them to a modem for conversion into sound.

The sound waves leave the computer center, enter the telephone system, and soon arrive at your modem. Your modem converts them back into electrical pulses and feeds them to your computer, where a micro-chip turns them into human-readable characters and displays them on your screen. At that point, you can either send the characters to your printer or record them on a disk. Or you can just let them scroll off into space.

From Periodical to Platter to Printout

The electronic delivery system we've just described is the centerpiece of the online information industry. As noted in Chapter 1, the industry has been developing since 1972. That was the year the first passwords were issued for the RECON system that the Lockheed Missiles and Space Company had developed for NASA in 1968. RECON stands for "Remote Console Information Retrieval System," and the remote termi-nals it employed represented a major advance. Prior to that time, if you wanted to get information into or out of a mainframe computer you had to be on-site at the computer center with access to the machine's main console, card readers, magnetic tape drives, and drives capable of read-ing punched paper or Mylar® tape. Still in use today, RECON is the father of the commercial system operated by Lockheed's DIALOG In-formation Services, Inc.

There is nothing that is information industry-specific in what we've discussed so far. The same communications links, computer hardware, and disk packs are used in many industries. What is unique about the information is the kind of information that is stored on those disk packs, how it is formatted, and the capabilities of the software running on the mainframe systems.

If you're going to use these systems effectively and feel comfortable doing so, it is essential to know a thing or two about them. The best way to do that is to consider the process by which information becomes available online in the first place. That's what we'll do next, as we peer over the shoulder of someone considering the creation of a new data-base.

Present at the Creation: The Story of ADAM
The process starts with the desire of some man, woman, or company to make a particular body of information available for electronic search-ing and delivery. Why? To make a buck, of course. Hopefully lots of bucks, since ours is an information economy, and people will pay good money for good information.

Databases can best be thought of as *products*, and as with magazines, books, or manufactured goods, most are created because someone per-ceives an unfilled gap in the market. On the surface, at least, the raw economics of it look very good. Once printed information has been digitized into a pattern of bits and stored on a platter, what could be more profitable than selling that same pattern in the form of electronic impulses over and over again? No ink. No paper. No postage.

Let's assume the prospective database creator in this case is a fellow who has worked for several years in advertising and marketing. He knows from personal experience how crucial it is to have the right information at the right time in those fields. What is needed, he feels, is a master database of marketing information that would let a user instantly obtain the latest information on new product announcements, plans for new ad campaigns, current market share and demographic information, analyses, informed opinion, and everything else he has wished he had instant access to during his career—a database, in short, that would have all the answers for someone in the marketing or advertising professions.

He even has a name for the product. Following the practice of many existing databases, he has chosen a "friendly" acronym. He has decided to use the name ADAM for "Advertising, Demographics, and Marketing." When it finally becomes available, ADAM will join ERIC (Educational Resources Information Center), PETE (Peterson's College Database), MARC (Machine Readable Cataloging), LISA (Library and Information Science Abstracts), and the rest of the kids online.

Content and Coverage

The next thing our friend must decide is exactly what ADAM will contain. This is without a doubt the most crucial step, since the decisions made here influence absolutely everything else from the initial and ongoing costs of creating and maintaining ADAM to its competitive position in the information marketplace. This step is also the most difficult, since there are no rules. ADAM can cover anything its creator chooses, from magazine articles and press releases to doctoral dissertations and train schedules.

Other database creators have had things a lot easier, since many of their products are essentially online versions of single publications. The *Harvard Business Review* database (Chapter 13), the *New York Times* database (Chapter 14), and many of the directories of people, companies, and organizations discussed in Chapter 15 are all good examples.

Single-source databases like these are also easier to market to potential users. Because lots of people are familiar with the source publications, no one has to spend a great deal of time explaining or figuring out what the database covers. This is obviously not the case with our mythical ADAM database or with such very real products as Magazine Index, PTS PROMT (sic) or ABI/INFORM, each of which covers hundreds of diverse magazines. Consequently, as we'll see in Part III, one of the first things you should ask when approaching a database for the first time is: Where does the information come from?

To keep our example simple, we'll assume that our database creator has decided that ADAM should cover all of the major advertising and marketing journals *(Advertising Age, Sales and Marketing Management*, etc.), plus the leading trade magazines for every major industry. He might include *Variety* and *Billboard* for the entertainment industry, for example, as well as such publications as *Progressive Grocer, Nation's Restaurant News, Publishers Weekly*, and *Computer Retailer*. He might also include selective coverage of *Business Week, Time, Newsweek*, and *U.S. News and World Report*. Or he might not. Again, there are no rules.

When Should Coverage Begin?

We will assume that ADAM will cover a total of 300 publications. The next question is: How far back should the coverage go? Should it start at the current year or go back to 1980, for example? Should coverage of each magazine begin in the same year or would it be all right to go back, say, three years for some but only one year for others?

There are no easy answers here either, and we won't belabor the point. The important thing is to be aware that due to competition, the costs of database preparation, maintenance, and storage, and many other factors, different database producers have chosen to begin their coverage with different years. As noted elsewhere, it is usually not enough to know that a given database covers, say, *Business Week*. Often it is important to ask: When does the coverage begin?

The Question of Format

The next major point to be decided is the form the online information should take. Suppose you were to search ADAM for references to ice cream. You would enter a command like FIND ICE CREAM. The computer would conduct its search and tell you how many references to "ice cream" are in the database. In online argot, each reference is called a "hit." If you wanted to look at your hits, you would next enter a command like DISPLAY.

Let's suppose that you got five hits on "ice cream." You enter a command to look at the first reference. What do you suppose would then be displayed on your screen? Your instinctive answer would probably be "Why, the complete article, of course." You might be right. But more than likely, you would see something else.

The nature of the source material is ultimately the determining factor, but in general there are three main types of database formats:

bibliographic, full text, and statistical. As you can see from Figure 2.1, statistical databases are essentially collections of numbers like stock quotes, demographic tables, production and consumption statistics, and so on. This is clearly not a relevant format for ADAM.

——— Figure 2.1. Statistical Databases: Nothing but Numbers ———

The Consumer Price Index (CPI) maintained by the U.S. Bureau of Labor Statistics is probably the quintessential statistical database. With the exception of the few words of text used to label the contents of a table, it contains virtually nothing but numbers. For example, here's the CPI, by quarter (Q1, Q2, etc.) for the years 1979 through 1983 just as you would see it on your screen:

CONSUMER PRICE INDEX FOR ALL URBAN CONSUMERS SUBFILE
ALL ITEMS;
U.S. CITY AVERAGE;
UNADJUSTED DATA

INDEX (1967 = 100)

YEARS	Q1	Q2	Q3	Q4
1983	293.0	296.6	NA	NA
1982	283.0	287.3	292.8	293.4
1981	262.9	269.0	276.7	280.7
1980	236.5	245.0	249.6	256.2
1979	207.0	214.1	221.1	227.6

SOURCE: U.S. BUREAU OF LABOR STATISTICS   DIALOG FILE 175
DATES AVAILABLE: (1966–JUNE 1983)

Searching for and downloading this information from DIALOG took less than a minute and cost under $2.00. Extending the list backward to include years before 1979 would have cost a few cents more. Please see Chapter 18 for more information on the CPI database.

File, Record, and Field

As with all databases that cover magazines, newspapers, journals, and similar publications, ADAM will be either a bibliographic or a full-text database. However, before we can explore these alternatives, we must pause for a moment to get righteous about our terminology.

Online databases, like those you might create yourself with PFS:File, dBASE III, or some other personal computer database management package, are called "files." Each complete item in the file is called a "record." And each piece of information in the record is called a "field."

> **Online Tip:** Occasionally you may hear the term "unit record" as well, but this is a rapidly fading holdover from the days of the punched 80-column cards one was admonished never to fold, spindle, or mutilate. At that time, each punched card typically contained a single record, and the term "unit record" was used to refer to both the information and the card itself. Similarly, fields are sometimes called "data elements," a term that is also gradually fading from use.

The easiest way to keep these terms straight is to remember the classic example of a collection of canceled personal checks. All the checks together constitute the file. Each individual check is a record. Each piece of information on a check (the date, the payee, the numerical amount, etc.) is a field.

In Figure 2.2, for example, all of the download text constitutes a single *record* in the mythical database *file* we've called ADAM. The *fields* include the article title, the name of the journal, the publication date, the volume number, the issue number, and the page numbers. The summary paragraph is also considered a field, as is the complete collection of "keywords" at the end of the record.

———————— **Figure 2.2. A Complete Record from ADAM** ————————

Here is a complete record from our mythical ADAM database. Notice that the record has three main sections: the bibliographic citation, the abstract summarizing the original article, and the keyword list.

Upscale Ice Creams Melt the Competition
Nation's Restaurant News
June 16, 1986 v. 20   no. 25   p. 1,4

According to the Washington, D.C.-based International Association of Ice Cream Manufacturers, "superpremium" ice cream is the fastest growing segment of the frozen dessert market. While overall frozen dessert sales have increased only 2% per year, superpremium sales (ice cream with more butterfat and less air than traditional products) have been growing at 10% to 15% a year. Most leaders in retail grocery sales have already opened "dip stores," a move that has prompted traditional chains like Baskin-Robbins to add "gourmet" flavors. The article includes an overview of some of the major superpremium manufacturers (Haagen-Dazs, Ben & Jerry's, and others).

KEYWORDS: food—desserts, dairy products, market information, shelf space, trade associations, fast food, yuppies, health concerns—cholesterol.

The Bibliographic Format

All records in a bibliographic database contain at least two components: a "bibliographic citation" or "bibcite" and a list of keywords. The bibcite format will be familiar to anyone who has ever used a library card catalog or prepared a bibliography for a term paper. It includes the article title, the author's name, and all relevant facts about the source publication.

In Figure 2.2, the bibcite occupies just the first three lines of the download text. As you can see, it includes everything you need to know to quickly locate the original article in a library or order a copy from a "document delivery" service of the sort described in Chapter 4. But it doesn't contain any real information.

Nor does it contain enough information to make it practical to search for this record. Remember, computers are nothing if not literal-minded. If a word does not exist in a record there is no way the machine can find it, and the bibcite alone doesn't give you much to work with. For this reason, the creators of bibliographic databases almost always add a field of keywords. These words may also be called "indexing terms" or "descriptors."

If ADAM is to be a bibliographic database, its creator would probably hire a staff of professional indexer/abstracters to prepare the material. These folks would read each source article and decide which keywords best describe its contents, the issues, topics, or concepts it covers, and where it fits in the overall scheme of things. The keywords the indexer/abstracter decides upon may or may not appear in the source article. It isn't likely, for example, that keywords like "dairy products," "trade associations," or "fast food" would appear in the article cited in Figure 2.2. But as you can infer from the summary paragraph, each of these concepts is relevant and likely to be of interest to ADAM users.

Controlled Vocabularies

How does the indexer/abstracter know which words to choose? Why is it "dairy *products*" and not "dairy *industry*," for example? The answer is that indexing terms are almost always drawn from a pre-defined list of words called a "controlled vocabulary." The complete controlled vocabulary used to index a database is called a "thesaurus."

For example, John Wiley & Sons, producer of the Harvard Business Review Online (HBRO) database, has established a list of 3,500 "authorized index terms" that includes everything from "ordnance" to "x-ray apparatus." The words "ammunition" and "x-ray machine," in contrast, are not on the list and are thus not used as keyword descriptors. The only way to determine this fact is to look up "ammunition" in the HBRO thesaurus, where you will be told, "See *ordnance*." Needless to say, if you plan to do much searching of a database that uses a controlled vocabulary, it's essential to have a copy of its thesaurus. Wiley sells the 400-page HBRO thesaurus for $50.

Including Abstracts—The Other Bibliographic Option

A record consisting of a straight bibliographic citation and a list of key index words can be quite serviceable. Indeed, when the information industry was starting and computer storage costs were high, it usually wasn't economic to offer anything but bibcites and keywords. Then too, communications speeds were four to six times slower than they are now, making it impractical to transmit significant quantities of text. There were few complaints from end-users, however, since most were librarians with easy access to the source material and since online databases represented such a leap forward.

Some commercial databases, like Information Access Company's (IAC) Magazine Index, still offer nothing but bibcites and keywords. But it is much more typical these days for the producer to include short summaries of the source article as well. These are called "abstracts," and as you might expect, they are typically prepared by the same professionals responsible for indexing a database.

In Figure 2.2 the abstract is the paragraph of text between the bibcite and the keywords, and as you can see, it gives you a much better idea of whether it would be worthwhile to obtain a copy of the source article. Indeed, a good abstract may very well contain exactly the fact, figure, or statistic you're looking for and thus eliminate the need for the source article entirely.

As noted, the abstract itself is considered a field in the record, and it is almost always searchable. That means that you would get a hit on the record shown in Figure 2.2 if you searched on "superpremium," "fastest growing segment," "butterfat," "dip stores," "gourmet," or any other word or phrase in the abstract. The industry usually refers to both bibcite-only and bibcite-cum-abstract products as "bibliographic databases."

The Full-Text Format

Finally, there is the full-text format. Technically, any database that contains a complete copy of some kind of source material can be called "full text." Thus, since the Marquis Who's Who database discussed in Chapter 15 is an online copy of its source volumes, it is a full-text database. Usually, however, the term is applied only to databases that offer complete magazine, newspaper, or other articles online. For example, IAC's Magazine ASAP™ database contains the full text of over 100 publications dating back to 1983.

Full-text records typically contain bibcites and keyword fields as well as a verbatim copy of the source article. The only source material you won't find are graphics, charts, photographs, and other forms of illustration that at this writing cannot be effectively transmitted online. However, most full-text records will inform you if the source article includes this kind of material.

Full-Text Versus Bibliographic: A Brief Comparison

The Sex Appeal of Full Text

No one creating a database today can afford to ignore the full-text alternative. For one thing, it is what new users and others not steeped in the ways of the information industry *expect* to find when going online. It is instantly gratifying and undeniably convenient. And from a marketing standpoint, it's the sexy, "in" thing to offer right now. But it may not be the best information alternative, either for users or for database producers.

Storage costs have fallen. But disk packs aren't free, and space still rents by the megabyte. At this writing, ADAM's producer could expect to pay anywhere from $1.25 to $10 or more per month per megabyte, depending on whether he owned the equipment himself or rented space on someone else's system. As a yardstick, the editorial matter in a daily newspaper can require anywhere from 500 to 300 megabytes of storage a year. Those costs not only continue but continue to grow as more information is added to the database.

If ADAM is to be a full-text database, its creator will also have to pay copyright royalties to the publishers of the original material. But that expense is minor compared to the costs of converting printed matter to magnetic form. This can be done in a number of ways. Unfortunately, none of them is as easy as one might think.

Great advances have been made in optical scanners in recent years, and more and more databases are being created directly from the computer tapes used to drive typesetting equipment. But at this writing, most data is still keyed in by hand.

Keying It Twice

Saztec Corporation of Rolling Hills Estates, California, is one of the leading firms in the data-entry industry. In addition to facilities in Kansas City and Dayton, the company has offshore operations in Singapore, Scotland, and the Philippines. Among other things, it is responsible for keying in many of the 140 periodicals offered by Magazine ASAP.

The process is labor-intensive. According to Tom Reed, the firm's president, "Everything is keyed in twice for accuracy. After the initial operator is finished entering the text, a verification operator loads some special software and re-keys everything from the original text. This is called 'over-keying' the document."

Most companies in the industry do some form of over-keying, though their techniques may vary. Typically, although the verification operator's screen appears normal, the software keeps a copy of the file created by the first operator in memory. When there is a discrepancy between what's in memory and what was just entered from the keyboard, the computer stops and notifies the operator. The operator then investigates and makes the necessary correction.

Online Tip: Saztec Corporation also does a lot of work for Mead Data Central (Chapter 9) and Business Research, producers of the Investext database (Chapter 16). It can convert most typesetting tape into a format required by the database vendors, and it is exploring the use of optical scanners. "If the scanners on the market today could do even half of what their manufacturers claim they can do, we'd use them," Tom Reed says. "Essentially we and every other successful company in this business have to offer a full range of services, since any given database may include material from a wide variety of sources." For more information contact:

Saztec Corporation
27520 Hawthorne Blvd., Suite 170
Rolling Hills Estates, CA 90274
(213) 544-0337

At this writing it is doubtful that even 30 percent of available databases are full-text products. But consumer demand, the continuing drop in storage costs, and the increasing use of computerized typesetting in the publishing industry all point to a large increase in that percentage. The text may be on a CD-ROM disk (*C*ompact *D*isk-*R*ead *O*nly *M*emory, the term for laser-read video disks) instead of online. But one way or another it will be available.

That's all to the good, of course. Magazine ASAP, for example, can instantly provide you with the full text of tens of thousands of articles at a cost of $7 each (plus connect time and telecommunications network charges). No delays. No trips to the company or public library. No need to send away for the article. Just the information you want when you want it. What businessperson wouldn't pay $7 to have an important article in its entirety delivered instantly to his or her screen?

Bibcites and Abstracts: A Better Alternative

As a new online searcher it is tempting to believe that because it is more "complete," a full-text database is ipso facto better than one offering bibcites and abstracts. But that is definitely not the case. In fact, much of the time exactly the opposite is true.

A database of abstracts is usually much easier to search. We'll have much more to say about this in Chapter 5. For now, take it on faith that unless you are looking for a very specific and unique combination of words, searching a full-text database can be treacherous. With so many words, the potential for unexpected (and thus irrelevant) combinations and occurrences of your search terms is enormous. You can easily end up retrieving and paying for articles that have nothing to do with your subject of interest.

Abstracts can also save you both time and money. For example, if you wanted information on the annual sales growth of superpremium ice cream, which would you rather read, a complete 1,000-word article or a short, fact-packed abstract of the article like the one shown in Figure 2.2? Which would you rather pay, as much as $7 for the full text or about 60¢ for the bibcite and abstract?

Online Tip: Of course, a poorly prepared abstract is no good at all, and it is important to be aware that even the best abstracts are necessarily subjective. Most are created by trained professionals, but each individual may interpret the same source article differently. Many databases cover the same publications, but each may emphasize different aspects of a given article. Thus an abstracter working for Database A may choose to highlight points that an abstracter covering the same article for Database B may choose to ignore, and vice versa.

You can make this work to your advantage. Since each abstract is likely to tell you something unique about the source document, it is often very helpful to look at two or more abstracts of the same article. Please see Figure 13.1 in Chapter 13 for a real-life example.

On Becoming an Information Provider

Finally, our friend must decide how ADAM and the information it contains will be sold. He *could* do it himself. But even if he managed to get together the $30,000 to $50,000 needed to buy the hardware required for a small system, he might not want to be bothered with details like billing, credit checking, and customer service. His best bet would probably be to try to persuade DIALOG, BRS, Dow Jones, or some other database vendor to handle these details for him.

That would make our friend what the industry calls an "information provider" or "IP" ("eye-pea"). In many respects, IPs are to the database vendors as authors are to publishers. The one supplies the information and the other handles the marketing. Vendors charge users by minute of connect time and pay a royalty to the IP based on the number of minutes someone spends accessing his database. Royalties are negotiable, of course, and the differences among royalty rates is one of the reasons why a database vendor like DIALOG may charge you $15 an hour to use one database and $75 an hour to use another.

According to LINK Resources, Inc., a New York-based consulting firm that closely follows the online field, in 1985 IP royalty rates were typically around 20 percent, though as the supermarket services compete for the most desirable databases that figure could rise to 28 percent or more in years to come. As with any other product, it may or may not be in an IP's best interests to negotiate an exclusive distribution deal with one of the vendors. In the next chapter we'll look at how database vendors price and sell the information supplied to them by the IPs.

...3...

How Information Is Sold:
Single-Subject Databases, Database Vendors, and Costs

nyone can sell information online. The basic hardware required to "put up a database" is so cheap that your brother-in-law or your next-door neighbor or the kid down the street with the $150 Commodore 64 system can sell information electronically. Whether they can sell it at a profit or not is a different matter. But at least some entrepreneurs are giving it a try by establishing computer bulletin board systems (BBSs) in bedrooms and basements across the land and charging callers to use them.

Of course most of the thousands of BBSs in North America and around the world are operated as a hobby, not as a money-making enterprise. And most serve as forums of communication and exchange points for public domain software, not as distributors of information in the classic sense of the word. But while a system like DIALOG or NEXIS may crown the totem pole and your favorite BBS may occupy a spot much nearer the earth, all are carved out of the same woody fiber. From top to bottom, they represent the entire range of electronic information marketing alternatives.

Any number of firms have purchased either micro- or mini-computers and the additional equipment needed to put up a database and offer it to the public. Some have rented space on large systems that normally focus on commercial billing applications and sold subscriptions just as they would if the database resided on a computer that they owned. The key point is that however they handle the hardware end of things, these companies usually fall into the category of "single-subject databases."

Entertainment Information from BASELINE
An excellent example is a product called BASELINE. This database

34

is the premier database of the movie and entertainment industry. Its files contain cast and crew credits for every feature film released in the United States "between 1970 and last week," plus data on films going back to 1913. All American musical stage productions between 1900 and August 1984, including Broadway, Off-Broadway, Off-Off Broadway, and major regional theater productions are covered as well. So are television series, pilots, and specials dating from 1974, the names, addresses, and contact person for over 100 motion-picture production companies, and a lot more.

BASELINE charges a monthly subscription fee of $75, but that includes one hour of online time, a monthly newsletter and "in-production" report, telephone support, and customized research reports. A consumer-oriented version is planned for the future. For more information, contact the company at:

> BASELINE, Inc.
> 838 Broadway, 4th Floor
> New York, NY 10003
> 800-CHAPLIN
> (212) 254-8235

Online Tip: Stewart Brand's POINT Foundation has been a leader in the new trend toward regional, independent online services. In 1985, Brand's magazine, *The Whole Earth Review*, set up The WELL (Whole Earth 'Lectronic Link) in a back room at its Sausalito editorial offices.

According to Matthew McClure, the system operator, The WELL consists of a VAX 750 and two Eagle Fujitsu 450-megabyte drives with a dozen telephone lines and an equal number of Hayes modems. The initial cost was close to $100,000, though Mr. McClure says that due to price cuts and new technology a similar system would now cost 20% to 25% less.

"We also installed a Telenet PAD at a cost of about $8,000 to permit subscribers to access the system more cheaply—$4 per hour from anywhere in the country, compared to paying long distance rates." (A PAD is a "packet assembler/disassembler" port that connects packet switching networks like Telenet to a host computer.) The WELL has the capacity to handle 25 to 30 callers at once, but demand is so great that "We're probably going to have to add another system relatively soon," says Mr. McClure.

The WELL is primarily a communications and conferencing system, though with different software the same hardware could be

Online Tip (cont.)

used to market online information. Given its regional orientation—
and the region it is in—it is not surprising to encounter some of
the country's leading computer luminaries online. Their WELL
names include LEE, PAUL, JDVORAK, WOODY, CRUNCH,
SACKS, ASK, NEEDLE, LMAGID, and many others.

A subscription to The WELL is $8 a month, plus $2 per hour for
connect time. If you use Telenet, the total connect time cost is $6
an hour. There is no extra charge for 1200 bit-per-second communications. To sign up online, use your modem to dial
415-332-6106 and answer the prompts. Have your MasterCard or
Visa handy. For more information contact:

> The WELL
> Whole Earth Review
> 27 Gate Five Road
> Sausalito, CA 94965
> 415-332-4335

A Snapshot of Eight Major Systems

Single-subject databases have a great deal to offer. Certainly if you
are interested in one and only one kind of information they are often
your best and sometimes only alternative. (The online database directories discussed in Appendix B contain complete write-ups of most databases in this category.) However, if you need to have access to all kinds
of information—everything from American Men and Women of Science
to an investment banking concern's report on an obscure but hot new
company—you'll need to subscribe to one or more of the encyclopedic or
"supermarket" systems.

We'll be mentioning single-subject databases of interest as we go
along, but we will be concentrating on eight major systems that are
likely to be of greatest use to you. We will refer to them as "database
vendors," not because it is a particularly felicitous term but because it is
the most descriptive of the various labels currently applied to such systems. Since we are going to be discussing them from now on, a quick
snapshot showing where the eight vendors fit in relation to each other
would be helpful:

- **DIALOG®, the Knowledge Index™, and the DIALOG Business
  Connection™** (Chapter 7)
  DIALOG is the main system. Some of its more than 250 individual

databases are available only on DIALOG. Some can be found on other systems as well. Most offer bibliographic citations and abstracts, though a number of full-text databases have been added in recent years. The Knowledge Index (KI, pronounced "kay-eye") offers about 40 of DIALOG's databases on an after-hours basis at reduced rates. The DIALOG Business Connection offers a dozen or more of the most business-oriented databases on DIALOG in an easy-to-use, menu-driven format. It is supported by a communications software package that is offered at a net cost of $45.

• **BRS/SEARCH™, BRS/BRKTHRU™, and BRS/After Dark™** (Chapter 8)

In the broadest sense, BRS is very similar to DIALOG. The main difference is that BRS offers about 100 individual databases. Again, some are exclusive and some are available elsewhere. The main BRS system is specifically designed for information professionals. BRS/BRKTHRU ("breakthrough") is designed for businesspeople and non-information professionals. BRKTHRU is menu-driven and full of helpful prompts, making it much easier to use. BRS/After Dark is the company's after-hours, reduced-rate service. It is a menu-driven system, and it includes about 50 of the main system's most popular databases.

• **ORBIT® Search Service (SDC)** (Chapter 10)

The ORBIT Search Service, as it is now called, is produced by System Development Corporation (SDC), a subsidiary of the Pergamon Group. You may still hear it referred to as "SDC," however. ORBIT is a command-driven system (as opposed to menu-driven) offering over 70 individual databases, many of them exclusively. DIALOG, BRS, and ORBIT are the "Big Three" of the "traditional" (mainly bibliographic citations and abstracts) online information services.

• **NEXIS® from Mead Data Central (MDC)** (Chapter 9)

Mead Data Central, or "MDC," is a subsidiary of the Mead Corporation, the Dayton, Ohio-based paper and forest products company. It has always specialized in full-text databases. Its LEXIS® system (not discussed in this book) contains so much full-text legal information that it can virtually eliminate the need for an extensive law library. The NEXIS system offers the full text of hundreds of magazines, newspapers, wire services, and industry newsletters. The only bibliographic citations and abstracts on the system are those found in The Information Bank section, a collection of databases MDC acquired from the now defunct New York Times Information Service.

- **Dow Jones News/Retrieval Service® (DJN/R)** (Chapter 10)

  The Dow Jones News/Retrieval Service offers about 35 separate databases or services. None of them is bibliographic in the classic sense of the word. About 15 are produced in-house by Dow Jones and follow their own special formats. They include a variety of stock quotes, news, and the full text of the *Wall Street Journal*. The remainder are also available on other systems.

- **VU/TEXT™** (Chapter 11)

  The main focus of VU/TEXT is regional newspapers. A subsidiary of the Knight-Ridder Company, it offers the full text of about 25 metropolitan papers (Knight-Ridder's and others'), but it also offers stock quotes, Predicasts' PROMT, ABI/INFORM, and a few other bibliographic databases that are available on other systems.

- **NewsNet®** (Chapter 11)

  NewsNet offers full-text access to more than 300 trade, industry, and investment newsletters—the sorts of publications that typically charge $250 or more a year for subscriptions to their printed versions. More than 40% of NewsNet newsletters have no printed counterpart and are available only on the system. NewsNet offers other features and services as well, but neither these nor the newsletters are bibliographic.

- **Wilsonline™** (Chapter 11)

  A service of the H. W. Wilson Company, Wilsonline offers about 20 databases. Virtually all of them are produced in-house and correspond to one of the printed reference works Wilson has published for years, including the *Readers' Guide to Periodical Literature*. All Wilsonline databases are bibliographic.

Database Vendors from Two Perspectives

Cutting a Deal and Consumer Impact

As noted in Chapter 2, a database producer who persuades DIALOG, BRS, ORBIT, NEXIS, or some other vendor to sell his product becomes what the industry calls an IP or "information provider." There are certain pluses and minuses to IP status, and both have an influence on what you will encounter as an information consumer.

First, the disadvantages. A prospective IP approaching a database vendor is like a clothing manufacturer approaching a major department store chain. If the database is hot and in great demand, he can probably cut a pretty good deal with not just one but all of the majors. If his position is not quite that strong, he may have to accept a lower royalty rate and agree to offer the product exclusively on one system.

We've oversimplified things here, of course, but whether for these or more subtle reasons, some databases are available on virtually every major system, while some can be found on only one. From the perspective of an information consumer, this cuts both ways. On the one hand, the more vendors that carry a database, the greater the chance that you will have access to it. You may also find that because of differing royalty arrangements you can use a database more cheaply on one vendor's system than on another's. Though not a commercial enterprise, the IRS TAXINFO database discussed in Chapter 18 is a good example. On DIALOG you would pay $36 an hour, plus telecommunications costs, regardless of the time of day. On BRS/BRKTHRU, the total cost is $45 during the day, but only $21.50 at night.

"Same" and "Identical" Are Different
On the other hand, the existence of the "same" database on different systems can set a trap that's very easy to fall into. At this writing, the complete IRS TAXINFO database contains the full text of the agency's 71 best-loved publications for individuals. That is what is available on DIALOG. However, although the database has the same name on BRKTHRU, the version available there contains only 66 of the 71 publications.

Similarly, the full-text Information Access Company (IAC) databases Magazines ASAP and Trade and Industry ASAP were brought up on BRS in the spring of 1986. But at this writing, they do *not* include the five *Time-Life* magazines found in DIALOG versions of those same databases. Variety of this sort does not help matters.

Or consider ABI/INFORM (Chapter 13), the Bell & Howell-owned database that covers such key publications as *Institutional Investor*, *Monthly Labor Review*, and nearly every business publication with the word *Journal* in its title. On the VU/TEXT system, the ABI/INFORM database goes back to January 1978. But on BRKTHRU the file goes back to August 1971.

The missing six-and-a-quarter years may not make a difference to you on any given search. But suppose that at some point it is important to go back as far as 1970 to develop a complete history of a competitor. You know you're going to have to do some of the work the old-fashioned way. Imagine how you'd feel if after searching ABI/INFORM on VU/TEXT and completing the job by hand in the library you learned that a more extensive version of the database was available on DIALOG or BRS.

Unless you happen to be having an affair with the librarian, wasting all that time is enough to make you cry. At this writing, none of the vendors tells you if what they are offering is actually a sub-set of a more extensive database. They simply tell you when coverage begins, or in the case of IRS TAXINFO, how many documents are in the file. The lesson then is this: All databases are *not* the same, even if there's no difference in the name.

Online Tip: Your best bet for discovering the extent of a database's coverage is to contact the database producer directly. Ask how far back the main file goes in its fullest implementation and how frequently it is updated. Then ask how far back it goes on the vendor you want to use, and how frequently it is updated there. The ABI/INFORM database cited above, for example, is updated weekly on DIALOG and monthly on all other systems.

It is unfortunate, but at this writing you cannot rely on any single database directory to give you all of the information you need. The Cuadra *Directory of Online Databases* will tell you about updating frequency, but not about time-span limitations. Knowledge Industry Publications's *Database Directory* cites the coverage limitations but not the differences in updating frequency. See Appendix B for more information on these directories.

Product Differentiation and the Consumer

Going with one of the major vendors reduces the need for an IP to produce his own documentation. Indeed, the common search language used by a major vendor is one of the advantages it offers both IPs and the public. However, many database producers do feel the need to prepare extensive manuals. As we'll see later, it is often vital to obtain a copy for the database you want to search. Some IPs also offer free telephone support to people who want to search their products.

Nor does a vendor relationship eliminate the need for an IP to advertise, just as a clothing or cosmetics manufacturer might advertise to encourage people to go to a department store to buy a product. At this writing, database advertising has a long way to go before it will rival ads for soap, cereal, or CompuServe.

Competition is also the reason that some IPs have taken steps to differentiate their products from others. This, too, has a direct effect on you as an information consumer.

If you're an IP and your product is but one of more than 250 on the vendor's electronic shelf, it's easy to get lost. In some cases you may be on a system with some other database that covers many of the same magazines and other source material. At this writing, for example, no fewer than 19 databases offer some form of coverage of *Business Week*. *Forbes* can be found on some 18 databases, and *Fortune* on about 23.

How can an IP persuade customers to spend their connect-hour dollars searching his database and not the other guy's? The answer is to find a way to differentiate the product from the others and tell people about it as often as possible. Is it cheaper? Are the abstracts more complete? Does it offer the full text of articles instead of an abstract and a bibcite? Is the information more current due to more frequent updates than everyone else's?

The Time Factor and Special Fields

Perhaps the database goes back further in time than that of the competition. The Management Contents database, for example, covers *Business Week* back to September 1974. The ABI/INFORM database takes it back to August 1971, while Information Science Abstracts goes all the way back to January 1966. The first two databases are available on DIALOG, BRS, and ORBIT, among others. The third database is only on DIALOG.

An IP might do something special with the format of each record to make it especially useful to his target audience. With this in mind, Cleveland-based Predicasts, Inc., has pioneered the use of "event codes" and similarly unique fields in all of the databases in its PTS (Predicasts Terminal System) family. For example, like some 17 other databases, PTS MARS (Marketing and Advertising Reference Service) covers *Advertising Age*. And like the others, each record contains fields for article title, author, a series of keyword descriptors, and so on.

Where MARS parts company with the rest, however, is in its use of special fields for such "events" as "New Product Introduction," "Orders & Contracts Received," and "Marketing Procedures." In addition, there are special fields for ad slogan ("The one beer to have . . ." etc.), celebrity spokesperson, agency name, and more. There are also some 50 "concept codes" developed in conjunction with members of the advertising industry ("advertising by medium," "targets and markets," "the regulatory environment," etc.).

There are other unique fields as well. The point is that by incorporating fields like these, MARS has made it easy for customers to conduct very fast, very precise searches of *its* collection of advertising information. In addition, the special fields serve as a customer guarantee that if a crucial piece of information like a slogan is mentioned in the source article, it will be reproduced in the MARS record. Conceivably a different database might include a sentence like "New slogan announced by firm's president" in its abstract but neglect to provide the actual words.

Customer Convenience Is the Key

Although on the surface the relationship between IPs and database vendors is similar to that of a manufacturer and a major department store chain, the intangibles of the relationship are quite different. *Collegial* is the word that comes most readily to mind, and it really is appropriate. Many of the people in this corner of the electronic universe are not only very bright, they are also very committed. They know they are not selling pipe fittings or pet food. Most are in the business because they enjoy dealing with facts and ideas. The atmosphere has more in common with a university faculty meeting than with an electronics trade show. In public at least, relations among IPs and between IPs and vendors appear more than cordial.

That's probably as it should be, since the existence of database vendors generates a lot of pluses for IPs and consumers alike. A vendor frees an IP from all hardware-related concerns, allowing him to concentrate on what he does best—producing databases. Nor does the IP have to worry about search software, billing, or customer support. The IP must provide the vendor with some information about the database and how it is set up so the vendor can pass this along to the consumer. But he or she doesn't *have* to do much more than that, though many do.

Those benefits also work to your advantage as a consumer. A single subscription can give you access to one to two hundred or more databases, each of which can be tapped with the same search language. There are many other benefits as well, and we'll explore them in the next chapter. Right now, the question is: How much is all this wonderful electronic information going to cost?

Tools to Make Sense of It All

If you have received the free vendor information packets we suggested you order at the beginning of this book, you should now have sitting in front of you or on the hall table or wherever, a stack of brochures, catalogs, flyers, and sundry other materials. (You *did* order the information, didn't you? If not, turn back to the Online Tip at the end of the Introduction to Part I and do so now.)

A lot of this information probably won't make much sense if you're new to the field. In fact, a lot of it won't make much sense even if you've had some experience. The reason is that as in the early days of personal computing, there are no standards where vendors are concerned. Just as CP/M, TRS-DOS, Apple DOS 3.3, and every other operating system uses a different technique to accomplish the same thing, each database vendor has its own method of handling accounts and delivering information.

This makes it very difficult to compare costs. And as previously noted, there is no way to tell whether the XYZ database on Vendor A is identical to the XYZ database on Vendor B without doing a lot of digging. Unless and until the equivalent of an IBM/MS-DOS standard emerges among database vendors, you'll need a set of tools to cut through the confusion. That's what we'll start to build now.

All of your interactions with a database vendor fall into one of three areas: Account-Related, Search-Related, and Information Delivery. Costs, standard system documentation, and billing methods fit under the Account heading, for example, while customer support, training, and supplemental database materials are almost always Search-Related. Similarly, almost any feature a vendor offers can be legitimately assigned to one of these three categories.

The balance of this chapter will address the Account-Related matters. It will show you how to figure out what you will be charged on any vendor's system. The chapter concludes with an optional section designed to bring you up-to-speed on the matter of downloading and the controversy surrounding it in the industry.

Chapter 4 continues the tool-building by focusing on Search-Related matters and Information Delivery. It will show you what you can expect from a database vendor and how to make the most of it. The chapter concludes with the Key Question Checklist, a comprehensive summary designed to be used to analyze any single-subject database or database vendor.

ACCOUNT-RELATED MATTERS
Subscriptions and System Manuals

As most people know, after the packet switching network has connected you to an online service, the next thing you must key in is your account number to tell the system who you are. That's usually followed by your secret password to assure the system that it is really you. This is what it means to have a vendor subscription and in some cases, as with DIALOG, subscriptions are completely free. You could call up DIALOG tomorrow, open an account, and when your number and password come in the mail, sign right onto the system. DIALOG even gives you $100 in free connect time to get you started.

What they *don't* give you, however, are the manuals and explanatory booklets and materials you need to do anything more than make a fool of yourself frittering away that free time. Those cost about $50 to $75, depending on what you decide to buy. So with the free connect time you

end up slightly ahead on the deal. And if the guy or gal down the hall
has already purchased the necessary manuals, you end up way ahead.

   A more common vendor practice is to charge a subscription fee of
around $50 and include account setup and a manual as part of the deal.
Depending on your needs, you may then wish to purchase additional,
expanded documentation to help you search a particular database offered by the system. Subscription plans designed for large institutional
users are also available on many systems. These may require a commitment of a certain amount of usage per month. Under such contracts,
you are billed for that amount whether you use it or not.

   Or they may involve placing money on deposit with the vendor as a
guarantee of a certain amount of annual usage. Vendors typically offer
discounts of 20 to 40 percent for these or any other type of plan based
on volume usage. An annual commitment of $3,000 on DIALOG, for
example, earns a discount of $4 off the regular connect-hour rate for any
database. If you agree to place $5,000 on deposit, the discount is $6 an
hour. And so on.

   If you work for a qualifying institution, you may be eligible for an
educational discount on some systems. And if you subscribe to the
printed version of the Wilsonline databases or a newsletter available on
NewsNet, you will pay less than non-print subscribers.

   Some systems also impose monthly minimums. BRS/After Dark requires you to use $12 worth of time a month, for example. NewsNet and
VU/TEXT charge monthly subscription fees of $15 and $10, respectively, to maintain your account. Dow Jones charges $12 a year.

Online Tip: Any time a minimum or usage commitment is involved, be sure to ask what you get for your money and what costs
count toward the total figure. To take a simple example, when
BRS/After Dark was first introduced, "communications costs" (the
cost of using Telenet, Tymnet, or some other packet switcher) did
not count against the $12 monthly requirement. Before the policy
was changed, it thus cost you an additional $6 to $12 to get on the
system so you could use your $12-worth of time each month. Sim-
ilarly, the $100 of free connect time that DIALOG gives all new
customers and its commitment discounts do not include communications costs and some other charges.

Usage Costs

   To serve your information needs, database vendors must obviously
incur certain costs. They have to pay for their computer or "host sys-

tem." And there are disk packs, software, maintenance, computer center and customer support personnel, plus all the traditional business expenses of rent, advertising, and taxes. As discussed, they have to pay the database producers royalties earned each time you access a database, and of course they have to make a profit. In addition, someone has to pay the packet switchers for the use of their networks.

Given these facts, one would think that deciding how much to charge would be fairly straightforward. In reality, exactly the opposite is true. You don't have to spend much time perusing the rate cards of the various vendors to realize that the information industry hasn't the slightest idea how to price its products.

• Connect-Hour Charges

Increasingly vendors are performing the long division for you and expressing this charge as cost per minute. But the concept is the same. Most charge you a certain amount for each minute you are connected to their systems, though their policies differ when rounding off fractions of a minute. You don't have to be doing anything to incur a charge. As long as the connection is open, you are at the very least using packet-switcher resources and occupying a port on the host system.

Due to differing royalty arrangements with the IPs, the actual connect-hour amount varies with the particular database you are using at the time. It is also worth noting that some vendors quote a single connect-hour rate that includes everything. Others quote a basic system connect rate, a database royalty rate, and telecommunications costs. To get the *actual* cost you must add all of these components together.

• High-Speed Surcharge

If you use a 1200 bit-per-second (bps) modem, you may pay double the 300 bps connect-hour rate. If you use a 2400 bps modem, the rate may be triple. Part of the reasoning here is that although you are paying twice or three times as much at a higher speed, you are receiving the information four to six times faster.

• Prime-Time Premium/Off-hours Discount

These are two sides of the same coin. From one perspective, you pay a premium to access a vendor's system during your regular business hours; from another, you receive a discount off the "regular" rate if you wait until the midnight hour, or at least until the close of business. Vendors like BRS/BRKTHRU, Dow Jones, and NewsNet offer these discounts because they have excess capacity during non-business hours. One can't just shut a computer system off for the night and go home. Since the system must be up and running anyhow, it might as well be generating some revenue.

• "Type" or Display Charge

The word *type* is a throwback to the days of the printing dumb terminals. Though many vendors still use the term, it is fortunately being replaced by the more accurate word *display*. Both terms refer to displaying information retrieved from a database on your screen. Other vendors call this charge a "hit charge" or a "citation charge." Since display charges are assessed in addition to connect-hour charges, when they were introduced they were generally viewed as a way to raise prices without being obvious about it.

This kind of charge is usually found only on a bibliographic database. As discussed below, display charges come in several varieties and often depend upon how much of a given record you elect to view.

• "Print" or Offline Print Charge

Databases that have display charges usually give you the option of having a record or parts thereof printed offline at the vendor's computer facility instead of displayed on your screen. The hard-copy printout is then mailed to you by the vendor. When terminals were dumb and communications speeds were limited to 300 bits per second, offline printing was more relevant than it is today, though it is usually still cheaper than displaying a record online.

• Per Search Charges

Mead's NEXIS is the only major database vendor to use this method. As applied by Mead, it in effect charges you $7 each time you hit the <ENTER> key to transmit a new search command—either that or $3 each time you modify a command you already have working. This is in addition to a $20-per-hour basic connect-time rate and a $10-per-hour telecommunications rate. Confusing as it is, this policy is better than the "database resource" charge Mead used to impose that billed you 45¢ for each 25,000 times a search word occurred in a database.

• Computer Resource Charge

None of the vendors presented in this book levies this kind of charge, but one day you may encounter a vendor who does. It is a combination of the amount of memory required and the number of operations (not instructions) the host computer must perform to satisfy your request. It is often quoted in terms of "CPU time." A CPU is the computer's central processing unit, and the time involved is usually fractions of a second.

1200 bps: Premium or Penalty?

The argument that you should pay more to be able to receive information four to six times faster than at 300 bps appears to make sense until you stop to ask, "Just how much information am I really going to be downloading?" When sending or receiving substantial quantities of text—say, 10 or 12 single-spaced pages or more—a higher speed can save you a considerable amount of time.

Most searches, however, involve downloading only a few paragraphs of information. Yet on systems like Dow Jones and NewsNet, if you sign on at 1200 bps (or 2400 bps), you will pay the higher rate for the entire session, including the time required to enter and modify your search commands and the time the host computer spends looking for hits. In a ten-minute session, you might spend only three minutes actually downloading retrieved information and thus benefiting from a higher speed. The rest of the time you'll be sitting there with lower speed communicators, waiting for the host system to give you the results of your search request. But you'll be paying more for the privilege.

Connect Time and Assumed Value

Vendors and IPs never stop to consider that there is only so much information one can absorb, regardless of how fast it is obtained. And you will rarely, if ever, hear vendors justify high-speed premium charges on the basis of increased costs. That's because there aren't any to speak of, and the costs that are involved are rapidly falling. Instead, they may point out, the way a parent might point out to a child, that your time has value and you should be willing to pay more to be able to spend less of it online.

Pricing on the basis of the assumed value of the product to the customer, instead of on the basis of production costs, also plays a major role in setting the connect-hour rates charged for using different databases. If the IP feels that the information in a database can make you or save you a lot of money, you will be charged accordingly. On DIALOG, for example, Investext is $95 an hour, and Thomas Register Online is $100. In contrast, Books In Print is $65 an hour and the Encyclopedia of Associations is $48 an hour.

Perhaps the creators of Investext and Thomas Register have to do more work to prepare their databases? They might, but as we will see in the relevant chapters, the information on Investext consists of reports and analyses supplied by some 30 or more investment banking firms. Thomas Register Online corresponds to the 13-volume printed

Thomas Register of American Manufacturers, a reference work the firm has published for many years. All that is required to make either collection of information available electronically is the addition of some fields and keywords and some reformatting. Neither firm has to build a database from scratch.

The Encyclopedia of Associations also corresponds to a printed work of the same name. And Books In Print embraces some 14 R. R. Bowker volumes *(Subject Guide to Books in Print, Children's Books in Print,* and so on). But look at the difference in price compared to the two investment- and business-oriented databases. All of these are excellent databases, but giving everyone the benefit of the doubt, it is impossible to believe that the two more expensive products are really that much more expensive to produce. One can only conclude that the database creators have set their prices on the basis of what they think the information will be worth to you.

In principle there's nothing wrong with that. Consultants and newsletter publishers have been pricing their services that way for years. The danger is that an assumed value is a "guesstimate" at best. Guess correctly and you maximize your profit. Guess wrong and you price yourself out of the market. Because of close contact with their clients and subscribers, consultants and newsletter publishers can quickly adjust prices to match the market. But a database producer doesn't have that kind of relationship with his customers and, with the vendor as a middleman, he lacks that kind of control.

Obsessive Possessives

Judging from their pricing policies and the articles and letters they've written for information industry trade journals, database producers often appear to be a bit frantic about pricing. Many seem like someone who's in debt to a loan shark and waiting for the "sure thing" he bet on to pay off. That's an exaggeration, but there's more than a kernel of truth in it. Creating a database involves considerable up-front expense. If one could phase in an information product gradually as the number of paying customers grew, pricing wouldn't be such a worry. But you can no more offer half a database than you can offer half an automobile. The whole thing's got to be there at once, whether or not there are enough customers to pay for it.

It is fair to say that database producers expected the demand for online information to grow far faster than it has to date and they invested on that assumption. What everyone, including writers on the subject, failed to allow for was the PC learning curve. We forgot that a new computer user needs a considerable amount of time to become comfortable with his or her equipment. Until that happens, online communications is virtually out of the question.

Producers also seem to have forgotten the age-old truth of "elasticity of demand." That economic concept can be translated as low price/high demand and high price/low demand. It should be of particular interest to database producers, since online information is largely a fixed-cost business. Whether a database is used by one customer or 1,000, the cost to the producer is the *same*. Realizing this, one would think that IPs would price their products to stimulate demand. But to date that has not happened.

Accurate as they are, all of the industry's arguments about how much time and money online information saves you compared with doing research by hand do not make up for the fact that it is *perceived* as being expensive. That discourages the kind of spontaneous use that leads to large connect-time profits. It also prevents more people from developing the skills and comfort level needed to make information retrieval a regular part of the workday.

As a result, at this writing, no one in the industry is making any serious money. But they've all got serious expenses. Unfortunately, in order to stay in the game until the boom arrives producers have not only set their prices too high, some have adopted an almost obsessive possessiveness about the information in their databases. We'll have more to say about this when we explore the downloading controversy at the end of this chapter.

Pay for Display

Display charges are almost always associated with bibliographic databases, and it's easy to see why. As you will recall, a bibliographic record is by its very nature divisible into discrete fields. It is thus relatively simple to impose a charge for each field a customer asks to have displayed.

It works like this. You enter a search command and the system goes away and locates the records containing your hits. Then, like a casino dealer holding his cards close to his vest, the system says in effect, "I've got all the fields for the records you asked for right here. But it's gonna cost'cha. Now, which cards would you like to see: Just the title and author? Just the title and abstract? The title, author, abstract, and indexing keywords? The full text of the article? Come on, ante up. I ain't got all day." As noted previously, under this system the more you ask to have displayed, the more you will pay.

BRS/BRKTHRU, for example, offers three display options (short, medium, and long). ORBIT offers four (Print Scan, Print Trial, Print

Standard, and Full). And DIALOG offers Formats 1 through 9. BRS/
SEARCH has a similar arrangement. On DIALOG, Format 1 displays
only the accession number DIALOG assigns to each record. Format 9
displays the full text of the magazine article or other source material in
those databases that offer this option. In between are options for virtually every combination of record components you can imagine.

Formats 1 through 9 on DIALOG apply to offline printouts as well. In
both cases, the database creator determines how much information is
actually parceled out in each format and how much you will pay. Format
details are provided in the documentation for each database. (See Figure 3.1.) The rate cards for most bibliographic databases quote only the
cost of displaying or printing the full record (bibcite, abstract, indexing
keywords, etc.). The prices for the other formats are typically available
only online. (Please see Figure 3.2. for a sample.)

_____ Figure 3.1. ABI/INFORM DIALOG Format Details _____

Here are the components of the eight DIALOG display formats as
implemented on ABI/INFORM, a database covering some 660 trade,
business, finance, and marketing journals and magazines. Though the
contents of each format are up to the database producer, the following
arrangement is typical. There is no Format 9, DIALOG's full-text format, because ABI/INFORM contains only bibliographic citations and
abstracts.

Format 1	DIALOG accession number
Format 2	Full record, except abstract
Format 3	Bibliographic citation
Format 4	Abstract and title
Format 5	Full record
Format 6	Title and DIALOG accession number
Format 7	Bibliographic citation and abstract
Format 8	Title and indexing (keywords)

_____ Figure 3.2. ABI/INFORM Prices on DIALOG _____

As a single line of very fine print on the DIALOG rate card points out,
"Unless stated otherwise, a 'full record' is Format 5. Prices for output in
other formats are available online by using '?Ratesn' where 'n' is the file
number." On DIALOG, ABI/INFORM is File 15. Shown below is what
the system produces when you key in ?RATES15. Remember that the
$81 per connect hour is in addition to telecommunications costs of be-
tween $6 and $18 an hour, depending on whether you use DIALOG's own

packet switching network or someone else's. Remember too, that "display" and "type" refer to looking at a record on your computer screen. "SDI" is a current awareness service explained in Chapter 4.

Rates15: ABI/INFORM. The cost of searching in File 15 is $81 per connect hour and $.60 per full record (Format 5) PRINTed offline. Cost of offline prints in other formats:

	Cost/Print
Format 1	$.024
Format 2	.30
Format 3	.30
Format 4	.45
Format 5	.60
Format 6	.24
Format 7	.45
Format 8	.30

Online TYPEs/DISPLAYs in File 15 are $.50 per full record. Cost of types/displays in other formats:

	Cost/Type/Display
Format 1	$.00
Format 2	.25
Format 3	.25
Format 4	.25
Format 5	.50
Format 6	.00
Format 7	.50
Format 8	.00

Monthly invoice amounts are adjusted for partial item printouts.

***

SDI service available on ABI/INFORM at rate of $9.95 per monthly update. High volume discounts available.

Billing Options and Diverse Other Points

All of the database vendors discussed in this book are eager for your business. However, as with anything else, much depends on the luck of the draw—specifically, who happens to pick up the phone when you call the marketing department for more information or to set up your account. Though not always the case, many marketing representatives are more accustomed to dealing with public and corporate librarians. If you're an executive or a businessperson, you cannot necessarily count on them to anticipate all of your needs. So ask. In addition to the various subscription options discussed earlier, ask about:

• *Billing options.* Many vendors will now automatically bill your credit card each month. Others offer only direct billing.

• *Billing detail.* Just about every system automatically sends you an itemized bill listing the amount of time spent using each database and the applicable rate, telecommunications costs, display or print charges, and so on.

• *Billing by cost center.* To take advantage of quantity discounts, don't automatically open an account on your own. Instead, see if your co-workers in other departments would be interested in joining you. Then contact the vendor to see if you can arrange for a master bill broken down by your cost centers to make it easy to apportion the charges while still earning any applicable discounts.

When it comes to saving money, it never pays to be shy. So tell the marketing rep that you're really interested in keeping costs down and ask what he or she can recommend.

Online Tip: Considering the complexity of their pricing schemes, it is surprising that vendors don't offer complete "For Example" work-ups of the costs of a typical online session. Interviews with various vendors lead one to conclude that this lack is not deliberate. Most of them simply haven't thought of it. *You* should think of it, however.

When you talk to a vendor marketing rep, go down the list of Usage Costs presented earlier and inquire about each one. Take notes. Then ask the individual to cost out a typical online session, emphasizing that you want to know *all* the costs.

"The Price Is Not *Right," and a Prediction*

Although it is of incalculable value, electronic information today is priced too high. Too high to stimulate maximum usage. And too high to generate maximum profits for vendors and database producers. If you work for a large company, bank, or accounting firm, you may think nothing of spending $2,000 to $20,000 a year on electronic information. From your perspective, you may think it cheap at the price.

Compared to what you would have to spend to obtain the information any other way, it *is* cheap. The problem is that the vast majority of businesspeople, large and small, never make that comparison. They don't even know they need the information, let alone the relative costs of obtaining it. In short, the "end-user" the industry claims to be enthusiastically courting doesn't understand the product, how to use it, or what it's good for. All the potential customer understands is that it is going to cost him anywhere from $75 to $100 an hour. Add to that the sense of being nickeled and dimed to death every way you turn with display charges, packet switching charges, and premiums for higher speed communications, and you do not have a recipe for success.

Somewhere there is a correct price, a price where both the demand curve and the profit curve intersect at the highest possible point. Without the aid of expensive marketing studies, one can make a pretty good guess at where it is. Simply look at H & R Block's CompuServe.

CompuServe began at about the same level as its chief rivals, Dow Jones and The Source. But with over 330,000 subscribers, it has long since pulled ahead to become the largest online service in the industry. CompuServe's financials are not made public, but clearly the company is doing something right. And as CompuServe spokespeople acknowledge, the service is most definitely profitable.

CompuServe subscriptions list for about $40, but they include over $30 worth of connect time and a $10 manual, so in essence they are free. The average CompuServe connect-hour cost, at all speeds and time periods, is $11.75 an hour. But CompuServe has nothing like the database creation expenses found in this part of the industry. So to cover these costs, let's double that figure to $23.50 an hour. Round it up, and you've got $24 an hour.

At that price a new user can afford to take the time to really get to know a system or a database, and an experienced user can comfortably test "I wonder if . . ." scenarios with the data. Is it do-able? Apparently it is. By sheer coincidence $24 an hour is exactly the price charged by DIALOG's Knowledge Index. And it includes everything. No extra charges for the amount of information you display. No extra charges for telecommunications costs. No handling fees or monthly minimums.

Will that price be adopted by the information industry? It's hard to say, but it certainly seems likely that something along those lines will take place. It will have to, regardless of whether today's IPs feel they can afford to sell their wares for that price. Even under current pricing policies, demand is growing. Consequently, at some point it seems inevitable that the MLSs, who are in it for love, will be replaced by MBAs, who will be in it for money.

As was the case in the microcomputer hardware and software industries, those companies who don't adapt will be cloned out of existence.

Current IPs have no lock on their source material. As we said at the beginning of this chapter, *anyone* can put up a database. McDonald's, Southland (7-Eleven Stores), Federal Express—business annals are filled with examples of smartly managed firms with vision seizing an opportunity and revolutionizing an entire industry. If and when that happens here, some information providers will have to fight to survive. At the very least, most will be forced to change their policies and lower their prices.

The Downloading Issue

"Terms and Conditions"

If there's one topic that's guaranteed to break the ice at parties in the information industry it is the issue of downloading—the practice of capturing information as it comes in from a database and storing it on a disk. You have only to review the IP-supplied statements in the DIALOG publication "Database Supplier Terms and Conditions" to get a sense of what we mean. Some IPs simply note that their database is copyrighted. But some flatly prohibit the duplication "in hard copy or machine readable form" of any portion of their databases without prior written consent. That means no printouts. No capturing to disk. Just read—fast—as the information scrolls up your screen. And take notes.

Others go on at great length stipulating whether or not you can save their information to disk or make a hard-copy printout of it, the number of printouts you can make, who can read them, and so on. Elsewhere in the industry there are vendors and IPs who graciously allow you to download items, but not "a substantial portion." And you may store it to disk temporarily, but in no case for a period longer than 30 days.

Still other database producers have made ominous rumblings about imposing a "downloading surcharge." Presumably, if you signed on and simply read or printed out the information, you would pay one fee. But if you planned to save the information to disk, you would pay the fee plus the surcharge. Needless to say, the plan needs work on the enforcement end of things.

As absurd as some of these terms and conditions are, they pale next to the draconian measures advocated by some IPs. Consider the Electronic Communications Privacy Act currently making its way through both houses of Congress (House Resolution 3338 and Senate 1667). This act is designed to extend to electronic mail the same privacy protections that apply to paper-based mail, an unquestionably laudable goal.

However, as the Information Industry Association's (IIA) "Friday Memo" put it in its October 11, 1985, issue, "One of the by-products of the bill in its present form is that unauthorized downloading of a database or part of a database would become a felony." There is also language permitting online systems like BRS or DIALOG to turn over the names of the people who have used a given database to the producer of that database. [For more information on the bill, contact Mr. Paul G. Zurkowski, President, Information Industry Association, Suite 800, 555 New Jersey Avenue, N.W., Washington, D.C. 20001, (202) 639-8262.]

The Three Major Concerns

Even if the provisions of this bill are changed or if the bill itself never makes it into law, the very fact that it has been introduced indicates that there is something fundamentally wrong with some sections of the information industry. What are the concerns that would lead companies to set absurd terms and conditions or support such a bill? Basically, IPs are worried about three things.

First, they are worried that you will download their information, photocopy it, and distribute it within your company. That's convenient for your co-workers. But since those people will not be signing on and downloading the information themselves, some IPs see it as a loss of revenue. Everyone who benefits from the information, they reason, should have to spend the time and money required to search for and download it.

Second, they are concerned that an information center manager or department head will sign on, download their databases, and store them on a hard disk. Once on the disk, the information would be available for local search and retrieval by company employees at any time. No need to sign on again. No need to pay royalties for each use of the database.

Third, they fear that some fly-by-night operator will conduct a massive download of their records, disguise them with reformatting, and resell the results as his own database.

Where Has Sense Gone?

This last concern can reasonably be dismissed as highly improbable. Not because pirating a database wouldn't be attractive to a thief, but because there is very little chance that he would get away with it. No one can download an entire database without raising eyebrows at the vendor's computer shop. And no one can profit from such a gambit without openly advertising the stolen product's availability.

The first two concerns don't hold much water either. The fact that they are raised is but one more confirmation that the information industry has precious little understanding of its "end-users." If every manager in a company had to take the time to sign on and download information or do without, most would do without. The IPs "lost revenues" due to printouts and photocopies are thus largely chimerical.

The concern about companies establishing an in-house or departmental database for free, any-time searching fails to take into account the effort and expense such an undertaking would involve. To be of any value such a database would have to be huge. As cheap as hard disks are, storage expenses would be considerable. More importantly, someone must be paid to maintain the database, signing on and downloading updates as they are added by the IP, and someone would have to offer the equivalent of customer support to employees. For most companies it simply doesn't make economic sense.

The Ultimate Answer

Believe it or not, the answer to all of these worries and concerns is simple. As in any industry, there are many companies in the information field who do not know what business they are really in. They *think* they are selling information. And that misconception governs everything from display charges to downloading policies. What the information industry is *actually* selling is service. Once that realization is reached, everything else falls into place.

Instead of prohibiting customers from photocopying and distributing printouts, IPs should make it easy and encourage the practice. As a manager, imagine being able to sign on to a system each day to pick up a customized report containing just the information you need, attractively formatted for easy printing and distribution. Imagine an information "site license" under which you could locally store and use as much of an IP's database as you wanted each year.

The IP could sell you the search software and possibly the hard disk itself with the information already loaded. A database producer could even offer to customize his product to meet your company's specific needs. A regular updating service would be a natural offering as well. Fees would be charged for every level of service, of course, and most companies would be glad to pay them. Best of all, most of those fees would go directly into the producer's pocket, since the database vendor would no longer be in the loop.

CD-ROM Offerings on the Beam

Happily, a number of companies have already begun to move in this direction, though not in quite the manner outlined above. For example, Datext, Inc., a subsidiary of the communications giant Cox Enterprises, offers a CD-ROM disk package designed to work with an IBM or compatible personal computer. The disk reader itself is included, and customers may choose any or all of four subject disks containing over a quarter of a million pages each. Databases covered include DISCLOSURE II, Investext, PTS PROMT, ABI/INFORM, Media General, and Marquis Who's Who in Finance and Industry. Subscriptions include regular monthly updates—they send you new disks—and at this writing, prices range from $9,600 to $19,600 a year, depending on how many subject disks you want.

Information Access Company (IAC) has taken a similar approach with its InfoTrac™ product. The company can supply the video disk player and all of the interface cards, cables, and software needed to connect it to multiple IBM or compatible PCs. Drawn from IAC's bibliographic and full-text electronic products, four CD-ROM databases are available. These include one for legal publications, one for government publications, one containing the full text of the last 12 months of the *Wall Street Journal*, and the business and general interest InfoTrac database. Monthly updates are included, and annual subscriptions range from $4,000 to $11,500, depending on the databases selected and the amount of additional hardware you need.

Here are the addresses to contact for more information on both products:

DATEXT, Inc.
444 Washington Street
Woburn, MA 01801
(617) 938-6667

InfoTrac
Information Access Company
11 Davis Drive
Belmont, CA 94002
(800) 227-8431

Whether via CD-ROM or magnetic media, on-site databases of this sort represent a very positive first step. But much more needs to be done. Truly, the possibilities are endless—once the industry realizes what business it is really in and instead of fighting the tide begins to make the most of it.

...4...

What to Expect from a Database Vendor:

Services, Support, and Document Delivery

One of the secrets to easy, effective online information retrieval is to take full advantage of the services offered by the various database vendors. In some cases, for example, obtaining the information you want is as easy as calling a toll-free number, explaining your request to a customer service representative, and then signing on and keying in the phrases and commands he or she suggested. Many times the representative will have a terminal by the phone and be able to test the search strategy as it is developed. This is not a substitute for learning how to search yourself, but it can save you a great deal of time with complex queries.

In this chapter, we'll show you what you can expect from a vendor and suggest ways to use these resources most effectively. We will do it by addressing the remaining two components of our database vendor analytical tools—Search-Related matters and Information Delivery. The chapter concludes with a Key Question Checklist that you can use to quickly bring yourself up to speed on any database vendor. We will be using a slightly modified version of it ourselves in profiling the vendors in Part II.

SEARCH-RELATED MATTERS
Differing Search Language Capabilities

There is no need to be concerned with the details just yet, but you should know that the search languages offered by each vendor differ in power and capability. A system like DIALOG may have 50 different commands one can use to enter or focus a search, while The Knowledge Index may offer only five. Or consider the matter of "truncation," a term we in the microworld would translate as "using a wildcard."

Most vendors allow you to search for a truncated word like REAGAN*, where the asterisk or some other character is used to symbolize "any characters." (This command would retrieve articles mentioning Reagan, Reaganite, Reaganites, Reaganaut, Reaganomics, and so on.) That's called "right-hand truncation" for obvious reasons. But only the BRS search language permits you to also search for *MATE (retrieving references to stablemate, roommate, classmate, and so on) using "left-hand truncation."

The vendor's search software also influences the fields you will find in each record and what you can do with them. The ABI/INFORM database, for example, is available on nearly a dozen systems, including DIALOG, BRS, and ORBIT. On all three systems you can enter a command to limit the search to articles published in one particular year. You can also limit a search to a particular range of years. This is easiest to do on DIALOG because the search language lets you specify the range in a single command. Entering PY = 1983:PY = 1985 sets the range of the search between "publication years." The same results require two separate commands on BRS and three on ORBIT.

That's helpful, but suppose you want to limit your search not only by year but by month as well. This is hardly unreasonable, since INFORM is a database of magazines and you might very well want to see how the major weekly magazines covered an event you know took place in a certain month. Although all three systems will let you do this, you must search not for the month and year of publication, but for the month and year the abstracted records were added to the ABI/INFORM database.

Since the lag time between a magazine's publication date and the time INFORM is updated with its records is rarely more than four to six weeks, this doesn't present a major problem. It is a twist you've got to watch for, however. And should you want to cover yourself and search for a *range* of update dates, you could do so on ORBIT and DIALOG, but not on BRS. (INFORM added a publication date field in June 1986).

As it happens, ABI/INFORM is also available in the Reference Service section of NEXIS. And here things are so much simpler, since on this system, the ABI/INFORM database includes a searchable field for publication date. Entering DATE AFT 7-1-86 AND DATE BEF 8-1-86 would limit the search to articles *published* during July 1986. Just so you don't get bored, however, NEXIS refers to fields as "segments" and uses the term "document" instead of "record."

Differences in search language capabilities may or may not be important to you. If you plan to labor over a really artistic search each time you go online, you will obviously want the most extensive palette of commands available. But for most people the fundamental search commands available on all systems will be more than enough. Systems like NewsNet and the Knowledge Index, for example, offer good sets of basic commands but none of the more elaborate variations found on the bibliographic databases. As a result, they are notably easy to learn and use.

Search-Aid Features

Vendor-Supplied Database Documentation

There are two main categories of documentation in this field. One is the system documentation that explains how DIALOG, NEXIS, or VU/TEXT operates, the commands and features that are available, how to enter a search, and so on. And the other is the database documentation that explains the particulars of a specific database available from a vendor. The system documentation is always found in the manual you receive with your subscription. Documentation for the various databases may be in that manual as well, or you may have to order it separately.

The type of database documentation and what you can expect to find depend on the vendor and on the kind of information the specific database contains. For example, since NewsNet focuses almost exclusively on newsletters and since newsletters all consist of headlines and paragraphs of text, if you know how to search through one newsletter, you know how to search through all newsletters. The system documentation thus tells you everything you need to know to search any NewsNet newsletter, each of which can be thought of as a "database." The only additional documentation required is a three- or four-sentence description of each newsletter, what it covers, and how frequently it is issued.

The situation is very different on a system that covers the range of databases found on the Big Three bibliographics. TRADE-MARKSCAN™ (Chapter 17) and Trade Opportunities (Chapter 17) are both available on DIALOG, but they are totally different products. The former contains every trademark on file with the U.S. Patent and Trademark Office. The latter consists of purchase requests by the international market for U.S. goods and services and is supplied by the Department of Commerce. Obviously their records will use different formats and have different fields.

DIALOG explains the formatting and fields used by each of its databases in its "Bluesheets." A complete set of these double-sided pages printed on light blue stock is included with the main DIALOG manual. The front of the Bluesheet for TRADEMARKSCAN, for example, contains headings for File Description, Subject Coverage, Sources, DIALOG File Data (dates covered, number of records in the file, etc.), and Origin (address, toll-free numbers, telex, and other contact information for Thomson & Thomson, the company that produces the database).

The back contains a Sample Record in which all of the fields are labeled so you know where to look for them. There is also a summary of the various fields you can search. There are nearly 30 of them, ranging from "Serial Number (PTO Application Number)" to "Class Number" to "Series Code" and "Year of First Use (of Mark)." Finally, there is a summary of the DIALOG format options and what information will be displayed in each case. Five DIALOG formats are available.

The Bluesheet for Trade Opportunities follows the identical pattern. Here, though, there are only a dozen or so searchable fields, ranging from "Business Name" to "Product Code" to "Type of Opportunity." Six DIALOG display/print formats are available.

IP-Supplied Database Documentation

Every vendor offers something similar to DIALOG's Bluesheets. On the main BRS system, single-sheet summaries are called "BRS Aid-Pages." The four-page summaries printed on tan stock for the Knowledge Index manual are called "Database Briefs." The Database Descriptions (on "DIALOG blue" stock) in the VU/TEXT manual run four to six pages.

In some cases, these pages may provide all the database documentation you need. However, if reading about all of the fields for serial numbers, special codes, and the like in TRADEMARKSCAN or Trade Opportunities makes your head spin, hang on. There's more to the story.

Generally, single-sheet summaries like the blues or the AidPages are intended as quick-reference sheets. You're not supposed to know what all of the codes and special fields mean the first time you look at them. The quick-reference sheets are intended to be used with more extensive booklets and manuals for each database.

DIALOG, for example, offers a "Database Documentation Chapter" for virtually every database on the system. Each sells for $6 and the typical length is 30 pages. The one for TRADEMARKSCAN is nearly 70 pages long. The Trade Opportunities chapter is 22 pages. Prepared by the resident DIALOG expert on the database from material supplied by the information provider, the chapters explain each field in detail. Sample searches, tips for searching, controlled vocabulary terms, and full-record printouts are all included.

ORBIT sells manuals for its databases for $7.50 each. But generally the other systems do not offer the equivalent of DIALOG's database chapters. Instead, they direct you to the IP for additional documentation. The BRS/BRKTHRU manual, for example, includes a single double-sided page for each database on the system. These are designed for quick reference only. But where applicable, there is a heading for "Search Aids" followed by the title of a manual or book or other document available from the database producer.

The BRKTHRU page for PTS/PROMT, for example, lists the *PTS Users Manual* as a search aid. The address for the information provider (Predicasts, Inc.) is given, but not the phone number. Nor are there any prices. As it happens, Predicasts not only has a toll-free phone number, it also offers a manual called the *PROMT User Guide* ($40), the *PTS Company Directory* ($50), and a variety of free brochures and helpful publications. (In this industry you should always simply assume that companies have toll-free numbers, even if they aren't published in every instance. Whenever no 800 number is given, call 800-555-1212, the AT&T toll-free information number, and ask.)

Other information providers may not publish such extensive documentation, but almost everyone has something. And it's almost always worthwhile because it goes into such detail about what's in the database, how often it's updated, why you should avoid searching on certain fields, and so on. Though this IP-supplied documentation is rarely cheap, it can save you many connect-time dollars and loads of online frustration.

Online Tip: Whether you plan to search a database on DIALOG or on some other system, you can benefit from the appropriate DIALOG database chapter. You don't even need a DIALOG subscription, though since it doesn't cost you anything, you might as well sign up while you're at it.

Contact DIALOG at the number or address given below and ask for a copy of the DIALOG Publications Catalog. Then order the publication called "Search Aids for Use with DIALOG Databases." The cost is $6 and you can charge it to your major credit card. At this writing, the item number is 0600003-5.

The catalog is 58 pages long, and it includes a complete summary and description of all the guides, manuals, newsletters, and brochures available from *both* the IPs and from DIALOG. Prices, addresses, and toll-free numbers are also included. For the Predicasts databases alone there are some 13 publications, including a free bimonthly newsletter.

The Publications Catalog also includes information on ordering the DIALOG Database Chapters discussed above. Although their quality may vary slightly, these are generally a real value at $6 each. The information they contain about a database can be essential, regardless of the vendor you use. The 28-page chapter on ABI/INFORM, for example, is useful for searching that database in BRS, the Knowledge Index, VU/TEXT, or any other system. You may even find that for your purposes it supplies enough information to eliminate the need for the $47.50 *SearchINFORM* manual sold by the database producer.

> Publications Distribution Center
> DIALOG Information Services, Inc.
> 3460 Hillview Avenue
> Palo Alto, CA 94304
> 800-334-2564
> 415-858-3719

Database of the Vendor's Databases

Each of the Big Three bibliographics has a separate database that serves as a master index to their systems. On DIALOG, it is called DIALINDEX™ (File 411) and can be searched for $35 an hour with no display charges. The BRS/SEARCH equivalent is CROSS (as in "cross-reference"), and ORBIT's is DBI ("Data Base Index").

These three databases are designed to help you decide which databases to search on their respective systems. Without going into detail, you basically key in your search strategy (RADIAL AND TIRES AND SAFETY, for example), and the system will tell you how many hits the strategy generates in each of the available databases. This not only makes it easy to check what you think are the most likely databases, it also makes it easy to take a flyer on some unlikely ones without spending much money. Once you have identified the most fruitful search strategy and the databases containing the most hits, you can key in a command or two and go search those databases for real.

The capabilities of these three files do vary. ORBIT's DBI file does not permit much more than entering a few keywords, while the other two let you refine your complete search strategy. On DIALOG and BRS you can also temporarily store a successful strategy on the system, move to the real databases, and run it again by keying in just its assigned label.

Vendor-Produced Search-Aid Software

Of the eight vendors considered in this book, four offer some kind of communications software package designed to help you use their systems. More may follow in the future since these products fit naturally with the vendors' main business. They are nicely packaged and produced, but with the exception of the programs offered by Dow Jones, in general they are nothing to write home about.

Most are basically just bread-and-butter communications programs that have been customized to automatically dial and log you onto the host system and let you issue complicated commands by hitting single keys. They may include some pleasant cosmetics and one or two unique features, but generally anyone who uses a keyboard macroing program like ProKey, SmartKey, or NewKey and a basic communications program can do the same thing. And while you may be able to use them for other communications tasks, you may find that few support the XMODEM or Kermit error-checking protocols needed for uploading and downloading software, spreadsheets, and the like from BBSs, CompuServe, and corporate mainframes.

Like the others, NEXIS has a communications package. But Mead deserves kudos for taking the additional step of making a special arrangement with Microstuff, producer of the best-selling CrossTalk communications program. Beginning with CrossTalk Version 3.6, all copies of the program now include a special script file for use with NEXIS. So if you've become accustomed to CrossTalk, there is no need to learn a special package to access NEXIS.

Dow Jones deserves special mention because the numerous software packages it offers are not only designed to mesh closely with the Dow Jones News/Retrieval Service, they are also designed to perform offline processing of the information you have downloaded. Available for Apple, IBM, and other machines, programs like the Dow Jones Market Microscope™ or Market Analyzer™ can go in and download stock quotes and financial data and then help you make sense of it once you've signed off.

Though none of them has been a roaring success, some software houses have produced special software designed to help you use one or more online information systems. These so-called "front-end" packages tend to be much more elaborate (and expensive) than the vendor-produced programs. We'll look at them in a later chapter.

Vendor- and IP-Sponsored Training

Some vendors offer demo disks to acquaint you with their systems before you sign on. And DIALOG supports a wide range of low-cost ONTAP™ practice databases. These are mini-versions of various databases available for practice searching at a connect-time cost of $15 an hour (plus telecommunications). They contain only a small fraction of the information available from their full-cost parents.

Just about everyone in this corner of the electronic universe offers some form of training. And that includes not only the vendors but the database producers as well. You may not know it, for example, but the first Monday of each month is actually "DIALOG Day." This is when DIALOG holds its free introductory sessions at its offices in major U.S. cities. There are also free "Brown-Bag Lunch" sessions (you pack your own) conducted during the noon hour at various locations.

But that is just the beginning. DIALOG also offers a range of half- and full-day seminars costing $55 to $125. The seminars include personalized instruction, materials, and on-site practice time, and they may be geared for beginners, advanced users, or subscribers interested in a particular subject area. Most are approved for continuing education credits. BRS, NEXIS, ORBIT, VU/TEXT, Wilsonline, and Dow Jones have training programs as well.

Vendor-sponsored training normally emphasizes how to use a system's features most effectively when searching a given set of databases or searching in general. But as mentioned, many of the IPs offer seminars, workshops, and training sessions as well. These programs focus intensely on the content of one or more databases, how they are indexed, why certain things are included and other things left out, unique features, and lots of helpful hints and search tips. Among the information providers who also hold seminars, for example, are ABI/INFORM, DISCLOSURE II, Standard & Poor's, TRADEMARKSCAN, the Electronic Yellow Pages, Predicasts, and many more.

Consider Information Access Company (IAC), for example, the producer of such products as The Magazine Index, The National Newspaper Index, and Trade & Industry ASAP. In 1986 the company conducted at least 36 full-day seminars in various cities around the United States. IAC charges $50 for the session, and users receive a workbook, practice time, and discounts on IAC search guide publications. There is a Basic Course focusing on seven IAC databases, and a Business Applications Course focusing on Management Contents, Industry Data Sources, and four other IAC products. Both are available in DIALOG and BRS versions. And both assume that you have had some previous experience on one of those systems.

As a subsidiary of Ziff-Davis, IAC has so many top-quality database products that it is rather like the Procter & Gamble of the information industry. It has the financial backing, the variety of products, and the vision to do things in a big way. Consequently, the extent of its training program is probably not typical. But many other IPs come close.

Customer Support, Toll-Free Numbers, and Newsletters

How do you find out about vendor training sessions? You check the vendor's newsletter. What about IP-sponsored training? The answer is the same. Only here you may have two newsletters to check, the one from the vendor and one published by the IP. As with training, customer support and related services run on two parallel tracks in the information industry. Both vendor and IP are involved.

Each vendor handles its newsletter differently, but nearly every vendor has one. DIALOG's "Chronolog" is a fat, 8½-by-11-inch booklet that contains information about new databases that have been added to the system and announcements of DIALOG training schedules in the U.S., Australia and New Zealand, Europe, and elsewhere. (The South American announcements are written in Spanish. Some European announcements are in French.) Subscriptions are $25 a year.

Also included are announcements of IP-sponsored seminars, summaries of changes and enhancements to the DIALOG search language, and tips on searching various databases. Most issues also have two or more new or updated Bluesheets bound into them (perfed and punched for easy installation in your manuals). An annual "Index to the Chronolog" is also issued each year.

The monthly "BRS Bulletin" performs a similar function for that system, with separate sections devoted to BRS, BRS/BRKTHRU, and BRS/After Dark. ORBIT publishes the "Searchlight" every two months for the same reason. Dow Jones publishes a full-blown magazine called *Dowline*. NewsNet offers the monthly eight-page "NewsNet Action Letter." And so on.

Vendor newsletters are sent to you automatically because of your subscription. After all, they know where you live. IP newsletters are almost always free as well, but normally you have to contact the IP directly to get your name on the distribution list. (You'll find contact information in each of the chapters in Part III.) As you might imagine, the IP newsletters focus exclusively on the IP's products. And that's all to the good. The vendor publications don't have the space to devote to all of the changes that may have been made to the databases you are interested in. Indeed, things change so quickly in the electronic universe that oftentimes an IP newsletter is the only way to keep up-to-date on a particular database.

Finally, all vendors and many IPs offer toll-free customer support numbers. They may not always be available every time you need them, but at the very least they are there for you eight hours out of every business day. Many of these firms have been in business for years, and unlike some personal computer software houses, they've got telephone support down to a science. They are truly the great unknown resource of the online world.

To make the best use of them, and to be fair to the person on the other end of the line, don't be a "RFM" (pronounced "riff-im" and short for "read the effing manual!"). Do your homework and try to acquire at least a basic understanding of the system and/or the database you are using before you call. But at the same time, there's no reason to hesitate when you have a question. If you want to know how to do something on BRS, give them a call. If you need help formulating a search strategy on an IAC database, call *them*. They are there to help, and in our experience the customer support people at the vendors and at the databases are highly professional, pleasant, and genuinely interested in helping you solve your problems.

INFORMATION DELIVERY
Special Display Options

Tagged Output, Sort, and Report

In addition to the standard formats discussed earlier, some databases, including the Big Three bibliographics, offer a variety of other display-related options. VU/TEXT, for example, lets you command the system to display records ranked by the number of times your search terms appear in each document. NEXIS lets you display the longest documents first or vice versa. You can also sort by date and some other options depending upon the database.

DIALOG, BRS, and ORBIT let you sort a range of documents by one or more fields when the information is displayed on your screen or produced as an offline printout. You might have records sorted by the author field and, within that group, by the publication year. Or you might identify your top 50 competitors and ask that they be sorted in descending order by annual sales. Unfortunately, not all databases permit sorting. The only way to tell is to check the DIALOG Bluesheet or other database documentation. (Or call Customer Service.) And while all three vendors can produce sorted printouts, at this writing only DIALOG can do so for online displays as well.

You may also be able to customize the online display format. Both Wilsonline and ORBIT let you specify any combination of printable fields, for example. And on ORBIT, you can have the system spell out the fields ("AUTHORS," instead of "AU") and display them in a left column matched to the field information in a right column. BRS and ORBIT records are always displayed with the field labels. DIALOG's usually aren't, though the company has recently added a "tagged output" display option that lets you request field labels.

On some DIALOG databases you can produce customized tabular reports by telling the system which fields you want displayed and in what order. This makes it easy to go into Moody's Corporate Profiles (Chapter 16), one of the databases that supports the REPORT feature, and produce a table containing a company's name, ticker symbol, cost of sales, net income, long-term debt, price/earnings ratio, and any other key fact in a record. Once the data is in tabular form, it is a relatively easy matter to import it into Lotus 1-2-3 for additional processing.

You could do the same kind of thing in the Electronic Yellow Pages (Chapter 15). The REPORT feature makes it easy to produce a table listing the name, city, state, and phone number of every company that meets your search criteria. In this and several other databases containing address information, there is a LABELS feature that will automatically display address information in a mailing label format. If you like, you can even order DIALOG to print the results offline on pressure-sensitive label stock.

With the exception of DIALOG's REPORT feature, customized display options and offline printing are less important today than they were when most searchers had only printing dumb terminals. With a personal computer and a decent word processing program you can easily reformat downloaded data any way you wish, though you may not want to take the time to do so. Other PC programs may be able to sort your downloads seven ways from sundown. However, you should still make a point of investigating your online options, since you never know when one of them may come in handy.

Online Tip: If you are going to be doing any online sorting, or for that matter if you are going to be downloading a relatively large amount of information, try to do it during a system's off-peak hours. When a lot of people are using a large computer simultaneously, the system usually takes longer to satisfy any one person's request. Your downloads and sorts may thus take longer during peak usage periods. And since time is always money when you are online, you may end up paying more than you would if you could wait until the system is less heavily loaded.

Off-peak times will vary with where you live. On most systems, for example, off-peak for East Coast users is any time the Westerners are in bed or eating their oats . . . brown rice, granola, or whatever passes for breakfast west of the Nevada state line. For Westerners, off-peak time is after the Easterners have unplugged their nervous systems from the jangle of the cities and are sitting peacefully in their railway or subway cars wondering why their train has suddenly stopped between stations. If you live in the middle of the country, you have a window of opportunity when either coast goes to lunch.

Current Awareness or "SDI" Services

Selective Dissemination of Information (SDI)

Many vendors offer a feature that the industry refers to as Selective Dissemination of Information or an "SDI" service. This is a ridiculous term. It serves only to prove that computer users aren't the only ones capable of sinning against the English language. Fortunately, some vendors are now using the term "current awareness service" to refer to the same thing, though through long tradition "SDI" is well entrenched.

In addition to representing an imaginative, natural use of online information technology, SDI services are really neat. Suppose your company manufactures potato peelers and your R&D department is currently working on a revolutionary twin-blade design. The first blade will depress the potato skin, smoothing it out for the second blade, which will cleanly slice it off. For easy peeling, you're planning to impregnate the two blades with Teflon®.

It's a hotly competitive field. And though you read *Potato Peeler Age* religiously, you can't read everything. So you go online with DIALOG, BRS, ORBIT, NewsNet, NEXIS, and other vendors and develop a search strategy that retrieves information about relevant subjects (steel alloys, Teflon, methods of impregnation, etc.). This produces exactly the kind of information you're looking for. The trouble is, you don't want to be bothered signing on to all of those systems every month to run that strategy against your selected databases.

That's where SDI comes in. An SDI feature lets you store your search strategies on a system indefinitely. Then, each time your chosen databases are updated, the vendor's system automatically runs the search. You might think of your saved strategies as a satellite in geosynchronous orbit over the database. As soon as the satellite detects an incoming update, it zaps it and sends it to the vendor's printing facility. From there it's a short hop into an envelope and into the mail. The "net

net" is that every time new potato peeler information is added to a database, a copy of it appears on your desk a few days later.

SDI services are not free. Normally there is a charge for storing your SDI "profile" (the saved search strategy) on a system. And there is usually a charge each time the strategy is run against a database, whether or not any hits are generated. Offline printout and postage charges apply as well, of course. NewsNet's SDI feature is called News-Flash, and SDI on NEXIS is called ECLIPSE ("Electronic CLIPping SErvice"). Not all systems and not all databases on all systems support an SDI feature. But those that do can save you a great deal of time if you need to stay up-to-date on a subject.

Document Delivery

"Document delivery" is the industry's term for the service of sending you a photocopy, facsimile, or actual copy of the source document from which an online abstract or bibcite was derived. It is no exaggeration to say that if you are willing to pay for it, you can obtain a copy of *anything* that is referenced online. That includes magazine articles, conference papers and proceedings, video and audio tapes, patents, complete books, chapters from books, maps, monographs, charts, architectural diagrams—if it exists anywhere in North America, you can have it in your hands tomorrow morning. If it exists anywhere else in the world, you may *still* be able to have it by tomorrow, though in most cases it will take a day or so.

For example, suppose you were interested in standards pertaining to the purity of paraffin used to seal jelly jars. You might sign on to DIALOG and begin to use the Standards & Specifications database produced by the National Standards Association, Inc. (NSA). In a few moments you've got three citations on your screen referencing standards issued by the Food and Drug Administration and two trade associations. You'd like copies of each.

At that point, you have only to key in the word KEEP, hit <EN-TER>, and key in the command ORDER SPECS. That transmits your document delivery request to the NSA document delivery division ("SPECS"). If it is received by 2:00 P.M. Eastern time, a photocopy will be shipped to you via UPS or first-class mail the same day. All orders are processed within 24 hours.

NSA can do this because it has over a quarter of a million documents in-house, and since it is located in the Washington, D.C., area it can easily obtain any it does not have. The cost ranges from about $5 to $30 per document, depending on whether the standard was published by the federal government or a private body. Delivery via Federal Express is extra.

The Worldwide Document Delivery Network
This example is only the smallest tip of the iceberg. To fully appreciate the power at your command, you have to know about the worldwide document delivery network. DIALOG, BRS, and ORBIT, as well as vendors not considered in this book, have features designed to help you tap this network. If you don't subscribe to a system with a document delivery feature, you can easily tap into the net on your own.

The network is vast indeed. There may be 3,000 databases, but there are over 8,796 public libraries in the United States alone, according to Mary Jo Lynch, Director of Research at the American Library Association (ALA). This does not include university or specialized libraries, and it does not include the tens of thousands of elementary and high-school libraries, some of which can be quite sophisticated. But libraries are only the beginning.

Online Tip: The ALA operates what may be the fastest-growing network in the library/information community. Open to libraries, corporate information centers, and individuals, ALANET is based on the Dialcom system. In addition to special ALA bulletin boards and customized interactive forms, it provides access to a variety of newswires, ABI/INFORM, and electronic mail/telex interface, the Business Research and Intelligence Network (B.R.A.I.N.), and a gateway to VU/TEXT. For more information, contact:

> Mr. Joel M. Lee
> ALANET System Manager
> American Library Association
> 50 East Huron Street
> Chicago, IL 60611
> (312) 944-6780

There are professional societies, government agencies, and antiquarian book dealers. There are firms that will produce complete photocopies of any of the 100,000 to 500,000 out-of-print books in their collections. (Softcover binding is included; hardcover is $6 extra.) Other companies specialize in supplying copies of U.S. government documents (court decisions, agency filings, Congressional committee reports, etc.).

Still others do the same for documents produced by non-U.S. governments. This doesn't scratch the surface of what's available. The list of document sources is virtually endless.

A Range of Choices

Document sources and delivery services overlap so much that it is difficult to put each organization into a neat category. But to give you a general idea of where everything fits, imagine that you have done an online search and obtained a citation for an article in some obscure magazine. Since you've got the citation, you have all of the reference information needed to track the article down (title, author, publication date, etc.). What can you do to obtain a copy of the article?

You can go to your local library. If it is not there, the librarian can check the various "Union List" volumes that detail the holdings of other libraries in the area, region, or state. If one of them has the publication, the librarian can send them an interlibrary loan (ILL) request asking them to send a photocopy. (You will be charged for photocopying and postage and may or may not have to pay a small service charge.) If none of those libraries has the article, your librarian might go online with OCLC, Inc., a nonprofit library service organization, in Dublin, Ohio.

OCLC maintains a database called the Online Union Catalog covering the "serial" (magazines and journals) collections of some 6,000 member-libraries in the U.S. and nine other countries. In the library profession it is something of an unwritten rule that if you receive an interlibrary loan request from any other library, you honor it, regardless of the requesting library's location. More than likely, someone will have what you seek, though it may take weeks or even months to make its way to your desktop.

The Database Producer Option

Another alternative is to contact the producer of the database from which you received the citation and ask *them* for a copy. Though it wasn't always the case in the past, database producers have increasingly begun to offer document delivery. The services offered by ABI/INFORM are typical.

The company will send you a copy of any article published since 1975 in any of the more than 650 magazines covered by the ABI/INFORM database. The cost is $8.25 regardless of the length of the article, and postage to addresses in the U.S., Mexico, and Canada is included. (Shipments elsewhere are sent by airmail and cost an additional $2.) You can place your order by telex, toll-free phone number, or facsimile machine, and orders received by 2:00 P.M. Eastern time will be shipped the following workday. Rush service is available for an additional $5 per order, regardless of the number of articles in the order, plus express delivery charges.

You can pay by Visa, MasterCard, or American Express. Or you can ask to be invoiced. If you are willing to place a minimum of $100 on deposit with the firm, the cost per article drops to $6.75.

Specialty Suppliers

Another alternative is to contact a firm that specializes in nothing but document delivery. University Microfilms International (UMI) is among the leaders in this area. Owned by Bell & Howell, UMI is the largest directly licensed (copyright cleared) distributor of periodical articles in the world. The company's collection covers nearly 9,000 publications, some of which date back to 1912 or earlier.

UMI guarantees a 48-hour in-house turnaround for any article dating from 1978 to the present. (If they don't make it, you don't pay for it.) Pre-1978 articles take an average of three to five days. "Rush service" (ships within 24 hours) and "rush overnight" (ships by overnight express carrier) are also available. And if your firm has a CCITT Group 3 or 4 facsimile machine, you can elect to have the article faxed to your location.

You can place your order using any of nearly a dozen electronic systems, including OnTyme, ALANET, OCLC, EasyNet, DIALOG, and the main BRS system. Or you may use UMInet, the company's own system based on Tymnet. (UMInet mailboxes are available at no charge.) In most cases, you will be prompted to enter the necessary article ordering information. You may also place orders via telex, fax, or regular mail.

Costs vary with the method of order placement. Ordering via electronic mail is the cheapest method, since no one at UMI has to rekey the data into the company's system. Payment is by deposit account (minimum of $200), major credit card, or check. There are discounts if you set up a deposit account. But assuming you placed your order using an electronic mail system and are paying by credit card, you would be charged $8 for each post-1978 article and $11 for each pre-1978 article. That includes all copyright fees and first-class postage. (There is a $2.25 charge per article to cover airmail costs for shipment outside of the U.S. and Canada.)

For more information and a copy of the free 30-page UMI Article Clearinghouse catalog listing all of the journals covered, contact:

University Microfilms International
300 North Zeeb Road
Ann Arbor, MI 48106

(800) 732-0616
(800) 343-5299, in Canada
(313) 761-4700

Though it is a leader in supplying journal articles, UMI isn't the only firm in its field. And articles are only one area that companies specialize in. Other companies focus on technical and scientific papers. Some limit themselves to government publications. There are firms who can get you a copy of virtually any foreign patent. And there are companies who deal exclusively in financial information on non-U.S. companies. You name it, and a specialty firm somewhere can supply it.

Online Tip: To our knowledge, there is no consumer's guide to help you choose a document delivery service, but someone has done a directory. For the past several years The Information Store, Inc., has published *Document Retrieval: Sources and Services*. The book sells for $60, plus shipping and handling ($1 book rate/$5 first class/$18.50 airmail overseas) and tax if you live in California.

Over 250 document delivery services are covered, and contact information, rates, fulfillment time, ordering procedure, and types of materials supplied are provided for each. The book is indexed by type of information and type of publication. There are 17 firms listed under PATENTS, for example, and five under METAL-LURGY. Other headings include "JOURNAL ARTICLES," "COURT DECISIONS," "SCIENTIFIC CONFERENCE PRO-CEEDINGS," and so on.

For more information, or to order, contact:

The Information Store, Inc.
140 Second Street, Fifth Floor
San Francisco, CA 94105-3715
(415) 543-4636

Online Tip: One of the best sources of document delivery information is the "Document Delivery" column found in each issue of *Online* magazine. In recent years the column has been written by Antoinette W. Colbert. Ms. Colbert has had long experience in the information brokerage and document delivery business, first with Information On Demand and currently with Dynamic Information

Corporation. Some of the sources she uncovers are inspired, and her comments on the strengths and weaknesses of various suppliers are invaluable.

Most medium- to large-sized libraries have back issues of *Online* for you to look at. (An electronic version of the publication is available on DIALOG as File 170, but sadly it does not include the "Document Delivery" column at this writing.) But since *Online* is one of the leading magazines in the electronic information field, you might also want a subscription. It is issued six times a year. Institutional subscriptions are $78, but subscriptions for individuals are only $39. Contact:

Online, Inc.
11 Tannery Lane
Weston, CT 06883
(203) 227-8466

Information Brokers and Intermediaries

Considering the huge number of document sources and suppliers, locating the right one can be a real challenge. Consequently it is not surprising that there are any number of firms who can take this chore off your hands. As information specialists, these firms know the network and the suppliers. All you have to do is contact them, tell them what you want, and they'll figure out where to get it and how to get it to you. You may hear such firms referred to variously as "information intermediaries," "fee-based information services," "information brokers," "information consultants," or "information specialists."

The terminology and lines of demarcation get a bit hazy at this point, however. Some companies are set up to respond to your request for a specific document. You would normally contact one of these organizations after you had conducted an online database search and determined exactly which documents you wanted. Other companies are set up to respond to your request for information on a particular topic. They will interview you about the kind of information you want, conduct the necessary searches, contact the appropriate document suppliers, and deliver the documents to you. This is usually what is meant by the term "information broker," and we'll discuss such services in greater detail in Chapter 6.

In practice, both types of companies perform both types of services. So probably the best rule of thumb is to find a company that offers you excellent service at a fair price and stick with it. As is the case with your main attorney or accountant, your main information firm may call in or refer you to a specialist if there is something it is not well qualified to handle.

Another advantage of doing most of your business with the same firm is the possibility of quantity discounts. But whether you handle things that way or on an on-demand basis, you won't necessarily pay more than you would contacting the information suppliers yourself. Dynamic Information Corporation, for example, can fill many information requests at a cost of $4.80 per article, plus 20 cents per page for photocopying. Depending on where the company must go to obtain the source document, a price of $7.50 per article and 35 cents a page, or $10 and any pass-along costs, may be charged. (An additional dollar or so may be charged to cover copyright fees where applicable.)

"Economies of scale is the key," according to Randy Marcinko, Dynamic's president and founder. "We handle so many requests that we can afford to price our services lower. That and the fact that we are almost totally electronic."

A chemist by training, Mr. Marcinko founded Dynamic out of frustration with the difficulties in obtaining the technical documents he needed. The company has established a worldwide network with contacts or personnel in many major cities, including Tokyo, Zurich, and London. Many of its locations are equipped with fax machines, which leads to some interesting possibilities.

"Say you need a copy of a patent, diagrams and all," says Mr. Marcinko. "You would contact us here in California with your request and we'd have one of our people in Washington, D.C., obtain a photocopy of it from the PTO (Patents and Trademark Office). The patent would be zapped back here. We'd verify that it was indeed what you requested, and zap it to the fax facility nearest you for delivery. Or if you've got a Group 3 or Group 4 machine of your own, we could send it directly to your office."

The cost for this document delivery wizardry is $7.50 plus 35 cents per page for pulling and photocopying the patent, plus 85 cents per page for ZAPping it. Hand delivery via Federal Express is an extra $5. Rush service (24 to 48 hours) is an additional $7.50, and emergency rush service is available. (Mr. Marcinko's firm once obtained documents from Tokyo in time to hand them to an attorney in California as he was entering the courtroom.)

Dynamic is the authorized supplier for a number of databases, including the entire Information Access Company collection (Magazine Index, NEWSEARCH, etc.), the Microcomputer Index, and International Pharmaceutical Abstracts. That means that while other services can obtain documents referenced in these databases from other sources, Dynamic is probably the only service capable of supplying everything found there. Information Access Company, for example, has placed its entire collection of magazines in Dynamic's hands.

For a price list and additional information, contact:

> Dynamic Information Corporation
> 333 Twin Dolphin Drive, Suite 250
> Redwood City, CA 94065-1027
> (415) 591-5900

Copyright Fees and the Copyright Clearing Center

After nearly two decades of legislative effort, the 94th Congress passed the Copyright Act of 1976 on September 30, one day before it adjourned for the year. The act represented the first comprehensive revision of United States copyright laws in 50 years, and it spoke to the question of photocopying. The law has all kinds of special provisions and exemptions regarding the photocopying of documents. Much depends on who is doing the copying and why and whether the copying is systematic or "spontaneous."

The details need not concern us here. What's important is that under the law a magazine or other publisher has the right to either refuse permission or negotiate a royalty payment for the privilege of duplicating works for which it holds the copyright. Technically, document delivery services are supposed to seek permission from and/or pay royalties to the publisher of every article they supply to you.

If the prospect of hundreds of document suppliers having to locate and negotiate separate arrangements with tens of thousands of publishers sounds like an administrative nightmare, you're right. Consequently, in 1977, in accordance with the expressed desire of Congress, an organization called the Copyright Clearance Center (CCC) was established by authors, publishers, information industry people, librarians, and others interested in the photocopying issue.

The goal of the CCC is to serve both publishers and photocopy users by streamlining the royalty payment process. Every time UMI, The Information Store, or Dynamic Information Corp. copies an article for you, it checks to see if the publisher is a member of the CCC. If it is, the document delivery service makes a note of the article and pays a certain amount to the CCC, which then passes it along to the appropriate publisher. Copyright clearance fees may be added on to the price the document supplier quotes you, or they may be built in. (Dynamic charges $7.50 for articles referenced in the Microcomputer Index, for example, but $2.50 of that is the copyright fee.)

Not all publishers charge a copyright fee. And not all publishers belong to the CCC. By the end of February 1985, according to Eamon T. Fennessy, president, the CCC had approximately 1,050 registered publishers—up from 525 in 1980—and about 1,900 registered users. Publishers and users presumably have a variety of reasons for not joining, but the end result has been a less than spectacular growth rate.

That may change with a new site licensing plan introduced in the summer of 1985. Under the plan a company can pay a single annual fee for the privilege of making unlimited internal-use copies of articles from nearly 10,000 journals, books, and magazines. Perhaps mindful of the fact that six technical publishers brought suit against Texaco charging "large-scale, covert, unauthorized photocopying of protected material" in 1985, Warner-Lambert, Exxon, and other large companies have signed on.

At this writing, however, no document delivery service is in the program. Services that supply photocopies in accordance with the law must still send itemized reports and payments to the CCC or to publishers with whom they have agreements. And as noted, both the clearance charges and the administrative costs are passed on to the customer. Understandably, these services tend not to think highly of competing firms whose less than scrupulous observance of the law allows them to undercut their price or to charge the same price and pocket the built-in clearance fee themselves.

For more information on the CCC and its programs, contact:

> Copyright Clearance Center
> 27 Congress Street
> Salem, MA 01970
> (617) 744-3350

Where Do the Database Vendors Fit In?

Database vendors don't do document delivery. Their role is to make ordering a copy of a document referenced in one of their databases as convenient as possible, and they do it through electronic mail. The vendors thus offer you a tangent to the document delivery network, but as we've seen, you're free to tap the network on your own.

Of the vendors considered in this book, only DIALOG, the Knowledge Index, BRS/SEARCH, and ORBIT offer a document delivery feature. This will undoubtedly change in the future. But at this writing, if you're using ABI/INFORM on VU/TEXT or BRS/BRKTHRU, you'll have to sign off and find a document supplier if you want a photocopy of an INFORM article.

DIALOG has long had the most convenient, best-developed online document ordering feature. The company has arrangements with nearly

80 document suppliers, each of whom has been assigned an easily re-membered name. For instance, by entering SPECS after .ORDER in the example at the beginning of this section, we told DIALOG that we wanted to order the target documents from the National Standards Association. We could have entered UMIACH to order from UMI, INFO-STOR to order from The Information Store, DYNAMIC to order from Dynamic Information Corp., and so on.

As part of the system manual, DIALOG supplies you with what it calls its "Yellowsheets." There's a Yellowsheet for each document delivery firm accessible via the ORDER command. Each sheet summarizes the firm's capabilities, areas of specialty, prices, and special services, and tells you whom to contact for more information. As with the Bluesheets, updates and new Yellowsheets are mailed to you with each copy of the "Chronolog" newsletter.

On DIALOG you are free to specify any Yellowsheet document supplier you choose. On the Knowledge Index, all document delivery chores are handled by Information On Demand (IOD), a leading information broker and document delivery service. The only exception is document delivery for the ABI/INFORM database, which is handled by the database producer.

At this writing, the document delivery features on BRS and ORBIT are considerably less well developed. ORBIT has arrangements with about 30 suppliers. Your options on BRS are pretty much limited to the companies who produced the databases, though it became possible to order from UMI in 1985. If you know the electronic mail address of suppliers like IOD (TJ52) or The Information Store (T19I), you can also order from them.

The problem is that, at this writing, you can't simply "KEEP" your search results and bibcites and tell a company that that's what you want to order. Both BRS and ORBIT require you to send an electronic message to the supplier and to rekey all of the bibliographic information needed to order the article. (BRS has announced plans to let users automatically request cited articles from UMI.) You must also key in your name and address for each order. On BRS you have only 12 lines of space per message. And neither system lets you redisplay and edit your order or verify that it has been picked up, both of which you can do on DIALOG. Until the situation improves, you may want to download your bibcites, sign off, and tap into the document delivery network yourself.

Conclusion

The Key Question Checklist that follows presents all of the various topics we have been discussing in a single, unified format. It's designed to be used as an analytical tool that can help you quickly nail down the

specific details of any electronic information service. The next chapter
will move the final major building block into place. It will show you how
to begin searching online and make any database sing your tune.

THE KEY QUESTION CHECKLIST
How to Quickly Analyze Any Information Service

This checklist is designed to be used as a tool to help you get up-
to-speed on any seller of electronic information, whether it's a single-
subject database or a database vendor. Not all of the question will apply
in every case, of course. But if you use this checklist as a guide when
reviewing materials supplied by the seller or when contacting customer
service for more information, you will be able to quickly see where everything fits and determine whether a given vendor meets your needs.
We're going to use the word *database* here to refer to all kinds of electronic information, including things like Dow Jones stock quotes, News-
Net newsletter, and classic bibliographic databases.

Preliminaries

Let's assume that there is a particular kind of information you want
to have access to right now. Part III of this book can help you locate
specific databases that cover the subject you are interested in. But you
should also consult one or more of the database directories described in
Appendix B. All of them have subject guides that will refer you to databases in your area of interest, and all of them will tell you which vendors carry which database.

It's important to be aware, however, that no printed publication in
this fast-moving field can ever be absolutely up-to-date. Sometimes
databases move around from one vendor to another. Sometimes they
disappear. But because it is in the best interests of a database producer
to have his product up on as many systems as possible, it is more usual
to find that a given database has become available from additional vendors since the directory or book went to press.

Even if you do not currently have a pressing information need, you
may still want to subscribe to one or more database vendors so that
they will be instantly available to you when the need arises sometime in
the future. One way or another, when you are considering a vendor, you
want to know:

☐ What databases (or other kinds of information) are available on the system?

You can find the answer to this question in the vendor's promotional literature or the (usually free) vendor catalog. Since additional databases may have been added since the catalog's publication, however, you may want to check with the vendor's customer service representatives as well.

☐ Which database(s) are you interested in?

• Is the version of the product that is available from this vendor the full implementation of the database?
  —How far back does its coverage extend?
  —Are there any publications or other items missing from this version?

• Does the database as it exists on this system have any special fields or other features not found on other vendors' systems?

• How frequently is the database updated on this vendor's system? Are updates more frequent on some other system?

Whether these questions matter to you or not will depend on the kind of information you're after. But as noted elsewhere, the content and coverage of a database can vary with the vendor. For answers to these questions, your best bet is probably the customer service or marketing department of the *database producer*, not the vendor.

Account-Related Matters

Subscriptions

☐ What subscription options are available and what do they cost?

• If you commit to one level of annual usage but at year's end find you have used more, do you automatically earn the discount applicable to the next higher level of usage?

• Can you pool your usage with members of a group to qualify for a higher discount?

• Are educational discounts available?

- Are there any minimum usage requirements? If so, which costs count against the minimum and which do not?

- Is there a monthly subscription or account maintenance fee?

- Is a low-cost, after hours subsystem like the Knowledge Index or BRS/After Dark available? Does it have the database(s) you need?

System Manuals and Documentation

☐ Is the system manual included in the price of the subscription? What does it include? If not, what does it cost?

☐ Is there a pocket reference guide or quick-reference sheet summarizing all crucial commands and how to use them?

☐ How and how often is the system documentation updated? Will you be notified online of any system or command changes?
   If there is an online updating feature, find out how it works and be sure to check it regularly. Print out the update information and store it with your system manual until a new edition is issued.

Usage Costs

☐ Do any of the following charges apply?

- Telecommunications charges (Tymnet, Telenet, etc.)

- Connect-hour charges
   —System or "basic" connect hour
   —Database-specific connect hour

- Other database-specific charges

   DISCLOSURE II, for example, carries a $2 to $6 access fee for each search on Dow Jones. The full-text IAC databases charge $7.50 for each full-text article retrieved. This is in addition to system and database connect time.

- High-speed surcharge (for 1200 or 2400 bps communications)

- Off-hours discount

- "Type" or display charge

- Offline print charge

- Per search charges

- Computer resource charge

☐ Are there any other charges for using the system?

☐ What would an itemized list of *all* the costs involved in a typical search look like?

☐ Can you obtain complete pricing information for a system's various databases online?

☐ Does the system provide an online estimate of costs before and a cost summary after a search? (DIALOG, ORBIT, and VU/TEXT currently have this capability, but others may add it in the future.)

☐ What billing options are available?

- By credit card

- By invoice

- By deposit account

- How extensive is the billing detail?

- Itemization by cost center (account number or password itemization)

Search-Related Matters

System and Search Language

☐ Is the system menu-driven, command-driven, or is there an option to switch from one mode to the other?

Menu-driven systems are easy to use but slow and possibly not as powerful as command-driven systems. Command-driven systems tend to be fast and powerful but challenging to master. Ideally, you will be able to use menus to get to know a system but have the option of switching to command mode after you've gained some experience.

☐ How powerful is the search language?

• Can you search by specific fields?

• Can you conduct a "full-text" search?

This is a tough one to call, since power and ease of use are generally at opposite ends of the spectrum. If you can search by a specific field, you can locate information very efficiently and economically. But you'll have to do a lot of head work before you sign on, and you'll have a lot of commands and command arguments to worry about.

A full-text search is less precise and generally more costly, since it usually turns up a lot of information you are not interested in. But it is very easy to use. You simply key in the name, word, or phrase you are looking for and let 'er rip. It's a meat-ax approach, but if you can afford to pay for all the "false drops" (irrelevant hits), you'll usually get what you're after.

Search-Aid Features

☐ Does the vendor publish booklets, guides, or other information focusing on a specific database? If so, what points are covered and what is the cost?

☐ Does the database producer offer additional documentation, thesauri, controlled vocabulary lists, tip sheets, or other aids? What do they cost and what do they cover?

The most efficient way to answer this question is to contact the IP directly. (The database vendor should be able to give you the phone number if you don't have it already.) Most IPs who offer additional manuals and documentation have brochures describing their contents, what they cost, why they are useful, and so on. If you search a given database frequently, this kind of documentation is absolutely essential. But since it tends to be quite expensive, we suggest that you send for explanatory material before sending in your money.

☐ Does the vendor offer search-aid software?

Software that is designed to help you search a particular vendor's system can be helpful, but we suggest you proceed with caution here.

Send for the vendor's descriptive and promotional literature first. Then try the system using your favorite communications program. Ask yourself how much time or effort the vendor-produced search-aid software would save you. Then make your decision. Unless the deal being offered is completely irresistible, we suggest that you deflect any attempts to get you to buy special software at the time you sign up. The programs may be good, but who wants to master a different communications program for every system?

Training

☐ What kinds of user training are available and what do they cost?

☐ What does each session involve? What materials and free connect time are provided?

☐ Does the database producer offer training as well? If so, what does it cost, when is it offered, what's included, etc.?

☐ Is there any sort of self-paced floppy disk-based program? Is there a videotape or cassette program?

Customer Support

☐ Does the *vendor* offer a customer support number? Is it toll-free in your area? During what hours is customer support available? Can they help you design your search strategies?

☐ What about the *database producer?* Is there a toll-free hotline? When is it available and can customer support representatives help you design your search strategies?

☐ Does the vendor publish a newsletter? How often is it issued and is it free?

☐ Is there a database producer newsletter? Is it free?

Information Delivery

Online Display and Offline Print Options

☐ How is information displayed on the system? Are there eight or nine formats or just three (short, medium, and long)? How can you find out what portions of a record are displayed in each format for each database?

☐ Can you order the system to tag each field with a label when displaying records? Or is that the default?

☐ Can you tell the system to display your hits in a particular order (most recent to oldest, longest or shortest first, sorted by some particular field, etc.)?

☐ Are there any special "report" options to let you specify which fields will be displayed and where they will appear? Is this feature available on your target database?

☐ What offline print options are available? Special mailing label stock? Delivery via electronic mail? Which is the cheaper alternative: online display or offline print?

Current Awareness or "SDI" Services

☐ Does the vendor have an SDI or current awareness service?

• If so, how does it work? How often will it be run, and what extra charges are involved?
   —Charges for storing your SDI profile online
   —Charges each time an SDI search is run

• What are the limitations on SDI profiles? How sophisticated may the search logic be in you SDI profile?

• Does the database you are interested in support an SDI feature?

Document Delivery Features

☐ Can you place an order for a document online?

• What limitations apply? Can you choose from a range of document suppliers or are you limited to just one?

• What is the document ordering process? Do you have to key in all necessary document reference information as well as your name and address, or will the system handle those chores for you?

...5...

How to Look It Up Online:
Tools and Techniques for Searching Any Database

There are two essential elements to successful online searching. The first is your mental approach to the problem at hand. The second is your familiarity with the tools available to get the job done. The mental element is the more important of the two. Indeed it may be the most important factor of all. It's certainly the most difficult to explain, which is probably why articles about online information retrieval tend to skip over it and concentrate on search commands and other tools.

In this chapter, however, we'll start with a discussion of how to develop the proper mental approach; then we'll discuss the major tools and techniques you need to start searching. We will use DIALOG as our main example; however, the concepts and approaches apply to *all* databases, even those that, like NewsNet, NEXIS, VU/TEXT, and most of Dow Jones, are not based on bibliographic citations and abstracts.

We'll conclude with a step-by-step guide to conducting a successful online search as illustrated in Figure 5.2. We will be referring to that figure frequently in this chapter, so we've placed it at the very end for easy reference.

PRELIMINARIES

Open a manual published by one of the database vendors and you'll find a great deal of information about search language, command syntax, and all the wonderfully intricate things you can do with the system. Unfortunately, if you are new to the field, an explanation of a full-powered search language in all its glory is about the last thing you need to see. The concepts are new. The commands are strange. And everything appears to have equal weight—you have no idea which portions of the manual are important and which commands and features you can safely ignore.

Ignore Everything

We suggest that you begin by ignoring *all* of them. We'll show you how to get started and what commands to look for later. For the moment, accept it on faith that if you can use a computer program like PFS:File, dBASE, or Lotus, you won't have much difficulty learning to use DIALOG, BRS, or ORBIT. Or any other information retrieval system. In fact, the computer programs may present the greater challenge.

Instead of trying to master all the commands at once, learn the commands *as you need them*. After you've done a little searching and gotten a feel for what it's like, after your mind has become actively engaged, you'll begin to ask questions: "I wonder if there's a way to focus my search on a particular magazine. . . . How can I search a range of dates instead of just a single year? . . . Is there a way to focus on the subject of plastics *without* including PVC or Styrofoam?"

You will discover that there are ways to do all of these things, and many more besides, on almost every system. But by waiting until you actually need these tools to find out about them, you will prevent the occurrence of that helpless, I-can-never-learn-to-do-this feeling that's inevitable if you try to absorb everything at once. Equally important, you'll have a strong motivation to learn the command since you will need it to solve a problem. You'll also have a much better sense of where it fits in the overall framework of the system.

Call Customer Service

The best way to find the answers to questions about how to use a system is to start by spending just a few minutes with the database vendor's manual, then *call Customer Service*. The information industry, unlike the computer hardware and software industries, has always put a heavy emphasis on telephone support. They've got the toll-free lines, the trained staff, and the years of experience to do the job right. It's part of what you're paying for when you use an online system.

This is such an important resource that we've included the relevant toll-free numbers and hours of availability in each of the vendor profiles in Part II. Often a customer service representative will not only tell you what commands to enter, he or she will enter them at a nearby terminal to test them for you and make suggestions on how to improve the results. You can then hang up, sign on to the system, and enter the same commands "cookbook" fashion.

IP Support

The vendor's hotline is only your first option. There is an entire second level of customer support provided by the database producers. Many IPs publish and sell their own reference manuals. The manuals and other materials explain how the database is set up, what it includes, and how to use any special codes or controlled vocabulary terms for precision searching. Many IPs also maintain their own customer support hotlines, many of them toll-free. (You'll find the relevant phone numbers and discussions of most IP manuals in Part III.) In fact, though it will stunt the growth of your information retrieval skills, you can often phone an IP with nothing more than a question like "How can I find information on Company X?" and receive a complete, blow-by-blow set of instructions on what commands and search terms to enter on a given system.

MENTAL APPROACH
The Five Rules of Search Success

Imagine that you've been parachuted into the central reading room of the Library of Congress in Washington for a night raid on its strategic information reserves. Your mission, should you decide to accept it, is to come out with everything you can find on industrial robots, particularly as pertains to their use in automobile assembly lines. Should you fail, your secretary will disavow any knowledge of the mission. "Impossible," you say. "Where in the world do I begin?"

• Rule 1: Respect Your Opponent

You begin by developing a healthy respect for your opponent—the vast quantity of information that's out there. With so much information now online, it is exceptionally easy to simply dive in and drown.

Consider all the various forms information on industrial robots could take: general interest, trade, and technical newspapers and magazines; specialized newsletters; doctoral dissertations; conference proceedings; books; government studies; films, filmstrips, and video tapes. Multiply all of these by the number of industrialized countries in the world, and you can begin to appreciate the scope of what's available on this topic alone.

• Rule 2: Define Your Target

One of the biggest mistakes new searchers make is to go online without a clearly defined idea of what they're after. If you do this, your information opponent will swallow you alive. For example, we searched *Business Week* on the ABI/INFORM database (See Figure 5.2) and discovered that there were nearly 19,000 articles containing the word *industrial*, over 1,200 containing the word *robot* or *robots*, and 150 containing the phrase "industrial robot(s)." That's one magazine out of the 680 that ABI/INFORM covers, and we limited things to just the last two and a half years.

You may have an image in your mind of what you want to know about industrial robots, but a database computer is just a dumb machine. It will gladly do your bidding. But you've got to tell it *exactly* what you want. When a computer comes back with too many hits on a topic, you can't say, "C'mon, you know, 'industrial *robots*,' like they use to put cars together. Get with it!"

Consider just a few of the various topics and subtopics that might be relevant to industrial robots: cost-savings, mean time to failure, maintenance expense, labor relations, occupational safety, use on assembly lines, use in hazardous applications, use in Japan, manufacturers of, planned acquisitions of, history of, industrial robots and the future, and so on.

Get the image of what you want out of your mind and translated into words on paper. Those words (search terms) are your weapons, and you create them by asking yourself questions: What subtopics could exist? Which ones am I interested in? Which ones do I want to avoid?

• Rule 3: Consider the Source: Who Would Know?

From your vantage point at the center of the Library of Congress, you now have a greater awareness of the quantity and variety of information that surrounds you. You've also clarified your target. You're ready to start searching.

You *could* start with a methodical inventory of the resources at your disposal. The card catalog over here, the magazine and newspaper racks over there, several thousand books from A to Absinthe in the stacks across the room, right next to several thousand more from Absolute to Accipiter.

It's much more productive to ask yourself, "Who would publish this kind of information? And how would each type of publication treat the topic?" In other words, instead of allowing your actions to be limited and channeled by what happens to be close at hand, whether it's a collection of databases or a collection of books, take control of the situation. This forces you to focus on the *source* material, and that has a number of benefits.

First, it emphasizes the fact that the information in an online database, whether it corresponds to a printed publication or not, has to come from somewhere. It isn't enough for an IP to say, as many do, "We've got a business database! Come search! Come search!" If information is to have any value, you've got to know where it came from. Is it from a reasonably impartial government study, a guaranteed-to-be-partial trade group, a reputable magazine or some rag you've never heard of, a newspaper with a particular viewpoint to sell, or what? Would you make an important decision or a substantial investment on the basis of a report from some firm you'd never heard of? Of course not.

Second, focusing on source material is one of the most important steps you can take toward insuring successful online searches. For example, *Business Week, Scientific American, Automotive Industry*, and *The New York Times* could all be expected to publish information on industrial robots. And you know, almost without thinking about it, that each one is going to take a different angle on the story.

Business Week would probably supply lots of business-oriented, industry-impact statistics. It might also single out a few key robot manufacturing firms and interview their executives. *Scientific American* might mention the economic implications as well, but it would focus on the technical aspects of how such robots work. As a trade journal, *Automotive Industry* could be expected to contain performance statistics, operating costs, announcements of planned installations, and labor union reaction to specific robot-related issues. The *Times* coverage would be similar to that in *Business Week*, and though it wouldn't be as deep, it would undoubtedly cover "impact on society" issues.

Certainly there would be some overlap in the kinds of coverage, but in general, this kind of logic is sound. If you know from years of reading *Business Week* that it could be expected to produce exactly the kind of article you want, it surely makes sense to search a database that covers *Business Week* and comparable publications.

• Rule 4: Don't Go Online Unless You Have To

Databases don't always offer the easiest solution to your information problem. It is crucial to be aware that an electronic database is only one of many options, part of a continuum of information tools that includes all of a library's standard reference, index, and directory volumes (some of which are online), encyclopedias and handbooks, the card catalog, inter-library loan programs, and every other library resource, especially the librarians. This continuum also includes the telephone and the U.S. mail.

There are lots of times when you *will* have to go online, of course. But when you've got a question, you might also ask yourself: "Who would know about this kind of thing?" One of your friends, contacts, or business associates? Maybe they know somebody who knows somebody you could call. No luck? Okay, let's go online. But instead of trying to find the actual information you need, consider using the online tools to find an expert who can tell you what you want to know.

When you're looking for an expert, you'll frequently discover that the nation's magazine and newspaper reporters have done much of the work for you. If you search for even general stories on a topic, you'll find that most will quote one or more experts and cite his or her credentials and affiliations. The stories will also give you important background information and alert you to issues you may not have considered. When you use a database in this way, it doesn't much matter whether the abstract or referenced article contains the exact facts and figures you're after. If it contains the name of an expert or recognized authority, you've got the entry point you need.

Sign off the system, pick up the phone, and call directory assistance to get the telephone number of the university, corporation, consulting firm, or other organization with whom the individual is associated. You may have to make several calls. The expert may or may not be able to help you. But the chances are that he or she knows someone who can and probably has that individual's phone number in the Rolodex. When you do make contact with the right person, you'll be able to ask questions and explore topics in a way that you will never be able to do with a computer, the inflated claims of artificial intelligence promoters notwithstanding.

Elementary, My Dear Database

When searching for information, it generally makes good sense to turn first to those publications and sources you know best. But of course no one can be familiar with every information source. The real challenge, and much of the satisfaction, comes when you apply your Holmesian powers of deductive reasoning. For example, if you're aware that almost every industry has a trade journal of some sort, you can deduce that one exists for the industry you are interested in without ever having seen or heard of it. Similarly, you can assume that most industries have at least one trade association. Even if it is a small industry, you can assume that some investment banking concern has prepared a detailed report on it, or on one or more of its leading companies. You can also assume that it falls under the jurisdiction of a governmental body somewhere that has probably prepared a report on it.

What are the names of the leading companies? Who are the executives of those firms? Is it possible that one or more of them has been quoted in a national magazine? In a local or regional newspaper? Have any of them written a book on their experiences? As we'll see in Part III, you can obtain all of this information and much more from online databases.

On Becoming an Information Detective

Information retrieval, in short, is anything but a passive activity. It is a skill that requires imagination, brainstorming, curiosity, and an ability to combine and extrapolate what you know into areas you have never explored.

For example, consider the problem of getting financial information on privately held companies, discussed in Chapter 16. Because they do not sell securities to the public, privately held companies are not required by law to publicly reveal their balance sheets, income statements, and other financial data.

At first blush, you might think, "Well, that's that. No way to get the information." But one shouldn't give up so easily. Instead, ask yourself: "Are there any circumstances under which a private company might voluntarily report its financials to someone? How about when it is applying for a loan? Come to think of it, don't most companies at one time or another have to fill out a credit report before their suppliers will do business with them? Who would have that kind of information?"

If you're a businessperson, you can probably make a pretty good guess at the answer: Dun & Bradstreet, the country's largest credit reporting organization. Certainly it is worth a phone call to Dun & Bradstreet to see if the information you want is available. Knowing what you now know about electronic information, it is also worth checking one or more database catalogs to see if the information is online.

Either way, you would almost certainly discover a file called D&B-Dun's Financial Records. Available on DIALOG, this file contains financial information, sans credit and payment history, on some 700,000 firms, 98% of which are privately held. If you need credit and payment history information as well, you can get that through the NewsNet gateway to TRW, D&B's main competitor. The cost is $29 per report.

Of course things rarely work out as neatly as in this example. And no one is suggesting that you should have been able to arrive at the same solution on your own. The point is the process. The most successful searchers are those who adopt the creative, imaginative approach of an information detective.

• Rule 5: Know Your Database

Let's assume that you've unbuckled your parachute and buried it deep within the Library of Congress stacks. You've decided to start your search for information on industrial robots in the automotive industry by going online and searching publications like *Business Week*. You notice a PC and modem conveniently located on a nearby reading table. You boot up and see a blinking cursor on your screen. Now what?

How do you know which databases to search? How do you know

which ones cover *Business Week* and similar publications? It would be wonderful if there were a master database of databases that could give you an instant list of every database that covers a specific topic or every database that includes a particular publication. Someday such a product may exist, but there is no such thing today.

Instead, there are printed database directories, several of which are also online. There are the vendor catalogs with their short descriptions of the databases on their systems. There are lists of the journals covered by individual databases, available from database producers. There is a *Directory of Periodicals Online* published by Federal Document Retrieval, Inc. (see Chapter 13 for details). And there are DIALINDEX, CROSS, and DBI, the files maintained by DIALOG, BRS/SEARCH, and ORBIT to help customers choose a database on those systems. (DIALINDEX is not available to DIALOG's Knowledge Index customers, however, and CROSS is not part of BRKTHRU.)

You might start by consulting one of the printed database directories. All of them are indexed by subject, but the subject headings are broad: real estate, science and technology, news, research in progress, and so on. Some of the database write-ups they contain mention the journals covered, but you can't count on it, and only a selected list is given in any case. You'll find the names of the major database directories, along with information on their availability for online searching, in Appendix B.

The directories are very helpful, but if you're a new searcher, you might be better off starting with the chapters in Part III of this book and with the catalogs and other information you should by now have received from the database vendors we suggested you contact. When you've found the databases that sound like they would cover the publications and topic you are interested in, phone or write the database producer for more information. Be sure to ask for the list of publications that it covers.

Ultimately, the only way to become an effective searcher is to become familiar with the databases and online systems that focus on your fields of interest. Remember, each database is a separate product, just as each computer program is a separate product. You can't expect to bring yourself up to speed on all of them overnight. As with computer software, you will probably begin by using two or three databases fairly frequently and thus get to know them well. Gradually you'll branch out, and as your familiarity grows you'll add more databases to your repertoire.

Whichever databases you decide to start with, the chapters in Part III will speed you along your way. You may find they contain most of the information you need to start searching immediately. But remember, there's no substitute for the information and journals lists available from the database producer.

TOOLS AND TECHNIQUES
Fields Are the Key

As you will recall from Chapter 2, databases like DIALOG, BRS, and ORBIT consist of files, records, and fields. Most other databases use similar divisions, though they may not call them by those names or permit you to search them in the same way. Of these information components, the most important are the fields. Indeed, it would be nice if we could make the word *field* on this page blink on and off in emphatic red neon. It's the key to the whole shootin' match. Records are what you are after when you search a database, and fields are the only way you can hit them.

Clown in a Cage
It's like the carnival game where the object is to dump the pretty girl, good-looking guy, or some other clown into the water by hitting a target with a baseball. You know someone's there. You can see him through the protective cage. But you'll never knock him into the pool unless you hit the target.

In the carnival game there is only one target. In a database record there are many. That's important, because the more fields a record contains, the more precisely you can focus your search. Needless to say, the number of fields a record contains is up to the database producer.

Imagine a database created from your address book or Rolodex cards. If there is a field in each record for "Phone Number," you could tell the database software to retrieve every record containing the phone number "800-555-1212." That's not terribly useful. After all, how often do you know someone's phone number but not their name?

Suppose we break up the phone number into more precise fields. Suppose we restructure the records so that there is a field for "Area Code" and one for "Phone Number." If you were planning a trip to Los Angeles and wanted to be sure to call all of your friends when you're there, you could easily produce a comprehensive list. Simply tell your database software to retrieve every record in the file in which "Area Code = 213."

Now, look at the record from ABI/INFORM that's shown in Figure 5.2. The abstract paragraph starts with the words, "Just as Ford Motor Co.'s assembly line . . ." Each of the single lines above the abstract is a searchable field: title, author, journal name, publication date, code number, International Standard Serial Number, document type, and language. "Availability" means you can order a photocopy of the original article from ABI/INFORM, and in this database it is not searchable.

The abstract also represents one searchable field. So if you happened to search on the term "automaking," you would hit this record, since that word can be found in the eighth line of the abstract.

The DESCRIPTORS field is also searchable. As you know from Chapter 2, the descriptors are anything but a random ad hoc collection of words. They are keywords that have been chosen from a predefined list by professional indexer/abstracters and assigned to the record.

The last searchable field is CLASSIFICATION CODES. To make retrieval even easier, a number of database producers assign special codes to their records. Sometimes the identical set of codes is used by several producers, but more often each producer creates and defines a unique list. INFORM's coding system is explained in Chapter 13. Here we will simply point out that the codes are hierarchical, meaning that the more non-zero digits a code includes, the more specific the topic to which it refers. Code 5200 refers to the broad heading of "Communication & Information Management." Code 5240, the first one listed in the record shown here, refers to "Software & Systems," a subtopic of the Code 5200 topic. All of this is explained in the user's manual published by ABI/INFORM.

Online Tip: Starting with the June 1986 update to the file, ABI/INFORM began including two additional fields and two new Industry and Marketing Classification codes. The two new fields are Company Name (/CO and CO=) and DUNS number (DN=), the "Social Security" number assigned to most corporations by Dun & Bradstreet. The two new codes were 8301 for Advertising Agencies and 8302 for Software & Computer Service Industry.

The point is that these fields are your targets. Throw the right words or code numbers at them and the record will be dumped in your lap. In a moment we'll show you how to select the right words and how to enter them into the system. But before we can do that there are two other topics to explain.

DIALOG's Basic and Additional Indexes

To search ABI/INFORM on DIALOG, you first look up the database in the catalog and note its file number (File 15). Then you sign on to DIALOG and enter BEGIN 15. That puts you into the database. Next, you enter your search terms with the command SELECT followed by the term. You may also enter the command SELECT SETS. The command may also be referred to as SuperSELECT or SELECT STEPS. This is the command you should probably use. It tells the system that you want it to assign a set number to the results of each search term. That saves you the trouble of retyping each search term when you enter subsequent commands, since you can use the set number (S1, S2, S3, etc.) instead. We'll have more to say about this later when we explain Figure 5.2 in greater detail. Both commands may be abbreviated to S and SS, respectively.

We've said a lot about fields, but suppose you signed on and simply entered SELECT ROBOTS. What would the system do? The answer is that it would search the Basic Index. Every file on DIALOG has a Basic Index consisting of one or more of the fields in each record. It's kind of a preselection of fields, which one can only assume is intended as a convenience.

The fields that are included vary with the file, but they are always listed on the appropriate DIALOG Bluesheet. In the case of INFORM, the system would search the abstract, descriptors, and title fields, since they compose the Basic Index for the file. Everything else—the fields for author, classification code, journal name, and so on—is considered part of the Additional Indexes group.

Online Tip: In our opinion, the Basic Index on DIALOG is not convenient at all. In fact, it is a drawback because it complicates things. If you want to search for articles in a particular magazine, for example, you can enter JN = (for "Journal name equals") followed by the name of the magazine. You can do this because the journal name field is one of the Additional Indexes. But if you want to search for a particular descriptor, say "automated," you must use a suffix instead of a prefix and enter it as AUTOMATED/ DE, all because the descriptor field is part of the Basic Index. Wouldn't "DE = AUTOMATED" make more sense? Unfortunately, that's not the way it works.

ABI/INFORM is also available on BRS/BRKTHRU, where it has approximately the same searchable fields. But on BRKTHRU, when you enter a search term without qualifying it in any way, the system searches all of the fields, not just a basic index selection.

Field Abbreviations and Labels
Each field in a bibliographic database, whether on BRKTHRU,

DIALOG, ORBIT, or some other system, has an assigned abbreviation. You'll find these on the DIALOG Bluesheet for each database and in the documentation supplied by the other database vendors. In Figure 5.1, for example you'll find the field abbreviations for all searchable fields in the ABI/INFORM database. You can generate an instant list of the searchable fields for any database on DIALOG by entering the command ?FIELDn, where *n* is the file number. You can do this at any time, regardless of the file you happen to be searching.

———— Figure 5.1. ABI/INFORM Fields on DIALOG ————

You can enter the ?FIELDn command at any time on DIALOG to get a list of the searchable fields for any file on the system. Notice the abbreviations that are used for ABI/INFORM fields below and the examples that are included.

```
??FIELD15

?FIELD15
Prefix-Coded Fields (EXPAND or SELECT)
```

Field Name	Example
Author	AU = MORANT, ADRIAN?
Classification Code	CC = 9170
CODEN	CD = TPEMAW
Classification Name	CN = ADVERTISING AGEN?
Company Name	CO = BROADVIEW FINANC?
D-U-N-S Number	DN = 05-944-1428
Document Type#	DT = JOURNAL PAPER
Journal Code	JC = TEM
Journal Name	JN = QUALITY PROGRESS
Language	LA = ENGLISH
Publication Date@	PD = 860101
Publication Year	PY = 1986
International Standard Serial Number (ISSN)	SN = 0040-263X
Update	UD = 8601W1

Basic Index Fields (SELECT only)

Field Name	Example
Abstract	CELLULAR (3N) COMMUNICAT?
Company Name	BOSCH (1N) ROBERT/CO

```
Descriptor*        MOBILE (W) RADIOS (W) TC/DE
Title              MOBILE (W) MARKET/TI
```

DT= JOURNAL PAPER is the only document
    type used at this time.
    Over 99% of the records are indexed
    to LA=ENGLISH.
@ Also cascaded to four digits,
    e.g., PD=8601.
* Also /DF.
** Sortable Fields** Online (SORT) and
    offline (PRINT).
    AU, CO, JC, JN, PD, PY.
    SORT 4/ALL/AU/TI
    PRINT 5/3/ALL/JN

What's in a Field?

If fields are your targets and keywords (search terms) are your weapons, the next point to consider is how you choose the right fields and select the right words to hit the records you want. Not surprisingly, there's more to this than meets the eye, for the fields and words you choose influence each other.

The place to start is with the question: What kinds of words can I search for in each field? You will find complete explanations of the type of information you can expect to find in each field in the appropriate DIALOG documentation chapter for the database. All such chapters begin with a general explanation of the file and the Basic Index. They then explain each searchable field in turn. The chapters always conclude with several search examples and a list of an additional documentation or search-aid material that may be available.

This is why we recommend DIALOG database chapters so highly. The documentation from other vendors carrying the same databases cannot compare. With minor translations, you can use the DIALOG chapter as a guide to searching the database on any other system. Here we'll look at the general categories of information you can expect to find in various fields with the understanding that you should consult the DIALOG database chapter and any additional documentation from the IP for specific details on any database.

Controlled Vocabulary

As explained previously, many IPs use limited lists of words and phrases to tag records that refer to articles on particular topics. Sometimes an IP will start with a widely used list like the Library of Congress Subject Headings (LCSH) explained in Chapter 12 and modify it to suit. Other IPs will create a list from scratch. The words themselves may be called indexing terms, descriptors, or something else, but all of these names refer to the same thing. Together, the words on an IP's list are called a "controlled vocabulary" because a professional indexer/abstracter may use those words and only those words when assigning indexing terms to a record. The one instance where this is not the case is in the IDENTIFIERS field found in some DIALOG databases. When used, identifier fields contain supplemental words that are not part of the official controlled vocabulary.

The specific words on a controlled list don't make all that much difference in and of themselves. You can think of them as code numbers if you like. The crucial point is that the IP uses a particular defined list. Thus if you search the ABI/INFORM descriptor field for "automobile manufacturer," "car," or "assembly line," you will not find any records. Those terms are not in INFORM's controlled vocabulary list or "thesaurus." But if you search the field for "automobile industry," you will have much joy since that term *is* on the list.

The only way to obtain the thesaurus for a database is to contact the database producer. In most cases you'll have to pay for it, though it will probably come as part of a complete manual. The vendors do not supply database thesauri.

Unique Code Numbers

The code number concept is the same as that of a controlled vocabulary. As discussed in Chapter 13, ABI/INFORM and the various Predicasts, Inc., databases, among others, make extensive use of code numbers. There are codes for companies, major topics, subtopics, "events" like the announcement of a new product, codes for specific types of products, and so on.

The code numbers can be used exactly as you would use controlled vocabulary terms. You look up the topic you want on an IP-supplied list, note the corresponding code, and enter the numbers in your search statement.

The main advantage of codes is that they tend to be quite precise and they are usually hierarchical. Thus, as noted previously, with ABI/INFORM you can say, "Give me every record with an assigned classification code starting with 52" and pick up every record in that broad category (Communication & Information Management). The codes may be "cascaded" as well, as is the case with Predicasts databases. See Chapter 13 for a complete explanation.

"Universal" Codes

Databases may also incorporate as searchable fields certain widely used and universally accepted codes. The codes may have been developed by the U.S. government, international standards organizations, or private companies. The most widely used code sets include:

• **SIC Codes—Standard Industrial Classification Codes**

Usually pronounced "s-eye-see" codes. Originally produced years ago by the Office of Management and Budget (OMB) for statistical purposes, SIC codes have been widely adopted throughout the economy as a convenient means of classifying goods and services. These are four-digit hierarchical codes (each digit to the right signifies a greater degree of specificity). For example, Code 54 is the broad major group code for food stores. Code 542 narrows things down to meat and fish markets. Code 5422 is more specific still: freezer and locker meat provisioners.

To information professionals, SIC codes have two drawbacks. First, they are not specific enough for many retrieval purposes. Second, the code list is not updated and revised fast enough to keep up with new businesses and products. At this writing, the last major revision of the codes was published in 1972. (The revision scheduled for 1982 was canceled.)

To help ease the situation, the Census Bureau in 1982 created a seven-digit coding system for the principal products and services of U.S. manufacturing and mining industries. The system "represents an extension, by the Bureau of the Census, of the four-digit industrial classification" as defined by SIC codes. In other words, the first four digits are the same as SIC codes. The additional three digits provide greater specificity.

Online Tip: For those who are already familiar with the SIC system, the Census Bureau codes cover major groups 10 through 39. You can get a list of them for $6 from the Government Printing Office (GPO). The title to ask for is *1982 Census of Manufacturers and Census of Mineral Industries: Numerical List of Manufactured and Mineral Products* (Reference Series: MC82-R). See Chapter 18 for contact information and other details on ordering documents from the GPO.

The complete list of four-digit SIC codes is available from the U.S. Government Printing Office (GPO). Contact the GPO and ask for the *Standard Industrial Classification Manual*. It's 650 pages long, hardbound, and weighs in at 2 pounds 14 ounces. The cost is $15. A 15-page supplement prepared by the Office of Federal Statistical Policy and Standards (Commerce Department), which now has responsibility for the SIC project, is also available for $2.75. As an alternative, you might want to consider ordering a copy of the list created by Predicasts, Inc. Predicasts codes correspond to the SIC list to four digits, with three additional digits added by the company. The list is widely accepted and used by many companies for internal operations. See Chapter 13 for details.

• MSA (formerly SMSA)—Metropolitan Statistical Area

These codes were introduced in June 1983 by the Census Bureau as a replacement for Standard Metropolitan Statistical Area codes. An MSA is a geographic area with a "large population nucleus that includes sur- rounding counties which have a high degree of economic and social inte- gration with that nucleus." Basically, your major cities and surrounding suburbs, each group of which has been given a code number by OMB. There are over 300 of them.

Some database manuals have complete lists of the MSA codes. But you will also find them in the *BLS Manual of MSA Codes: Metropolitan Statistical Areas (as defined by OMB June 30, 1983), Primary Metro- politan Statistical Areas, Consolidated Metropolitan Statistical Areas.* Variant Title: *B.L.S. Manual of M.S.A. Codes.* Write to: Commis- sioner, Office of Field Operations, Bureau of Labor Statistics, 441 G Street, Washington, D.C. 20212.

• ISSN and ISBN—International Standard Serial Number and International Standard Book Number

The "serial" here is serial as in magazine and other regularly issued serial publications. These are unique identifying numbers assigned un- der the auspices of the International Standards Organization of the United Nations. See Chapter 12 for a more complete explanation.

• DUNS or D-U-N-S Number—Dun's Universal Numbering System

Created by Dun & Bradstreet as part of its credit reporting opera- tion, a DUNS number is like a Social Security number for a company or business establishment. This is an especially convenient system since, when a database uses DUNS numbers, you don't have to search for a company using every possible variation of its name. With a DUNS number there can be no doubt. There is no relationship between the DUNS number of a parent corporation and its subsidiaries. The num- bers are randomly assigned. (See Chapter 16 for more information.)

Inverted Files and the EXPAND Command

The majority of codes and controlled vocabulary terms you can use to search various fields can be found in the manuals and documentation published by the database producer. If you were interested in finding the abstracts in the ABI/INFORM database that referred to articles about car companies, you would first open the *SearchINFORM* manual that ABI/INFORM sells for $47.50. The manual contains an 8,000-word thesaurus of controlled vocabulary terms. As noted previously, the correct term to use in the descriptor field in this case is "automobile industry." You would then sign on to DIALOG and BEGIN 15 to get into INFORM and key in SELECT AUTOMOBILE INDUSTRY/DE.

That's the least expensive way to do it. But there is an easier way. With the DIALOG EXPAND command you can rapidly check to see if any term is in a database's controlled vocabulary. You can do many other things with EXPAND as well, but we'll stick with this one for the time being. Similarly, you can use the ROOT command on BRS/SEARCH, the STEM command on BRS/BRKTHRU, and the NEIGHBOR command on ORBIT. Virtually everything we are about to say about EXPAND applies to these systems as well.

Inverted and Linear Files

The key to understanding the EXPAND command is the concept of the "inverted file." When a database is loaded into an online system, every record it contains is given an "accession number," which we can think of as its address. This is so the system knows which disk drive, which cylinder of the disk, and so on to go to to find it again. All of the records in the database make up what can be called the "display file." The display file is a linear or sequential file, and it is the source of the information you see on your screen when you look at a record online.

However, at the same time the display file is loaded, a second file is created. To make this file, the records are torn apart word-by-word, and the words are reassembled in alphabetical order. Each word on the list carries the address of its parent record and its numerical location within the record. This is the inverted file. Since it contains virtually every word in the display file, plus a certain amount of software overhead, it is usually about 120% the size of the display file. This is the file that is searched when you SELECT a keyword.

Conceptually, if you enter the word TANGERINE, the database system zips through the alphabetical inverted file, locates that word, notes the record address attached to it, and goes and gets the record that contains it from the display file. In information industry terms, the system can only find words that have been "posted to the index" (made a

Essentials

part of the inverted file). Thus "hits" are often also called "postings."

Actually, there is more than a single inverted or "index" file for each database. There is one for each searchable field. Also, the mainframe search system software uses sophisticated algorithms to get close to the target word without having to scan the entire list. Since even full-text databases are treated this way on systems like DIALOG, BRS, and ORBIT, it normally doesn't take any longer to search a full-text file than one consisting solely of bibcites. The mainframe search system never has to read through every word in a sequential file looking for a match the way many personal computer database programs do.

Checking It Out Online

When you enter the command EXPAND followed by a search term on DIALOG, you are actually asking the system to show you an inverted file for the database. For example, here are several terms in the Library of Congress LC MARC database discussed in Chapter 12. The terms are all alphabetically close to "conglomerate corporations," the term we expanded:

?EXPAND CONGLOMERATE CORPORATIONS

Ref	Items	Index-term
E1	76	CONGLOMERATE
E2	1	CONGLOMERIT CORPORATION
E3	68	*CONGLOMERIT CORPORATIONS
E4	1	CONGLOMERATE MERGERS
E5	1	CONGLOMERATE MERGERS : CAUSES, CONSEQUENCES, A
E6	1	CONGLOMERATE MERGERS—THEIR EFFECTS ON SMALL B
E7	9	CONGLOMERATES
E8	1	CONGLOMERATES AND MULTINATIONALS IN INDIA : A
E9	1	CONGLOMERATES AND THE EVOLUTION OF CAPITALISM
E10	1	CONGLOMERATEURS
E11	1	CONGLOMERATEURS AND THEIR CONGLOMERATES : DIVE
E12	1	CONGLOMEROID

The "items" column refers to the number of records in the database that contain the index term shown in the rightmost column. Note that EXPAND causes the system to look for literal match-ups with what you key in. Thus if you entered CONGLOMERIT CORPORATION? above, you would see "E3 0 *CONGLOMERIT CORPORATION?" but the surrounding words on the list would still appear.

DIALOG always lists your EXPAND term as E3, marks it with an asterisk, and shows you the two terms preceding it on the index list. The system presents a total of 50 terms for each EXPAND, displaying them about 12 at a time with a prompt to hit a key if you want to continue. That makes it easy to cruise through the list.

EXPANDing by Field

If you enter an EXPAND term without qualifying it, as we just did, the system displays the inverted file for the Basic Index. But you can also EXPAND by field. As with ABI/INFORM, there is an author field (AU) in this database. For example, suppose you wanted to find books written by Peter F. Drucker. Should you search on "Drucker, Peter." or "Drucker, Peter F." or "Drucker, P.F."? Let's EXPAND on the AU field to find out:

```
?EXPAND AU= DRUCKER, PETER
```

Ref	Items	Index-term
E1	1	AU=DRUCKER, MORT
E2	16	AU=DRUCKER, PETER FERDINAND
E3	0	*AU=DRUCKER, PETER
E4	1	AU=DRUCKER, REUVEN
E5	1	AU=DRUCKLER, JENS

Nope. "Drucker, Peter" is not the right form of name to use. Had you simply signed onto the database and entered it after a SELECT command, you would have gotten zero hits. But as you can see, there are 16 records in this database listing "Drucker, Peter Ferdinand" in the author field. Actually, you don't even have to know the author's first name. Keying in EXPAND AU = DRUCKE would have also led to the complete proper name.

Sleight of EXPAND

You might think of EXPAND and the terms it presents as sort of a dictionary sitting at your side as you sit at a database's control panel. You can turn away from the control panel, open the dictionary, and look something up at any time. But to use what you've looked up for searching, you've got to turn back to the panel and key it in. Entering the command SELECT signals to the database that you've closed the dictionary and are back on station.

If you want to retrieve records containing CONGLOMERATE CORPORATIONS, you've got to get that phrase into your search stream. There are two ways to do this. You can either enter SELECT followed by the phrase. Or you can save yourself some keystrokes and simply enter SELECT E3, the reference number for the phrase from your EXPAND list. The system will blink and notify you in seconds that you have 68 hits. Those are the same 68 revealed by the EXPAND command, but now they're in the search stream and you can go to work paring them down by adding qualifiers.

Just remember that the system resets the list each time you do an EXPAND. Or to put it another way, each new EXPAND cancels the one that preceded it.

Entering Search Terms

We've looked at the idea of fields. And we've looked at the kinds of information you can expect to find in various fields. The final step is to actually enter the terms you want to search for in the database.

There are a number of general points to keep in mind here. The first is that there are some words you may not use. The industry calls them "stop words" or "noise words." The exact list varies with the system, but it usually includes words like these: the, to, with, from, for, of, that, who, and all of the Boolean operators (AND, OR, NOT). Should you need to use a stop word as part of a search term, some systems will let you search for it if you set it off in quotation marks ("The Man Who Came to Dinner").

The second and even more crucial point is that computers are absolutely dead-bang literal-minded machines. To a computer, one string of characters is like every other string of characters. So if you enter a misspelled word, you won't get any hits, since the machine will look for exactly what you enter.

There is a corollary to this as well. Any time it is possible to spell or abbreviate a name or a word more than one way, you can assume that both or all variations have been used in the database. For example, look at the abstract in Figure 5.2 and consider the potential variations in the terms found in just the first sentence: Ford Motor Co. or Company, US or U.S. or United States, General Motors Corp. or Corporation, Saturn Corp. or Corporation or perhaps "Division" or "Company" or something else. Government agencies are another good example: SEC, S.E.C., and Securities and Exchange Commission all refer to the same agency, and all three variations may be used in the same database.

The best way to deal with this problem is to pause and think about potential variations and abbreviations. Then make liberal use of the EXPAND command to check for them. As your system manual explains, you can pick up any quantity of EXPAND "E" numbers and put them into your search stream. You can also pick up a range of these numbers by using a colon (SELECT E7:E12).

A Question of Quality

The question of quality is something that the industry doesn't talk much about. But the fact is that due to data-entry errors, most databases are littered with landmines that can easily blow up in an unsuspecting searcher's face. If someone has miskeyed or misspelled a word when entering the record, you may end up retrieving and paying for it even if it isn't remotely related to what you are searching for.

One can deal with that. A far more troubling problem is the database's unintended use of Stealth technology to make records invisible to conventional search techniques. For example, the REMARC database described in Chapter 12 includes all the works catalogued by the Library of Congress (LC) from 1968 back to the sixteenth century, some 5.2 million volumes in all. When the file was searched on this author's rather unique last name, an 1834 history of York County, Pennsylvania, turned up as did an 1892 pamphlet by a great-grandfather and namesake. But there was also a record that is of interest for more than just personal reasons:

0622392 LCCN: 37008722
The life of Bishop J. J. Glossbrenner, D. D., of the United brethren in Christ, with an appendix containing a number of his sermons and sketches
Drury, Augustus Waldo,,1851-
Dayton, Ohio, Published for J. Dodds by United brethren publishing house, 1889, xv, 17-391 p.incl. front. port. 19cm.
Place of Publication: Ohio
LC Call No.: BX9877.G6D7
Languages: English
Document Type: Monograph
Geographic Location: United States
Named Person: Grossbrenner, Jacob John bp 1812-1887
Descriptors: United brethren in Christ-Sermons; Sermons, American

First, look at the "Named Person" field (second line from the bottom). The record is presented exactly as it was downloaded from REMARC, and the named person ("Grossbrenner") is obviously wrong. If you were to search with the command SELECT NA = GLOSS? to tell the system to search that field for anyone whose name began with GLOSS followed by any other letters you would *not* retrieve this record.

The mistake could have been made by the person who keyed this information into the database. Or that data-entry operator may simply have duplicated a mistake made in 1889 when the original LC card from which the REMARC record is derived was typed up. However such mistakes happen, there is virtually no way to catch them. How can you think of every possible misspelling of a name or a word?

Nor is REMARC unique. *All* databases are to one degree or another plagued with this problem. You have only to look at Figure 5.2 for another example. We EXPANDed the partial word AUTOMOB in ABI/INFORM, but as you can see by looking at E4, there is at least one record in the database where "automobile" has been keyed in as AUTOMOBIEL. And we've got our doubts about E12. Unless a new compound word has been invented, it should probably be AUTOMOBILE WORKERS. We don't know anything about these two records (E4 and E12). But we do know that if you spelled the word(s) properly, you would *not* retrieve them.

Of all people, writers know how easy it is to make typing mistakes. And even the most eagle-eyed proofreader misses something now and then. It is easy to be sympathetic with the beleaguered data-entry operator responsible for keying in database information. But that doesn't solve the problem.

The solution is twofold. First, as an information consumer, resist the temptation to put away your natural skepticism and simply accept whatever you download as the final word. It may be impractical to verify everything. But if the information is crucial, spot checks of its validity are definitely in order. If money is involved, as with a potential investment, an even higher degree of vigilance is essential.

Second, use the EXPAND command to check for misspellings. As the example in Figure 5.2 demonstrates, unless the word has been completely murdered, a misspelling should appear alphabetically close on the list to the correct form.

Wildcards (Truncation)

What personal computer users call "wildcards," the information industry refers to as "truncation." The concepts are identical. For example, when an MS-DOS user wants to copy every file that ends in ".BAS" from the disk in drive A to the disk in drive B, he or she keys in COPY A: *.BAS B:. That tells the computer's operating system that it doesn't matter what's to the left of the dot (period), as long as "BAS" is to its right, and it saves a lot of time, since the alternative would be to laboriously key in a COPY command for every complete filename.

In the online field, the same technique is used both to save time and to allow for possibilities. For example, it would not normally make good sense to search for ROBOT when you know that the records you want *could* contain not only ROBOT but also ROBOTS. To allow for that possibility on DIALOG, you use the question mark as the truncation or wildcard character. Keying in ROBOT? will retrieve every record with ROBOT, ROBOTS, ROBOTICS, or any other word with any number of characters after ROBOT.

This is called "right-hand truncation," and there are a number of variations. The search term WOM?N, for example, would retrieve both WOMAN and WOMEN. The search term ROBOT? ? would retrieve words containing only one character after the "stem," so you'd get the singular and the plural but not ROBOTICS. Code numbers can be truncated as well. Searching ABI/INFORM on SELECT CC = 53? would hit all records to which the more specific classification codes 5310, 5320, 5330, and so on had been assigned.

Unfortunately, each database has its own truncation character. BRS and Dow Jones use the dollar sign ($), NewsNet uses the asterisk (*), and so on. BRS also offers "left-hand truncation," so you can enter the very heart of a word framed on either side by truncation characters.

Positional or Proximity Operators

On systems like DIALOG, you can also specify where you want one search term to occur in relation to another search term. Do you want "industrial" to appear before and right next to (adjacent to) "robot?"? Is it okay if a certain number of other words are sandwiched in between them? What about having them occur within five words of each other and in any order, ROBOT first and INDUSTRIAL second or vice versa? DIALOG offers you at least seven basic permutations, and other systems do likewise.

In our opinion, these are the kinds of commands you can safely ignore when you are just starting. The only one that's really important is the "W" (with) operator as in INDUSTRIAL(W)ROBOT?. It's nice to know the others are available should you need them, but using them generally takes too much mental energy. In some DIALOG files, you won't even need the "W" operator because you will be able to search by phrase ("industrial robot?") instead of by word.

Boolean Operators and Nesting

If there's one thing database vendor manuals love to go on about it's "logical" or "Boolean" operators (AND, OR, NOT, XOR, etc.). You sometimes get the impression that the authors would be drummed out of the manual-writers union if they didn't include complicated discussions of search logic laced with plenty of Venn diagrams—those intersecting, variously shaded circles you learned about in sophomore geometry. Forget it!

Well, no, don't *forget* it. It's a worthy concept. But don't let it spoil your day. Be aware that you can get so tangled up in Boolean logic and AND/OR/NOT operators that you may never go online. AND means a record must have *both* terms in it. OR means it can have *either* term. NOT means it can*not* have the specified term.

Different people have different philosophies of searching. The simplest and most effective, we feel, is what might be called the bowl-of-fruit approach: apples AND oranges AND grapes AND pears. The idea is to enter a search, note the results, and keep ANDing things to the results until we come up with a manageable number of records we know contain all of our search terms. If you have to think about what your records should NOT contain (NOT lemons NOT bananas NOT mangoes) at the same time, OR what they might *also* contain, things can get rather complicated. Consequently, we suggest that you start with AND and use the other operators only when it is obvious that you need them.

You can also forget about much of the material most manuals contain concerning "nested" search terms like SELECT (SOLAR OR SUN) AND (ENEGY OR HEAT). These things are fine for an information professional, and you may want to use them yourself someday. But for the nonce, put them on "hold." As we'll see in a moment, you can accomplish the same things without all that MENTAL AND (ENERGY OR EFFORT OR WORK).

Online Tip: Most vendors supply quick reference cards or booklets with their documentation. But if you regularly search several systems, keeping all the commands straight can be a real problem. Online, Inc., the publisher of a trade magazine of the same name, has done something about this. It has created The Online International Command Chart.

This is a spiral-bound affair similar in format to a calendar. The leftmost column gives the operation name ("Logon"), and succeeding columns give the required commands for up to 16 different systems. Included are DIALOG, BRS, ORBIT, VU/TEXT, QL Systems, InfoGlobe, NEXIS, DATA-STAR, and a variety of European systems. There are 41 commands in all, "from Logon to Logoff."

The cost is $40, but if you order more than one at the same time, each additional copy is $25. Visa, MasterCard, and American Express are accepted. For more information, contact:

Command Chart
Online, Inc.
11 Tannery Lane
Weston, CT 06883
(203) 227-8466

HOW TO ATTACK A DATABASE MANUAL
The Eight Crucial Commands

There used to be a reading and study technique taught in elementary schools called S.Q.R: Survey, Question, Read. The thought was and is that the best way to read a book or a chapter is not to plunge in at page one but to survey the terrain first. Then ask yourself questions about the topic being covered and the coverage itself. Then, and only then, begin reading.

S.Q.R. is an excellent way to attack a database vendor's manual. You've now got the tools and concepts needed to make sense of most of it. All that's lacking is a list of the most important commands. When you strip away all of the advanced commands and fine-tuning features, there are about eight basic things you need to know to use any system.

These are the things you should look for when you are performing S. and Q. and the things you should zero in on when doing R.:

1. How do you get into a particular database or file?

DIALOG uses BEGIN followed by the file number. BRKTHRU requires a mnemonic abbreviation like NOOZ for the National Newspaper Index, or lets you choose from a menu. Dow Jones requires the command //QUOTES for its stock quote database but also offers menus.

2. How do you begin a search?

On the Knowledge Index and Wilsonline you enter FIND. On BRKTHRU and After Dark you are prompted to "Type in Search Term." On VU/TEXT you enter S.

3. How do you specify the specific field you want to search?

BRS systems use dots after the search term while DIALOG uses field name prefixes or suffixes. In the ABI/INFORM database on BRS, the name of the source publication can be found in the "Source" field (SO), but on DIALOG the field is called "Journal Name." Thus, these commands are equivalent on the two systems: BUSINESS WEEK.SO and JN = BUSINESS WEEK. VU/TEXT uses an "at sign" (@) followed by the field number (found in the documentation for each database) to specify a field. On NEXIS you can specify the "segment" and use parens: DATELINE (OHIO).

4. What truncation or "wildcard" characters are used?

VU/TEXT and NewsNet use an asterisk (*). DIALOG uses a question mark (?). BRS and the Dow Jones //TEXT database use a dollar sign ($). Wilsonline uses the hatch mark (#) and the colon (:).

5. How can you search for a phrase of two or more adjacent words?

DIALOG uses parentheses and a W (W). ORBIT uses just a matching set of parens with a space in between ( ). Wilsonline has a special "Stringsearch" command.

6. What tools are available to narrow down the results of a search?

This is where the AND operator really comes into its own, for it lets you add more and more stipulations until the specifications become so stringent that only a few records can meet them. Most systems have an AND operator.

7. How do you display results?

On NewsNet you can look at newsletter headlines or read the whole articles to which they refer. BRKTHRU and After Dark offer short, medium, and long display formats. DIALOG databases may have as many as nine or ten display options.

8. How do you sign off and stop the connect-time meter from running?

NewsNet's command is OFF. DIALOG's is LOGOFF. Dow Jones requires DISC (for "disconnect"). The quickest way to double the cost of your search is to wait until you're ready to leave a system before you go rooting through the system manual to find out how to get off. Always note the exit before entering the theater.

FREE TEXT SEARCHING

So far we've concentrated on the idea of specific fields, on the various terms or codes you might look for in those fields, and on the ways you might enter the terms. You should know, however, that you can also do a free text search. Free text searching refers to searching the text of a record without zeroing in on a particular field and without using a controlled vocabulary term. You might think of it as searching paragraphs, whether they are part of the abstract or part of a full-text (complete article) record, using whatever terms occur to you. On the face of it, you'd think this would be the easiest technique of all. Ironically, it is among the most difficult and calls for the most work on your part.

Free text searching can be treacherous. Our language is so rich and so varied that the same word can have many different meanings depending on the context in which it is used. For example, suppose you're after information on job actions and strikes. And suppose you enter SELECT JOB AND ACTION? AND STRIKE?. That tells the system that you want only records containing all three of those terms. Now suppose the database includes a record in which a person is quoted as saying, "We've got a job to do. We must take action now and strike while the iron is hot!"

Your search logic will retrieve that record. Which could be great if the person being quoted was a latter-day John L. Lewis. But suppose it's a newly appointed government official stating his views on import quotas, tax reform, or women's rights. Suppose it's the president of a fast-food company talking about taking advantage of a perceived opportunity to beat out the competition.

Surprised? Damn right. But this kind of thing happens all the time when you go online. The industry calls them "false drops," records that were retrieved with legitimate search logic but have nothing to do with what you're after. We like the term "search surprise" because in truth, you never know what you're going to pull up out of a database. It is simply the nature of the beast and yet one more reason to respect your opponent.

Even the best searchers will generate their share of false drops. In fact if they don't, their search logic is probably too narrowly focused to be as comprehensive as it should be. Or there is something else wrong. Our point is that free text searching is False Drop City. If you wander in unaccompanied by a field search or without a highly specific free text term, it is an automatic signal to all the online gremlins in creation to rain false drops down upon your unsuspecting head.

Properly used, free text searching can be an important retrieval tool. But before you venture forth, give some serious thought to coming up with the most specific, unique, proper name or term that is still relevant to your topic. If possible, use field searches first as preliminary screens to narrow down the number of hits.

HOW TO SEARCH ANY DATABASE
Zen and the Art of Information Retrieval

In the following section we're going to put it all together, using the search reproduced in Figure 5.2 as an illustrative example. We will be focusing on DIALOG, and by extension, BRS and ORBIT, the other two classic bibcite and abstract database vendors. However, with appropriate modifications to allow for the differences among systems, the same steps can be used to search any database. The process starts with:

The Five Rules of Search Success
Rule 1: Respect Your Opponent
Rule 2: Define Your Target
Rule 3: Consider the Source: Who Would Know?
Rule 4: Don't Go Online Unless You Have To
Rule 5: Know Your Databases

No problem with Number 1. If you don't have a pretty good idea of what you're up against by now, there's nothing we can do to help you. For target definition, let's assume that you're interested in industrial robots because you're thinking about installing them at your plant. There are lots of things you will eventually need to know about the topic, but right now you don't know enough to know what questions to ask. All you know is that the automotive industry seems to have had some success with robots. That's fine. INDUSTRIAL ROBOTS AND AUTOMOTIVE ASSEMBLY LINES is a good place to start.

Who would know about such a thing? Car companies, of course. And makers of industrial robots. Car companies have large, well-paid public relations and public information staffs. Bet they'd have some information for you. Why not give them a call? You may get bumped around to several offices, but eventually you'll find someone who can help you. When you do, explain what you're interested in, and ask the individual to send you some information.

There's no way to tell what that information will consist of. There might be press releases and photocopies of articles published in various trade magazines. It may be nothing but a corporate annual report. But more than likely there will be something you can use: the names of the companies who make the robots, the names of the people at GM, Ford, or Chrysler who are in charge of robot-related projects, the name of one or more trade journals, and so on. Your next step might be to contact one or more robot manufacturers. (The Thomas Register Online database described in Chapter 15 is designed to provide precisely this kind of information.)

Should you go online? Sure you should. The materials you receive from the firm's you've contacted can help you refine your search. But you want to know a lot more about the topic, and a database search is ideal for that kind of application. But which database should you choose?

Before choosing a database, stop for a moment and ask yourself about the *kind* of information you want. Do you want a *Scientific American*-type treatment or the kind of article you'd expect *Business Week* to do?

Whatever you decide, by asking yourself these questions you have automatically made the database selection process ten times easier. We'll assume that you've opted for *Business Week*, at least to start. So the question now is: Which online databases cover *Business Week* and similar publications?

If you're brand new to the field, there's no way for you to know off the top of your head. But there are people you can ask and, as noted previously, directories you can consult. The *Directory of Periodicals Online* discussed at the beginning of Chapter 13 is an invaluable resource, for example. The chapters in Part III, the catalogs from the various vendors, and the journals lists from the database producers are also good sources. And of course a reference librarian at your corporate information center, in the MIS department, or at a major library may be the biggest help of all.

Many of these folks have the skills to go online and conduct a search for you. You may want to take advantage of that fact at a later date. But when you're trying to get a handle on a topic, when you're not exactly sure yourself what you're looking for, you need to be able to play interactive "I wonder if . . ." games online. Should you later decide to enlist the skills of a professional, you will then be able to give the individual a much clearer idea of what you want and don't want.

TWELVE STEPS TO ONLINE INFORMATION RETRIEVAL

Yes, it's beginning to sound like a crazy Chinese herbalist and sex therapist has gotten loose on these pages. But lists can be wonderful things, and frankly we know of no better way to cut through the fog that surrounds information retrieval. So sit back, sip your Lapsang Souchong, and attend The Twelve Steps.

• **Step 1. Select your database.**
We've covered this pretty thoroughly. All that remains to be said is that you may eventually want to search *several* databases. Be aware, however, that at some point you're going to encounter diminishing returns. As noted in a previous chapter, overlapping coverage is fine, since one IP's abstracts can complement another's. But if you search more than a few databases you can very quickly end up with more information than you can successfully digest and you will have lost much of the benefit of using online systems.

• **Step 2. Check the documentation.**
Please, please, please do not omit this step. Discipline yourself to do it every time until you know the database so well you don't have to

think about it. Which fields are searchable? Can you search by phrases or must you use words and proximity operators? What kinds of information does each field contain: words, code numbers, dates, controlled vocabulary terms?

• **Step 3. Meditate.**
Seriously. You may not be a Ninja warrior preparing for battle, but it's not a bad analogy. If you ride in like a cowboy with six-guns blazing, firing off search terms as they come into your head, you'll stir up a lot of dust, expend a lot of ammunition, and be presented with a hefty bill but very little relevant information when you're done.

Think about the topic beforehand. Let your mind run free and flow into the subject. What do you know and what can you extrapolate about industrial robots? Aren't they used extensively in Japan? Yes. So some of your hits are going to deal with robots in Japanese factories and warehouses. But isn't there something about American companies counting on robots to help them compete with Japanese firms? Yes. So some of your hits will focus on international competition.

It may be that neither of these topics is of interest to you. Or they may be exactly what you're interested in. Either way, by meditating on the problem first, you will be better prepared when you go online. You might want to be prepared to add the term AND AMERICA? or some other term that would eliminate references to Japan (NOT JAPAN?). Similar types of questions can be asked of the searchable fields. Should you limit the search to a particular range of years? Is there a company name you should definitely include? Are there any code numbers that can make things both easy and precise?

Try to develop a list of search words that come close to defining what you want. Some searchers try to think in terms of synonyms. We prefer an approach that's closer to free-association. Ultimately you'll develop a technique that works best for you.

Think about the source material and types of magazines or whatever you are searching. Then pick the words that you feel could logically be expected to appear in the kind of document you're looking for. The process is similar to writing up a bid specification. The document you want will have this, this, and this. It will be published between these dates. It will deal with such-and-such a topic, and so on.

Of course, if you make the requirements too stringent, you won't get any bidders (hits), and if you make the specs too broad you'll get every Tom, Dick, and Harry and his brother. There is also a very good possibility that the precise document you envision does not exist. But you have to start somewhere and doing things this way is likely to be much more productive than simply lunging into a database with a bunch of search terms in your hand.

• Step 4. Select your fields.

We can't tell you what fields to search, since they vary so with the database. The author (AU) field may be virtually useless in a database of general-interest magazines, but crucial in a database of book titles. If you use a DUNS number you obviously don't have to also specify the company's name. As noted, doing a free-text search on the abstract field can be tricky and is best done in conjunction with at least one other field. The documentation is your best guide to selecting the fields most likely to retrieve what you want. We would only add that as a rule, use just three or four fields and choose the ones that let you be as specific as possible without getting zero hits.

• Step 5. Write out your first search statement in full.

Don't try to keep all of your search terms and search logic in your head. Free yourself of them by putting them on paper. When you are actually online, you'll have many other things to think about, and unless you're awfully quick, you don't want to be thinking about all the various words and commands you could use while the meter's running.

Keep a pad of paper and a pen within easy reach, as well. You will need them.

• Step 6. Check the display options and verify how you sign off.

The ultimate point of going online is to display the records that your search statements have selected. Make sure you know what formats are available and what pieces of information are included in each format as it applies to the database you're going to search. Again, this is not the kind of thing you want to look into while you are connected and paying for online time. The same thing goes for making sure you know how to sign off.

• Step 7. Set your computer to capture incoming information.

This is so important that it's worth the emphasis of making it a separate step. Generally it doesn't pay to keep your printer toggled on during an online session. Printers slow things down and thus eat up connect time. During your search you may want to dump a screen to the printer for easy reference. So leave it on and enabled, but don't toggle the printer echo on from within your communications program.

Floppy disks are cheap and erasable, however, so it definitely makes good sense to capture your entire online session. Open your capture buffer or set your communications program to dump to disk or do whatever else is necessary to put the machine in "record" mode. You can always go back into the file and delete the portions you don't want with a word processor. In addition, a record of a complete online session can be a wonderful self-teaching tool, since you can review it to see where you went wrong, the number of hits on a term that you did not follow up on, etc. If you have a hard disk, tell your system to capture to it, since less time is required to write to a hard disk than to a floppy.

• Step 8. Sign on and EXPAND your search terms.

At this point we pick up the example in Figure 5.2. Since we are going to be referring to it quite a bit, you might want to take a moment to peruse the entire search session displayed there to get a preliminary idea of what we'll be discussing. Then start at the top with "BEGIN 15," the command that tells DIALOG you want to start searching File 15 (ABI/INFORM).

Skip over the date, time, and other information, and note the next command: EXPAND AUTOMOB. By entering this command at the DIALOG question mark prompt, we told the system to look for AUTOMOB in the inverted files for the fields in its Basic Index. As the ABI/INFORM Bluesheet points out, these fields include the abstract, the company name, the descriptor, and the article title. There is no way to focus on just the descriptor or just the abstract field with INFORM. Note that there are 1,669 hits on AUTOMOBILE INDUSTRY, the term that is closest to what we were after. The same term could have been found in the controlled vocabulary list in the *SearchINFORM* manual.

We made a note that that was the proper term to use and then moved on to the actual search logic.

• Step 9. Enter your first search statement and note the results.

For the purpose of this demonstration we decided to focus only on *Business Week* and only on issues published between 1984 and 1986. Thus we entered SELECT SETS JN = BUSINESS WEEK AND PY = 1984:1986. Notice that in response to the SELECT SETS command, the system assigns a set number to each element in the statement. Reviewing the results, we find that there are 9,659 records with BUSINESS WEEK in the journal field (JN), 91,110 records for articles published between our specified years, and 2,217 records where these two fields intersect.

That's a good first cut and it means that we are now dealing with a limited universe of 2,217 articles instead of the more than 320,000 that are in the ABI/INFORM database.

• **Step 10. Add qualifiers to narrow the search.**
Some searchers like to put all of the qualifiers they can think of in their initial search statements. Many of the commands that clutter the vendor system manuals are designed to make this possible. For our money this makes things needlessly complex and eliminates much of the interaction that is the essence of the "I wonder if . . ." approach.

We prefer to think of searching as a process similar to repairing a household appliance at a well-equipped workbench. There are certain tools (search terms and search logic) you know you're going to need to open the case or remove the housing. But from then on there are no definitive steps to follow. At this point we've got the case off and are peering into the machine's innards to try to get an idea of the situation.

Now it's time to reach for a tool that looks like it might do the trick. Let's cull out all the records in our set of 2,217 that refer to articles dealing with the automobile industry. Using the abbreviation for SELECT SETS (SS), this time we apply the ABI/INFORM authorized descriptor AUTOMOBILE INDUSTRY. As noted earlier, specifying the descriptor field requires use of the /DE suffix. Note that instead of rekeying all of the search terms in set three, we merely used its number (S3).

Now what have we got? Set 5 (S5) with 72 hits. That still sounds like a lot, but we know from experience that that's not bad. After all, we're not finished yet.

Hoping for Bingo we took our newly reduced set of 72 records and told the system to search it for occurrences of INDUS-TRIAL(W)ROBOT?. Since we did not specify any field for this new term, the system automatically searched every field in the Basic Index. This was in effect a free text search, since INFORM abstracts are often short articles in themselves.

Look at the results. There are 150 abstracts in the database in which the term INDUSTRIAL(W)ROBOT? appears in the Basic Index. But there are none with all the terms we have specified. Was a search term misspelled? Should we sign off, review the session, and sign back on again with new terms and refined logic? What went wrong?

Nothing really. Since we've always heard the machines referred to as "industrial robots," we simply assumed that that was the term to use. Obviously it wasn't. It was the wrong tool for this particular job.

"I wonder if . . ." a broader term like ROBOT or ROBOTS would do the trick. Sure enough, telling the system to check our 72-item set (S5) for *that* word yielded three hits (S11). We're almost home.

• Step 11. Display results.

This is the easy part. There's nothing like conducting a search that appears to be on the beam and yields a manageable number of results. Here you have merely to key in TYPE 11/5/1 to display the first record in Set 11 using Format 5. That is the full-record format for many DIALOG databases.

Except in full-text databases like Magazine ASAP where the full-record format costs $7 and involves downloading the complete article, we prefer to always look at the full record when displaying results. It's a bit more expensive (the one shown here costs 50¢), but it can save a lot of time and possibly money as well. If you look at a more limited format and decide that on that basis you want to see the full record, you'll pay for the display of the same information twice.

Besides, by reviewing all of the fields in a record you can often discover search terms and concepts you hadn't thought of. Although we were aware of GM's new Saturn operation, for example, we had never thought about it in terms of industrial robots. Perhaps by incorporating SATURN in a search statement you would discover a whole range of information about the latest robot technology. "I wonder if . . ."

• Step 12. Logoff and write your capture buffer to disk.

You already know about logging off and stopping the clock. The only point to be added is that you shouldn't hesitate to logoff and logon frequently in the course of a search. There is no minimum charge or other cost penalty each time you logon. With DIALOG and most other databases, you pay only for your actual connect and telecommunications time. It is thus much better to logoff and review the results at leisure than to try to play "Beat the Clock" while you are online.

Closing a capture buffer and writing it to disk or otherwise making an orderly exit from your online session is something that's easy for a new communicator to forget to do. Because of the way most personal computers do things, if you neglect this step, you may lose all of the material you have downloaded, and the information that has already been written to disk may be rendered inaccessible.

Conclusion

Although we have reproduced only one of the three records retrieved, all were typical of what one could expect from a broad search of this type. It is not the ultimate article on industrial robots in the automotive industry. But it's a good lead to additional information. The abstract also gives you enough information to decide whether you want to order a photocopy of the original article, look for it in your company files, or pass it by.

Certainly there is a lot more searching to be done. But as you search, you remember that the definitive article as you envision it may not exist. With all the information that's out there it may seem like a paradox that no one has written the one article that can fill all of your needs. But it is really yet one more confirmation of that fifth force of nature, "the information force." There are so many variables and so many possible configurations. If you're looking for statistics, market share, names and addresses, corporate earnings, or any other specific, narrowly defined fact, it's a different story. As we'll see in Part III, you can find all of these things with relative ease.

But when you are looking for general information on a subject, you will get a different type of result. If the "perfect" article exists, there's a good chance that you'll find it online. But it is more likely that you will pull the information you need out of a collection of documents and thus create your own "perfect" article.

Finally, it's important to point out once again that there is no one correct way to search. Someone else might have done things in a different order and used a completely different approach than that illustrated in Figure 5.2, though the results would have been essentially the same. As you become more familiar with the online world, you'll develop your own style.

Ultimately, no one can teach you how to search. We can describe the databases, show you the tools, and suggest ways to use them. But to really learn, you have to go online. And as with any other skill, to become proficient you have to practice.

— Figure 5.2. A Complete ABI/INFORM Search on DIALOG —

```
?BEGIN 15
        DDMMMYY 11:53:03 User000000
     $0.00    0.002 Hrs File1

File 15:ABI/Inform — 71-8N/MMM, Week 3
(Copr. Data Courier Inc. 19—)

     Set  Items  Description

?EXPAND AUTOMOB

Ref   Items  Index-term
E1        1  AUTOMIZATION
```

Fig. 5.2 (cont.)

```
E2        1  AUTOMIZED
E3        0  *AUTOMOB
E4        1  AUTOMOBIEL
E5     4353  AUTOMOBILE
E6      135  AUTOMOBILE DEALERS
E7      145  AUTOMOBILE FLEETS
E8     1669  AUTOMOBILE INDUSTRY
E9      446  AUTOMOBILE INSURANCE
E10     113  AUTOMOBILE LEASING
E11    1708  AUTOMOBILES
E12       1  AUTOMOBILEWORKERS

        Enter P or E for more
?
?SELECT SETS JN=BUSINESS WEEK AND PY=1984:1986

    S1     9659   JN=BUSINESS WEEK
    S2    91110   PY=1984:1986
    S3     2217   JN=BUSINESS WEEK AND PY=1984:1986

?SS S3 AND AUTOMOBILE INDUSTRY/DE

           2217   S3
    S4     1669   AUTOMOBILE INDUSTRY/DE
    S5       72   S3 AND AUTOMOBILE INDUSTRY/DE

?SS SF AND INDUSTRIAL(W)ROBOT?
             72   S5
    S6    18832   INDUSTRIAL
    S7     1254   ROBOT?
    S8      150   INDUSTRIAL(W)ROBOT?
    S9        0   S5 AND INDUSTRIAL(W)ROBOT?

?SS S5 AND ROBOT?

             72   S5
    S10    1254   ROBOT?
    S11       3   S5 AND ROBOT?

?TYPE 11/5/1

 11/5/1
85005280
        How GM's Saturn Could Run Rings Around Old-Style Carmakers

        Whiteside, David; Brandt, Richard; Schiller, Zachary; Gabor, A.

        Business Week n2878 (Industrial/Technology Edition) PP:126,128

        Jan 28, 1985

        CODEN: BUWEA3
        ISSN: 007-7135
```

JRNL CODE: BWE
DOC TYPE: Journal paper
LANGUAGE: English   LENGTH: 2 PAGES
AVAILABILITY: ABI/INFORM

Just as Ford Motor Co.'s assembly line became the mainstay of industry in the US, General Motors Corp.'s new Saturn Corp. subsidiary may pave the way for the elusive "factory of the future." GM's Saturn subsidiary is a $5-billion bid to try to revolutionize automobile manufacturing. The details have not been finalized, but GM is attempting to assemble the most advanced manufacturing technology possible. By replacing the assembly line with a fully computerized production system that extends from the dealer to the factory floor, GM is hoping that it can close the estimated $2,000-per-unit gap between its production costs and those of Japanese competitors. Saturn would change nearly every aspect of automaking operations. It is expected to tie together GM's collection of advanced technology in robots, machine vision, and computers, which the company has assembled over the past few years. Saturn's objective is to reduce costs on all fronts. The system will bring component production and assembly together on one site.

DESCRIPTORS: Automobile industry; Case studies; General Motors-Detroit; Subsidiaries; Automated; Production; Systems

CLASSIFICATION CODES: 5240 (CN = Software & systems); 5310 (CN = Production planning & control); 8680 (CN = Transportation equipment industry); 9110 (CN = Company specific)

...6...

Search Aids:
Front-End Packages, EasyNet, and Information Brokers

E ver since the first bibcite got up off its disk drive and sallied out into the communications stream, database producers have been looking for a magic formula to make their product not only palatable to their customers but also a veritable cinch to use. Many seem possessed of the notion that if they could just hit upon the right software interface, users would swarm to their databases for the answers to the ultimate questions of life, the universe, and everything. The field of information needers would at last be unified with the field of information providers, and you wouldn't be able to reach them on the phone, they'd be so busy counting their money.

It hasn't happened, though not for want of trying. Well-financed companies backed by the most savvy of venture capitalists have gone belly-up in the attempt. "Never" is a very long time, and anything can happen. But from our perspective, information is a force of nature, and you fight it, channel it, or try to control it at your peril. Perhaps someday, when the laws of information are better understood, it really will be possible to ask any question of a box sitting on your den table and receive the answer you seek. But don't hold your breath waiting for it.

People, on the other hand, are another story entirely. What seems far more likely than the development of an all-seeing, all-knowing computer is the rapid growth of a largely new profession: the independent information intermediary. As information consciousness rises due to the easy availability and increased use of information, it is inevitable that the demand for people with skills to get the requested information will rise as well. At this writing, these professionals are variously referred to as information brokers, specialists, or consultants. We'll discuss how and when to take advantage of their services at the end of this chapter.

First, however, we'll look at the search-aid software that exists and at some of the packages available to deal with what you download. All of the software discussed in this chapter is designed for use on an IBM-PC or compatible.

Front-End Software

A number of vendors and database producers have created specialized software packages to make their products easier to use. For example, there is SearchHelper™ (Information Access Company), Wilsearch™ (Wilsonline), microDISCLOSURE (DISCLOSURE II), Version 1.4 (NEXIS), DIALOG/Link and the DIALOG Business Connection™, and a range of programs from Dow Jones. Since these are noted and discussed in the relevant chapters of Parts II and III, we won't consider them here.

Other programs are available from independent software producers. These are almost always called "front-end packages." Generally, front-end packages do four or five things. They allow you to key in your search terms and logic before going online. They will automatically log you onto a system and upload (transmit) your prepared strategy. Once you are online and are looking at the results generated by your strategy, the front-end package may offer you a descriptive menu from which you can choose your next command or allow you to enter a "native" (regular) system command from the keyboard. All packages permit you to download (capture) records and store them to disk.

Once you are offline, a package may offer post-download processing options. It might offer a word processing module for use in removing unwanted characters or records. It might make it possible for you to search your stored records much as you would on a commercial online system. In some cases there's an accounting function to make it easy to track the amount of time and money you have spent on a search so that you can bill a client.

This last feature highlights an apparent paradox. Although many packages are ostensibly designed to make online systems easier to use, today most are aimed at specialists and information professionals, the very people one would think would be least in need of user-friendly front-ends. It wasn't always so.

The In-Search/Pro-Search Saga

When In-Search was introduced by the Menlo Corporation in the spring of 1984, it was billed as the ultimate end-user (that's you) answer. In fact it was the most talked-about program in the electronic universe. In-Search could only be used with DIALOG. But the program made descriptions of DIALOG databases and their Bluesheet information instantly available at the touch of a few keys. Among its seven floppy disks were disks for various information categories (arts, education, and social sciences; business, government and news; etc.). The manual was excellent, the packaging superb: molded plastic function key overlay; high-quality, high-concept slipcase; the whole nine yards. Unfortunately, end-users stayed away in droves.

The company then introduced Pro-Search, a package that could search BRS as well and had the ability to translate the commands of the system you knew into those of the one you didn't. You could search either system using either Pro-Search menus or "native mode" commands. An accounting reports feature was added to make it easy to track monthly costs by client, charge code, or specific search session. It became possible to download updates to the software directly from Menlo's own system. Unfortunately, it wasn't enough to keep Menlo afloat. In-Search is now dead and Pro-Search is now marketed primarily to information professionals by Personal Bibliograpic Software, Inc. The cost is $495, with quarterly updates available at $150 a year or $50 apiece. Contact:

> Personal Bibliographic Software, Inc.
> P.O. Box 4250
> Ann Arbor, MI 48106
> (313) 996-1580

The Sci-Mate® Packages

Sci-Mate®, from the Institute for Scientific Information (ISI), is another leading package. But it too is aimed at specialists, particularly researchers and medical doctors. There are three separate programs in the complete package: the Sci-Mate Searcher, the Sci-Mate Manager, and the Sci-Mate Editor. Each sells for $399 separately or $359 each if you buy two or all three. Your total cost could thus range from $399 to $1,077.

The Sci-Mate package was developed for researchers who want to keep up with the literature in their fields using online and other resources and do file management offline. The Searcher program has the ability to access DIALOG, BRS, ORBIT, Questel, or the National Library of Medicine (NLM) database. It presents you with essentially the same menu of commands regardless of the system you are on. Sci-Mate Searcher has an option for BROWSE, for example. If you select this while connected to DIALOG, it issues the EXPAND command. If you select the same menu item while on BRS, it issues the ROOT command.

The Sci-Mate Manager will retrieve records stored to disk while you are offline. The records may come from an online system, or they may have been entered at the keyboard in the form of notes or other text. One way or the other, the Manager lets you create and maintain your own personal library of references that you can search and retrieve at any time. However, you must signify where each file and each record begins and ends. In other words, you must review and slightly process your records after you download them.

The Sci-Mate Editor has the capability of using the raw data in your records to create bibliographic citations in the format required by major journals *(The Journal of the American Medical Association, Nature, Science,* etc.). It does this most easily when the records have been downloaded in "tagged" format in which each field carries a two-character label (AU, JN, AB, etc.). Should that download format not be available, you must go through each record and add those tags. For more information, contact:

Institute for Scientific Information, Inc.
3501 Market Street
Philadelphia, PA 19104
(215) 386-0100

SearchWorks

SearchWorks, a program from Online Research Systems, Inc., may be the most sensible package of all. Information brokers and others who do online research for a fee will find it of greatest value. But even if you have no plans to become a broker, if you search DIALOG, BRS/ SEARCH, ORBIT, or the National Library of Medicine (MEDLINE), it is worth looking into. Instead of trying to wrap everything in the cotton wool of online menus, SearchWorks makes the manuals and quick reference cards for all of these systems available to you at the touch of a few keys.

This feature is available to you whether you are keying in a search statement while offline or while you are connected to one of the host systems. For example, if you're familiar with DIALOG but want to search ORBIT, you can set things up such that when you need to know the proper command for something, the program will display the DIALOG command (the one you know) and its equivalent on ORBIT. Short explanations of the command and the various ways to use it are also included.

SearchWorks can handle full-text records, but it is really designed for bibcites and abstracts. It automatically opens a capture file whenever you tell it to log you onto a system. But while you can upload any number of prerecorded search statements, you will probably want to key in most of your own commands during the session. The program includes a "backscrolling" feature to let you review information that has already scrolled off the screen.

If the records have been downloaded in "tagged" format such that each field carries a two-character label (AB for "abstract," SO for "source publication," etc.), you can tell the program to replace those tags with any word you want before it prints the records. You can sort the records alphabetically on the basis of a single field. Or you can ask that they be printed in ranked order on the basis of the keywords you specify and the relative weight you assign to each one. Up to 99 terms can be specified and assigned weights of between one and nine.

Finally, you can have all of the records printed with an accompanying cover sheet that includes a headline and information about the search, the client's name, and so on. The cover sheet can include the cost of the search as well. If you like, you can include an index of keywords that lists the record numbers where they can be found. There is an accounting function as well.

The slipcased manual, while extensive, could be better organized and offer greater detail. But telephone support is available Monday through Friday from 1 P.M. to 5 P.M. Eastern time if you have any problems. The cost for SearchWorks is $149, plus $10 shipping and handling. For more information contact:

> Online Research Systems, Inc.
> 627 West 113th Street, Suite 4F
> New York, NY 10025
> (212) 408-3311

The Most Sensible Approach for Most People

All three of the commercial programs we've considered have something to offer, and if they sound like they might be of interest you should definitely contact the software vendors for more information. However, if you are not an information professional or professional researcher, the most important kind of search-aid software you can get is available free for the cost of a disk or in return for a modest voluntary contribution.

As discussed in the previous chapter, online searching is an interactive procedure. You should always know what your first search command is going to be before you sign on, but you can't know what your second command will be until you look at the results generated by your first. All front-end programs do a great job of automatically logging you onto a system and transmitting your prepared first search statement. But after that, realistically, you're pretty much on your own.

In our opinion, it is foolish to pay for features like these when you can get the same thing and much more besides for much, much less with user-supported software. As explained in *How to Get FREE Software*, user-supported programs, or "freeware" as they are sometimes called, are available from user groups and computer clubs around the country. They are copyrighted but freely distributed, usually for the cost of a floppy disk. The instruction manual is usually on the disk as a text file that you can print out. If you like the program, you are requested to send a contribution to the program's author. In return you may receive a typeset manual, notification of software updates, telephone support, and other benefits.

Three of the programs in this field that carry our highest recommendation are Qmodem, NewKey, and FANSI-CONSOLE™. Each is of commercial quality, and each would carry a much higher price were it available from your local computer store. You may not need all three of them, but you should know that they exist, since they can save you hours of time and untold frustration whether you are online or doing something else with your computer. Each can be ordered directly from its author as well as from users groups.

Qmodem

Qmodem Version 2.0 is the full-featured communications program for IBM-PCs and compatibles discussed in Chapter 1. It uses the same commands familiar to users of PC-TALK, the first "freeware" program created. With its script language, it can automatically log you onto any system and execute commands at any time you specify, whether you are present or not. What's of greatest interest here, however, is the fact that you can load strings of characters into the ten function keys in any of their four modes (straight, shifted, ALT'd, CTRL'd) for a total of 40 possibilities.

This means that with some one-time preparation work, you could arrange for F5 in one of its possible modes to always issue an equivalent command. When you are on DIALOG, hitting F5 might issue the EXPAND command. When you are on BRS/BRKTHRU, hitting a shifted F5 might issue the STEM command. On ORBIT, an ALT'd F5 might issue the NEIGHBOR command, and so on. Qmodem also has a backscrolling feature to let you look again at text that has disappeared from the screen.

CrossTalk offers similar backscrolling and keyboard "macroing" features. "Macro" is short for "macro expansion," and it refers to the ability to in effect expand a single keystroke (like hitting a function key) into a string of characters. Other commercial programs may have these features as well. So if you like the program you're using, there's no reason to change. However, if your favorite communications program does not offer macros and backscrolling, you might consider Qmodem or one of the programs described below.

NewKey

The first is NewKey, written by Frank A. Bell and available from FAB Software. NewKey began as a user-supported equivalent to Pro-Key, SmartKey, and similar commercially available macroing programs. It works in much the same way. You toggle on its "record" mode with [<ALT><=>]. Then you hit the target key, followed by the characters you want to load. When the last character has been entered, you hit [<ALT><->] to toggle off the record mode. You can save your key definitions to disk and load them any time. You can look at a list of your macros and any descriptive tags you may have added to remind yourself what they're for. You can create complete, automatically executing macro "scripts," load any key in any mode (shifted, ALT'd, or CTRL'd) up to a maximum of 32,000 characters, and do much more.

The cost is $7.50 plus $2.50 U.S. shipping and handling, for a total of $10 when ordered from FAB Software. That's for Version 2.4, which you may also find in user group collections. The latest edition, Version 3.0, adds even more features and power. This version is not user-supported software, but it's cheap at $24.95 (plus $2.50 U.S. shipping and handling) and includes a 75-page printed manual and telephone support. You can order directly from FAB. "Foreign orders must be paid in U.S. dollars with a check drawn on a U.S. bank or through the U.S. branch of a foreign bank, or through an international money order." Contact:

> FAB Software
> P.O. Box 336
> Wayland, MA 01778

FANSI-CONSOLE™

It is impossible to say enough about FANSI-CONSOLE™, the "Fast ANSI X3.64 console driver" from Hersey Micro Consulting, Inc. In essence, it gives you complete control over every aspect of your screen and keyboard. You'll find reviews of the program in *Lotus Magazine* (June 1985, page 8) and *PC-World* (February 1986, page 282). Here we will limit ourselves to the FANSI feature you'll find most valuable while you are online: backscrolling.

FANSI loads in when you boot up, so the program, FCON-

SOLE.DEV, must be on your boot disk and a line reading DE-VICE = FCONSOLE.DEV (followed by various parameters) must be in your CONFIG.SYS file. Once FANSI is loaded, you can hit your Scroll Lock key at any time to stop the display and then use your arrow and page keys to scroll back through the lines that have disappeared from your screen. If you forgot to record something, you can use other keys to "clip out" the text and write it to disk as a file. Hit the Scroll Lock key again, and you're back where you started.

According to Hersey Micro Consulting, FANSI works with Qmodem and most other communications programs, including CrossTalk. (The only problem point on CrossTalk is VT100 emulation.) Whether you're in DOS or online, you'll find that FANSI's one-key backscroll feature is so habit-forming that using a machine without it becomes a real chore.

The program is available with an abbreviated but quite functional on-disk manual from users groups for the price of the disk, or direct from Hersey for $25. If you like the program and want to become a registered user, an additional $50 brings a fat, slipcased three-ring manual, a quarterly newsletter, and telephone support. You can buy the whole package at once for $75. Both prices include U.S. shipping via UPS. Visa and MasterCard are accepted. Foreign orders are possible as well, but contact the vendor for details. Contact:

Hersey Micro Consulting, Inc.
P.O. Box 8276
Ann Arbor, MI 48107
(313) 994-3259

Online Tip: There is a drawback to FANSI: It is so powerful that it is inevitably more than a little "bytehead" in its approach. There are a number of solutions, however. If you obtain a copy from a users group, see if you can find a member who is a knowledgeable FANSI user to help you set it up. If that is not possible, order the complete package from Hersey, review the manual, and take advantage of the customer support hotline.

If you have the program right now and want to use it immediately, add the following line to your CONFIG.SYS file:

```
DEVICE=FCONSOLE.DEV /L=1 /R=100
```

Put the program FCONSOLE.DEV on your boot disk with your newly edited CONFIG.SYS file and reboot. To test it, key in DIR and hit the Scroll Lock key before the directory has finished dis-

---

Online Tip (cont.)

playing. Use the arrow keys to scroll through the display. Hit the
Scroll Lock key again and the directory will continue displaying
where it left off. The L enables the Scroll Lock key pause function.
The R allots space for 100 recalled lines. You set this number anywhere from 50 to as many lines as you have memory for.

Post-Download Processing Software

There isn't space to go into detail, but two programs that should be
on anybody's search-aid software consideration list are ZyINDEX and
F.Y.I. 3000 Plus. Both make it possible to search a text file on your
hard or floppy disk almost exactly as you would when searching a commercial database. The programs don't care where the file came from. It
could be a collection of records you have downloaded, manuscripts, business letters, ASCII spreadsheet files, or something else.

The key point is that you never have to go back through the downloaded or other file to tag search words or otherwise process records.
You simply turn the file over to ZyINDEX or F.Y.I. for a one-time
indexing procedure during which a compact inverted index file is prepared containing every significant word in the file. Once that's been
done, you can locate any information in the file using the same type of
search commands and search logic you would with DIALOG, BRS, or
some other system.

For example, with ZyINDEX you can use parentheses for nested
searches, wildcard truncation characters, proximity operators to locate
words that are adjacent to or within a certain number of other words of
each other, and the standard AND, OR, NOT Boolean operators.

ZyINDEX comes in three versions. The main difference between
them is the number of files they can handle. The Standard Version
($145) can handle 500 files. The Professional ($295) handles 5,000. And
the Plus Version ($695) handles 15,000. The Plus version is designed for
use on a network of up to five workstations. The version most people
buy is the Professional, but if you buy the Standard version you can
upgrade at any time by returning the software and paying the difference plus a handling charge. None of the versions is copy-protected,
so using the software from a hard disk is no problem. In fact, although
ZyINDEX can be used with a floppy-based system, a hard disk is
strongly recommended.

F.Y.I. 3000 Plus is an improved version of an earlier program. Many
of the improvements were added specifically to match ZyINDEX's ca-

pabilities. The cost is $395, and the program can handle a database of up to 65 million characters. We suggest that you send for information on both programs. Contact:

> ZyINDEX
> ZyLAB Corporation
> 233 East Erie Street
> Chicago, IL 60611
> (312) 642-2201

> F.Y.I. 3000 Plus
> Software Marketing Associates, Inc.
> 4615 West Bee Caves Road
> Austin, TX 78746
> (512) 346-0133

Online Tip: How about full-text retrieval for $40? That's what Eric Balkan's Total Recall™ program can do. Total Recall handles up to 254 files totaling a maximum of one megabyte of storage, and it lets you search with AND, OR, NOT, create your own list of stop words, use wildcards, and more. For an additional $10, Mr. Balkan will include a copy of his database of some 3,000 movies (film, stars, date, etc.) which can be used with the program. Contact:

> Packet Press
> 14704 Seneca Castle Court
> Gaithersburg, MD 20878

EASYNET
Also Known as InfoMaster or IQuest

Wouldn't it be great if people who needed information could use their computers to dial a number, key in their credit card number, and gain instant access to 16 or more online vendors offering some 700 databases—without having a subscription to any of them? If callers don't know which databases to choose, they'll be presented with a series of menus to help them define the kind of information they want. The system will then select a database for them. If callers want to search a specific database, that's fine too. They'll be able to key in as much of the database name as they can remember and the proper connection will be made. As for entering a search statement, there'll be simple commands and lots of helpful menus to guide the caller.

This is the essence of EasyNet, a product of Telebase Systems, Inc. of Narberth, Pennsylvania. In the information industry, a system that gives you access to another system is called a "gateway," and EasyNet is hands-down the ultimate database vendor gateway. You can connect with EasyNet and access databases that are on BRS, VU/TEXT, DIALOG, NewsNet, and ORBIT, as well as those on DataTimes, Data-Star, Datasolve, Questel, Pergamon, ADP, and other vendors not featured in this book. You do not need a subscription to any system. Nor do you need a system manual. In fact it would do you no good at all.

Whether EasyNet selects the database or you choose one yourself, you will be prompted to enter a single search statement. You can use AND, OR, and NOT, a wildcard character (/), and parentheses for nested searches. When you hit <ENTER>, the system will display the search statement for your confirmation. If you confirm, it will then go away and conduct a search of the selected database for you. If you entered the term MARKET SHARE and the database being accessed requires "(W)" or some other connector to be inserted between two search words, EasyNet will do it for you.

EasyNet conducts the search on the chosen system, signs off, and brings back up to ten short-format results. The actual contents of the results vary with the database, but the publication, title, date, and author fields of a bibliographic citation are typical. EasyNet shows these to you and asks if you would like to see their associated abstracts. You may select the ones you want to see by entering the number of each result. EasyNet then goes away again, reconducts the search on the host system, and brings back the chosen hits in a lengthier format. Through it all, you are never in direct contact with the host system. Please see Figure 6.1 for an illustration of how all of this works.

Means of Access

You can dial EasyNet directly via a toll-free "800" number, go in through Telenet or Tymnet, gain access through CompuServe where EasyNet is called IQuest, or make a connection through Western Union's EasyLink system where it is called InfoMaster. You'll pay about 20¢ per minute in connect time and $8 per search. Different vendors have different policies, but when all things are considered, the price works out about the same. One successful search will deliver from one to ten citations to your screen, but if the search is not successful, you pay only for your connect time. Viewing the abstracts associated with the citations typically costs $2 apiece. If you want to look at additional citations, the search will be conducted again and you will be charged another $8, only this time EasyNet will come back with the *next* ten citations.

Sound pretty good? There is no doubt about it, it *is* an interesting idea, and Telebase Systems gets high marks for thoughtfulness, user friendliness, and overall implementation. Each user, for example, is served by a dedicated computer (a board-level supermicro CPU) for improved response time. When DIALOG is down for the weekend, the system dynamically reconfigures to access Data-Star in Switzerland for many of the databases it would normally go to DIALOG for.

The prompts and menus are good, though experienced online users will find them time consuming. EasyNet customer support is excellent, and it's available round-the-clock. When you have a question you have only to key in SOS and a Telebase specialist will come online to assist you. You may also use a toll-free customer support phone number.

EasyNet, in short, really is very easy to use. However, even Telebase Systems does not maintain that EasyNet as it is now configured is the ultimate answer. At this writing users may choose from one of two versions of the system. With EasyNet I, the system prompts you through a set of menus and uses your responses to choose a database. Databases are chosen from a limited list of about 100, not from all of those available. With EasyNet II, you enter the name of the database you want to search, and Easynet picks the vendor.

In both cases the major drawback is that you can enter only one search command. It can be quite lengthy, to be sure, but it is very time-consuming and rather expensive at $8 a shot to successively enter commands and look at results as one would when connected directly to a vendor's system. There is also next to no flexibility in how you display results. You either get a bibcite or the full record. (Full-text records are treated somewhat differently.)

Telebase has an answer to this. It's called EasyNet III, and it should be available as you read this. Version III will offer a common search language for use on all 700 databases, simultaneous multiple database (cross database) searching, variable downloading formats, and more. Experienced searchers will be able to enter the commands they know for, say, DIALOG and have them automatically translated into whatever is required for the target database. According to Marvin I. Weinberger, senior vice president, "We haven't done even one percent of what we plan to do. We hope to go far beyond what EasyNet is today."

A Database Is a Database Is a Database?

EasyNet is the brainchild of Dick Kollin, President of Telebase Systems, Inc. Mr. Kollin has deep roots in the information industry. He created Magazine Index, for example, and co-founded Information Access Company (IAC). He helped develop IAC's SearchHelper software. He was also a senior vice president with the Institute for Scientific Information, where he helped develop the Sci-Mate package discussed earlier. EasyNet was developed by Mr. Kollin under the sponsorship of the National Federation of Abstracting and Information Services (NFAIS). DIALOG, BRS, ORBIT, and most of the other giants of the field have endorsed it.

Everyone would like to see EasyNet succeed. However, at this writing, the key to using EasyNet is to remember that it is an evolutionary product. If you are new to the information field, there are some things to keep in mind to use the system more effectively.

First, EasyNet gives you access to over 700 databases, but it tells you almost nothing about them. The company publishes a free "Database Directory," which you might want to ask for, but the publication contains at most two or three sentences describing each offering. The directories supplied by Western Union and CompuServe are no better. Since providing even 200 words of description for each of 700 databases would require a small book, this is understandable. Possibly the chapters in Part III of this book can be of some help. But what's the point of having access to 700 databases if you can't tell one from the other?

Online Tip: As it happens, EasyNet gives you access to three of the leading database directories. Choose EasyNet II, the option to select your own database, and key in either CUADRA or KIPD or DATABASE OF DATABASES. These are the names of the Cuadra Directory, the Knowledge Industry Publications Directory, and the directory published by Martha E. Williams, a noted authority in the field. When prompted to do so, enter the word or phrase that best describes the subject you are interested in. We used the word BIOGRAPHY and had good results with all three of them. The cost per search will be $8, but you will not have to view the abstracts since the names of the relevant databases are displayed as part of the initial citations.

A Small Matter of Price

Second, there's the matter of cost. Uniform pricing for all databases is certainly a welcome change from the tangled, Byzantine policies of the various vendors. But information prices are too high as it is. And with all the middlemen who have to be paid—Telebase Systems, the database vendor, and the database producer—EasyNet is even more expensive. For example, we signed on, selected the ABI/INFORM database and responded to the prompts to tell EasyNet to search *Business Week* for ROBOT/ AND AUTOMOBILE INDUSTRY. (As noted, the slash is EasyNet's wildcard character.) We got three hits ($8) and elected to look at all three associated abstracts ($6), for a total cost of $14, plus connect time.

Since EasyNet conducted the search on BRS, we signed onto BRS/ BRKTHRU and conducted the same search of ABI/INFORM. We got four hits, three of which were identical to those EasyNet delivered. Perhaps EasyNet searched different fields. Whatever the case, neither we nor Customer Service were able to account for the disparity. The BRS search was conducted after hours and required a total of five minutes. At 44¢ a minute, the total cost was $2.20. There are no display charges for ABI/INFORM after hours.

To be sure, EasyNet offers 24-hour customer service and adds other value. And certainly one would have to be familiar with BRKTHRU and online searching to do what we did without spending a lot of time poring over the system manual. But a difference of $11.80 on a single search is enough to make anyone swallow hard. Particularly when you consider that with *its* menus BRS/BRKTHRU is nearly as easy to use as the Telebase product.

Zero Hits? What Do You Mean, "Zero Hits"!

Third, there's the matter of the effectiveness of the EasyNet information retrieval process itself. On one occasion we tried to use EasyNet to retrieve a record from the BBC Summary of World Broadcasts database. It was a summary of a radio broadcast originating in Iran, and we had used the BBC database on NEXIS to obtain it. On EasyNet we pretended that we were looking for information on one of the specific topics covered by that broadcast. But despite the hard-copy printout we had in hand, we could not locate the identical information with Easy-Net. That's an interesting test, perhaps. But suppose it were for real. Suppose you were the one doing the searching and suppose you didn't have the advantage of knowing with absolute certainty that the information was there. No hits. Well, there must not be any information on the topic.

At other times we did not have to pretend. On the spur of the moment we selected the Cuadra Directory of Online Databases database and keyed in the search term ROBOTS. Zero hits. Apparently there are no databases devoted to mechanical men. But there is one on BRS that we know of for sure and a check of the printed Cuadra directory uncovered three others. What went wrong? What went wrong was we didn't search on ROBOTICS, a word that appears in all of the Cuadra database write-ups. To be safe we should have searched with a wildcard (ROBOT/) on EasyNet. But ROBOTS was the first term that came to mind, as it might to anyone else who wasn't thinking like a searcher at the time.

Finally, before doing the cost comparison discussed previously, we set out to duplicate the DIALOG and ABI/INFORM results of robots in the car industry discussed in Chapter 5. Our mistake was in not reviewing that search first. We entered what came naturally: INDUSTRIAL ROBOT/ AND AUTOMOTIVE INDUSTRY. Zero hits. Nothing. Yet we knew the information was there. Examining a printout of the previous search, we immediately saw the mistake. As noted in Chapter 5, ABI/INFORM doesn't use "automotive"—it uses "automobile" as its controlled vocabulary descriptor. Searching again with that modification yielded the results discussed for the cost comparison.

But how would one know to use "automobile" instead of "automotive"? You don't have the ABI/INFORM manual. You've probably never heard of Data Courier, Inc., the database producer. There is no way to check the database index with the equivalent of an EXPAND on EasyNet I or II. And if you truncate the term to AUTOMOB/ and don't think to include INDUSTRY, you *might* get hits on ROBOT/ and automobile dealers, automobile fleets, automobile garages, automobile insurance, and automobile leasing, as well as automobile industry. All of those terms are in the INFORM controlled vocabulary and thus in the records in the INFORM database.

It may very well have been ineptitude on our part. But EasyNet isn't supposed to be for "ept" people. Quite the contrary. What happens if you sign on, enter the best possible search statement you can, and EasyNet says there is no information on the subject? What happens if you get a bunch of hits but they all turn out to be "search surprises" containing nothing but irrelevant information for which you are charged $8? These are troubling questions that hopefully will be addressed by EasyNet III.

When It Was Good

Even at its present stage of development, however, it is impossible to dismiss EasyNet out of hand. About 50% of the time it produced some very good results, as demonstrated in Figure 6.1, and it did so with an ease unmatched by any other system. EasyNet does indeed have the ability to pull up a single fact or a range of citations to get you started on researching a topic. (Photocopies of cited articles can be ordered online. ISI and UMI handle document delivery.) Just remember that EasyNet is not the final word.

It is also true that if you had to subscribe to all of the systems Easy-

Net can gate you into, you'd have little money left in your bank account and/or room on your bookshelves for anything but manuals. It's fun to search TASS or The Manchester Guardian or Banque: French Banking Law or any of the other databases available on systems to which you do not subscribe.

At this writing EasyNet, though expensive, is certainly worth a try. More importantly, it is worth watching, since it appears to be on the right track. For more information, contact CompuServe, Western Union EasyLink, or EasyNet itself at:

> EasyNet
> Telebase Systems, Inc.
> 134 North Narberth Avenue
> Narberth, PA 19072
> (215) 649-217
>
> 24-hour Customer Service:
> (800) 841-9553
> (215) 296-1793

Online Tip: If you do not currently subscribe to CompuServe or EasyLink and you want to use EasyNet immediately, there are three alternatives. Dial your local Telenet node, hit <ENTER> twice, key in D1 as your terminal identifier, and enter C 21549 at the at sign (@) prompt. Dial your local Tymnet node, wait until garbage begins to appear on your screen, hit <A>, and key in EASYNET at the login prompt. Or dial (800) EASYNET. Have your MasterCard, Visa, or American Express card ready.

Telenet numbers are available from Telenet Customer Service at (800) 336-0437. Tymnet Customer Service is (800) 336-0149, worldwide. Both can help you log on if you're having trouble.

Figure 6.1. Looking for Market Share on EasyNet ──────

We signed onto EasyNet with the goal of finding out what share of the fast-food market Burger King holds vis-à-vis McDonald's and other major competitors. It seemed reasonable to assume that a new user would not know which database to ask for, so we told EasyNet to do it for us. EasyNet then presented the following sequence of menus:

```
PRESS              TO SELECT
   1   Subject
   2   Person
   3   Place
   4   Organization
   H   Help
Total charges thus far :          $0.20
— > 4


PRESS              TO SELECT
   1   Corporations
   2   Colleges and universities
   3   Foundations/Grants
   4   Associations
   H   Help
Total charges thus far :          $0.20
— > 1


PRESS              TO SELECT
   1   Basic background information
   2   Financial information
   3   Credit reports
   4   Stock and investment
   5   Family tree
   6   Information about the industry
   7   other choices
   H   Help
Total charges thus far :          $0.40
— > 6


This database carries a surcharge
of $ 5 for this search.
Do you wish to continue ? (Yes/No) — > Y


Enter your specific topic.

(type H for important examples)
    or B to back up)
```

— > BURGER KING AND MARKET SHARE   ←——— This is what we entered.

```
Is:
BURGER KING AND MARKET SHARE
   Correct ? (Yes/No) — > Y
```

EasyNet informed us that it was going to search the PTS/PROMT database on BRS. It presented a disclaimer ("We have no reason to believe . . . that errors exist in the data . . . have no liability . . . etc."). The system also told us when it had accomplished the step of accessing the network, selecting the database, and so on. It then showed a line of asterisks as it began to retrieve information. Then there was this:

Search completed . . . .

There are 33 item(s) which
satisfy your search phrase.

We will show you the most recent 10

You may wish to PRINT or CAPTURE this data if possible.

Press (return) to see
your search results . . .—>

For reasons of space, only four of the ten hits EasyNet gave us are presented here. Note that Heading #2 looks particularly promising:

Heading # 1   Searched: MMM DD, YYYY
You may stop this display with control c

AN 132471. PROMT. 8612.
SO Nation's Restaurant News. Mar 10, 1986. pp 1, 143.
TI Industry sales slump stings the Big Three burger chains.

Heading # 2

AN 1310742. PROMT. 8607.
SO Nation's Restaurant News. Feb 3, 1986. pp 2.
TI Fact file: Chain market share leaders
        Top 10 chains in market share, 1985 (%).

Heading # 5

AN 115993. PROMT. 8500.
SO Advertising Age. Mar 11, 1985. pp 88.
TI BK launches dawn attack on McMuffin.

Heading # 8

AN 1047504. PROMT. 8400.
SO World Food Report (Incorp Eurofood). Apr 25, 1984. pp 6, 7.
TI Fast food & catering: Italy: Burger invasion begins.

PRESS   TO
    1   Review results again
    2   See abstracts   (need heading #'s $2.00 each)
    3   Order reprints   (need heading #'s)
    4   See next 10 headings   ($8.00 extra)
    5   Start a new search
    6   Leave System
Total charges thus far : $14.00   <—— $8 for the search, $5
                                                 for the surcharge, and $1
                                                 for connect time so far.

We opted to look at the abstract for Heading #2. EasyNet accessed the database again, repeated the search-and-retrieval process, and then saw the following:

You may wish to PRINT or CAPTURE this data if possible.

Press (return) to see
your abstract(s) . . . —>

Heading # 1   Searched: MMM DD, YYYY
You may stop this display with control c

AN 1310742. PROMT. 8607.
SO Nation's Restaurant News. Feb 3, 1986. pp 2.
LG English (EN).
TI Fact file: Chain market share leaders
       Top 10 chains in market share, 1985 (%).
PN *Eating-Places (PC5812000).
EN *Market-data (EC600).
CN *United-States (CC1USA).
CO McDonalds DN: 00-790-0947 CUSIP: 580047 TS: MDD. Burger-King.
   KFC. Wendys-International DN: 05-285-6671 CUSIP: 950590 TS:
   WEN. Hardees-Food-Systems. Pizza-Hut DN: 00-725-0046 CUSIP:
   725845 TS: PIZA. Contract-Food-Services.
   International-Dairy-Queen CUSIP: 459373 TS: INDQ. ARA-Services.
Big-Boy-Restaurants
PD 860203.
AB Fact file: Chain market share leaders
   Top 10 chains in market share, 1985 (%)
   McDonalds   7.6
   Burger King   3.0
   KFC   2.1
   Wendy's   2.0
   Hardee's   1.5
   Pizza Hut   1.4
   Marriott   1.0
   Dairy Queen   1.0
   ARA Services   0.9
   Big Boy   0.8

Press (return) to continue . . . —>

Not bad. Not bad at all. Having gotten what we signed on for, we left the system. The following cost summary was then displayed:

Charges:

EasyNet Access:
   Telecommunications $1.40

Database Charges:

1	Searches:	$8.00
0	Reprints:	$0.00
0	Express Reprints:	$0.00
1	Abstracts	$2.00
	Surcharges	$5.00
Total Charges:		$16.40

How to Hire an Information Professional

Research and information retrieval are like anything else: there's a time when it's best to do it yourself and a time to call in the pros. Unfortunately, there is no way for us to tell you which path to take every time. In matters of personal finance, for example, some people enjoy playing the market and overseeing all of their own investments, while others are happy to pay someone they trust to do it for them. But both groups might very well turn to an independent financial consultant for help in devising an overall personal financial plan and strategy. Others may have developed the necessary expertise to handle everything on their own, while still others may have no plan at all and be flying strictly by the seat of their pants.

As far as information is concerned, the important thing to know is that there *are* alternatives. As information consciousness rises, particularly throughout corporate America, the need for information intermediaries—specialists skilled in the fine art of research and information retrieval—will rise as well. It is already happening.

The number of people calling themselves information specialists, consultants, brokers, and freelance librarians has increased so rapidly in recent years that no one can say for sure just how many there are. At this writing, it is probably less than 1,000. There is no dedicated trade or professional society and no agreement on the profession's proper name. We will use the term "information broker" because that is what seems to be used most frequently in the literature. But it is an inaccurate description that hopefully will one day be replaced by something better.

There have always been professional researchers and information consultants of one sort of another. What's new is the easy availability of online information sources. People who would shun the deep, dusty stacks of a major-league library are only too happy to call themselves information brokers, sit in their sunny home offices, and go online for a fee. There's nothing wrong with this, of course, and many of these people perform a valuable service. But when dealing with an emerging profession that has yet to develop tests and minimum competency certifications, it is wise to proceed with caution.

What Services Are Available?

The first thing to be aware of is the range of services available. FIND/SVP, the creator of the database of market research reports discussed in Chapter 17, is one of the biggest information brokers. In addition to a large, full-time staff of professionals and a worldwide network of affiliates, it maintains one of the largest private business libraries in America.

The company's Quick Information Service is designed for specific queries requiring just a few hours of research. Callers are asked the nature of the question and then transferred to a specialist from one of six subject groups. These include consumer, industrial/technical, health care, and business/company/financial. The central search group handles biographical, demographic, education, political, publishing, information about the arts, and other areas not covered by the other groups. The retrieval section handles requests for copies of reports, books, and other documents and purchases of product samples and other items ("even theatre tickets!"). The firm once successfully located the front end of a 1977 Toyota for a client.

The FIND/SVP Research Projects Service specializes in preparing "customized, interpretive, analytical research studies." Industry overviews, opinion and market surveys, special studies "for acquisition analysis, business expansion, new technologies, and new products," and virtually any other type of customized research is included. There is a translation service and an Information Tracking Service (current awareness) as well. Monthly minimum guarantees ("retainers") start at $100 a month, but $300 to $400 a month is more typical. Research time is billed at between $38 and $90 an hour, depending on the complexity of the inquiry. For more information, contact:

> FIND/SVP
> 500 Fifth Avenue
> New York, NY 10110
> (212) 354-2424
> Telex: 148358

Information On Demand, Inc.

Information On Demand, Inc. (IOD) in Berkeley, California, is an excellent example of a more conventional information broker. Founded in 1978 by Sue Rugge and now associated with the Pergamon Group of Companies, IOD does many of the same things that FIND/SVP does, but the emphasis is different. As its name implies, IOD has always been oriented toward finding answers to specific questions. For example: Is there a market for Christmas trees in Hawaii? What are the current trends in the Brazilian construction industry? By what process can platinum be extracted from catalytic converters? The firm's sales literature points out that it has successfully answered these and many similar questions in the past.

IOD employs a staff of full-time professional researchers, many of whom have a Master of Library Science (MLS) degree, and it maintains accounts on more than a dozen database vendor systems. But, like all top-quality information brokers, it does not rely upon online resources alone. IOD conducts traditional library research, phones and interviews experts, and uses the full range of other research tools as well. Research services are billed at $75 per hour, plus costs, with a two-hour minimum.

IOD also puts a strong emphasis on document delivery ("doc-del" in the biz). It has a network of runners stationed near major libraries around the country, and of all the information brokers it has been the most aggressive in pursuing electronic ordering. You can place an order with IOD from virtually any system, including The Source and CompuServe, and bill it to your credit card. Costs start at $14 per document (up to 20 pages, 25¢ per page thereafter) and include all copyright royalties and delivery by UPS or first-class mail. For more information, contact:

Information On Demand, Inc.
P.O. Box 9550
Berkeley, CA 94709
(800) 227-0750
(415) 644-4500

Independent Information Brokers

By far the majority of information brokers are independent consultants. Though some operate as one- or two-person firms, many hold full-time jobs. Some are reference librarians at public and university libraries, law librarians at major law firms, or corporate librarians at company information centers. Although the typical independent information broker can handle a wide variety of requests, most tend to have one or more specialties: chemistry and pharmaceuticals, law, patents and trademarks, scientific and engineering topics, foreign trade, government information and statistics, management and business information, and so on.

The services you can expect from an independent broker vary. Some may offer only online research services and only on a limited number of systems. Others may combine databases with conventional library research. Most do not offer their own document delivery service, though of course they know how and from whom to order copies. Typical research costs range from $25 to $60 an hour, plus database connect time and other expenses.

Online Tip: Maureen Corcoran, President of the Online Connection, is among the first to offer an interesting extension of traditional information brokerage services. Ms. Corcoran has been a professional, full-time information broker for many years. She says, "I always try to be sensitive to my clients' needs. So when some of my corporate clients began to say, 'We'd like to be able to do some of the things you're doing internally, but we don't know where to begin,' I took note."

According to Ms. Corcoran, most companies can fill 95% of their online information needs with 20 to 50 databases, and of these most will use three to five 80% of the time. "The question is: *Which* 20 to 50 databases and *which* three to five should they pick? What's the smartest, most cost-effective way to set things up?" Ms. Corcoran reports that she now spends most of her time analyzing a company's needs and showing clients what to do to establish internal online information programs. For more information, contact:

> The Online Connection
> P.O. Box 1702-195
> 3702 N.W. 6th Street
> Gainesville, FL 32602
> (904) 375-4001

How to Find an Information Broker

The best way to find an information broker is through a referral from a friend or business associate. The advantage is that your friend can give you an appraisal of the individual's work and presumably would not steer you wrong. The disadvantage is that a skilled information broker is a strategic resource and you can't expect someone with whom you compete to pass that kind of information along unless you are very good friends indeed. Since most brokers don't advertise and get most of their clients by referral, finding the one you need can require some effort.

Professional Librarians

Fortunately, a number of resources are available. One place to start is with your local library or, if you live in a small town, the library of the nearest city or university. Your quest may end there as well, since many libraries offer what amounts to a fee-based information service. (In some locations, it's free.) In return for a small overhead fee, plus any online costs, a reference librarian may be able to serve as the only information broker you need.

In fact, if you are impressed with the person's capabilities, you may be able to hire him or her on a freelance, after-hours basis. This has a lot of advantages if you can pull it off. You know going in that the individual has the skills of both an online searcher and a professional librarian. And who is likely to know a library better than someone who works there?

DIALOG Yellowsheets and CompuServe

Another source is the DIALOG Yellowsheets. As explained in Chapter 7, these firms specialize in document delivery. But many of them offer online research services as well. Whether these services are mentioned on the Yellowsheet or not, it might be worth contacting a firm that specializes in delivering documents related to the field you're interested in. Still another source is the Work-at-Home Special Interest Group (SIG) or "forum" on CompuServe. Operated by Paul and Sarah Edwards, two of the leading figures in the work-at-home-with-computer and telecommuting field, this SIG is often a meeting place for freelance information brokers. (See *The Complete Handbook of Personal Computer Communications* for more information on the CompuServe SIGs.)

The Burwell Directory

The only directory available at this writing is the one produced by Helen Burwell. It's called the *Directory of Fee-Based Information Services* ($24.95, plus $2 shipping and handling), and it contains nearly 545 listings of information brokers in 30 countries. That number is sure to grow, for Ms. Burwell is actively seeking to list every bona fide information broker. Each entry provides the company name and a paragraph or two describing the types of services offered and any areas of specialization. The book is indexed by services, by subject speciality, and by personnel. Canada, Western Europe, Japan, Africa, Australia, and Asia are also covered.

Ms. Burwell also publishes a newsletter called "The Journal of Fee-Based Information Services." There are six issues a year and subscriptions are $35. If you subscribe to the newsletter or purchase the directory, you may contact Burwell Enterprises at any time for the names of brokers who may meet your needs. Referrals are also available to non-subscribers at a flat rate of $25. Here are the American and European addresses to contact:

> Burwell Enterprises
> 5106 F.M. 1960 West
> Suite 349
> Houston, TX 77069
> (713) 537-9051

> Johan Van Halm & Associates
> P.O. Box 688
> 3800 AR Amersfoort
> NETHERLANDS
> 033-18024

Marquis PRO-Files Online

Perhaps the quickest, easiest way to locate an information broker is to use information technology itself. Marquis Who's Who, Inc., has created the *Marquis Who's Who Directory of Online Professionals*. The book sells for $65, plus $3.50 shipping and handling. It doesn't list everyone in the online industry, but at 830 pages it is the most comprehensive directory available. More importantly, it is available for searching online as DIALOG File 235, Marquis PRO-Files.

As with all *Who's Who* publications, a listing is purely voluntary, and prospective listees are sent questionnaires. One of the categories listees were asked to fill out was "Current Online Function." And among the choices were "Information Broker" and "Intermediary Searcher." Another category was "Subject Expertise." This makes it a snap to find an information professional who wants to be listed as an expert in a particular area.

Sign on to DIALOG. Enter BEGIN 235 and then enter SS FN = INFO BROKER to pull up all those records listing "info broker" as their current online function. Then enter SS S1 AND SJ = CHEMISTRY (or whatever other subject area you are interested in). At that point, you can pick out just those information brokers with expertise in chemistry who live in a particular state or who meet some other qualification. See the DIALOG Bluesheet (explained in Chapter 7) for more details.

Here is an abbreviated sample search and single record for an information broker who lists chemistry as a specialty:

?BEGIN 235

File 235:MARQUIS PRO-Files 1985
Copr. Marquis Who's Who, Inc.

	Set	Items	Description

?SS FN = INFO BROKER

                S1   370   FN = INFO BROKER
?SS S1 AND SJ = CHEMISTRY

                       370   S1
                S2   1021   SJ = CHEMISTRY
                S3   67   S1 AND SJ = CHEMISTRY

?TYPE 3/5/1

3/5/1
151173   OP01   BIOG UPDATE: 19840000
   Radding, Shirley B
FUNCTION: cons (04); info broker (05)
EMPLOYMENT SECTOR: pvt
ONLINE EXPERIENCE: 05   (10 or more yrs)
ONLINE SYSTEMS USED:
   Chem Abstracts Service (05);
   DIALOG Info Services, Inc (12);
   NLM (31)
SEARCH HOURS/MONTH:61-80
EQUIPMENT USED:
DATABASES USED:
   CAS ONLINE (036);
   CANCERLIT (032);
   CA SEARCH (030);
   COMPENDEX (058);
   CLAIMS/US PATENT ABSTRACTS (053);
   CLAIMS/CHEM (049);
   MEDLINE (137);
   INSPEC (115);
   TOXLINE (212);
   NTIS (154)
DATABASE SUBJECT EXPERTISE:
   chemistry & chem engring (07);
   electronics & elec engring (13);
   materials scis (21);
   medicine & biosciences (24);
   toxicology (34)

(record continues with address and contact information)

How to Choose an Information Broker

Even the most reputable of information brokers would agree that today the byword must be: caveat emptor. Anyone can call himself an information broker, whether he's had years of online and library research experience or bought his first modem only last week. There's no way you can tell from a simple listing whether the individual is a seasoned professional or simply someone who is going to learn the online trade at your expense. The only way to tell for sure is to talk to the person, and even then it is best if you know something about information in general and online information in particular.

You should be suspicious, for example, if someone who quotes a flat price without discussing the problem with you first to try to get a handle on what you want and what obtaining it will involve. There are other questions to ask as well, both of yourself and of the prospective information broker:

• Are you simpatico?

Ideally, the person you want will be in tune with your way of thinking and expressing yourself. The best research librarians and information brokers have an uncanny ability to get inside their clients' heads and, through the questions they ask and their own native intelligence, reach the point where they can anticipate your needs. The ideal information broker is the person who would do what you would do when online or researching a topic if you had his or her skills.

• Does the individual plan to do a presearch interview?

This is a sine qua non. A good information broker will take the time to interview you, whether in person or on the phone, to try to determine exactly what you want and need.

• What research resources will the individual use?

As noted previously, some information brokers limit their service to online searching only. Others use library and other conventional techniques as well. Neither approach is necessarily better than the other. It all depends on what you want. But you should definitely make sure that the broker plans to do the kind of research you want before going much further.

• Does the individual have an area of special expertise?

Many information brokers are generalists and they are quite effective. But if you need searches on chemical formulas, patents, legal matters, or some other specialty area, you need someone who knows the field and has done similar searches before.

• Which databases do they plan to search and what other steps will they take?

You may not be in a position to judge the validity of their answer. But that doesn't matter a great deal. What you're after here is a sense of whether they know what they're doing. If you want a list of all books published on a particular topic, for example, and they hesitate when you ask them this question or say they'll have to get back to you, it is not a good sign. As we'll see in Chapter 12, books are among the easiest things to track down, and any information broker worth his or her salt will know about the Library of Congress database and the Books in Print database.

• What exactly will you receive?

It is very important for both parties to have an exact idea of what will be delivered once the search process is finished. Will it be a simple list of bibliographic citations? Will it be an executive summary or report supported by printouts of the online research? An analytical report? Or what? Ask if the individual can forward some samples of research reports done for previous clients.

• What will it cost?

From this perspective, hiring an information broker is no different from contracting with any other professional. The nature of information is such that one cannot purchase it by the pound. Generally, information brokers charge by the amount of time required, plus any applicable online or other costs. Some brokers mark up online charges by 10% to 15%. Others bill you exactly what they are billed. Don't be shy about asking. What do you charge per hour? Do you mark up online and other costs and, if so, by how much? Do you have a set minimum fee, regardless of how much time the job takes?

If you have never used an information broker of any kind before and have no feel for what things should cost, set a modest maximum price (confirmed in writing) over which you will not go. Make certain that you understand what you will receive for that amount of money. Indeed, a good broker should ask you how much money you want to spend on the search.

• Is confidentiality likely to be a problem?

It shouldn't be. But if the research you are requesting is confidential, it wouldn't hurt to make sure the individual is aware of that fact. And certainly he or she should inform you if one of your competitors is also a client.

• What formal training and work experience have they had?

This one is rather tricky. If you're the kind of employer who likes to pigeonhole people, then fine; ask them if they have an MLS, and don't hire anyone who doesn't. Be aware, however, that by doing this you will automatically cut yourself off from the services of many individuals with fine, intuitive minds who may be better suited to the job at hand.

A better alternative would be to give the person a chance if he or she seems competent. Give the person an assignment where the amount of money you're committed to is clearly defined. You might discover a real gem. If he or she doesn't work out, go to someone else the next time.

• Does the individual have any references?

This too is tricky because everyone has to start somewhere. If the person doesn't have any references, he or she should be honest about it and tell you so. It may not matter to you if everything else seems right, but it doesn't hurt to ask.

Evaluating Results

When you receive the information broker's report, you'll naturally be eager to read it for the information it contains. But there are other things to look for as well. Good information brokers will tell you which databases they searched and how far back in time they went. But more importantly, good information brokers will tell you what they *didn't* do. They will indicate where they stopped searching and why (usually because further searching would have led to diminishing returns). They will indicate other topics or avenues that they could pursue in the future should you so desire. The difference between an experienced searcher and an inexperienced one is that the inexperienced one isn't aware of what he or she missed or what else could have been retrieved or the other research options available.

You're Paying for Expertise, Not Information

When you hire an attorney, an investment advisor, or any other professional, you're paying for time and for expertise. If an attorney or an investment counselor did his or her best for you, would you refuse to pay because you didn't win the case or because the investment did not pay off? Perhaps you would if you thought you could get away with it. But you know within yourself that you'd be wrong.

Unfortunately, some brokers report that some of their clients are reluctant to pay them if the research does not generate the desired information. Leaving aside the matters of contracts, commitments, and letters of agreement, this shows an ignorance of the realities of information. Sometimes the specific information you want does not exist, at least not in a form that can be retrieved with relative ease by even the most experienced information professional. But that knowledge itself is information, and it can have value. If you were contemplating writing a doctoral thesis or applying to patent a new product, the lack of information on such things could be the best news possible.

Of course, just as when dealing with a medical problem, you may want to get a second opinion, whether from another information broker or professional researcher, or by some other means. But if you have agreed to pay someone to research a topic for you, for heaven's sake live up to your agreement, just as you would want your customers to do when dealing with you. And if you want to continue to be able to avail yourself of a particular information broker's services, make a point to pay the individual promptly. Remember, he or she may have signed onto DIALOG, BRS, ORBIT, or some other system and incurred expenses on your behalf. But the database vendors don't send their bills to you. They send them to the information broker, who must maintain a good credit rating to have continued access to these and other systems.

On Becoming an Information Broker

If you are considering becoming an information broker yourself, a number of resources are available. Sue Rugge, the founder of one of the most successful information brokerage firms, has summarized her experiences and offers tips for starting your own information brokerage in two audiotapes called *Information Gathering and Brokering for a Fee*. The cost is about $30, and a hard-copy version is available as well. Contact:

Ms. Sue Rugge
1626 Chestnut Street
Berkeley, CA 94702
(415) 524-3212

At this writing, there are at least two books on the subject. One is called *The Information Broker's Handbook: How to Profit from the Information Age* by John H. Everett and Elizabeth Powell Crowe. This is a comb-bound, photo-offset book of about 150 pages. Research techniques are considered, but the emphasis is on the business side of things (sample contracts and agreements, business letters, fee structures, etc.). The cost is $24.95, plus $2 postage and handling. Visa and Master-Card are accepted. Contact:

> Ferret Press
> 4121 Buckthorn Court
> Lewisville, TX 75028
> (214) 539-1115

We have not seen the second book, but it has gotten good reviews. It is called *The Information Brokers: How to Start and Operate Your Own Fee-Based Service* by Kelly Warnken. The book is 154 pages long and costs $24.95 in hardback, $15.95 in paper. It is published by R. R. Bowker and can be ordered from any bookstore.

Ms. Warnken and Katherine Ackerman have in the past conducted seminars on the topic in various U.S. cities. Ms. Ackerman is associate editor of *Link-Up*, one of the leading consumer-oriented magazines in the field. Both women are information brokers of long experience. For more information, contact:

> Katherine Ackerman and Associates
> 403 Oxford Street
> East Lansing, MI 48823
> (512) 332-6818

Part II:

—PROFILING THE MAJORS—

INTRODUCTION

The chapters in Part II of this book profile eight of the major vendors in the electronic universe. Among them they provide access to nearly 1,000 leading databases, full-text newsletters, newspapers, magazines, and other information collections. If the information you want exists online, there's a very good chance that it will be available through one or more of these eight systems. To find out, contact the vendors directly. All have toll-free customer service or other numbers, and each will be happy to send you a copy of its most recent database catalog.

Each database write-up starts with a section that includes the vendor's address, customer service numbers and hours, the system's hours of operation, means of access, and a connect rate summary. If you subscribe to several systems, you'll find these quick-reference sections especially handy, since vendors rarely provide all of these vital statistics in one place. The balance of each write-up uses the Key Question Checklist presented in Chapter 4 as a basic template for bringing you up-to-speed on a given vendor.

International Access

There are undoubtedly some exceptions, but generally you can access the vendors profiled here from virtually every country on earth. Most systems have a "dial-up" number that connects directly with the host computer. Several have In-WATS (Incoming Wide Area Telephone Service) "800" numbers for their U.S. customers. DIALOG even makes it possible to connect with its computers through the Telex I and II (TWX) networks.

More than likely, though, the least expensive way to contact one of

157

these vendors from abroad will be through a packet switching network. Whether you live in a non-U.S. country or are an American planning to be traveling abroad, the process of connecting with U.S.-based packet switchers requires a bit of explanation.

In the U.S., anyone can buy a modem, subscribe to a database vendor, and access that vendor's system by dialing a (usually) nearby Tymnet or Telenet number. (In July 1986, the U.S. Justice Department gave final approval to the merger of GTE's Telenet and United Tele-communication's Uninet networks. Operated by the newly formed U.S. Sprint company, the combined network retains the Telenet name.) These networks operate only within U.S. borders, and the cost of using them is usually passed on to the customer as part of the bill issued by the database vendor.

Non-U.S. countries have domestic "public data networks" (PDNs) as well, and they too operate only within their national borders. Connections between two countries are handled by yet another class of network known as international record carriers or IRCs. The major IRCs include ITT, RCA, TRT, FTC (owned by McDonnell Douglas, the same company that owns Tymnet), Telenet's international division, and WUI (Western Union International, a subsidiary of MCI Corporation).

Thus, someone in Paris who wished to logon to DIALOG in Palo Alto, California, would connect with TRANSPAC, the French public data network. TRANSPAC would connect with one of the international record carrier networks, and the IRC would connect with one of the U.S. packet switchers, who would then connect with the DIALOG computers. (For hard-core technies only: The IRCs follow the CCITT X.75 network-to-network protocol, while the U.S.-based networks use the CCITT X.25 network-to-host protocol to make their connections.) In order to do this, the caller must have an account with both TRANSPAC and DIALOG.

The Crucial Role of the PTTs

In almost every non-U.S. country, the telephone and public data networks are owned and controlled by the national government through agencies known generically as PTT (Postal, Telephone, and Telegraph) authorities. Thus, if you live outside the U.S., you must contact your local PTT office to set up an account that will let you use your nation's data network. Usually it's a relatively simple matter of providing a billing address and possibly paying a small fee.

Once your account has been established, the PTT will issue you a "Network User Identifier" number or "NUI." This is the account number you will enter each time you connect with your country's PDN. You will also need to establish an account with the database vendor you want to access. The following chapters provide both the U.S. address and the addresses of any non-U.S. offices the vendor may maintain. When you contact them, be sure to ask for an explanation of what you must key in at each step of the logon process, starting with the moment you dial the phone. The U.S.-based vendor will bill you for usage and for U.S. telecommunications costs. Your national PTT will bill you for the use of its network and for international communications costs.

The policies of the PTTs vary widely regarding data communications. In some countries, if you want to use a modem you must pay a one-time licensing fee to the PTT. In other countries there is an annual or a monthly fee associated with the NUI account. In still other countries, you must lease the modem directly from the PTT.

The charges levied by the PTTs for the domestic portion of the link-up also vary. There may be hourly connect charges, and there may be "traffic charges" measured in "kilocharacters" or "kilopackets." Some PTTs also levy a tax on communications costs as well. IRC charges are set by international tariff agreements.

For U.S. Citizens Traveling Abroad . . .

If you are going abroad and you want to be able to access a database vendor or other online system in the U.S., it is best to plan ahead, since policies and procedures are not as simple abroad as they are in this country. Fortunately, both Tymnet and Telenet have international specialists on staff who can help you make your preparations. You can contact them at the following addresses:

> International Sales Office—Suite 200
> TYMNET, McDonnell Douglas Network Systems
> 2080 Chainbridge Road
> Vienna, VA 22180
> (800) 368-3180
> (703) 356-6993

> International Services
> Telenet Communications Corporation
> 12490 Sunrise Valley Drive
> Reston, VA 22096
> (703) 689-6300

Undoubtedly the simplest procedure is to bring your U.S. modem with you and make your connection by dialing the vendor's direct or In-WATS phone number from wherever you happen to be abroad. This is also the most expensive option, and you should definitely make sure that the procedure is legal in the country you will be visiting. If you will be taking a modem with you, it is also advisable to bring a receipt or other document proving that you bought the modem in the U.S. for your own use and do not intend to resell it inside the country. Non-U.S. customs officials have been known to confiscate modems that lack such documentation.

Regardless of where you are, if you are calling a U.S. data network or database vendor directly, you will be able to use your U.S. "Bell standard" modem. But you should be aware that while U.S. and Canadian modems and networks follow the Bell standard, the rest of the world uses modems and networks that conform to standards set by the CCITT, the Consultative Committee on International Telephone and Telegraph communications, an arm of the United Nations.

If you are going to be connecting through another country's PDN, you will need a CCITT-compatible modem. A CCITT V.21 modem, for example, communicates at 1200 bps. CCITT V.22 *bis* is the standard for 2400 bits per second. Many top-of-the-line U.S. modems now offer both Bell and CCITT compatibility.

In addition to the modem, you will need an NUI account number to gain access to the local PDN. Here again, policies vary with the country. In some cases a billing address within the country is sufficient. In others you will need to establish a bank account in the country as well. PTT approval for your network user ID can take anywhere from a few days to several weeks.

In some countries special agreements have been signed to expedite this process. For example, Tymnet has established NUI exchange programs with about half a dozen countries, including the United Kingdom and Japan. Designed for the user who must go abroad on a moment's notice, this program allows Tymnet to issue you a NUI and bill you directly for the costs you incur using a non-U.S. data network. Some database vendors have also established communications networks abroad. DIALOG's DIALNET network, for example, can be accessed directly from numbers in the U.K.

The X.121 Address

In addition to having an NUI and a CCITT modem, callers from abroad must know the proper "X.121" address of the system they want to connect with. Like all "X" and "V" designations, this too is a CCITT-recommended standard. In this case, the standard specifies a 14-digit number that you might think of as an international ZIP code for database vendors and host systems. The number is also referred to as an "NUA" for "network user address." As defined by the CCITT, the first four digits are the "data network identification code" or DNIC ("dee-nick"). Since most countries have only one data network, there is usually only one DNIC per country. But in the United States, where there are many privately owned networks, each of the major PDNs has been assigned its own DNIC. Telenet's DNIC is 3110, Tymnet's is 3106, and so on. This is necessary so that a call coming in from abroad can be routed to Telenet, Tymnet, or whatever other carrier the caller specifies once it arrives on U.S. shores.

The significance of the remaining ten digits can vary with the network. But for U.S. networks, the next three digits are usually the telephone area code of the host system. For example, since DIALOG is in Palo Alto, its area code is 415; NewsNet is in Philadelphia and its area code is 215. The next five digits are the actual network address of the host. In international communications, if the address does not occupy five digits, zeros are used to bring the total up to five. The final two digits are optional, but when they are used they refer to the port address of the host.

You should always check with the online system you wish to access to get the proper X.121 address, since they do sometimes change. However, as an example, if you were to sign on to DIALOG using Telenet in the U.S., you would enter the telephone area code and DIALOG's network address: 41520. (On Tymnet you would enter "Dialog," and the network would translate this into the numerical address.) If you were to sign on to the same system from abroad via Telenet, you would enter Telenet's DNIC first to specify that system (3110), followed by the telephone area code (415), followed by three zeros to round out the network address to five digits, followed by the address itself (20), followed by, in this case, a two-digit port address (04). The grand total would look like this: 31104150002004.

Which IRC? Which U.S. Carrier?

Does it make a difference which international record carrier transports your call to the U.S. or which U.S. carrier you specify with the DNIC? Understandably, both Tymnet and Telenet answer this question differently. According to Tymnet, five of the six major international record carriers use Tymnnet-supplied equipment. And as mentioned earlier, FTC Communications is owned by Tymnet's parent, McDonnell Douglas. It is suggested that this can make for a smoother interconnect between the IRC and the U.S.-based Tymnet network.

Telenet's answer is based on its status as an international record carrier with some 22 direct connections between foreign countries and the U.S. Where those direct connections exist, a higher quality of service may be possible because fewer "hops" or network interconnections are involved. If a British caller selects Telenet as the IRC on a call, the call goes from the British network to London, where it is connected to Telenet's IRC facilities. From there it goes up to the InfoSat satellite and back down to the Telenet gateway facility in Reston, Virginia, and from there, into the U.S. Telenet network. In contrast, if a different IRC is used, the call arrives at that company's U.S. gateway and must be connected to Telenet's gateway before going on into the Telenet network.

You must always select a U.S. carrier with the DNIC portion of the X.121 address. But you may or may not be able to select the IRC to be used as well. The PDNs in some countries offer you a "Carrier Select" option each time you sign on. In other countries, or in the absence of your specification, the IRC will be selected by a random rotary designed to apportion the business equally among the various IRCs. However, although it isn't widely known, in some cases you can ask the PTT to code the NUI it issues so that a particular IRC will automatically be used to transport all of your calls. Usually this involves adding a digit or two to the NUI number.

Since book publishers generally frown on sending authors on globe-trotting tours to sample the world's data communications connections, we are not in a position to test any of the above. However, these points are of more than passing interest, and you may want to consider them if you plan to do any communicating from abroad.

Free Online PTT Information

We strongly advise phoning Tymnet or Telenet at the numbers given above for the latest information. However, both systems do maintain free online systems containing rate information, the contact person and address of a country's PTT authority, and more. To gain access to these systems, dial and connect with Tymnet or Telenet as you normally would. Then follow the steps outlined below.

For Tymnet, simply key in the word INFORMATION when you see the "please log in:" prompt. That will log you into the Tymnet Information Service and cause a menu to be displayed on your screen. At this writing, item 4 on the menu will select "INTERNATIONAL ACCESS INFORMATION."

For Telenet, key in MAIL immediately after the Telenet "at sign" (@) prompt. (No spaces.) Respond to the "User name?" prompt with INTL/ASSOCIATES. Then respond to the "Password?" prompt with INTL. (This will not show up on your screen as you key it in.) That will log you into the Telenet International Information System and generate a menu with nine selections pertaining to international access.

Online Tip: At the risk of confusing the issue, you should know that in some cases you can also use the telex network to make contact with a packet switcher like Telenet. ITT's InfoTex, RCA's Data-Link, and WUI's Telelink, for example, have the ability to convert telex Baudot code into ASCII and back again and smooth out the speed differences between the 50 baud communications rate of a telex machine and the much higher speeds of a packet switching network. For technical reasons, 50 baud on a telex machine equals 400 characters a minute. (See *The Complete Handbook of Personal Computer Communications* for more details.) In other words, telex is S-L-O-W. But you can do it.

You can even use the telex-to-Telenet connection to access the Telenet International Information System described above. The only difference is that instead of keying in MAIL, key in 202141. (You may also use 202142.) Then proceed as above.

...7...

DIALOG®, the Knowledge Index™, and the DIALOG Business Connection™

DIALOG Information Service, Inc.
3460 Hillview Avenue
Palo Alto, CA 94304
(800) 334-2564
(415) 858-3810
Telex: 334499 (DIALOG)
TWX: 910-339-9221

CUSTOMER SERVICE

From all 50 states:
(800) 334-2564

From Canada: (415) 858-0321,
                          collect

Available continuously from
3:00 A.M. Monday to 3:00 A.M.
Saturday, Eastern time.
Daylight saving time is
observed.

From other countries, phone
your local office. (See end
of chapter for contact
information.) Or call
(415) 858-3810.

Hours of Operation
—All hours are given in Eastern time.—

DIALOG and the DIALOG Business Connection
NOTE: DIALOG always operates on Eastern time.
Daylight saving time is not observed.

Available	Not Available
Continuously from 5:00 P.M. Sunday through 8:00 P.M. Friday	8:00 P.M. Fri.–8:00 A.M. Sat.
	8:00 P.M. Sat.–5:00 P.M. Sun.
Sat.: 8:00 A.M.–8:00 P.M.	

The Knowledge Index

NOTE: The following are your *local* times. Daylight saving time is observed. KI is available from North America and from London.

Mon.–Thurs.: 6:00 P.M.–5:00 A.M.	"KI," DIALOG's low-cost
Fri.: 6:00 P.M.–midnight	after-hours service,
Sat.: 8:00 A.M.–midnight	offers access to about 35
Sun.: 3:00 P.M.–5:00 A.M.	databases. It is not
	available during regular
	business hours

Access: Telenet and Tymnet at $11 an hour. DIALNET, the company's own network available from London and in 60 or more U.S. cities, at $8 an hour. In-WATS at $18 an hour. Gateway through LEXIS/NEXIS at $12 an hour. (No prior PTT arrangement needed.)

Connect Rate: Varies with the database, but averages about $75 an hour, plus telecommunications costs. There is no plain system rate since you are always in a database of some kind. Unless you specify otherwise, you will automatically be placed in ERIC ($30 an hour) when you sign on. No off-hours discount. No extra charge for 1200 bps. Knowledge Index has a flat rate of $24 an hour, including telecommunications. Business Connection is $84 an hour, plus telecommunications and display charges.

What's on the System?

It is impossible to say enough about DIALOG. It is quite simply the world's premier electronic information system. No one else offers such a wide selection of databases. And no one else can match the breadth, depth, and quality of its training, search aids, and customer support. But DIALOG's supremacy is more than a matter of size. The company is clearly possessed of a vision of what an information service should be.

And while every system has its faults, in almost every respect DIALOG executes superbly.

According to Roger K. Summit, president of DIALOG Information Services, Inc., the company's mission statement reads "to develop and provide services which utilize the information storage, manipulation, and communication capabilities of computer and telecommunications technologies in the provision of increasingly effective access, presentation, and dissemination of civilization's recorded knowledge." You can skip the gobbledygook at the beginning. The last three words are the key to understanding what DIALOG comprehends.

As the leading vendor, DIALOG pretty much has its pick of available databases, and consonant with its mission statement, it has chosen those offerings that best cover particular segments of the world's knowledge. Almost all of the leading databases are here, many of them exclusively. In fact, about the only things you won't find are the full text of *The New York Times* and the full text of the *Wall Street Journal*. These are available only through NEXIS and Dow Jones, respectively.

At this writing DIALOG offers some 250 databases, but DIALOG typically adds 30 to 40 new databases each year. Since quite a few of the ones currently on the system are discussed in detail in Part III and since no partial list can convey the size and scope of the system, we offer instead a list of subject categories and the number of databases that can be found in each one. Drawn from a promotional brochure, the categories and classifications are DIALOG's own. The list includes neither the various ONTAP™ practice databases nor databases added since this particular brochure went to press:

DIALOG Category	Number of Databases
Business, Industry, Corporate	62
Science, Technology	30
Education, Reference	27
Humanities, Social Sciences	24
Law, Government, Intellectual Property	21
Energy, Environment, Agriculture	16
Medicine, Bioscience	15
News	7
Chemistry	6
People	5

The Costliest System?

DIALOG, in short, is comprehensive. But it is also expensive. As in any store that offers an especially broad selection, it costs money to maintain an extensive inventory of information. Making the system available 24 hours a day during the week with round-the-clock, toll-free customer service and all of the support features we will discuss later costs money as well.

How much money? Well, as is always the case, it varies with the database. Vendor-to-vendor comparisons are very tricky since so many different charges, subscription options, and other variables can apply. However, since the ABI/INFORM database is available on so many systems, we can use it as a rough benchmark.

Assuming you want to search INFORM during regular business hours, that you have a subscription that does not involve an annual commitment or advance deposit, and that you are using the least expensive packet switching option, here are the total hourly rates and full-record display charges on four systems that carry INFORM:

	Per hour	Per record displayed
DIALOG:	$89.00	50¢
VU/TEXT:	$83.50	40¢
ORBIT:	$80.00	30¢
BRS/BRKTHRU:	$70.00	33¢

DIALOG tops the list. But even with this simple benchmark, some caveats must be added. The full ABI/INFORM database made available by Data Courier, Inc., goes back to August 1971, but the version on VU/TEXT reaches back only to 1978. Also, updates are added weekly on VU/TEXT and DIALOG, but monthly on BRS and ORBIT. We should also point out that like many databases, INFORM is considerably cheaper on after-hours systems. On DIALOG's Knowledge Index the rate is $24 an hour with no display charges. On BRS/BRKTHRU, the after-hours rate is $26.50 with no display charges.

As we said, price comparisons are extremely tricky. During prime time and including DialNet communications costs, Management Contents on DIALOG goes for $98 an hour, compared to $75 an hour on BRKTHRU and $90 on ORBIT. DIALOG charges $43 for the GPO Monthly Catalog; BRKTHRU charges $35. Yet where BRKTHRU charges $75 for Books in Print, DIALOG charges $73. And while the Dow Jones News/Retrieval prime-time, 1200 bps price for Media General is $158.40 an hour, DIALOG's price is $68 plus $1.50 for each record displayed.

This kind of variety can drive a writer to drink and cause a glazed condition to rapidly develop in a reader's eyes. So in the interests of everyone's personal health, we'll leave it there and simply say that in most cases you're not going to get a break on prices when you use DIALOG. However, DIALOG officials claim that their system has a consistently faster response time than others (as much as three times faster than BRS according to DIALOG's own tests), and if true, that can actually make DIALOG cheaper to use. In addition, DIALOG's customer support in every area is unmatched, and it offers round-the-clock access to more databases covering more subjects than anyone else in the business.

Background and Configurations

What is now DIALOG Information Services, Inc., a wholly owned subsidiary of the Lockheed Corporation, began as an in-house research project in 1963 when the Lockheed Missiles and Space Company established its Information Sciences Laboratory. The goal was to develop a system that would allow users to ask questions of a mainframe computer and receive a response in seconds instead of the days required using methods current at that time.

The research resulted in the first interactive information retrieval system. Lockheed brought the system up for its own internal use in 1965, and four years later won a contract from NASA to apply it to more than half a million documents generated by the space program. Lockheed called the system RECON (Remote Console Information Retrieval Service) and the command language used to run it "Dialog."

Other government agencies contracted with Lockheed as well, including the Atomic Energy Commission and the U.S. Office of Education. In 1972 the system was renamed DIALOG and, with a total of six databases, offered to information professionals and the general public. In 1981 Lockheed made DIALOG a wholly owned subsidiary, and in 1982, along with two other companies, it became part of the parent firm's Information Systems Group. The other two companies are CADAM, a developer of computer-aided design software, and DATAPLAN, a computer service bureau specializing in automatic flight planning.

At this writing there are three configurations of the main DIALOG product. First, there is the main system itself. This is referred to as either DIALOG Version 1 or Version 2, but don't let that confuse you. Basically, the company completely rewrote its software and began phasing in the results in 1984 as DIALOG 2. The new software adds many important features to the existing command language. As you read this,

DIALOG Version 1 will have ceased to exist. Everything discussed here refers to Version 2.

In addition to the main system, there are the DIALOG Business Connection (DBC) and the Knowledge Index (KI). DBC is a menu-driven system with special report-generation features. It offers over a dozen of DIALOG's most business-oriented databases at a single connect rate. KI is available only after regular business hours. It includes some 35 DIALOG databases and features a simplified command language and a low flat rate of $24 an hour, including communications.

The Man Who Invented "DIALOG"

With over 250 databases online, more than 80,000 subscribers in some 76 countries, and an average annual growth rate of 30% over the last decade, DIALOG has made huge strides toward fulfilling the goal set forth in its mission statement. Success on this scale is never the work of any one individual, of course. Yet more than anyone else the person responsible for making DIALOG what it is today is Roger K. Summit, the company's president.

Mr. Summit, who earned his A.B. degree from Stanford in 1952 and followed it with both an M.B.A. and a Ph.D., is of interest for at least two reasons. First, as a research scientist for Lockheed in 1962, he invented the DIALOG information retrieval language and has been involved with the system ever since. He was thus more than merely present at the creation of the online information industry. His work was an integral part of it.

Second, if a vote were taken, Mr. Summit would be the leading candidate for the title of "Dean of the Information Industry." Part of the reason would be his long experience and his credentials as the head of the largest database vendor. But the major factor would be a vision and sense of purpose that is rare in any industry. It may be an illusion, but unlike most online vendors, DIALOG seems to know exactly where it's going and how it is going to get there.

Yet Mr. Summit's published thoughts and analyses range far beyond the parochial concerns of a single company. He is aware in a way that few others seem to be of the revolutionary worldwide potential of online information. His opinions are always worth listening to. And since he is one of the leading figures in the industry, you are sure to encounter them sometime in the future.

Account-Related Matters

DIALOG Subscriptions

Since everything springs from the main DIALOG system, we will look at it first. Then we will present the DIALOG Business Connection and the Knowledge Index.

Subscriptions to the main DIALOG system are free. You have only to pick up the phone, call the toll-free number given at the beginning of this chapter, and a sign-up kit will be mailed to you immediately. The kit contains a 14-page, four-color descriptive brochure called "To Finish in First Place," a rate card, a publications catalog, some information on training options, and an order form for standard service.

New subscribers receive $100 worth of free connect time. A subscription to the monthly "Chronolog" newsletter is $25 a year. You also receive a mailbox keyed to your DIALOG account number on DIALMAIL™, an electronic mail, bulletin board, and conferencing system the company introduced early in 1985. Note that the free time is to be used within 30 days of the first time you sign on to the system. So don't sign on until you're ready to take advantage of it.

Billing is by direct invoice. And multiple passwords are available under each account (an annual $25 charge per password applies). Usage for each password is detailed separately on monthly statements.

Under the standard service agreement there are no commitments and no obligations. It's strictly pay-as-you-go. Two main discount contracts are available, however. If you agree to use a certain amount of connect time during a year, you receive one discount. If you place an amount equal to your estimated yearly usage on deposit at the beginning of your year, you receive an even better discount. Contracts begin at $3,000 and run up to $100,000 or more, and discounts start at $3 per hour and run to a high of $15 an hour. See DIALOG's "Service Agreement Options" flyer for details.

The Good News about the Guide to DIALOG Searching *Package*

Although subscriptions are free, you will have to purchase some documentation if you really want to use the system. The DIALOG Publications Catalog supplied with the start-up kit lists so many items that it can be a bit daunting. As we'll see later, you will eventually want to order some of these additional materials, but to get started you really need only one publication: The *Guide to DIALOG Searching* ($50 for North America and elsewhere by surface mail; $75 for Air Parcel Post elsewhere).

This is actually a complete package, and while the company may not be losing money on the deal, it probably isn't making any either. The package is massive. It includes two three-inch, three-ring notebooks and tabbed sections on how to use the system, plus all of the Bluesheets with their vital information on the contents, fields, and sample records for each database, plus all of the Yellowsheets describing the services of various DIALORDER™ document suppliers.

Also included is a 60-page booklet called "Search Aids List for Use with DIALOG Databases." This booklet lists all of the additional materials and manuals available directly from various database producers. You also receive a copy of the latest DIALOG Database Catalog (62 pages) with its descriptions and vital statistics for each database (period of coverage, frequency of updates, File Number, and other details). A new catalog is issued at the start of every year, with a mid-year supplement in July.

And you receive an 18-page booklet called "Pocket Guide to DIALOG Version 2," a wall chart listing DIALOG databases alphabetically on one side and by subject on the reverse, and a 15-page booklet called "DIALOG Basics" to help you get started searching the system.

A variety of shipping options are available, but DIALOG recommends Air Parcel Post if you live outside the U.S., Canada, or Mexico. Payment can be made by MasterCard, Visa, American Express, or by check or money order (in U.S. funds drawn on a U.S. bank).

The Bad News About the Guide

No one can accuse DIALOG of skimping. The company does an excellent job of providing you with all the tools and information you need. Unfortunately, it fails miserably when it comes to showing you how to use them. The 17-page "Introductory Overview" at the front of the *Guide* is a joke. After assuring you that "retrieval of information through the DIALOG system is a relatively simple procedure," it immediately presents a sample search of the National Technical Information Service (NTIS) database. Then it moves right into an explanation of how to display an online thesaurus of indexing terms. If you don't know about abstracts, bibliographical citations, and controlled vocabularies before opening the manual, you could be in big trouble.

It might be argued that DIALOG is intended for professional searchers and that the manual is intended to be used in conjunction with DIALOG training. But that doesn't explain why there is no system overview and summary of features, or why there is no reference to such basic tools as Bluesheets in the *Guide*'s index. Poor organization is poor organization, regardless of the intended audience.

The situation is exacerbated by DIALOG's chosen method of updating the manual. Subscribers periodically receive "Technical Notes" and

"Technical Memos" containing updated information. These arrive with the monthly "Chronolog" newsletter. The process has been going on for so long that there are now nearly as many pages of supplemental material as there are in the original manual, portions of which date back to 1979.

The Best News About the Guide

The best news about the *Guide* is that it is scheduled to be completely replaced. As you read this, a new DIALOG manual should be available. According to one DIALOG official, "It will be much more of a system guide than a technical manual and much more appropriate to the needs of all our users, particularly the nonspecialists." And a good thing, too, for as Roger Summit noted in the 1985 National Online Meeting, "Seventy percent of our 1984 sign-ups were direct users as opposed to information specialist intermediaries." By 1986, that figure had risen to nearly 80%. It is to be hoped that DIALOG will not allow another seven or eight years to go by before updating the new *Guide*.

Online Tip: Here's a trick that can save you a flat $15 an hour. Although DIALOG's sign-up materials don't mention the fact, there is no plain system connect rate. Whenever you are on DIALOG, regardless of what you are doing, you are always "in" a database and you are billed at that database's stated connect-hour rate.

In the absence of instructions to the contrary—and there is no provision for supplying such instructions on the sign-up form—you will automatically be connected to the ERIC (Educational Resources Information Center) database each time you logon to DIALOG.

Because ERIC is a government-created database no royalties are charged, making it among the cheapest on the system ($30 an hour). So if you are going to check the rates charges by any database, read the online "NEWS," or do anything other than actually search a database, it makes sense to do so in ERIC. And of course that's why DIALOG makes it your default database.

However, DIALOG also has some 18 ONTAP (ONline Training And Practice) databases (ONTAP ABI/INFORM, ONTAP PTS/PROMT, etc.). These contain no information to speak of and are designed solely for practice. But they cost only $15 an hour. If you put your request in writing when you sign up or at any time thereafter, you can make one of these low-cost ONTAP databases your

---

default database. (You can also send your request by DIALMAIL.
Send it to this address: DIALOG CUSTADMIN.)

Once you make the switch, you'll never pay more than $15 an
hour, plus telecommunications charges, for your nonsearch activities on DIALOG.

Usage Costs

There is no off-hours discount on DIALOG and no extra charge for
1200 bps communications. Generally, there are three main components
to the cost of a search. The first is the cost of access. Telenet and
Tymnet are all $11 an hour, while DIALNET is only $8 an hour. If you
live outside the continental United States, there will be additional
charges for using your locally available packet switcher as well.

Second, each "File" (database) has its own hourly connect charge.
These costs range from $15 an hour for one of the ONTAP practice
databases to $300 an hour for the CLAIMS/UNITERM patent data-
base. Most charges, however, are around $75 an hour.

Third, there are display charges. These charges are always quoted for
displaying the full record (bibliographical citation, abstract, indexing
words, etc.). But as noted elsewhere, DIALOG offers eight other formats for displaying various portions of a record. Each format is priced
separately. You can get a list of these charges by keying in ?RATESn
at any time, where *n* is the number of the target file. (Please see Figure
3.2 in Chapter 3 for an example of the costs of searching the ABI/IN-
FORM database.)

Full-record display charges are typically 30¢ to 50¢ each. But charges
of $4 to $20 to $100 are not uncommon. A full report from DIS-
CLOSURE/Spectrum Ownership, a database detailing the common
stock holdings of major institutions and anyone else with 5% or more of
shares outstanding, is $25. A report from Standard & Poor's Corporate
Descriptions, a database offering in-depth corporate background, balance sheet, and other information on more than 9,000 public corporations, is $3.50. A full-text article from the Harvard Business Review
Online is $7.50, and one from Magazine ASAP is $7, rates that compare
favorably with most document delivery alternatives.

It is important to be aware that you may never have to pay charges of
this magnitude, even when you are using these databases. Everything
depends on the specific database and the specific portions of a record
you need to see. DIALOG's public relations handouts claim that a typical search costs from $5 to $25, while its database catalog claims costs
of between $5 and $16.50 for a ten-minute search, including telecom-

munications charges. But there are so many variables, including the definition of "typical" and the skill of the searcher, that those figures are next to meaningless.

Search-Related Matters

System and Search Language

As you might expect from the system that started it all, the DIALOG search language is quite powerful and quite rich. All of the Big Three supermarket database vendors offer powerful languages, of course, and generally one would never select one over the other on this basis alone. The databases offered and the prices charged are much more important. Still, with the introduction of DIALOG Version 2 in December 1984, DIALOG has the newest software of the three, and it does have some nice features.

For example, DIALOG probably has a greater range of positional operators than any other system. You can specify that search words appear in any order, be adjacent to each other, be separated by no more than a certain number of other words, or appear in a particular field in a particular order. You can do the same thing with groups of words. The search statement (OIL OR PETROLEUM) (W) REFINERY, for example, will retrieve OIL REFINERY and PETROLEUM REFINERY. There are also negative proximity operators: PC(NOT W) JR will specifically exclude any records containing "PCjr."

On the system side of things, you can use the SET command to set the number of columns and lines on your screen, though if you prefer something other than the default values of 75 characters by 40 lines, you must do this each time you sign on. DIALOG does not save a user profile of your preferences. And you can summon up an estimate of your total session cost since logging on at any time.

The DIALOG manual current at this writing doesn't do a very good job of telling you what system commands are available, though this oversight should be corrected in the new *Guide*. Meantime, you'll have to really dig, for example, to discover that entering a BREAK after you sign on will stop the opening announcements from appearing. In the past it has been easy to conclude that entire dictionaries of commands exist but that they have never all been made publicly available in one place. The best way to solve the problem is to go into one of the low-cost ($15/hour) ONTAP practice databases and key in ?EXPLAIN. That's DIALOG's term for what most other systems refer to as "HELP." (?HELP on DIALOG generates a list of customer service phone numbers.) This will produce a long list of available "explain" commands, each one of which will generate an explanation, a list of subsidiary "explain" commands, or both.

Search-Aid Publications

DIALOG offers a greater depth and greater variety of support publications than any other online system. In fact, its materials are so good that even if you regularly search a given database on a different system, you can usually benefit from obtaining a copy of the relevant DIALOG publication.

It's important to remember that while there are many similarities among groups of databases and while DIALOG, ORBIT, or BRS may provide access to many of them with a uniform search language, each database is ultimately a separate product. In what might be called the "target acquisition" process that should precede every search, you need to know where the information in the database came from, how it is indexed, what a typical record looks like, the significance of each major field and what you are likely to find there, and so on.

This is the kind of information that search-aid publications are meant to provide, and you should try to be aware of the range of materials available to you. The most fundamental search aid on DIALOG is the Bluesheet for each database or file. As mentioned, a complete set of these is supplied with the *Guide* package. Updates and new additions are provided via the monthly "Chronolog" newsletter.

The Bluesheets can be useful in and of themselves, but they are really intended as quick-reference summaries of more extensive publications. Those publications are what DIALOG refers to as its database "chapters." You'll find a complete list of database chapters in the publications catalog that comes with your DIALOG subscription. There's one for virtually every file on the system, and each sells for $6.

DIALOG "Database Chapters"

DIALOG database chapters are published on 8½-by-11-inch stock, double-sided, and they range in length from about 25 pages to 50 pages or more. There is a heavy tabbed cover page, and the chapter itself is prepunched to fit in a three-ring binder. Usually, the first page or two of a chapter will be identical to its corresponding Bluesheet.

As an example, consider the kind of things you would learn from the DIALOG chapter for Moody's Corporate News—International:

• If you don't specify a field when searching this database, the system will consider the company name field, the event name field, and the textual abstract field.

- In the company name field, non-English company names are given in the original language.

- You can search more efficiently if you use Moody's event codes. There are over 80 of them representing such things as "IMF Credit," "New Holding Company," and "Telephone Number." The database chapter supplies a complete list.

Other fields and techniques are explained in similar detail, and there are lots of sample searches with accompanying explanations. Clearly, this is a vital document to anyone interested in obtaining financial and business information on any of the 4,000 corporations in 100 countries that the database covers. The same could be said of nearly every other DIALOG database chapter.

But there's more. As mentioned earlier, each new DIALOG subscriber receives a 60-page booklet called "Search Aids for Use with DIALOG Databases." This too is an invaluable document with no equivalent that we know of anywhere else. It lists and describes all of the supplementary documentation available directly from the companies that produce the databases found on the system. Turning to page 40, for example, we find that Moody's offers a "two-sided, single-page laminated guide for searching Moody's databases on DIALOG." Price: FREE. And there's a toll-free number to use in placing your order to boot.

The Electronic Yellow Pages also has a free mini-search guide. This explains how the database is "assembled and shows several search examples and techniques." There is also a free "Online Search Summary" (a "quick guide to the various searchable fields of EYP databases") and a free "Where-To-Find-It-Guide" listing all SIC (Standard Industrial Classification) codes used in EYP databases. Finally, for $29.95, there is the *Electronic Yellow Pages User Guide* offering "a complete discussion of the databases including . . . use of basic techniques, special features, and search tips and strategies."

Again, these offerings are not unusual. Most database producers, whether their product is on DIALOG or not, have some kind of additional documentation available. And often these materials can be crucial to anyone who does a lot of serious searching of a given database. Unfortunately, their existence is among the best-kept secrets in the information industry. Most non-information professionals simply aren't aware of them.

DIALINDEX and ONTAP Databases
DIALINDEX is a database (File 411) that contains nothing but the

index files from all of the other databases on the system. It doesn't contain any bibcites, abstracts, or other information. Its purpose is to allow you to determine the databases and search strategies that are most likely to produce the information you want on DIALOG. The cost is $45 an hour, plus telecommunications.

If you don't have any idea which database is most likely to hold the information you want, you can enter DIALINDEX and tell the system to search any one of some 76 subject categories. These range from DE-FENSE to NUTRIT to PEOPLE. Each category includes all appropriate DIALOG databases for that subject. Alternatively, you can select any number of specific databases against which to run your search strategy.

Most of the main search commands can be used in DIALINDEX, though there is no "set" capability. That means you cannot continually refine your strategy by combining new terms with sets of previous search results. However, DIALINDEX will quickly tell you how many times the terms in your search statement occur in a given database. And that will give you a much better idea of which database(s) and search strategies to use. You may save your search strategy using DIALOG's Search*Save™ feature, give it a name, and then go into one of the real databases and enter EXECUTE followed by the name of the strategy. There is no need to rekey your search terms.

As mentioned, there are also some 18 ONTAP (Online Training And Practice) databases, including ONTAP ABI/INFORM, ONTAP ERIC, ONTAP MAGAZINE INDEX, and even ONTAP DIALINDEX. These databases cost $15 an hour, plus communications. Each is in effect a miniature version of its full-sized parent. ONTAP MAGAZINE IN-DEX, for example, contains about 40,000 records, compared to the more than two million records in the parent file. ONTAP databases provide an excellent opportunity to hone your search skills and build your familiarity with the DIALOG system at very low rates. About the only thing you cannot do in these files is request an offline printout of a record. Everything else works just as it does on the main system.

Online Tip: Though traditional information industry people would probably blanch at such crass terms, DIALOG, in conjunction with its database suppliers, offers what amount to monthly specials and promotional sales. These usually take the form of a half hour or more of free time in a designated database, and over the course of a year their total value can add up to $400 to $500.

Of course a bargain's not a bargain unless you need the item, but whether you need the information or not, the monthly specials of-

Online Tip (cont.)

fer an excellent way to inexpensively sharpen your skills. Specials are announced in the "Chronolog" newsletter, in the screens that greet you when you sign on the system, and in the online news (?NEWS) section. Here's a sample:

*MAY 1-Up to $50 of free combined connect time and TYPEs or DISPLAYs is available in May for searching INVESTEXT (File 545).

***

*MAR. 1-In March, April, and May, Format 9 records from MAGAZINE ASAP (File 647), TRADE & INDUSTRY'S ASAP (File 648), MAGAZINE INDEX (File 47), and TRADE & INDUSTRY INDEX (File 148) may be TYPEd, DISPLAYed, or PRINTed for $3.50 each. This price is half of the regular price for Format 9 records.

DIALOGLINK™ Search-Aid Software

Early in 1986, DIALOG announced the first product in what will ultimately be a line of communications packages marketed under the DIALOGLINK™ name. The product is the DIALOGLINK Communications Manager ($95) for IBM/PCs, Compaqs, the AT&T 6300, and the OCLC M300. The program is designed to make it easy to log on to DIALOG, KI, DIALMAIL, or some other service and to facilitate your interactions with the system once you are there. Its two main features are a "type-ahead buffer" and a circular "retrieve buffer" (what everyone else calls a "capture buffer") that is always active when you are online.

The type-ahead buffer is essentially a character-prompted upload feature. You can prepare search strategy command lines before you sign on, and record them to disk as a file. There is a built-in word processor that responds to either WordStar™ control commands or the PC's arrow and other keys to let you edit your file.

Once you are connected, you can load the file into the program's type-ahead buffer, and from then on each time DIALOG sends out its main question mark (?), the program will upload one line from the file. Alternatively, when you are online you can create an on-the-spot file of command lines while the system is searching, displaying information, or doing something else. Each line will be sent in sequence in response to the system's main prompt.

You can look at anything in the retrieve buffer again, at any time, even after it has scrolled off the screen. The program's documentation does not tell you how many characters this buffer can hold. It simply says that its size is determined by the amount of memory in your computer. (That's too bad, since after the buffer fills up, each new character added pushes the oldest character out of the buffer and into space. This is what makes it a "circular" buffer.) While you are scrolling through the retrieve buffer you can selectively mark the lines or blocks of text you would like to have printed or saved to a disk file.

Lost in Translation

The program does perform as advertised, but its best feature is the "smart" logon capability that lets it automatically try various packet switching networks until it makes a connection. This portion of the program was licensed from and lifted virtually in toto from In -Search, a front end package marketed by the now defunct Menlo Corporation. Unfortunately, something seems to have been lost along the way, for while In -Search was snappy and responsive, DIALOGLINK's screen handling leaves much to be desired.

Whether you are viewing information coming in from an online service or scrolling back through the retrieve buffer, the display is so jerky that it is distracting. In addition, when you are using the type-ahead buffer while online, you will notice a significant degradation of performance as the PC's processor is forced to divide its time between handling those characters coming in through the communications port and those you are typing at the keyboard.

The feature is also unnecessary. Regardless of the communications program you are using, you can easily type ahead on DIALOG and stack up a series of commands just as you would on The Source, CompuServe, and most other online systems. Besides, the whole point of interactive online searching is to key in a command, view the results, and key in another command *based on those* results. Under the circumstances, the ability to "enter a strategy of 250 lines containing 80 characters each," as the manual puts it, seems rather pointless. There are other problems as well. The program does not support communications rates higher than 2400 bits per second, and it does not support the XMODEM or any other error-checking file transfer protocol.

In short, this is not a program you are likely to use for anything other than connecting with DIALOG services. And it doesn't offer anything that you can't do with CrossTalk XVI Version 3.6 ($99 from most mail-order firms) or dozens of other programs used in conjunction with Side-Kick or other software with which you may already be familiar.

Tracking Session and Monthly Time

The DIALOGLINK Account Manager ($45) is the second product in the nascent software line. Designed to work in conjunction with the Communications Manager, it is likely to be of most interest to information brokers and others who need to keep an accurate record of which databases were searched, when, and what the total costs were. The program can deliver summaries by individual online session, by the month, or by the portion of the month. You can purchase both programs for a combined total of $125, a savings of $45. A demo disk containing both programs is available for $10, which can be applied against the purchase price of the package. The disk will operate for two hours.

Training

Training at DIALOG is a worldwide operation. A recent issue of "Chronolog," for example, listed scheduled classes in Amsterdam, Basel, Berlin, Cologne, Copenhagen, Helsinki, London, Oslo, Paris, Rome, Stockholm, Vienna, and Villeurbanne. And that was just one month's European schedule. Courses are also given in the Middle East, Latin America, Australia, Canada, and Japan, as well as in most major U.S. cities.

The simplest form of training is DIALOG Day, a free two-hour demonstration of the system offered periodically throughout the world. Next are the free "Brown-Bag Lunch" sessions offered in Boston, Chicago, Houston, Los Angeles, New York, Palo Alto, Philadelphia, and Washington, D.C. These sessions give searchers a chance to chat informally with DIALOG staffers over the noon hour. DIALOG provides the coffee, you provide your own lunch and the questions. Schedules are announced in "Chronolog." Reservations are required for both types of sessions.

There are many types of full-day ($125) and half-day ($55) formal training sessions as well. Most are rated for from three to seven continuing education credits. Lunch and hands-on practice are provided for full-day sessions. Schedules are announced in "Chronolog" and online. If you key in ?TRAIN while online, you will get a list containing dozens of commands to be used in determining the current schedule of seminars by country, by city, by topic, and by virtually every other criterion you can imagine.

The entry point to DIALOG training is the full-day System Seminar. This session shows you everything you need to know about using the basic DIALOG system and it is a prerequisite for virtually all other DIALOG courses. ("Equivalent beginner training" can also fulfill the prerequisite.) The System Seminar offers a combination of lecture and hands-on practice. In addition, participants receive a training voucher worth $50 off the cost of any full-day advanced seminar or $25 off any half-day advanced seminar.

Online Tip: System Seminar participants also receive a password good for free practice time on DIALOG's ONTAP databases. The password is good for a limited number of days (usually 30). But if you call up and request a renewal, in most cases it will be granted. Since the company pays the telecommunications charges on these passwords, you can practice on DIALOG for free.

Advanced seminars include "Beyond the Basics," for people who really want to learn to make the system sing. You are encouraged to bring along search topics and questions to work on during the practice breaks. Other advanced seminars focus on business, chemical information, government information resources, humanities, legal applications, medical topics, patents, social sciences, and science and technology.

Customized seminars are also available. And while one might not join the DIALOG training staff to see the world, it could happen since DIALOG will fly its trainers anywhere there is a need and someone willing to pay the price.

Customer Support

DIALOG's customer support is excellent. At this writing we know of no one else who offers a 24-hour hotline during the week. And no vendor produces a better newsletter. As noted at the very beginning of this chapter, calls from the 50 United States are toll-free and Canadian subscribers may call collect.

If you live elsewhere, your best bet is to phone your nearest DIALOG representative. (See the list at the end of this chapter.) But you are perfectly welcome to phone Customer Service directly at (415) 858-3810. We are told that this is not uncommon. However, while the Customer Service staff can usually locate someone fluent in Spanish, Japanese, and French, you should be aware that there is no mechanism in place to serve non-English speaking callers. If you have the time, you might send your inquiry via DIALMAIL. Address it to DIALOG CUSTSERV, or to DIALMAIL number 9046.

The monthly "Chronolog" newsletter typically contains 20 pages of information designed to alert subscribers to new databases, new commands, price changes, new features, and so on. As with all vendor newsletters, there is an element of self-promotion designed to increase online usage. But "Chronolog" has a broader perspective than most, and the information it contains really is essential. We don't particularly care for the approach, but "Chronolog" amounts to a living manual.

The "Chronolog" arrives prepunched for notebook insertion, and you should definitely make a point of saving every issue. The pages are numbered consecutively throughout the year (87:1, 87:54, etc.), and indexes are issued for January through April and January through August, culminating in a comprehensive index at the end of the year. The full text of every "Chronolog" dating back to 1981 is also available online as File 410.

Information Delivery

Online Types and Offline Prints

As mentioned, in most DIALOG databases there is a display charge keyed to the particular portions of a record you ask to see. DIALOG has eight main formats and a ninth one for full-text databases like Trade & Industry ASAP. The Bluesheet for each database will tell you what fields of each record are included in each format. And entering ?RATESn, where *n* is the database number, will give you a complete summary of format costs.

Offline printouts are also available, and the price quoted on the rate card includes postage. In the past this has often been cheaper than paying "type" or display charges and paying for the connect time required to view a record. The downside is that you must wait for your information to arrive in the mail. Now, however, there is DIALMAIL, and it may be the best option of all.

DIALMAIL Delivery

DIALMAIL can be accessed through DIALNET or any of the packet switchers, and every DIALOG subscriber is automatically given a free mailbox number. Your new user information packet will include a booklet called "DIALMAIL Basics" (22 pages). Unfortunately, it is not very well written and you may be better off taking advantage of the extensive help explanations that are available online.

The DIALMAIL system greatly resembles MCI Mail, though it isn't nearly as flexible. It has MCI's capability of delivering either electronic or hard copy to your correspondents. But you cannot have such letters printed on your own letterhead as you can with MCI, and all DIALMAIL hard-copy letters are mailed from Palo Alto instead of from locations near your recipient, as is the case with MCI. At $20 an hour (a connect rate of $12, plus $8 for DIALNET access) with no per-character charges, however, DIALMAIL is considerably cheaper. Sending a 7,500-character electronic letter (the equivalent of about four double-spaced pages) would cost about 35¢ on DIALMAIL and about $1.05 on MCI Mail.

Although DIALMAIL-only accounts are available for those interested only in an electronic mail system, the company has yet to promote that fact. Consequently, the only people you can generally reach via

DIALMAIL are those who happen to be DIALOG or KI subscribers and thus automatically have an account. That places considerable limits on the system's value as a communications medium, whether for business or other uses.

In addition, the bulletin board and conferencing features seem to have been created from scratch by people completely unaware of more than a decade's worth of development work done in these areas by Turoff, Hiltz, Stevens, Johnson-Lenz, and others. DIALMAIL's offerings cannot compare to systems like EIES, PARTICIPATE, CompuServe, The Source, or even most public domain bulletin board system software. In short, at this writing, we feel that DIALMAIL's conferencing and bulletin board features are all but unusable.

But there is a major advantage to DIALMAIL and it is this: It is directly linked to the DIALOG information retrieval system and this can save you a great deal of money. Suppose you're using a full-text database like Magazine ASAP and suppose you've located a magazine article you would like to download. At that point you have a choice. You can request an offline printout, you can request an immediate display of the article, or you can tell the system to print the article "offline" via DIALMAIL. Here's how the costs compare.

We'll assume that the article is 2,000 words long. The traditional offline paper printout costs $7 per article, regardless of length. The display charge for viewing the article online is also $7, but here connect time and length become a factor as well. The total connect rate for Magazine ASAP accessed through the DIALNET network is $92 an hour or $1.54 per minute. Since a 2,000-word article (about 14,300 characters) would require about two minutes to download at 1200 bits per second (120 characters per second), the connect time required to read the article would cost you about $3. Add that to the $7 display charge and your total cost is $10.

However, the connect rate for DIALMAIL accessed through DIALNET is $20 an hour or 34¢ a minute. If you told the system to print the article via DIALMAIL, you would pay the offline print charge of $7. But you could then sign on to DIALMAIL and download the article for about 68¢. Your total cost would thus be $7.68.

Online Tip: How soon after entering PRINT VIA DIALMAIL can you expect to find the requested information in your electronic mailbox? Print requests are queued up and dumped to the mail system three times a day. DIALOG tries to meet weekday Eastern time deadlines of 10 A.M., 5 P.M., and 4 A.M. If you worked in New York City, you could place your DIALMAIL order in the

Online Tip (cont.)

morning and have the full text of the article in your electronic
mailbox by the time you were ready to head home for the day.

Tagged Output and the REPORT Option

In DIALOG-speak, "tagged output" refers to a bibliographic citation
and abstract displayed with each field labeled. BRS and ORBIT have
always displayed records with the author, title, publication, and other
fields labeled with a two-character identifier (AU, TI, PU, or whatever), but DIALOG didn't add this feature until early in 1985. Now the
system offers the best of both worlds. You can request format 5 to view
the full record untagged or format 4 to view it tagged with field identifiers that match the Bluesheet descriptions. Each field begins with a
two-letter code and ends with a vertical bar. The intent is to both improve readability and facilitate post-download processing. (You could
tell your word processing program to search for and display every occurrence of "AU" in a file, for example, to look at every name in the
author field of a large download.)

DIALOG has also introduced a REPORT display option for selected
databases that is especially convenient. The REPORT option lets you
specify precisely which fields will be displayed and in what order. And
as with most DIALOG databases, the output can be sorted online in
ascending or descending order. If you were using the Electronic Yellow
Pages, for example, you could easily produce a list of company names
and telephone numbers sorted alphabetically by state.

Because it is priced differently, REPORT can save you money as
well. For example, if you wanted to compare the net sales of the top ten
semiconductor companies versus their research and development expen-
ditures, you could go into DISCLOSURE II, conduct a search, and enter a command like this:

REPORT (set number)/1-10/CO,NS,RD

The set number would refer to a particular group of hits generated by
your search. The "1-10" tells the system to display items one through
ten. And the codes stand for the fields for company name, net sales, and
R&D. Field names and codes are given on the Bluesheets.

In DISCLOSURE you would be charged 10¢ per field, so your total
cost would be 10¢ × 3 × 10 = $3. If the REPORT format were not
available, the only way you could obtain the necessary information
would be to request the display of the complete records for all ten companies. At $3.50 per record, your cost would have been $35.

> **Online Tip:** DIALOG also does labels. If you like, when using the Electronic Yellow Pages databases, the Electronic Directory of Education, and several other "directory" databases, you can tell the system that you would like to have your search results printed on pressure-sensitive labels. (This is called "Format 10.")
>
> The labels are printed three up on 8½-by-11-inch sheets, 33 labels per page. There is a maximum of 5,000 labels for any one PRINT request, but you can ask for as many groups of 5,000 as you like. The cost is 10¢ per label, and as with all DIALOG offline prints they will be mailed to you, usually within 24 hours of your print request.

SDI and Document Delivery

DIALOG's Search*Save™ feature lets you save a search strategy temporarily, permanently, or as an SDI profile. In each case you may use the full power of the DIALOG language. There are no restrictions in the commands you can use in a saved search as is often the case on other systems.

You can also give each strategy a three- to five-character name instead of having the system assign each strategy a number. And you can add a short (240 characters) comment describing the purpose of the strategy. This comment will be displayed whenever you review your "saves" by listing their names with the RECALL command. There is no charge for temporary Search*Saves, but they are automatically purged after seven days. Permanently storing "saves" on the system costs 20¢ each, plus 10¢ per command line, per month. They can be released at any time.

At this writing some 56 databases offer an SDI feature. You are charged each time a database is updated. Fees range from $5 to $13 per update and include any number of search terms and a maximum of 25 printed full records. Additional records are billed at the standard offline print rate.

DIALOG has the most extensive document delivery service of any system in the electronic universe. It's called DIALORDER™ and it includes nearly 80 document suppliers, each of whom has a three- to eight-character mnemonic name (INFORM, CIS, METALS, etc.) and each of whom is profiled on a DIALOG Yellowsheet. The ordering procedure is simplicity itself. When your search turns up something you want, you enter KEEP. Then you enter ORDER followed by the name of the document supplier you have chosen.

That's it. The system takes care of sending descriptions of the items

and your name and address to the DIALORDER supplier. (On BRS and
ORBIT you must key in all of that information yourself.) If you like,
you can attach special instructions by keying them in after the
DIALORDER supplier's name. And you can order material not retrieved by a search by using the ORDERITEM command and following
it with the supplier's name and the item's specifications. This lets you
use the DIALOG information system as an electronic mail system to
contact document suppliers. Unfortunately, not all DIALORDER suppliers are reachable via DIALMAIL, and those that are don't use their
DIALORDER abbreviations as their mail address.

The DIALOG Business Connection™

"Watch Out Dow Jones!"

Some years ago Burger King (BK) ran an advertising campaign
featuring a Pepsi-style taste test and the tagline, "Watch out
McDonalds!" . . .

. . . We interrupt this paragraph to bring you a special DIALOG
Business Connection™ (DBC) bulletin . . . Burger King, a unit of the
Pillsbury Company, was after a bigger slice of the $30 billion-a-year
fast-food industry, an industry that accounts for some 12.5% of the 32%
of the food dollars that Americans annually spend on meals eaten outside the home. Due to heavy TV advertising and the offer of a free
hamburger to every customer who walked up to a Burger King counter
and said "The Whopper beat the Big Mac!" sales at U.S. locations
jumped 70%.

Unfortunately for BK, the triumph was short-lived. As of 1985,
McDonalds still dominated the U.S. restaurant industry with sales of
$1.674 billion, while Pillsbury was fourth with sales of nearly $749 million and a 4.51% market share. (The Number 2 and 3 spots were held by
DHI Corporation and General Mills.) . . .

. . . We now return you to the regular paragraph as it was originally
scheduled to be written . . .

. . . With the introduction of the DIALOG Business Connection in
April 1986, DIALOG may be in a position to send a similar challenge
rocketing toward Dow Jones and its News/Retrieval Service. In a word,
DBC is a winner.

• • •

Information power can be a terrible thing. Like comedian Steve Martin's sudden attacks of "happy feet," the temptation to go online and
find out can strike at anytime. Before you know it, you're typing in
keywords and waiting for the system to respond with the answers you

seek. We gave in to the temptation above because it offered an excellent way to demonstrate both the strengths and the weaknesses of the DIALOG Business Connection.

A DBC Overview

We'll explain in a minute. But first, some nitty-gritty details are in order. DBC is a special menu-driven system running on the main DIALOG computers. It is designed to make it as easy as possible for a businessperson to obtain some of the most frequently sought business information. DBC does this by corralling about a dozen DIALOG databases into one area and inserting a series of easy-to-understand menus between you and the information in its "raw" database form. Thus when you sign on, you are greeted with a menu that looks like this:

DIALOG Business Connection
Main Menu

1 Corporate Intelligence
2 Financial Screening (Public Companies)
3 Products and Markets
4 Sales Prospecting
5 Travel Planning: OAG Electronic Edition

Each selection leads to a subsidiary menu, and so on down the menu tree. At some point the system will prompt you for the company names, products, industries, or other subjects you want to investigate. Then it will go away momentarily and return with a customized menu containing the items it has found. At that point you can select the items you want to see, key in a list of their menu item numbers, and download the whole lot without stopping.

You don't have to know anything about files, records, and fields, or the commands needed to search them. If you can read a menu, you can use DBC to generate a financial profile of any publicly traded company, generate a list of every company that meets some financial criteria (debt-to-equity ratio, assets over a certain amount, operating revenue, etc.), develop a sales prospect list of every firm in a particular geographic area meeting your criteria, find out who makes what and how much of the market they hold, and much more.

At this writing, the databases involved are Investext, DIS-CLOSURE, Dun & Bradstreet, Electronic Yellow Pages, Media General, Moody's Investor Services, the Official Airline Guide, Predicasts PROMT, Standard & Poor's, Thomas Register Online, and Trinet. Each of these is profiled in Part III of this book. The regular DIALOG cost for using these databases ranges from $45 to $114 an hour. But

DIALOG Business Connection subscribers pay a flat rate of $84 an hour, plus telecommunications and any normal DIALOG display or print charges.

A subscription to DBC costs $145, and it includes a slipcased DBC manual and a copy of the DIALOGLINK communications program, plus $100 of free time on the service. Considering the previously discussed limitations of DIALOGLINK, however, it is important to point out that you can use DBC with *any* communications program. Current DIALOG customers can join DBC for $120 and receive the same benefits.

This is clearly just the beginning of what DIALOG feels will be a major information product. Other databases are sure to be added in the future. Stock quotes and online stock trading via Trade*Plus are already available on the main DIALOG system and they will probably have been made a part of DBC as you read this. (For more information on Trade*Plus and online stock trading in general, please see *The Complete Handbook of Personal Computer Communications.*) It also seems likely that DIALOG will apply the DBC approach to other collections of databases in the future.

Using the DIALOG Business Connection

The DIALOG Business Connection is a revolutionary product. No one else has anything like it, and no one else has ever so successfully married highly interactive, "intelligent" menus to a major-league information system before. It is still far too early to tell whether the DBC revolution will be exported to other systems and the industry as a whole, but the potential is there. Indeed, to use DBC is to sense that you have seen the future. And despite a few rough edges here and there, the future most definitely works.

Any businessperson who has ever been online before, whether with Dow Jones, CompuServe, or a bulletin board system, can stride into DBC with only the most cursory glance at the manual and come back with the information he or she seeks. The menus, prompts, and online help are that good. Someone who has never communicated before and doesn't have a feel for how online systems work will require a bit more time but will ultimately be just as successful.

There are at least two major caveats you should be aware of, however. The first concerns something that almost has the force of a natural law regarding information qua information. The second concerns certain failings and omissions in the otherwise excellent implementation of the DIALOG Business Connection product.

The Iron Law of Information Retrieval

In the personal computer world, there is always a trade-off between power and ease of use. In the world of electronic information, the trade-off is between flexibility and ease of use. A menu-driven system like DBC is wonderfully easy to use and completely satisfactory as long as what you want happens to be on the menu. The main DIALOG system can give you anything you want, but not without increasing the complexity of the search-and-retrieval process. The Iron Law of Information is this: The complexity of the retrieval process varies directly with the precision of an information request.

In short, DBC isn't going to fulfill all of your information needs, regardless of how many databases are added to the system. Nor will it free you from the need to raise your information consciousness. To have confidence in the information itself, you've still got to know where it came from, how the source database was prepared and by whom, how often the database is updated, and virtually everything else you would need to know if DBC didn't exist.

Unfortunately, the implementation of DBC current at this writing does not provide that kind of information and worse still, does not offer direct paths to obtaining it. For example, the DBC manual is well written and well packaged, and it does a good job of showing you how to move around the service. It even contains an entire chapter called "Where to Find It" that consists of an index of the DBC service. You can look up *divestitures* or *valuation analysis* and be told which section of DBC to check for that information.

Where the Implementation Fails

What the manual doesn't provide is adequate detail about the individual databases that participate in the service. It simply advises you to contact the database producer if you have any questions about any of the information you receive through DBC. DBC subscribers do not receive the "Chronolog," and they are not told about the existence of Bluesheets and database chapters. Yet because the manual fails to explain everything you see on the screen, you *need* these materials almost as much as a regular DIALOG subscriber does.

DBC insulates you from the complexities of keying in the search strategies and commands a professional searcher would use to reach the point where the desired information is about to be displayed. But after that, everything is the same. The information you receive online as a DBC subscriber is identical to what a DIALOG user would see on the screen. That means that at times there will be codes and references you won't understand—unless you have the Bluesheets and database chapters.

We could cite numerous examples. But instead, let's look at what might be called an annotated DBC search session. We wanted to find out what share of the fast-food market is held by Burger King. As you will see, the session highlights both the strengths and the weaknesses (both avoidable and un-) of the DIALOG Business Connection.

Searching for "Fast Food"

The information on Burger King and McDonalds in the paragraph at the beginning of this section was selected from the results of an online session that lasted less than 15 minutes and involved reviewing the titles of over 50 trade journal and newspaper articles, downloading eight of them, and requesting a tabular report ranking the top 50 companies in the restaurant industry. The total session cost was $45, but $25 of that was for the report, and most of the time spent online was spent waiting for DIALOG's mainframes to prepare the report.

Based on a cursory reading of the DBC manual, we knew that the place to look for this information was in the "Products and Markets" section, item 3 from the main DBC menu. Here's what was displayed after we made that selection:

Products and Markets
Application Menu

1 List of Manufacturers
2 Share of Market Data
3 Market Information
4 Product Design and
Processes
5 Facilities and Resources
6 Unit Costs and Prices
7 Analysts' Reports on
Industries

We selected option 2, "Share of Market Data," and the following screen appeared:

Products and Markets
Product Selection

Any of the following options can be used to select a product or industry:

A Standard Industrial Classification (SIC) Code.
   Enter 4 digits, or <return> for a series of menus to aid you in selecting the desired
   SIC code.

A Predicasts Product Code.
   Enter 2 to 7 digits.

A generic product name, e.g., plastic bags.
 Enter a product name or multiple names (synonyms) separated by commas. Use the
 plural form of the name, e.g. bags (not bag).

Okay, you're an executive of a medium-sized tool and die manufacturer. Do you know what an SIC code is? How about a Predicasts product code? If you don't, you can probably get by. You could key in "fast food" and come up with a list of the 50 most recent abstracts in the Predicasts database. But these are hard-core, industrial-strength information retrieval tools, and as you can see, even in a user-friendly system like DBC, there's no escaping them. In fact, if you want the system to produce a share of market report like the one shown below, you *must* use an SIC code as your search term.

If you've never heard of SIC and Predicasts codes before, you'll probably find that the DBC manual's explanation of them is barely adequate. It doesn't tell you how to order a copy of the SIC manual from the U.S. government, and while it suggests that you contact Predicasts, it doesn't tell you that the Predicasts thesaurus costs $50.

As you will notice above, if you hit <return> at this point, you will be taken to a series of menus that will help you locate the correct SIC code. Although these work fairly well, you might have to move back and forth through the menus until you locate the correct topics. If you were looking for fast-food restaurants, for example, you might choose "Services" from the opening SIC-finder menu, but this would not lead to restaurants. You would have to backtrack until you finally chose "Wholesale & Retail Trade" as your first path. That would ultimately lead to "Eating Places" and the proper code: 5812.

We cheated and looked up "fast food" in the U.S. government manual before signing on. The code was the same, 5812, but the government publication explained that this classification does not include restaurants and lunch counters operated by hotels or department stores. More to the point, there is no SIC code for just fast-food chains. That means that when we call for a share of market report, we're going to get the entire U.S. restaurant industry. Here's what was displayed when we entered 5812:

                    Products and Markets—Share of Market Data
                              Display Options

SIC Code(s): 5812

A Share of Market Report and 50 article summaries are available. The summaries will be
displayed most recent first. The first summary is dated March 10, 1986, and the last
summary is dated November 21, 1983.

1 Share of Market Report
2 Titles of Summaries
3 Full Summaries
4 Price and Source

We chose the "Share of Market Report" option. Then we waited. And waited. The monotony was broken only by the word "Processing" that DIALOG thoughtfully fired our way every 30 seconds or so. The total time required (late at night), was close to 15 minutes. Then the following appeared:

Align paper; press <return>
?

SHARE OF MARKET REPORT
INDUSTRY ANALYSIS BY COMPANY

5812 EATING PLACES

RANK	TRINET NUMBER	COMPANY NAME	SALES ($MIL)	SHARE OF MKT	CUMUL SHARE	NO OF ESTAB
1	03985	MCDONALDS CORPORATION MCDONALDS PLAZA OAK BROOK, IL 60521	$1674.0	9.70	9.70	17
2	01869	DHI CORP 16700 VALLEY VIEW AVE LA MIRADA, CA 90638	$1118.0	6.46	16.16	18
3	02673	GENERAL MILLS INC 9200 WAYZATA BLVD MINNEAPOLIS, MN 55440	$984.4	5.69	21.85	5
4	04979	PILLSBURY CO INC PILLSBURY CENTER MINNEAPOLIS, MN 55402	$748.9	4.51	26.36	35
.						
.						
.						
50	05190	R J REYNOLDS INDUSTRIES 1100 REYNOLDS BLVD WINSTON SALEM, NC 27105	$27.7	0.29	71.18	22

Cumulative Sales $12,017.5
Industry Sales $17,314.6
     Copyright TRINET Inc. 1985

Enter <return> to proceed
?

Now by anyone's standards, that *is* impressive. These reports always include the top 50 companies in the market. We've shown only the top four and the last one here. If you look at this report, however, with the goal of discovering Burger King's share of the fast-food market, some serious difficulties begin to appear. First, what's a "Trinet Number" (second column)? And what does "Cumulative Share" mean? How can General Mills hold a 5.69% share with only five establishments? And who in the world is DHI Corporation?

The answers to the first two questions can be found only in the Trinet database chapter. The DBC manual is silent on the matter. If you're in the restaurant business, you know the difference between company-owned stores and franchises and are thus aware that the five General Mills establishments represent only a fraction of the firm's restaurant-derived income.

If you want to know what restaurants General Mills, Pillsbury, and R. J. Reynolds own, you can use the DBC Corporate Intelligence section. There you will quickly discover that General Mills owns Red Lobster Inns of America Inc. and York Steak House Systems, Inc., among others, and that Pillsbury owns Burger King, S&A Restaurant Corp., and Haagen-Dazs Co. Inc., among others.

But what about DHI, Inc.? It's the second-ranked restaurant business in the country and who's ever heard of them? If you were to zip over to the Corporate Intelligence section of the DIALOG Business Connection and try to run DHI as you ran General Mills and Pillsbury, you would come up empty. No listing. No SEC filing. Nothing but the "Door and Hardward Institute" in Dun & Bradstreet Locations & Profiles.

Since DHI Corporation is evidently not a public company, there is no way to get information about it from DBC at this time. The reason it appears in the Trinet report is that Trinet covers *both* public and private companies, a fact the DBC manual fails to point out. (This information *is* in DIALOG's Trinet database chapter, however.) So we had to cheat. We logged onto DIALOG, entered the Trinet database, and keyed in SELECT TN = 01869 (the DHI Trinet number from the above report), and displayed the results:

```
0255492
DENNYS INC

HEADQUARTERS:

    DHI CORP
    16700 VALLEY VIEW AVE
    LA MIRADA, CA 90638
    Telephone: 714-739-8100

    TRINET number: 01869
```

Online Tip: This is for information detectives only. As we have emphasized throughout, information retrieval is anything but a passive act. It requires perseverance, a love of the hunt, a bit of imagination, and a familiarity with the resources at your disposal. It's a lot like computer programming in that respect, and it can be equally addictive.

But it wasn't addiction that caused us to pursue the DHI/Denny's question. (Honest!) We merely wanted to test the DIALOG Business Connection. The results were most gratifying.

Here's what we did. We went into the DBC Corporate Intelligence section and, having learned that DHI was actually the Denny's restaurant chain, searched for "Denny's." The search turned up 123 references, including "Denny's Discount City" and "Chuck & Denny's Chevron." But there were also scores of listings for various Denny's Restaurants locations.

We looked at one of these listings and—bingo!—the DHI Corporation was listed as the parent and the D-U-N-S (Dun's of Dun & Bradstreet) Corporate Number was provided (06-510-9423). Now, there is nothing you can do with that information on the DIALOG Business Connection.

But if you have a regular DIALOG subscription, you can check the DIALOG catalog for the Dun's databases, and consult the appropriate database chapter to find out how to search for a company on the basis of its D-U-N-S number. You can then sign on to the main system BEGIN 516, the file for Dun's Market Identifiers, and search for DC = 06-510-9423 to pull up all the information you need on the elusive DHI Corporation.

The share of market report, while interesting and undeniably impressive, wasn't quite what one might have been led to believe was possible on DBC. There was simply no way to make it precise enough to answer our question.

Fortunately, DBC offers another information alternative. If you look back to the example with "Display Options" in the heading, you'll see that DBC found us 50 of the most recent articles dealing with the "Eating & Drinking Places" classified under SIC Code 5812. This, as it turned out, was an information bonanza. We selected option 2 from the menu to display the titles of the article summaries, and here is the first screen that was displayed:

Products and Markets
Summary (50 summaries, most recent first)

Title
_____

1. Industry sales slump stings the Big Three burger chains.
2. Fact file: Chain market share leaders Top 10 chains in market share, 1985
3. Gloves come off in '86 market-share battle.
4. Baker: Sell more than just products on TV.
5. Jack's rolls out five new bigger hamburgers.
6. A commitment to change.
7. Church's purchasing Texas-based Tinsley's.
8. Menu line expansion more than adding food.
9. McD 1st in US to get new Coke.
10. Mac's ad bucks put bite on foes.

Article summary number 2 certainly looks promising. That's what we chose and here is what was displayed:

Article Summary section 1 of 1
1310742
   Fact file: Chain market share leaders Top 10 chains in market share, 1985 (%)

Nation's Restaurant News	February 3, 1986 p. 2
McDonald's	7.6
Burger King	3.0
KFC	2.1
Wendy's	2.0
Hardee's	1.5
Pizza Hut	1.4
Marriott	1.0
Dairy Queen	1.0
ARA Services	0.9
Big Boy	0.8

Copyright Predicasts 1986

All *right!* You can't always get what you want when you go online. But if you try sometimes, you do indeed! Almost all of the information on the fast-food industry in the opening paragraph of this discussion of DBC came from five of the 50 articles the system queued up for us. Reading them was like reviewing an intense five-year history of the battle of the burgers, and the time required to generate it was less than six minutes.

Online Tip: This won't make much sense to you until you become a DBC subscriber, but there is a trick to reading article summaries that the manual doesn't explain. DBC always selects the most re-

Online Tip (cont.)

cent 50 articles and it always displays the summary titles ten at a
time. If you want to look at all 50 titles, you can do so by pressing
your <ENTER> key at each prompt. You can then use DBC
menus to redisplay the titles.

There is a better way to do it, however. Hit your <ENTER>
key to review all five screens. But as each screen appears, make a
note of the item numbers that are of interest. They are numbered
consecutively from 1 through 50. When the last screen appears,
key in all of your selections separated by a comma. In other words,
the items you select do not have to be on the current screen. You
can choose summary 1 from the screen that shows summaries 41
through 50 and vice versa.

So how long did all of this take and what did it cost? The total time
required from sign on to logoff was 24 minutes, most of which were
spent waiting for DIALOG to create a report. By the end of the session
we had downloaded a report detailing the top 50 companies in the restaurant industry, selected 50 of the most recent and most relevant article summaries drawn from the more than 1,000 business and news
publications covered by Predicasts databases, reviewed the summary
titles, and downloaded five of the most promising summaries. The summaries turned out to be packed with facts and stats from reputable industry and trade journals. And the cost of the session, as automatically
reported by DIALOG at logoff, turned out as follows:

```
Menu system v. 3.8 ends.
        DD/MM/YY 23:27:34 User 000000
$32.85     0.391 Hrs FileDBC
 $2.35  Dialnet
$25.00  1 SHARE Reports
 $2.40  5 Types
$62.60  Estimated total session cost   0.391 Hrs.
```

The "Net Net"

The DIALOG Business Connection is a major step forward in the
quest to make the power of online information available to everyone.
The system was beta tested for nine months by some 40 companies prior
to its introduction on April 2, 1986. We looked at it a month and a half
later. As you read this, DBC will almost certainly have expanded its
offerings. And in all likelihood, DIALOG will have applied the concept
to at least one additional subject area.

DBC has its faults, but generally it is a *very* good system. If you are a businessperson with $120 to spend and an interest in or need for the power of electronic information, we suggest that you subscribe, with two caveats. First, bear in mind that no menu-driven system can ever give you everything you are likely to want. And second, don't subscribe to DBC directly.

Instead, subscribe to DIALOG and order the *Guide* and the database chapters for the databases covered by DBC. The price for the new edition of the *Guide* has not been set at this writing. But in the past the cost would have totaled about $122 ($50 for the *Guide* package and $72 for a dozen database chapters at $6 each). There is no continuing obligation and as mentioned, you receive $100 in free connect time. Then contact DIALOG and subscribe to the Business Connection. As a DIALOG subscriber you can do this for $120 and you will receive the DBC manual and DIALOGLINK software and $100 of free time on DBC.

DBC subscribers cannot get into DIALOG proper. But DIALOG subscribers can enter the Business Connection at any time by keying in BEGIN DBC. Thus if you subscribe to DIALOG first, you will have the best of all possible worlds. The main DIALOG system with its 250 databases will be at your disposal should you need to supplement what DBC has to offer. (For an extra $25, you'll receive the monthly "Chronolog.") And you'll have the database chapters needed to fully understand the information DBC provides. Your total out-of-pocket cost will be $242, but you will receive a total of $200 in free connect time. Since there is no continuing obligation of any kind, you really can't lose.

The Knowledge Index

The Knowledge Index (KI) is DIALOG's low-cost, after-hours system. The information it offers can also be found on the main DIALOG system, but KI differs from DIALOG in a number of ways. At this writing, KI offers some 35 databases. These include ABI/INFORM, the Harvard Business Review Online (full text), Peterson's College Database, Books in Print, Marquis Who's Who, the Information Access Company bibliographical databases (Magazine Index, National Newspaper Index, etc.), and the Standard & Poor's databases (S&P News, S&P Corporate Descriptions, etc.). Scientific, engineering, computer, and medical databases are available as well.

KI charges a flat rate of $24 an hour, regardless of the database you use. That price includes telecommunications costs, and there are no display charges. The search language is a stripped-down (simplified) version of the language used on DIALOG, but it is quite serviceable. You can use wildcards and you can search on a particular field (AU = Adams,

D?), and you can use the basic AND/OR/NOT Boolean operators. You can view your hits in one of three formats (short, medium, or long), and you can order copies of the documents referenced in the bibcites and abstracts you see online. Documents are supplied by Information On Demand. You can also directly connect with DIALMAIL. (DIALMAIL accessed via KI is $18 an hour.)

The KI start-up fee is $35 and it includes your manual (what KI calls its *User's Workbook*) and two free hours on the system. (This $48 credit is to be used within 30 days of your first logon.) There is no continuing obligation.

Online Tip: DIALOG offers a KI demo disk for $5. The disk includes a general introduction to the Knowledge Index, an interactive instruction module featuring the three main KI commands (BEGIN, FIND, and DISPLAY), and a small searchable database consisting of 54 abstracts from ABI/INFORM. You'll need an IBM or compatible with 256 and DOS 2.0 or higher. The disk works with color or monochrome displays.

If you are a current DIALOG subscriber, you may order a copy over the phone by calling the toll-free number and speaking with the Marketing Department. Just have your DIALOG account number ready. Alternatively, you may send a written request to the Publications Distribution Center at the main DIALOG address. You can send a check or a purchase order. Or you can charge it to your Visa, MasterCard, or American Express card. (Include the number, expiration date, your signature, and print or type your name.) California residents, add sales tax.

The manual is a three-ring, tabbed notebook, and it includes a four-page descriptive insert for each database. These inserts serve as both Bluepages and database chapters. There are also very good instructions on how to use KI. Billing is by credit card, but you can request direct invoicing. And you can put multiple passwords under a single account for a one-time fee of $25 per password. In return, KI will send you a manual for each password. KI subscribers also receive a quarterly newsletter called the *Knowledge Index News*.

Basically, if the databases you want to use are on the system, and if you are willing to wait until after 6 P.M. your local time to use them, you should probably subscribe to KI. The only way to gain access to some of these databases at a lower price is to subscribe to BRS/After Dark. But as we will see in the next chapter, After Dark subscriptions require you to use a minimum of $12 worth of communications and connect time a month.

DIALOG Worldwide

DIALOG has offices in Boston, Chicago, Houston, Los Angeles, New York City, Philadelphia, and Washington, D.C. But it also has offices in at least six other countries. The two companies in Japan are direct competitors.

Australia
Insearch Ltd./DIALOG
P.O. Box K16
Haymarket NSW 20000
Australia
Telephone: (02) 212-2867
Telex: AA27091 (INSRCH)

Canada
Micromedia Ltd./DIALOG
158 Pearl Street
Toronto, Ontario M5H 1L3
Telephone: (416) 593-5211
Telex: 065-24668

Europe
DIALOG Information
Retrieval Service
P.O. Box 8
Abingdon, Oxford OX13 6EG
England
Telephone: (0865) 730 969
Telex: 837704 (INFORM G)

West Germany
DIALOG Information
Services, Inc.
Tizianweg 2
4010 Hilden
West Germany
Telephone: 02103-69904

Korea
Data Communications
Corporation of Korea (DACOM)
The Business Office, 12th Floor
Korea Stock Exchange Building
1-116 Yeoeido-Dong, Yeongdungpo-Ku
Seoul, Korea
Telephone: 783-5201 or
5/783-6471
Telex: DACOM K28311

Japan
Kinokuniya Company, Ltd.
ASK Information Retrieval
Services Dept.
Village 101 Bldg.
1-7 Sakuragaoka-machi, Shibuyu-ku
Tokyo, 150
Japan (KIN)
Telephone: (03) 463-4391
Telex: J27655 (KINOASK J)
Cable: Kinokuni

Masis Center
Maruzen Co., Ltd.
P.O. Box 5335
Tokyo International 100-31
Japan
Telephone: (272) 7211
Telex: J26630 (MARUZEN J)
Cable: Moraya Tokyo

...8...

BRS/SEARCH®, BRS/BRKTHRU™, and BRS/After Dark™

BRS Information Technologies
1200 Route 7
Latham, NY 12110
(800) 227-5277
(518) 783-7251, collect
TWX: 710-44-4965

CUSTOMER SERVICE

(Eastern time)
Mon.–Fri.: 8:00 A.M.–1:00 A.M.
Sat.: 8:00 A.M.–5:00 P.M.
Sun.: 8:00 A.M.–2:00 P.M.

Hours of Operation
—All hours are given in Eastern time—

BRS/SEARCH and BRS/BRKTHRU

Available

Mon.–Sat.: 6:00 A.M.–4:00 A.M.
Sun.: 6:00 A.M.–2:00 P.M.
and
7:00 P.M.–4:00 A.M.

Not Available

Mon.–Sat.: 4:00 A.M.–6:00 A.M.
Sun.: 2:00 P.M.–7:00 P.M.
and
4:00 A.M.–6:00 A.M.

Non-prime time for BRKTHRU users begins at 6 P.M. *local* time during the week and ends at 4 A.M. *Eastern* time. Thus, if you live on the West Coast, non-prime begins at 6 P.M. your time and ends for you at 1 A.M. All weekend hours are non-prime, but during the weekend only Eastern time applies.

BRS/After Dark

Mon.–Fri.: 6:00 P.M.–4:00 A.M.	Mon.–Fri.: 4:00 A.M.–6:00 P.M.
Sat.: 6:00 A.M.–4:00 A.M.	Sat.: 4:00 A.M.–6:00 A.M.
Sun.: 6:00 A.M.–2:00 P.M.	Sun.: 2:00 P.M.–7:00 P.M.
and	and
7:00 P.M.–4:00 A.M.	4:00 A.M.–6:00 P.M.

After Dark is available weekday evenings starting at 6 P.M. your *local* time and running until 4 A.M. *Eastern* time. All weekend hours are Eastern time.

Access: Telenet, Tymnet, and BRSnet. On BRS/SEARCH, communications costs are $9 an hour, in addition to database royalties and system connect charges. On the other two services, communications costs are included in the quoted hourly charge. There is no extra charge for 1200 bps access. BRSnet is the firm's international network intended for subscribers living outside of North America. Available in more than 16 countries, the cost is $15 an hour. Direct dial ($3/hr.) and In-WATS ($26/hr.) access is also available, as is gateway service from Pergamon's Infoline system.

Connect Rate: Varies with the database on SEARCH and After Dark. On BRKTHRU it varies with the time of day as well, since there is a discount for using the system during non-prime-time.

What's on the System?

Because BRS offers so many different configurations of its basic product, we'll modify the Key Questions Checklist format somewhat in this chapter. Instead of detailing each offering individually, we'll consider the system as a whole. Then we'll conclude with some suggestions on choosing the BRS offering that's right for you.

As an organization and database vendor, BRS has a personality that is quite different from DIALOG, its chief competitor. Though it wouldn't be wise to push the analogy too far, in many ways BRS is to DIALOG what Apple is to IBM in personal computers. Both are after the same connect-time dollar and both offer many of the identical databases. However, while BRS is actively adding databases, with slightly more than 100 online at this writing, it has a long way to go to equal DIALOG's 250 or more. (ORBIT, with some 64 databases, is solidly in third place by this criterion.)

There are less definitive contrasts as well. Most vendors are interested in feedback from their subscribers. But BRS has a User Advisory Board that it takes very seriously. Board members are nominated and elected by BRS subscribers. Its business-oriented offerings, while certainly respectable, have long been overshadowed by its offerings for educators and medical professionals. BRS is moving rapidly to change this. But it is moving in other directions on other fronts as well, and as we'll see, that could be a problem.

Corporate mission statements seem to be very much in vogue in this corner of the electronic universe. No one has yet offered to boldly go where no man has gone before, but they do tend to have a majestic sweep. We saw what DIALOG had to say. Here is BRS's corporate mission statement: "To provide superior information products to selected markets without regard to the vehicle of distribution." At this writing, BRS Information Technologies is involved in a multiplicity of projects. These range from a joint venture with W. B. Saunders unit (BRS/SAUNDERS), the world's largest publisher of medical books, to a variety of CD-ROM-based undertakings (BRS/MD and others), to medical information processing software, to selling micro, mini, and mainframe computer versions of its main system search software.

All of this in addition to the company's core business of offering online information. It is impossible to say whether being involved in so many areas has strained BRS's resources. But if the past three or four years are any guide, BRS has at times suffered from a lack of focus and a lack of follow-through in its online offerings.

Three Configurations

Those offerings require some explaining. Essentially, there is one master BRS collection of databases that the company has chosen to present in a variety of configurations. The main system is BRS/SEARCH. This is the original BRS product, offering access to all databases, a complete search language, and no off-hours discounts. BRS/BRKTHRU offers virtually all of the same databases, a menu-driven system with most of the BRS commands, and discounts for after-hours usage. As we'll see in a moment, this is the product that is best suited to most personal computer users.

BRS/After Dark is very similar to BRKTHRU. The differences are that After Dark subscribers have access to only about 70 of the vendor's databases, they pay $12 a month as a minimum monthly usage requirement, and they can use the service only after 6 P.M. on weekdays and all day during the weekend. In return, they pay the lowest connect-time rates of all. BRS has other configurations, like BRS/COLLEAGUE and

BRS/SAUNDERS, but these are focused on medically oriented information and we will not consider them here.

A Bit of Background

What was originally known as Bibliographic Retrieval Services was founded in 1977 by Janet Egeland and Ron Quake, both of whom were employed by the Biomedical Communication Network of the State University of New York (SUNY) at Albany. The system is now owned by Indian Head, the U.S. arm of Thyssen-Bornemisza, a Dutch industrial conglomerate. Thyssen also owns Predicasts, Inc., creator of the PTS PROMT, MARS, and other databases, and Information Handling Services, a major player in the CD-ROM field, but together the three companies account for only about 3% of the conglomerate's annual revenues.

Undoubtedly because of its origins, BRS has always been exceptionally strong in the fields of medicine, science, and education. Its databases in these fields include MEDLINE, Chemical Abstracts, Drug Information Fulltext, and Psychinfo. But BRS has a great deal to offer searchers of all persuasions. Some of its databases are available nowhere else. And even those that can be found on DIALOG, the Knowledge Index, or some other system may be available more cheaply on one of the BRS offerings.

Among other things, for example, business users will find ABI/INFORM, the *Harvard Business Review*, Management Contents, and DISCLOSURE II and DISCLOSURE/Spectrum Ownership, each of which is covered in Part III of this book. There is also the Business Software Database, Corporate and Industry Research Reports Online, and Industry and International Standards.

Online Tip: There are at least two offerings that are worthy of special note. The information they contain is for a limited audience, but the approach is intriguing. One is the Superindex (SUPE). This database consists of the back-of-the-book indexes from nearly 2,000 professional-level reference volumes including such titles as the *Handbook of Analytical Toxicology*, the *Physicians' Desk Reference*, and *Physics Vade Mecum*.

You'd need access to a good library to locate the books themselves. But imagine how convenient it would be if the indexes of many more books were available online. Armed with your search results, you could go to a library knowing exactly which books you wanted to look at and which pages contain references to your topic.

The other offering is a series of databases designed to help users

Online Tip (cont.)

locate *materials* instead of facts, figures, and quotes and other "traditional" information. The Educational Testing Service (ETS) Test Collection, for example, is intended to aid teachers, psychologists, and counselors in locating commercially available tests and assessment tools. Other databases focus on audio-visual packages, educational computer software, and software in general. There are relatively few non-information catalog databases of this sort in the electronic universe, but the concept is so useful that there will likely be many more in the future. In the meantime, BRS is definitely the leader in this area.

How Do the Systems Differ?

Although you would never discover it from the company's literature, the main differences among the three BRS systems we are considering here fall into three categories: system features, search language, and price. For example, on BRKTHRU and After Dark you cannot save your search strategy when you leave one database to search another. There is no SDI service either, and no offline prints. These things are available only on the main BRS/SEARCH system, along with BRS's "X" databases, files containing only the most recent update of a given database.

Nor is there a LIMIT command to make it easy to limit a search to a particular range, like a range of dates. There is a way to do this on BRKTHRU and After Dark, but it takes more keyboarding and does not produce results as quickly as on SEARCH. At this writing, there is no file containing descriptions of every database. And you cannot try out your search strategies in CROSS, the BRS equivalent of DIALOG's DIALINDEX. Although it has been long expected, there is no electronic mail system either. Again, all of these features and databases *are* available on BRS/SEARCH.

Subscriptions and Costs

The costs for using any BRS system are always database-specific. The variables are whether or not you are assessed display charges for looking at a portion of a record, whether or not there is a non-prime time discount, and whether the quoted rate includes telecommunications charges.

We can best consider the cost differences by looking at the various subscription options. There are two main ways to subscribe to BRS/ SEARCH, though neither is likely to be appealing unless you plan to do a lot of searching. Subscription accounts, intended for libraries, institutions, and corporate information centers, call for advance deposits ranging from $750 to $3,800 a year. The more you put on deposit, the lower your search costs. Each deposit account includes up to five passwords, which can be used by five separate organizations electing to share the same subscription.

The second alternative is the Open Access plan under which the system is available on an as-needed basis, but the rates are the highest on the rate card. There is no start-up fee, but you must pay BRS $75 annually. A BRS/SEARCH manual is supplied free of charge to all new subscribers. Billing is by credit card or direct invoice. For purposes of comparison with the other BRS offerings, ABI/INFORM on an Open Access SEARCH account would cost a total of $79 an hour, plus display charges running as high as 33¢ per citation.

At the other extreme is BRS/After Dark. Here the total cost for searching INFORM is $15 an hour, and there are no display charges. After Dark subscriptions require a $75 start-up fee and the price includes your manual. But it also includes an obligation to spend $12 a month ($144 a year) on the system. Only a limited number of BRS databases are available (about 70 at this writing), and you can use the system only after 6 P.M. and on weekends. Billing is by credit card.

In the middle is BRKTHRU. The total cost of searching INFORM here is $70 an hour during prime-time, with display charges of 33¢, regardless of format. During non-prime-time, the hourly cost is $26.50 and there are no display charges. As noted, however, prices and display charges vary with the database. The cost of a BRKTHRU subscription is $75 and it includes your manual and a quick-reference card. There is no continuing obligation. Except for the limitations noted above, the only major file BRKTHRU does not offer is the Comprehensive Core Medical Library (CCML) database.

Other Details and Features

Each BRS service has a separate three-ring manual. The manuals tend to be well-produced and well-written, with lots of examples and sample searches. There is a handy die-cut tabbed pocket guide for BRS/ SEARCH and a quick-reference card for BRS/BRKTHRU. Each month subscribers receive the "BRS Bulletin," a 26-page newsletter on slick 8½-×-11-inch paper. Subscribers also receive a folder called "Added Attractions!" This contains BRS AidPages describing databases that have been added to BRS/SEARCH. AidPages are similar to DIALOG Bluesheets and are meant to be inserted in the SEARCH manual. The latest rate card for SEARCH, a publications order form, and one-page flyers may also be included.

Like DIALOG, BRS publishes database-specific booklets called "Database Guides" for many of its databases. These sell for $3.50 each. There are also training workbooks for SEARCH and a video tape/workbook package for BRKTHRU ($50), as well as SEARCH workbooks aimed at business, education, and biomedical users.

The search language on all three systems has its roots in the IBM "STAIRS" language, and it is quite powerful. BRS, for example, is one of the few systems to offer both right- and left-hand truncation. The company has an extensive SEARCH training program. Classes are conducted in major cities throughout the U.S., and in Ottawa and Toronto in Canada. There are regular courses for biomedical, business, education, and MEDLINE users, as well as two levels of introductory courses and one for advanced users. Some are half-day sessions ($55 per person) and some require a full day ($95 per person). On-site training at your facility is also available.

Customer support is available toll-free, and it is excellent. Over the years we have never asked its staffers a question they could not answer. They will be happy to help you design your search strategy on any BRS system.

BRKTHRU and After Dark offer three display formats: short, medium, and long. There is also a special "full" format for use in full-text databases. "Full" shows you just the paragraphs of a complete document that contain your search terms, and it is a nice feature since it can save you from needlessly downloading a very long but only marginally relevant article. SEARCH lets you use the same eight formats found on DIALOG, plus a ninth format that includes the bibcite and indexing words. In addition, you can tell the system that you would only like to see specific fields—BRS refers to fields as "paragraphs"—by keying in the two-character field identifier (like TI for the title, or AU, TI, SO for author, title, and name of the source document).

Online Tip: You can stop the display of records at any time by hitting your <BREAK> key on BRS. However, although the rate card does not mention it, you will be charged for some of the documents you originally requested but decided not to view. For example, if you entered a command to display 20 records and hit <BREAK> after looking at the first five, you would be charged for the display of three or four additional records.

Apparently this is not intentional. BRS itself evidently wasn't aware of the fact until users called it to the company's attention. But at this writing, that's the way it is.

Output on all BRS systems is tagged with two-character field identifiers, but there is no option for customized display layouts of such as those available with DIALOG's REPORT function. The company added a SORT capability to its SEARCH system in 1985. Prior to this time records could only be sorted for offline printout. BRKTHRU and After Dark do not have a sort function. SDI current awareness services are available only on SEARCH and only on certain databases.

Only SEARCH has a document delivery option (. . ORDER). Announced in the August 1985 "BRS Bulletin" with the headline "UMI Document Delivery Is Here," the service wasn't actually available to users until March 1986. This feature puts you in touch with the UMI Article Clearinghouse (Chapter 4), but ordering is not automatic. On DIALOG you have only to KEEP your hits and enter "ORDER" followed by the code for the document supplier you have chosen from one of the Yellowsheets. The system does the rest. On BRS/SEARCH, you must first enter the publication's ISSN (International Standard Serial Number) code and wait for the system to check to see if UMI handles that publication. If it does, then you must key in the volume, issue, date, title, author, and page numbers of the article you want. Though there is no official support for the practice, you can also order from information brokers and other document suppliers via the SEARCH electronic mail system, but you must know the target firm's "T" number (electronic mail address).

Which One Should You Choose?

The first question one must ask regarding BRS or any other vendor is: Does the system offer one or more databases I need right now or am likely to need in the future? The second question follows naturally: Is the same database(s) available on another system and if it is, how do the prices compare? Since all vendors are constantly adding databases to their collections, the only way to answer these questions is to get copies of their latest catalogs and price sheets, as we suggested in the Introduction to this book.

If BRS has what you want or need, you must then ask a third question: Which BRS offering should I choose? If money were no object, the clear choice would be BRS/SEARCH. The rates for the Open Access SEARCH option are the highest charged by the company, and there is that $75 annual fee. But you have access to the complete BRS system.

SEARCH is a command-driven system, but it is no more complex than DIALOG. And if you would prefer to give it a friendlier face, you can always key in MENUS to tell the system you'd like it to use the BRS/BRKTHRU menus and prompts during your current session.

(There is a $1 per session charge for this feature.) More importantly, as a careful study of several years' worth of BRS newsletters will reveal, SEARCH is obviously where the company's heart and mind lie.

Low-Cost, Low-Priority

For example, conversations with BRS marketing personnel leave the impression that After Dark had a dual mission when it was introduced some years ago. First, the company understandably wanted to tap new markets, and offering its services at reduced rates after 6 P.M. was a logical way to do this. But the second and possibly even more important goal was to use After Dark as a laboratory for developing a more user-friendly version of BRS, a project that eventually was introduced as BRS/BRKTHRU.

Unfortunately, after spending a couple of years and a couple of hundred dollars in monthly minimums, one gets the impression that After Dark is not only a low-cost system, it is also a low priority on the BRS agenda. As pointed out in Part I, it is vital to know what information a database contains and how its fields and records are arranged before you start searching. This is the kind of information found in DIALOG Bluesheets and Knowledge Index "Database Briefs." But although there was a tabbed divider in the After Dark manual for this information, the company did not supply it until a full two years after introducing the service.

That was in August of 1984 and the materials supplied covered the original 40 After Dark databases. By May 1986, After Dark had grown to cover some 70 databases, but no provision had been made for updating the database description portion of the manual. We asked BRS Customer Service, "What's a body to do?" They suggested inserting the "BRS Bulletin" pages that carry new database announcements.

The After Dark newsletter, "Datalines," was always published rather ˄ irregularly. Then it was reduced from its former eight pages to one or two pages bound into the BRS/SEARCH newsletter, the "BRS Bulletin." There is an online electronic newsletter as well, but experience has shown that it may go for months without an update, even when a variety of new databases have been announced in the printed newsletter. Nevertheless, if After Dark offers the databases you need, you probably won't find them available for less money anywhere else in the electronic universe. To get your money's worth, though, be sure that you plan to do at least $12 worth of searching every month to fulfill your After Dark minimum-use requirement.

BRS/BRKTHRU is the third alternative, and it is indeed much friendlier than SEARCH. You can drive it with commands or opt for menus and generous explanatory prompts. It's available during the same hours as SEARCH and offers virtually all of the same databases, with the added bonus of a non-prime time discount. And the manual is beautifully done. Presented in a padded three-ring binder of the size now used for most computer documentation, it is tabbed, typeset, and two-color.

BRS put a lot of resources behind its introduction of BRKTHRU in the spring of 1985, and the company has apparently made a major commitment to the project. It is a good system with a lot to offer. Yet at this writing some disturbingly familiar patterns have begun to reappear. The section in the manual describing individual databases does not include the most recent additions, but it is informative and as complete as possible under the circumstances, and one assumes that updates will be forthcoming.

Other sections are not as complete. More than a year after the BRKTHRU introduction, the tabs for several manual chapters covered but a single page reading: "Coming Soon . . . Information will be mailed to you just as soon as it is available." The "NewsBRK" newsletter now shares space (four pages) in the "BRS Bulletin" with After Dark. And at this writing the online BRKTHRU newsletter has not been updated in five months.

Two Databases to Help You Make Up Your Mind

If you're on the fence about whether to subscribe to BRS/BRKTHRU or not, here are two databases that may help you make up your mind. At this writing they are available only on the BRS system. Each is considered in more detail elsewhere in this book.

The first is the Index to Reader's Digest database. To be sure, *Reader's Digest* is indexed by other online databases as well, but none of the others do the job as thoroughly. Here you can locate material by subject, author, and title. But it is the subject indexing that you will find most useful because of the way it has been done. For example, the main subject of a 1982 article may be economics, foreign relations, or Ronald Reagan, but if it mentions or quotes John F. Kennedy, you will find a reference under "KENNEDY, John F.," as well as under the main topics.

There is also the fact that most printed and electronic magazine indexes cite only the major articles in *Reader's Digest*. But this database gives you subject access to such regular features as "Humor in Uniform," "Points to Ponder," "Life in the United States," and the rest. Even the cartoons are indexed.

This material has never been indexed before, and the fact that it is included makes the database an incredible resource for anyone who must write an article, preach a sermon, or give an after-dinner talk.

Need a joke, humorous story, quotation, or topical anecdote on computers, marriage, income taxes, or miracles? Simply search the database on the desired subject and you'll get a list of issue and page references. Someone will still have to go the library to look at the actual magazine, but even the smallest two-room library is sure to have *Reader's Digest* in its collection.

The second unique offering is KIPD (Knowledge Industry Publications Database), a "database of databases." As mentioned in Part I, the three leading printed directories of online databases are the ones published by Cuadra Associates, Martha E. Williams, Inc., and Knowledge Industry Publications, Inc. (KIPI). Cuadra is available in North America on the Westlaw system. Williams is on DIALOG. And the KIPI publication is on BRS.

With KIPD on BRKTHRU you an easily generate a list of all databases dealing with, say, metallurgy or the environment. Or you can find out if a particular publication, like *IRCS Medical Science* or *Hi Tech Patents: Fiber Optics*, has been turned into an online database. Unlike the other directories, KIPD includes the name and address of the relevant vendors with each database listing instead of putting this information in a separate section. And it includes vendor pricing information in each case as well.

Short of going to the library, the least expensive way to get your hands on the printed version of KIPI's directory is through the company's Database Service. For $120 you receive a copy of the latest directory (750 pages) and six months of the "DataBase Alert" newsletter. (A year's subscription, including two issues of the directory, is $215. See Appendix B.) In contrast, searching the KIPD database on BRS/BRKTHRU is $60 an hour and 31¢ per document displayed during prime time, and $26.50 an hour with no display charges after hours. Depending on your needs, the online availability of the KIPI directory alone may be reason enough to subscribe to BRKTHRU.

...9...

Mead Data Central's NEXIS®

Mead Data Central
9393 Springboro Pike
P. O. Box 933
Dayton, OH 45401
(800) 227-4908

CUSTOMER SERVICE

U.S.: (800) 543-6862
Canada: (800) 387-9042
   In Toronto: (416) 591-8740
North America and overseas:
   (513) 859-5398

Available 24 hours a day, except between
10:00 P.M. Saturday and 6:00 A.M. Sunday.

Hours of Operation
—All hours are given in Eastern time—

Available

2:15 A.M.–2:00 A.M.
  Mon.–Fri.

2:00 A.M.–10:00 P.M.
Sat.

6:00 A.M.–2:00 A.M.
Sun.

Not Available

2:00 A.M.–2:15 A.M.
  Mon.–Fri.

10:00 P.M. Sat.–6:00 A.M. Sun.

Non-prime ("Off-Peak Hours") time runs from 7:30 P.M. to 7:30
A.M., *your local time* every day, including weekends.

211

Access: Telenet, Tymnet, Alaskanet, In-WATS, and Mead's own Mead-
Net.

Connect rate: Basic rate is $30 an hour ($20/hour in connect time plus
$10/hour for the packet switching networks). "File
charges" vary with the database and range from $7 to $30
per search. File charges are discounted 30% during non-
prime time. A 2¢ per line print charge may also apply.

What's on the System?

The keyword that best applies to Mead Data Central's (MDC) system
is *full text*. Although a number of full-text databases have recently
come on stream elsewhere, for years MDC had the full-text franchise
virtually to itself. Nearly everything about the system and how you use
it stems from the fact that it has been a full-text operation from the
beginning.

MDC is a wholly owned subsidiary of The Mead Corporation, a 140-
year-old Fortune 200 paper and forest products company based in Dayton, Ohio. What is now MDC got its start as OBAR, a legal research
service that began converting the complete record of Ohio case law into
machine-readable form in 1968 for the Ohio Bar Association. The Mead
Corporation liked the operation so much that it bought the company as
part of a planned diversification effort. It soon expanded its offerings
and introduced the result as the LEXIS® system in 1973. (LEXIS currently competes with a product called WestLaw from West Publishing
Company in St. Paul, Minnesota.)

The date is important because in 1973 there were no personal computers. Pocket calculators sold for what you would pay for a complete computer today. Consequently, to be able to offer LEXIS to lawyers far
and wide, Mead began to build and supply dedicated dumb terminals
and printers and plug them into its own MeadNet network. Known as
UBIQ terminals, the machines had dedicated keys bearing labels like
"Next Case" and "Next Page" and "Full" (full text) to make it easy to
tell the system what to do. The system still operates this way today,
whether you are using a personal computer or a dumb terminal.

Six years later, in 1979, Mead introduced NEXIS®. NEXIS was originally intended to complement the legal database by offering attorneys
access to general news and information. Both products can be accessed
on the same host system, and both use the same search software. Both
are full text.

In July 1984, "over 40% of NEXIS use [came] from the legal market,"
according to Jack W. Simpson, the company's president. But while the
percentage of NEXIS users who are in the legal profession may still be

quite high, in recent years NEXIS has moved to expand its offerings and make them more appealing to businesspeople. It has also completely revamped its pricing structure and, belatedly perhaps, gone full-speed ahead in making its system available to personal computer users.

In the words of a computer salesman we know, "that's goodness" because NEXIS has lots to offer. Perhaps its greatest prize is the full text of *The New York Times*. The final city edition is online in its entirety within 24 hours of publication, and the file dates back to June 1, 1980. That means the Sunday magazine, the book review, the Sunday regional supplements—everything. Nobody else has it.

At this writing nobody else has "The MacNeil/Lehrer NewsHour" either. NEXIS gives you the complete transcripts (typically 50 pages or so per program) from January 1, 1982 on. Transcripts are available within about 21 days of airing. "The Current Digest of the Soviet Press" is available as well, as is the full text of *InfoWorld*, the *Manchester Guardian Weekly*, and the Monitoring Service of The British Broadcasting Corporation (BBC), with its summaries of transmissions from the Soviet Union, Eastern Europe, the Middle East, the Far East, Africa, and Latin America.

There are over 50 full-text magazines, including *Aviation Week & Space Technology*, *Maclean's*, *Time*, *Newsweek*, *Sports Illustrated*, *Fortune*, *Forbes*, and *U.S. News & World Report*. There are some 16 wire services, 50 industry newsletters, a clutch of Federal Register and regulation-related files, at least four patent databases, the DISCLOSURE® Online Database, and the Trinet databases. There are also reports from 29 leading investment banking firms and brokerage houses. Although 15 of these reports and analyses are also available in the Investext database found on other systems, at least 12 of them are unique.

There is also the special AP Political Service with information on election campaigns, political issues, statewide referenda and propositions, national polls, and election calendar. MDC also offers versions of Information Access Company's full-text databases (Magazine ASAP and Trade & Industry ASAP), as well as the *Los Angeles Times*.

The complete *Encyclopedia Britannica* (Macro- and Micropedia, Book of the Year, etc.) is also available. But you can't have it. Unless you are using one of Mead's dumb UBIQ terminals, your electric bus will not stop at the *Britannica* station. And while the full text is online, even if you do have an MDC terminal, you can print only short excerpts containing your keywords. You can also view the article in full, but if you do this, you can't print it. Apparently afraid that people will steal its information, and worried that schools and homes will no longer buy its printed editions, the *Britannica* has placed so many restrictions on the use of its electronic product as to render its availability of no consequence.

Online Tip: Mead has a demo disk for IBM/PC users, and it is absolutely top-drawer. It does a good job of introducing you to NEXIS and LEXIS without overburdening you with details. And its use of graphics and animation is enormously clever. In fact, whether you're interested in MDC's products or not it's worth a look just to see how good a PC graphics presentation can be.

You'll need an IBM/PC or compatible with at least 192K and a color graphics card. At this writing, the disk is available free of charge. Contact:

> NEXIS/LEXIS Demo Diskette
> Mead Data Central
> P.O. Box 1830
> Dayton, OH 45401

Account-Related Matters

Subscriptions

NEXIS may very well be the easiest to use of all the major-league database vendors, especially for people who have never used an online system before. Part of the reason for this is that NEXIS deals in full text. (Everyone knows what a magazine or a newspaper article looks like, but few are familiar with bibliographic citations and abstracts.) And part of the reason is that unlike DIALOG, BRS, and ORBIT, NEXIS was from the beginning designed for what is now called the "end-user" instead of professional researchers and librarians. Once you sign on, you will wish that every system was as easy and natural to use.

The problem is arriving at the point where you can sign on. Mead has undergone tremendous changes in recent years, but at this writing it is still very much oriented toward large accounts. Although the system became available via personal computer in late 1983, the company is still burdened by an organizational and procedural superstructure that was created to do one thing: put UBIQ terminals and printers into large law firms and teach attorneys how to use LEXIS. At times it can almost be like dealing with the government.

Here, for example, is the procedure you must follow to get a NEXIS subscription. First, contact Mead in Dayton and ask for the location of the MDC office nearest you. (There are sales offices and learning centers in nearly 50 U.S. cities, an office in London, and one in Toronto at this writing.) When you contact your local office you will be assigned an account representative and be sent some literature. If you're interested, call back and tell the individual you'd like to sign up. You will be sent a subscription agreement and price sheet and a booklet called the "Library Contents and Price List." There is also an addendum for customer-provided equipment which you must sign if you plan to use a PC.

The forms must be signed (in duplicate) and returned to the local office along with a bank reference and two credit references. The whole packet will be sent to Dayton, and several weeks later the local office will be notified that you have been accepted as a customer.

The local account representative then gets back to you to schedule training. Sessions run about three hours and are almost always conducted at the local office. Only at the beginning of the training session do you receive your LEXIS/NEXIS ID number. You will spend about an hour of the session searching the system for information on your own questions. And you will receive an hour of free time to be used for practice on your own sometime within the following 14 days.

LEXIS subscribers have access to NEXIS and all other files and pay a monthly subscription fee of $125. Training for them is $75 per person. NEXIS-only subscribers do not have access to LEXIS, but their subscription fee is $50 per month and their training is free. Subscribers to both services may return for additional training at any time at no charge. Note that since company personnel tend to refer to the whole system as "LEXIS," make sure that you understand which system is being discussed when you call for more information.

System Manuals and Documentation

As a NEXIS subscriber you receive two main pieces of documentation: the 100-page *Reference Manual* and the 900-page *Guide to NEXIS and Related Services*. Both are perfect-bound, 8½-by-11-inch, typeset paperbacks. Neither contains any reference whatsoever to personal computers or how to sign on to the system. The reference manual does include an elaborate appendix about the care and maintenance of a Mead UBIQ terminal and its tabletop printer.

The reference manual contains 20 pages detailing the NEXIS search language. The remainder of the book is devoted to overviews and tips on using the various LEXIS/NEXIS databases and services. For its part, the Guide fills the same function as the DIALOG Bluesheets. Descriptions, the name and address of the IP, and the searchable fields of the records are presented for each database on the NEXIS system.

The Guide does not have a paginated index. Instead, filenames

(BUSWK for *Business Week,* for example) are printed vertically in a black block at the edge of the pages. To locate information on a particular file, you must literally thumb the volume, or refer to the paginated table of contents. To Mead's credit, much of the information in the Guide is available online, so you can instantly find out how far back a file goes, how often it is updated, and whether there are any additional IP-supplied manuals available for it.

When we inquired about the lack of information on how to sign on to the system, it was explained that this topic is covered in a subscriber's initial training. We were also told that, if you are using a UBIQ terminal, all you have to do is turn it on and it will automatically connect with the NEXIS system.

Usage Costs and Billing

As with everything else, Mead's pricing technique is completely different from the information industry as a whole. There is a $50 per month subscription fee for NEXIS subscribers. There is a $10 per hour charge for telecommunications (Telenet, Tymnet, MeadNet, etc.). And there is a basic connect rate of $20 an hour. This means an effective connect rate of $30. All charges are based on a transmission rate of 1200 bits per second.

In addition to the connect rate there is what MDC calls a "file charge." When you use NEXIS, the first search statement you enter is considered your search. Everything you tack on after that is considered a "modification." Each individual database has an associated file charge. The individual file charge for *The New York Times,* for example, is $7. The file charge for searching all 18 newspapers on the system—the so-called "PAPERS" group file—is $16. Each modification of the initial search strategy is $3, regardless of the database.

For example, if you selected the PAPERS group file and keyed in CAJUN you would be charged $16 as soon as you hit your <ENTER> key (what NEXIS refers to as your "transmit" key). The system would come back with perhaps 40 hits. And so on. Each time you enter an AND, a NOT, or some other connector to narrow the search, you will be charged $3.

Online Tip: If you were to search NEXIS the way you would search DIALOG, BRS, or ORBIT, at $3 per search modification, charges could mount up quite rapidly. However, according to one MDC official, "Search modifications are fairly common in LEXIS. But only about a third of our NEXIS subscribers ever modify their initial search statements." One can only surmise that either

NEXIS training is incredibly effective or that the majority of subscribers are using the system as a document delivery service instead of as an interactive database.

There are no charges other than the connect-time rate for actually
displaying the information you retrieve. But if you opt to download the
entire document all at once (Mead's "print doc" function), you will be
charged for the connect time required to transmit the article and record
it on disk *and* a fee of 2¢ per line. Mead uses 80-character lines. Thus, at
an average of seven characters per word, a 2,000-word article would
occupy about 175 lines and cost an additional $3.50 to download in this
fashion.

Two types of discounts apply. The first is the "Off Peak Hours" discount. Between the hours of 7:30 P.M. and 7:30 A.M. (your local time),
there is a 30% discount on file charges. For example, accessing *The New
York Times* during off-peak hours would cost $4.90 per search, plus $3
per modification, plus $30 an hour connect charges. There is also a
monthly volume discount schedule beginning with your 101st search and
ranging from 4% to 34%. Half of the rate card for new NEXIS-only
subscribers is devoted to "Equipment Charges" that apply to the installation of the UBIQ terminal, monthly rental fees, and charges for
moving the equipment from one office location to another.

You can get a summary of file prices while online, but the system
does not provide a DIALOG-style cost estimate at the end of a search.
It does, however, summarize the number of searches and modifications
you have entered and the total connect time spent for a session. Billing
is by direct invoice, itemized by each individual's password.

Search-Related Matters

"Version 1.4": The Best Way to Use NEXIS
NEXIS is far and away the slickest, most sophisticated system of
those considered in this book. And with the right software, it is a joy to
use. The right software in this case is Mead's own "LEXIS/NEXIS
Communication Software." That's its official name, but everyone refers
to it as "Version 1.4," the version current at this writing. This is an
improved version of the IBM/PC and compatibles package that Mead
used to sell for over $200. They are now virtually giving it away at a
cost of $50 for the first copy and $25 for each additional copy per
LEXIS/NEXIS account.

The program is absolutely superb. You can run it from your hard disk or leave it on a floppy. There is a well-thought-out configuration screen that lets you use your Up and Down arrow keys to move among settings and your Left and Right arrow keys to scroll through lists of possible settings. If you know the brand and model of your modem, the local phone number of the packet switcher you want to use, and your NEXIS personal ID, you can have everything set up in minutes.

There is a batch file on the disk called LEXIS.BAT that calls the communications program. But on general principles, we renamed it NEXIS.BAT. Thus, once Version 1.4 is configured, signing on to the system is as easy as keying in NEXIS. Everything proceeds automatically and the entire sign-on takes less than 30 seconds.

The IBM/PC-style slipcased manual explains how to use the program and generally how to use NEXIS. A template designed to fit over your function keys is provided, and it's crucial since all of your interactions with the system can be handled with the function keys in shifted, unshifted, and "ALT-ed" modes. (You can also use NEXIS by entering "dot commands," like ".NP" for "next page." But the function keys are more convenient.)

Now for the snazzy part. Version 1.4 lets your PC emulate a mainframe-style terminal. That means that individual words and sentences can be displayed with reverse video. So when you are browsing through a document that the system has retrieved for you, all of your search terms will be highlighted wherever they occur in the document. It also means that you have full-screen editing capability. If you want to change your search statement, for example, you can use the arrow keys to move around the screen and your INSERT and DELETE keys to edit the statement as you would with a word processing program. (Each time you edit and run a search statement, you are charged for a new statement. In other words, editing is more expensive than "modifying" by adding additional search words.)

CrossTalk, Jazz, and Plain Vanilla

You can also use Jazz on the Apple Macintosh and CrossTalk XVI Version 3.6 to access NEXIS. And you can use a wide range of terminal emulation programs. In fact, you can even use a plain vanilla communications program. As long as NEXIS receives the correct identification code for your terminal, it will configure itself to match your machine's capabilities. Contact Customer Service for details.

However, there are lots of reasons to use Version 1.4 wherever possible. Contrary to what you might expect, there is no need to be concerned about having to learn yet another communications program. Version 1.4 is a customized tool designed solely to get you into NEXIS and help you use the system while you are there. Thus, learning to use

NEXIS and learning to use 1.4 are essentially the same thing.

In addition, 1.4 has a number of important features that the others lack. CrossTalk supports both reverse video and color highlighting, but the INSERT and DELETE keys do not function when in editing mode. With other programs, keyword highlighting may be done with angle brackets (< >) instead of reverse video. Version 1.4 also has an important document-printing feature that we'll discuss in a moment. Most important of all, however, Mead isn't really set up to support a program like CrossTalk or Jazz. Mead's own Version 1.4 is so good and so inexpensive that it is really the only solution.

Online Tip: Beginning with CrossTalk version 3.6, Microstuff, the program's producer, began including script files for a variety of online systems. To get things set up for NEXIS, you have only to run the NEWUSER command file and select NEXIS from the menu that will appear. Respond to the prompts for your Telenet or MeadNet phone number and NEXIS ID, and CrossTalk will build the proper command file for you. The file works smoothly to automatically sign you onto the system.

CrossTalk also loads the function keys with the dot commands needed to use NEXIS, but no keyboard template is provided by Microstuff. A template does exist, however. And there is a Mead-produced manual for using CrossTalk. At this writing, only the manager at your local MDC office can supply these materials. Since your account representative may not be aware of their existence, be sure to ask if you decide to use CrossTalk instead of Version 1.4.

Online Tip: If you want to use NEXIS with a plain vanilla program (no brand-name terminal emulation or other special screen handling), as might be the case when you are traveling with a laptop computer or portable printing terminal, you need to enter .TTY01 when NEXIS prompts for terminal type. This will tell the host system that you are emulating a standard "telex"-style ASCII terminal. The communications settings to use are 7 data bits, even parity, and 1 stop bit. The system should be set for half-duplex and it should not echo characters back to the host. The X-ON/X-OFF setting should be disabled if possible.

This information was provided by a very knowledgeable customer service representative in Dayton. And it works like a charm, with one caveat. NEXIS does not echo characters. There-

Online Tip (cont.)

fore, depending on the system and software you are using, what you type may not be displayed on the screen when you are set for half-duplex.

If you are using a Hayes-compatible modem, you can easily remedy this situation by telling *it* to echo your characters by setting it to half-duplex. To do this, key in AT F0 O when the modem is in its command state. (You may have to enter + + + to put it into that state first.) You'll see some double characters while you are dialing Telenet, but once you are into NEXIS, you will see only single characters. You can then use NEXIS by keying in the appropriate dot commands.

System and Search Language

NEXIS offers a full-featured, full-powered command language. Unfortunately, NEXIS does not use industry-standard terms to refer to its information. Within the NEXIS "service," for example, there are several "libraries." There is a newspaper library, a magazine library, a wire service library, and so on. Each library contains any number of individual publications. The magazine library, for example, includes some 54 magazines. Each publication within a library is a "file." Thus there is a file for *Forbes*, one for *Time*, one for *Byte*, and so on, within the magazine library in the NEXIS service.

Mead calls each discrete article within a file—what other systems would call a record—a "document." Each division of the document—what everyone else calls a field—is what Mead refers to as a "segment." Standard NEXIS segments, for example, include publication title, date, section, headline, byline, body, and similar divisions.

Cross-File Searching

One of the most powerful and convenient features offered by NEXIS is the ability to do what the rest of the industry calls "cross-file searching." For example, you can search each publication file separately on NEXIS, but you can also search *all* of the files within a library at once. You do this by telling the system you want to search the library's "group file." Among others, NEXIS group files include PAPERS (newspapers), MAGS (magazines), WIRES (wire services), and NWLTRS (newsletters). Each of these corresponds to a complete NEXIS library.

In addition, there are specially configured group files that include publications selected from the NEXIS libraries. For example, the BUSINESS group file includes those magazines, newspapers, and newswires that deal primarily with business matters *(Forbes, Fortune,* PR Newswire, etc.). Other special group files do the same thing for finance, government, news, and technology.

If you want to be really comprehensive, you can tell NEXIS to search OMNI. OMNI is sort of a master group file that embraces all of the magazines, newspapers, newsletters, and wire services carried by the service—a total of more than 15 million documents.

At this writing, no other vendor offers such extensive cross-file search capabilities. To accomplish similar feats on DIALOG, BRS, or ORBIT, for example, you would have to search a database, temporarily store your search strategy, change to another database, recall the stored strategy, and search again. You would have to repeat the process for each database you wished to search. The reason NEXIS can be more flexible is that each publication is in effect a database and each is offered at the same standard price ($7 per search/$3 per modification). That's a pretty good trick, considering that NEXIS must negotiate royalty arrangements with the publisher of each newspaper or magazine to be able to offer its full text online.

As mentioned, NEXIS was the first system to be designed for use by someone who is not trained in library science. And the deeper you get into its search language, the more apparent this becomes. For example, you do not have to enter AND when you are searching for, say "solar energy." On many DIALOG databases you would have to enter: solar AND energy. Should you want to include a word like *and* in your NEXIS search statement, simply bracket the phrase with quotation marks. To find "The Good, the Bad, and the Ugly," you would enter exactly that. On DIALOG you might have to enter: Good (4W) Ugly. (Find *good* within four words of *ugly.)*

There are many other handy features as well. If a search word forms its plural by adding *s* or *es* or by changing the final *y* to *ies*, NEXIS will retrieve documents that contain them. The system will also automatically search for the single and plural possessives of a noun, which means you won't get tripped up because you forgot to allow for plurals in your search statement. For example, *investor, investors, investor's,* and *investors'* are considered equivalent. The system has other equivalents as well: *H.U.D.* and *HUD* are equivalent, as are *twenty* and *20, memorandum* and *memo,* and *pound* and *lb* or *lbs.* (If you don't want the equivalent to apply, you can just "NOT" it, as in: Pennsylvania NOT PA.)

You can limit your search to a particular segment (field), truncate words (wildcard search), conduct proximity searches, nest search terms in parentheses, and do just about everything else you can do on

DIALOG, BRS, or ORBIT. We have not done a point-by-point comparison, but you may be able to do more on NEXIS than on the other three. You can certainly do it more naturally.

Search-Aid Features and Training

NEXIS has a practice database that is billed only at basic connect rates. It also has sections it calls CAI (Computer Aided Instruction) and TUTOR, which attempt to teach the user the basics of framing a search strategy and using it on the NEXIS system. And there is PROFILE, a feature that tells you how far back each publication goes, how often it is updated, the publisher's name and address, and so on. CAI, TUTOR, and PROFILE are also billed at basic connect rates. Finally, there is a section called DEBUT that describes new files and features and serves rather as an online newsletter. There is a short printed newsletter as well called "NEXIS BRIEF."

The online help function is impressive. You can get help at any time by simply keying in H or HELP. The prompts and system messages are also exceptionally helpful since they explain what to key in to accomplish the next two or three paths you might want to follow. If you make a mistake, the system will come back with "NEXIS assumes you meant such-and-such" and give you the opportunity to affirm this assumption or deny it.

As you may have gathered, NEXIS is very big on training. A monthly schedule of training sessions is published and sent to most major accounts, but of course the information is also available at your local office if you call. There are specially focused sessions, but these tend to concentrate on LEXIS ("LEXIS and Tax Law" or "Litigation"). But all NEXIS training is free, unless you plan to make special arrangements for on-site training.

Toll-free customer support is available nearly round the clock, except when the system is down for maintenance. There is a special customer support section for personal computer users, one for LEXIS search assistance, one for NEXIS search assistance, and one for general questions. The LEXIS/NEXIS customer support staff includes seven attorneys, two paralegals, a registered nurse (to help users search Mead's medical databases), librarians, and men and women with banking and brokerage house experience (to help users search the company's investment and financial information offerings).

Information Delivery

Browsing and Reading

Nothing illustrates how well adapted the NEXIS tool is to full-text databases as its techniques for information display. It is the closest thing imaginable to being able to page through a document online we have ever seen. To begin with, if you have a lot of hits, you can tell the system to give you a CITE of each document. This includes the publication name, date, article title, author, and other bibliographical information. When you search wire service files, the first two to three sentences in the article will also appear.

Each citation has a number, making it easy to pick a document to look at. You can move forward or backward among your retrieved documents (articles) at will, regardless of what you happen to be looking at when you enter the command. You can also move forward or backward among the pages within a given document. When actually looking at your hits, you can choose to view the full text of the document or set the system for KWIC mode (Keyword in Context). In KWIC the system defaults to displaying your highlighted keyword surrounded on either side by 15 searchable words. However, you can enter a command to change that from one to 999 surrounding words.

In addition, you can decide exactly which segments (fields) you would like to have displayed. You are not locked into a set of predefined formats as with DIALOG, BRS, or ORBIT. At your command the system will give you a list of displayable segments for the document under consideration. You have only to key in the ones you want in the order in which you want them to appear. You can also sort several different ways, including by date and by length.

After you've read enough of the document to decide whether you want a copy of it or not, you can hit a key to tell the system to print it for you. If you are using the Version 1.4 program, you will then be given a choice of having it printed at Mead Data Central's facility in Dayton as an offline print and mailed to you, or having it printed on your own printer after you've finished searching.

Make your selection and enter "yes" to confirm the order, then continue searching. You only have to go through this dialogue once. After you enter your first print order, you may move from one file or library to another selecting documents to print and in effect putting them into your shopping cart. If you have chosen to do your printing on your own machine, when you sign off, NEXIS will ask you whether you would like to print the documents now or wait until your next sign-on.

Document-to-Disk

Whenever you decide to print your documents, you have only to toggle on Version 1.4's "document-to-disk" feature. This fools the NEXIS system into thinking it is talking to a PC printer. This saves on connect time since, while you are charged for the time required to transmit a document, it takes far less time to dump something to disk than to dump it to a printer. However, since Mead charges you 2¢ a line if you opt to do things this way, it may not be as cost-effective as it first appears. You can view and download a whole document with Version 1.4, CrossTalk, or any other program, but the process is not automatic and you will have to enter a response at the end of each displayed page.

If you choose to use Version's 1.4's document-to-disk feature, you can use the PRINTSES ("print session") utility supplied with the software to print the material once you are offline. Make sure your page is at the top-of-form in the printer, then key in PRINTSES followed by the name of the downloaded file. Articles are neatly printed with page numbers and headers citing the publication from which each came. When a document ends without filling a page, the system advances the paper to begin the next document on a fresh page.

The printout also contains a summary of the number of documents, the total number of pages, the library and file from which they came, the total time required to print, and a recap of your search strategy. The system runs so smoothly and is so well thought-out that it deserves the highest marks.

SDI: Electronic CLIPping SErvice (ECLIPSE™)

ECLIPSE™ is the NEXIS current awareness service and it is quite flexible with one exception. You can run a search, save it, and then tell the system to run it again on a regular basis. You can choose any files or combination of files you want. And you can ask the system to run your search strategy daily, weekly, or monthly. Searches are charged at the peak-hour file rate (usually $7 per file), but there is a 25% discount for weekly searches and a 60% discount for daily searches. Results are printed offline in Dayton at a cost of 2¢ a line and there is a $15 handling charge per mailed report. If you have a Mead stand-alone printer in your office, however, the system will automatically call it after it runs your strategy (ECLIPSE searches are done at 7:30 A.M. each morning) and print out any new articles in the format you request. Your costs here are for the search, the connect time, and communications charges. At this writing it is not possible to pick up your ECLIPSE results with your personal computer, and that is the service's main limitation.

NEXIS for Non-U.S. Subscribers

Mead Data Central has sales offices and learning centers in nearly 50 U.S. cities. Check your local phone book or call the toll-free customer service number at the beginning of this chapter for the number and address of the location nearest you.

If you do not live in the United States, the following information may be helpful:

Mead Data Central International, Ltd.
Sun Life Centre
Suite 1902, West Tower
200 King Street West
P.O. Box 81
Toronto, Ontario
M5H 3T4
Canada
(416) 591-8740

Mead Data Central
Tele Consulte
44, Rue du Four
Paris, France
75006
011-33-1-320-1560
(LEXIS only)

In Australia dial:
011-61-2-887-3444

Mead Data Central
International House
One St. Katharine's Way
London, England E1 9UN
44-1-488-9187

In Japan dial:
011-81-3-279-1577

...10...

The ORBIT® Search Service and the Dow Jones News/Retrieval® Service

The ORBIT® Search Service

ORBIT Search Service
SDC Information Services
2500 Colorado Avenue
Santa Monica, CA 90406
(213) 453-6194 (collect calls
accepted from Canada)
(213) 820-4111, ext. 6194
Or Customer Service numbers.
Telex: 65-2358
TWX: 910/343-6643

CUSTOMER SERVICE

9:00 A.M.–5:00 P.M. Eastern
(800) 336-3313, except in Virginia
(703) 790-9850, in Virginia

9:00 A.M.–5:00 P.M. Pacific
(800) 421-7229, except in California
(800) 352-6689, in California

Hours of Operation
—All hours are given in Eastern time—

Available

Mon.–Thurs. All day.
(except from 9:45 P.M.
to 10:15 P.M.)

Fri. 3:00 A.M.–8:00 P.M.

Sat. 8:00 A.M.–7:00 P.M.

Sun. 7:00 P.M.–3:00 A.M.

Not Available

Mon.–Thurs.
9:45 P.M.–10:15 P.M.

Fri. 8:00 P.M.–3:00 A.M.

Sat. 7:00 P.M.–8:00 A.M.

Sun. 3:00 A.M.–7:00 P.M.

Access: Telenet and Tymnet at $10 per hour or via direct dial.

Connect Rate: Varies with the database. Total charge consists of packet switcher costs, database rate, and any display or offline print charges.

What's on the System?

The ORBIT Search Service, as it is now officially called, is operated by System Development Corporation (SDC). SDC began as a division of the Rand Corporation, and one of its first tasks was to develop an information retrieval system for the Advanced Research Projects Agency (ARPA) of the Department of Defense. Another ARPA project, the ARPANET, was the first system to employ packet switching technology to connect widely scattered users, most of whom were on university campuses. ARPA is now called DARPA for reasons unknown. The Burroughs Corporation bought SDC in 1981 and sold it to the London-based Pergamon Group in October 1986.

Quantitatively the ORBIT Search Service is the smallest of the Big Three classic bibliographic databases. Qualitatively, the words that best describe it are "exclusive" and "technical." Of the 64 databases on the system at this writing, 32 are available exclusively through ORBIT. The system has more scientific and technical databases than any other kind, followed by engineering and electronics, energy and environment, and numerous industry-specific offerings. A database called SAE, for example, is prepared by the Society of Automotive Engineers. One called COLD covers the literature of Antarctica. APIPAT focuses on petroleum refining patents from the U.S. and eight other countries.

Some ORBIT databases are exclusive in another way as well. At least a dozen databases require special permission from the database producer. ORBIT tells you whom to contact to secure permission, but that's about all. You may have to purchase a subscription to the printed publication from which the database is drawn, though if you do you'll probably get a discount when you use the product online.

Account-Related Matters

Subscriptions and Manuals

There are three ways to subscribe to ORBIT, but each of them involves some kind of training package. The least expensive is the Workbook Package. The cost is $125, and you receive a workbook with step-by-step instructions and self-paced practice exercises, plus three hours of connect time on selected files.

The second option is the Training Workshop package at $150. Under this plan you and an associate attend a regularly scheduled ORBIT basic skills workshop presented "in major cities throughout the U.S. and the world." This is a full-day session (lunch is included in the price) involving demonstrations, instruction, and hands-on practice. You receive a training workbook and one and a half hours of free connect time on selected files for post-session practice.

The Custom Package is the third offering. This is a session for up to 12 people conducted at your facility and convenience. The training is customized to the needs of your organization, and free post-session practice time is included. The cost is $500, plus travel expenses for the trainer.

All three options include the *ORBIT System User Manual* (regularly $40) and a *Quick Reference Guide* (regularly $18 with binder) and five free individual database manuals of your choice. These regularly sell for $7.50 apiece. That adds up to $95.50 worth of documentation were you to purchase the items separately. The *Quick Reference Guide* contains three sections. There is a system basics section (blue sheets), a database description section (ivory sheets), and an online ordering section describing document delivery services (green sheets).

In April 1985, ORBIT discontinued its monthly minimum charges. In the past these were as high as $100 a month. But no more. Now you can subscribe via one of the training options and pay for things on an as-needed, as-used basis. If you plan to use ORBIT frequently, however, there are two main discount plans.

The Monthly Minimum Plan lets you commit to a certain amount of monthly usage in return for discounts. The minimum $200 per month commitment earns a discount of $2 an hour. The top discount of $15 an hour requires a commitment of $4,000 a month. The other alternative is an Annual Subscription Plan. The minimum subscription is $3,000 a year, which you can elect to pay quarterly, semiannually, or annually. Both options permit the assignment of an unlimited number of passwords for the same account.

Usage Costs

The basic charge for using ORBIT is made up of two components: Telenet or Tymnet access at $10 an hour and the database-specific connect-hour charge. There is no extra charge for 1200 or 2400 bit-per-second access and no off-hours discount. Databases sell for an average of $75 an hour, though some are as low as $50 and as high as $300.

There are also display charges and offline print charges. These range from no charge for displaying the bibliographic citation and 10¢ for the full record to $3.00 for each full record printed offline. Most display and offline print charges, however, are in the 25¢ to 35¢ range for full records. Postage is charged on top of the offline printout rate. Billing is by direct invoice.

Search-Related Matters

System and Search Language
ORBIT is entirely command-driven, and its search language is very powerful. In addition to proximity searching (not available on all databases), truncation, and field searching, and all the other features you would expect in a Big Three system, the language has some unique features.

For example, you can change a command name to some other name more to your liking. Or you can create a synonym for a command so you can use both it and the original. In both cases, your instructions will remain in force for the duration of your session. But you'll have to re-enter them the next time you sign on. There is also a command called "TIMEPROMPT" that can be toggled on or off. Its purpose is to notify you that the system is indeed working on your search, should your search take abnormally long. At each time interval, you can decide to cancel the search. Or you can ask not to be notified until the search is done.

You can choose to automatically receive a display of all of your accumulated charges each time you move from one database to another or stop searching. Or you can toggle the feature off. A variety of other cost-related commands enable you to ascertain how much money you have spent from virtually any point in your online session to the present.

Search-Aid Features
In addition to the database descriptions (ivory sheets) that are part of the *Quick Reference Guide*, there are database manuals for about 53 of ORBIT's databases. These sell for $7.50 each, and as noted, you receive five manuals of your choice with your subscription. Many of the individual database producers also have manuals, guides, and thesauri to help you, though they typically sell in the $50 range. ORBIT Customer Service can tell you who has what and how much it costs.

ORBIT also sells a program called SearchMaster for $300. This is a communications program with two main features. It can be set up to automatically log you on to DIALOG, BRS, ORBIT, and other systems. And it lets you prepare search strategies and search scripts offline to be issued at a single keystroke when needed. The program also has a module designed to help library patrons and others create a search command. The module asks you simple questions ("Last name of author?" "Date?" etc.) and then substitutes your answers for variables in previously prepared search strategies.

Training and Customer Support

In addition to the training/subscription options, ORBIT offers a variety of additional seminars. The Basic Skills for beginners lasts a whole day and costs $115, including lunch. There are full-day seminars on Advanced Skills, patents, and chemistry ($100 each). There is an ORBIT Refresher course, an ORBIT Timesavers (tricks and tips) course, and one on cross-file searching. All three are half-day sessions ($50). Free half-day classes include ORBIT Overview, JAPIO/CLAIMS Overview (this is an English-language database focusing on Japanese patents), and Engineering Overview. Courses are conducted in major cities in the U.S. and Canada on a very frequent schedule.

There are two Customer Support "Action Desks," one on each coast (McLean, Virginia, and Santa Monica, California). Each operates from 9 A.M. to 5 P.M. local time, and both are reachable by toll-free number. ORBIT also has offices in several other countries.

Information Delivery

Online Display and Offline Printouts

ORBIT may well offer the most flexible range of choices for displaying information online of any of the Big Three. You can look at the record title and indexing terms, usually at no charge, or you can display the entire record. Or you can use one of ORBIT's "Tailored Formats." This means you can tell the system exactly which fields you wish to have printed to create your own customized display. Or you can tell the system to use one of its standard formats but to add or exclude fields of your choice. There is also a PRINT HIT command that will display only those portions of a record containing your search terms. You can sort by any printable field. And everything that applies to online displays applies to offline prints.

SDI and Document Delivery

ORBIT has a well-developed SDI current awareness feature that is supported by more than half of its databases. The price for storing a search of any kind online is a nickel a word per month. This applies to the stored search strategy of an SDI as well. In addition, there are charges ranging from $2.95 to $7.95 each time a search is run, plus offline printing charges and postage. You can tell the sytem to automatically run the same SDI strategy against up to six databases.

ORBIT gives you access to about 35 document delivery services, each of which is described on a green sheet in the *Quick Reference Guide.* These include the British Library Lending Service, Dynamic Information Corp., Information On Demand, The Information Store, and other leaders in the field. Unfortunately, while you are charged only $40 an hour to enter your order online, you do have to key in all relevant information. There is no automatic ordering process at this writing.

ORBIT for Non-U.S. Subscribers

In addition to its two U.S. offices, SDC's ORBIT Search Service has offices and representatives in five other countries. If you live in Great Britain, Australia, Japan, Brazil, Hong Kong, or Asia, you may find it convenient to contact the appropriate address listed below:

Europe
SDC Information Services
Bakers Court, 4th Floor
Baker Road
Uxbridge
Middlesex UB8 1RG
U.K.
(0895) 37137
Telex: 8958961

South America
Barroslearn
Rua 24 de Maio 62-5.0
Caixa Postal 6182
Cep. 01000
Sao Paulo, SP
Brazil
(011) 223-6011
Telex: 01121770 PBAS BR

Australia
SDC Search Service
30 Alfred Street
P.O. Box 439
Milsons Point 2061
Australia
(02) 9229308 or (02) 9229302
(008) 226-474,
toll-free in Australia
Telex: BURAD AA23015

Japan
SDC of Japan, Ltd.
Nishi-Shinjuku Showa Building
1-13-12, Nishi Shinjuku
Tokyo 160, Japan
(03) 349-8520 or 349-8528
Telex: 2322262 SDC J J

For Singapore, Malaysia, Brunei, Hong Kong, Thailand, and Indonesia, contact:

Integrated Information PTE
Ltd.
Marketing Department
456 Alexandria Road
18-00 NOL Building
Singapore 0511
(65) 278-9811
Telex: RS 37071

The Dow Jones News/Retrieval® Service

Dow Jones News/Retrieval Service   CUSTOMER SERVICE
P.O. Box 300
Princeton, NJ 08540   (800) 257-5114
(609) 452-2000   (609) 452-1511

Mon.–Fri.: 8:00 A.M.–12:00 A.M.
Eastern
Mon.–Sat.: 9:00 A.M.–6:00 P.M.
Eastern

Hours of Operation
—All hours are given in Eastern time—

Available   Not Available

6:00 A.M.–4:00 A.M.   4:00 A.M.–6:00 A.M.
All days.

Non-prime time runs from 6:01 P.M. to 4:00 P.M. Eastern time, *not* your local time. Weekends and holidays are non-prime as well.

Access: Telenet and Tymnet. The company's own Downet is available in selected areas. You may also use ConnNet, for access from any city in Connecticut. Call Customer Service for locations and details for both services.

Connect Rate: // INTRO is free; other rates vary from $72/hour to $12/hour, depending on the database and the time of day. Telecommunications costs are included.

What's on the System?

DJN/R is *the* source for current information on financial markets. Lots of systems offer stock and commodity quotes, but no other system covers as many markets and no one does as much with them. The service is also known for the quality and accuracy of its information. DJN/R personnel constantly watch the quote wire, for example, and they'll phone the exchanges for confirmation should any figures appear out of line. (For more information on DJN/R financial databases, please see Chapter 16.)

There is a great deal of other financial information as well (Standard & Poor's, Investext, Media General, DISCLOSURE II, etc.), as we will see in various Part II chapters. In addition, you can do your stock trading on the system via Fidelity Investor's Express. You can scan for discounted prices on over 60,000 items and place your order online via Comp-U-Store. And there is a gateway service to MCI Mail. If you are a Citibank Direct Access (online banking with New York's Citibank) customer, you can not only access DJN/R through that system, but you may receive a 10% discount on your connect time as well.

Dow Jones & Company has its own news service with reporters in almost 100 cities worldwide. Dow Jones was the first private company to be licensed by the FCC to own and operate its own satellite earth stations, which it uses to link its offices and its 17 printing plants. As a result, Dow Jones News stories are usually available to DJN/R customers within 90 seconds of being filed by a reporter.

Dow Jones publishes a number of Canadian newspapers, *Barron's*, and *The Wall Street Journal*. The full text of the day's *Journal* is available online by 6 A.M. each business day. You'll find it in the //TEXT section of the service. (See Chapter 14 for more information.)

Account-Related Matters

Subscriptions

Individuals can subscribe to DJN/R in one of two ways. You can buy the Radio Shack Universal Sign-Up Kit for $19.95 (Catalog Number: 26-2224). This includes a subscription to both CompuServe and Dow Jones and an hour of free time on each system. Dow Jones will mail you your manual free of charge as soon as you send in the enclosed registration form. Under this option you will be charged a $12 annual service fee.

The second way to sign up is to purchase the Dow Jones News/Retrieval Membership Kit from the company or from your local retailer.

The list price is $29.95, and it includes the manual (regularly sold at $9.95) and five free hours of time on the system. (Be sure to use your free time within 30 days of receiving your password.) Under this option the $12 annual fee is waived for the first year.

Corporate subscriptions are also available for $49.95 per location. They include eight hours of free connect time and multiple passwords. Monthly itemized bills detail usage by password, making it easy to apportion costs. The annual service fee is waived for the first year under this option as well.

These are the DJN/R start-up packages. If you expect to use the service frequently, you may be interested in two add-on options. After you have purchased one of the start-up packages, you can opt for the Blue Chip Membership. This provides a one-third discount on non-prime time usage and eliminates the annual service fee completely. The cost is $95 a year. The Executive Membership plan offers a one-third discount on usage at *all times*. The cost is $50 per month per location, and there is no annual subscription fee.

Both Blue Chip and Executive members are guaranteed six hours of free usage each year (half an hour a month) in selected databases.

Usage Costs

On June 1, 1985, Dow Jones introduced what it considered a simplified pricing scheme. Unfortunately, the result was to make the service appear cheaper than it really is and to make it more difficult to figure out what you will be charged. The company likes to say that it has only two rates: 90¢ a minute during prime time and 20¢ a minute non-prime (6:01 P.M. to 4 A.M.). But at least nine of its databases carry surcharges of between 30¢ and 60¢ a minute. And as it notes in the small print, all of these charges refer to 300 bit-per-second ("baud") access. For speeds of 1200 to 2400 bps, multiply by 2.2.

When you add the surcharges to the basic rate, it becomes apparent that Dow Jones has two basic prime-time prices ($1.20/minute and 90¢/minute) and two basic non-prime prices (80¢/minute and 20¢/minute). The higher prices apply to databases like Standard & Poor's, Investext, Media General, and DISCLOSURE II. To more easily compare Dow Jones prices to those of other database vendors, you might want to refer to the following table when reviewing Dow Jones-supplied rate information:

Prime-Time Charges

DJN/R	Translation
90¢/minute	$54/hour at 300 bps $118.80/hour at higher speeds

$1.20/minute $72/hour at 300 bps
$158.40/hour at higher speeds

Non-Prime-Time Charges

DJN/R   Translation

20¢/minute $12/hour at 300 bps
$26.40/hour at higher speeds

80¢/minute $48/hour at 300 bps
$105.60/hour at higher speeds

Some databases have special additional fees. There is a $6 access fee for each company you search for in DISCLOSURE II ($2 during non-prime time), plus a $6 fee for each use of one of the Disclosure/Spectrum stock ownership files within the DISCLOSURE II database. If you want Real Time Quotes (no mandatory 15-minute delay), a stock exchange fee of $18.50 per month is charged.

You can elect direct invoicing or have all costs automatically charged to your major credit card. The rates quoted include everything. There are no type or display charges, no additional charges for telecommunications. As the rate card points out, there is a "one-minute minimum for each access of any billable database."

Search-Related Matters

System and Search Language
The DJN/R system itself is both menu-driven and command-driven. That is, if you want to move from one feature to another, you can call up a menu to guide you. But if you know the name of the feature ("WSJ" for *Wall Street Journal* highlights online, for example), you can simply enter two slashes and the target name (//WSJ) to be taken there directly.

As far as the search language is concerned, Dow Jones uses four main techniques, depending on the database. Some databases are completely menu-driven. If you wanted to read transcripts of the Public Broadcasting Service's "Wall Street Week," for example, you would be presented with a menu containing a choice for each of the last four shows. No searching is involved.

The most frequently used search technique is, as you might imagine, a corporation's stock ticker symbol. In many DJN/R databases, "searching" is a simple matter of responding to the supplied prompt with the correct symbol and a date range, where applicable. If you don't know the symbol to use, there is a database containing only stock symbols. Just enter as much of the company name as you are sure of and the database will come back with a list of candidates.

The third technique is used in the Dow Jones News database and involves both ticker symbols and unique Dow Jones "category codes." This database includes material drawn from *The Wall Street Journal* and *Barron's*, but the bulk of the information comes from the Dow Jones News Service (also known as the "Broadtape"). It is current from 90 seconds to 90 days (after that the information is moved to a database called the Dow Jones News Archive in the //TEXT section of the system).

The category codes are crucial to the effective use of Dow Jones News, and the manual provides a complete summary. Entering .I/CHM will retrieve articles on the chemical industry. Entering .I/FLX focuses on motion pictures ("flicks"). Similarly, if you want news on a specific company, you have only to enter a period followed by its ticker symbol (.IBM, .GAF, etc.).

The fourth technique is the search language used in the full-text databases *(Wall Street Journal, Barron's, Washington Post,* and Dow Jones News Archive). This is a full-blown search language of the sort you might find on a bibliographic database like BRS. In fact, it essentially *is* the search language used by BRS. Both systems use a modified version of IBM's STAIRS database language and pay IBM a royalty for the privilege.

In //TEXT you can conduct a full-text search or limit your search to various fields. Fields include the source publication and the publication date, which you may enter in either numbers or words (860324, 3/24/86, or March 24, 1986, are all acceptable). You can also search on the basis of ticker symbol or the Dow Jones category codes used in the Dow Jones News database.

Search-Aid Features

The Dow Jones manual is excellent. Published in a software documentation-style three-ring binder, it tells you virtually everything you need to know about what the databases contain and how far back they extend. There's a good index and there are lots of examples. Quick-reference cards, command summaries, and manual updates are regularly provided.

All of the //TEXT databases *(Wall Street Journal* full-text, etc.) and completely menu-driven services (like "Wall Street Week," the sports report, or the weather) must be used manually. However, Dow Jones has been a pioneer in introducing effective, easy-to-use "front-end" software packages. The company sells a number of programs that can automatically sign on, go into a database, download the necessary information, and sign off. Each requires some set-up work on your part, but once that is done, you really don't have to do much more than turn on your computer and modem. The front-end package will do the rest.

In addition, most such programs are designed to help you analyze or graph or otherwise *use* the data once you are offline. Programs are available for the Apple // series, the Apple Macintosh, and IBM and compatible PCs. The software sells for between $100 and $450. Here is a representative sampling of what's available:

• Dow Jones Market Manager and Market Manager PLUS.

Lets you create one or more portfolios (files) containing your securities. The program automatically accesses the Current Quotes database to update the value of your holdings. Once offline, you can use the program's other features to record your trading activities, calculate net profit, and handle other portfolio management tasks.

• Dow Jones Market Analyzer PLUS.

Designed for investors who favor technical analysis (Louis Rukeyser's "gnomes"), the program will automatically obtain a full year of historical data from the Dow Jones Historical Quote database. When you are offline, the program will display this data in seven or more types of charts (stock bar, oscillator, trend lines, etc.).

• Dow Jones Market Microscope.

Designed to automatically access the Media General database, this program lets you create an unlimited number of lists containing up to 50 different companies and/or industry groups. You can choose to retrieve as many as 20 of the 68 available Media General indicators for each list. When you are offline, you can print or view an alphabetical list of all stocks, select and print out only those stocks whose current prices are at critical levels, and perform a number of other manipulations.

• Dow Jones Spreadsheet Link.

This program is designed to download information from the current and historical quotes services, the Corporate Earnings Estimator, Media General, and the DISCLOSURE II database and store the results for direct importation into your spreadsheet program. Several sample templates are provided, but of course you may create your own. You will need VisiCalc, Multiplan, or Lotus 1-2-3.

Customer Support and Training

All active subscribers receive copies of the DJN/R magazine, *Dowline*. (You can contact the editors at no cost by messaging them via MCI mail. The address is DOWLINE.) Issued somewhat irregularly, this is a slickly produced publication that offers profiles of the DJN/R databases, tips on using the system most effectively, "reviews" of Dow Jones software, a Question and Answer column, and more. The free //INTRO feature on the system itself also offers a form of customer support in the announcements it provides regarding updates and changes to the system, special offers, training schedules, and so on.

Dow Jones holds regular training sessions and seminars in major U.S. cities. There are three basic types, and each runs approximately three hours. Seminar A, "Investing with a Personal Computer," demonstrates Dow Jones software. The cost is $15, payable at the door, and attendees receive a $25 gift coupon good toward the purchase of Dow Jones software.

Seminar B is aimed at corporate executives and focuses on the DJN/R service. The cost is $75 for your organization's first attendee and $25 for each additional person. Seminar C is aimed at home users. The cost is $25 per person (under 18 admitted free). Attendees of both B and C seminars receive a full free day online. Phone the main Dow Jones number [(609) 452-2000] for information on scheduled seminars. Or see // INTRO online.

Information Delivery

Dow Jones News/Retrieval has what is arguably the crudest system software in the entire online world. The simplest computer bulletin board program is smooth by comparison, and some of the free BBS software available in the public domain puts the DJN/R system in deep shade. All of this could change, of course, but at this writing every DJN/R subscriber must contend with the following problems:

- There are no -MORE- prompts. Information is formatted in pages and after one page has scrolled up your screen, the system simply stops. If you did not know to hit <ENTER>, you could easily assume there was a problem on the line and sit there with the meter running, waiting for Dow Jones to respond.

- Pages are formatted in lines of 32 characters each, with about 12 lines per page. You cannot get the system to display its information in lines of 65 or 80 characters.

- Much of the information is formatted so poorly that it is difficult to read. The use of all capital letters in some databases doesn't improve readability either.

- There is no way to get the system to scroll continuously (except in the TRACK service). The only way to avoid having to keep your finger on the <ENTER> key is to note the number of pages in the document or section and quickly hit <ENTER> a corresponding number of times.

- The system does not support the X-ON/X-OFF flow-control protocol. That's not a major problem until you use the DJN/R gateway into MCI Mail. Once there you will find that the lack of flow control makes it impossible to upload a letter previously composed offline.

As an online communicator, you can get used to anything. And in truth, if you know how to use CrossTalk, Relay, or any other communications program with a "script file" feature, or if you have a keyboard macroing program like SmartKey or NewKey, you can compensate for these problems. But it does add yet another layer of complexity to the process.

To complete our Key Question Checklist, Dow Jones does not offer a current awareness or SDI feature. And since all of its databases offer the full text of whatever they deal with, document delivery is not an issue.

...11...

VU/TEXT®, NewsNet®, and Wilsonline™

VU/TEXT®

VU/TEXT Information Services, Inc.
1211 Chestnut Street
Philadelphia, PA 19107
(215) 665-3300

CUSTOMER SERVICE

(800) 258-8080

Pennsylvania residents
call: (215) 665-3303,
3310, 3313

Mon.–Fri.: 8:00 A.M.–10:00 P.M. Eastern
Sat.–Sun.: 9:00 A.M.–6:00 P.M. Eastern

Hours of Operation: 24 hours a day, every day. Except that any given database may be down for half an hour each day for reloading. The down time will not take place during regular business hours.

Access: Telenet. Free passwords and unified billing are available to subscribers to QL Systems, Ltd., of Ottawa, Ontario, Datasolve's World Reporter, WESTLAW, and OCLC's (Online Library Computer Center) UNISON service.

Connect Rate: Varies with the database and your subscription option. The highest rate is about $100, the lowest, $5 (training and practice databases). Telecommunications charges are extra ($9/hr.) No extra charge for 1200 bps, but 2400 bps access is billed at 50% above the stated connect hour rate. There is no non-prime-time discount.

What's on the System?

If *The New York Times, The Washington Post*, the *Los Angeles Times*, and other major metropolitan dailies are the nation's head, the country's regional papers are its heart. They cover us where we live—in Akron, in Detroit, in Miami, in Wichita. Papers in these cities do a fine job of covering national and international news, of course. But they are not the place to look for a complete transcript of a presidential news conference. Most devote the bulk of their coverage to items of greatest interest to people who live in their circulation areas.

That means a great deal if you're from out of town. It means you can be sitting in your office thousands of miles away from Richmond or San Jose and by tapping a few keys find out who runs things in those two cities as well as who *really* runs things. If a competitor has built or closed a plant, if you want to know about pollution or quality of life, if you want to get an insight on the local labor situation, a local paper will give you the kind of depth of detail available nowhere else.

In short, if you want to know anything about a town that you could get from reading several years' worth of its local newspaper, you can do it on VU/TEXT. And as with all electronic information, you can do it *very* quickly.

VU/TEXT is a Knight-Ridder company, and while it will probably eventually carry all 30 Knight-Ridder papers, it has papers from many other publishers besides. The system grew out of an automated clipping file—what newspaper people call the "morgue"—set up by the Philadelphia *Inquirer* and *Daily News*. The software was acquired from QL Systems, Ltd., a company that had previously provided a similar service for the Toronto *Globe and Mail*. It is thus specifically designed for newspaper search and retrieval. And the emphasis has been on full text from the beginning. The system went up for internal use at the two Philadelphia papers in 1980, and VU/TEXT was set up as a commercial service in 1982. Since then it has become the premier online service in this area. (Though it is not without competition. As we'll see in Chapter 14, DataTimes covers many local and regional papers that VU/TEXT does not.)

In addition to the local and regional newspapers, there are at least 16 other databases on the system. These include the AP newswire, Facts on File, DISCLOSURE, ABI/INFORM, VU/QUOTE (stock and commodity quotes; 20-minute delay), and ECS Marine Credit Reports (financial, credit, and management information on international shipping companies). Many of these databases are considered in Part III of this book.

Account-Related Matters

Subscriptions and Manuals

There is no cost for a subscription to VU/TEXT, but you will definitely need the VU/TEXT manual ($35). This contains all the system documentation and bluesheets describing each of the more than 30 newspapers and 16 other databases on the system at this writing. Some of the bluesheet write-ups run to several pages. Most include complete lists of the applicable keywords (indexing terms) used in each database, as well as the names of a given newspaper's "sections" and sample records.

The manual is tabbed, nicely laid out, and well-written. There are plenty of examples, and at appropriate points red is used for highlighting or emphasis. It includes a step-by-step tutorial and an extensively annotated command glossary. There is also a Ready Reference Guide to keep by your machine. Again, it is well laid out and complete.

VU/TEXT offers two main subscription plans. Option I involves a commitment to a minimum of $60 per month in usage. Only the database connect-hour charges apply toward this minimum, however. Telecommunications charges are extra. In return for this commitment, Option I users pay an average of $10 to $15 less for their database connect hours. Multiple passwords are available at no charge, though you may want to order an extra manual or two depending on your situation. Also, each time someone signs on to VU/TEXT he or she has the option of entering a name, project or department number, or anything else that will identify the search. These identifiers are reproduced on the monthly bills to help you correctly apportion costs.

Option II is the open rate plan. There is no monthly minimum usage requirement. However, database connect-hour prices are $10 to $15 higher, and there is a $10 per month account maintenance fee. All billing under both options is by direct invoice at this writing.

Usage Costs

Under Option II pricing, the newspapers all cost either $90 or $100 an hour ($75 to $85 under Option I). Each of them is a full-text database, and there is no additional charge for displaying articles. Indeed, only three of the other databases (ABI/INFORM, PTS PROMT, and the Geneva Consultants Registry) have display charges. The cost is 40¢ per record displayed. Offline printing is 50¢ per page (two full computer screens), plus postage. The only exception is The Wall Street Transcript, which is $1.50 per page.

Volume discounts are available on some databases, and they go into effect automatically after five hours of connect time during the month. A discount schedule is available on request. Also, it is easy to see how much you have spent on any given search or during any given session. Simply enter TOT when you want to see your current itemized total charges.

Search-Related Matters

System and Search Language

VU/TEXT is almost completely command-driven. The screen that greets you on sign-on does list the various databases available and the codes you need to enter to access them, but that's about it. Although you can return to check a service code at any time, almost everything else the system does is by your command. You cannot set your page width in VU/TEXT. (Everything is 80 columns.) And you have only limited control over the number of lines displayed before the system pauses (23 or 10). But when viewing the results of your search, you can tell the system to display any document or range of documents continuously without pausing.

The search language is complete and it offers all the power you are likely to need. It appears to be a good compromise between power and ease of use. For example, unless you tell it otherwise, VU/TEXT automatically searches the full text of documents in its newspaper and other databases. You don't have to think about specific fields. However, if you want or need that kind of precision, a fully developed field-search capability is provided. There is a right-hand truncation feature and a word adjacency feature. Entering RONALD (space)/(space) REAGAN (RONALD / REAGAN) would retrieve "Ronald Reagan," for example. Proximity searching is available on most databases as well. Entering REAGAN /2 RONALD would retrieve both "Ronald Reagan" and "Ronald W. Reagan."

You can temporarily save your search strategies and assign each a number for reuse later. The strategies remain stored only for the length of your current session. And you can carry a given search strategy with you from one database to another. That means you can enter it once, run it against one newspaper, change to another newspaper, and run it again without having to rekey it. Without doing an exhaustive analysis, users certainly seem to benefit from the fact that the VU/TEXT search software was specifically designed for use with newspapers.

Search-Aid Features, Training, and Customer Support

There is no online "help" feature to speak of, though the Ready Reference Guide card that comes with your subscription is so good that you may not miss it. VU/TEXT does send you a copy of the ABI/INFORM booklet listing all of the journals that the database covers. However, if you are going to search INFORM frequently, you should probably buy the manual published by INFORM's producer. The same thing applies to PTS PROMT.

VU/TEXT holds User Workshops in major cities, including Boston, Chicago, Detroit, Houston, Fort Lauderdale, New York, Orlando, Philadelphia, Richmond, San Diego, Anchorage, Seattle, and Washington, D.C. The cost is $25 and sessions last approximately three hours. Contact Customer Service for schedules and details. Subscribers receive the "VU/TEXT Newsline" newsletter. Published about six times a year, it includes the same kind of announcements, search tips, and "war stories" found in most vendor newsletters.

Information Delivery

VU/TEXT has a number of interesting display options. First of all, the system automatically brackets all occurrences of your search terms in *asterisks* when it displays results. You can also ask to see just the pages of an article that contain your search terms. And you can ask that documents be displayed by order of the number of hits each contains ("weighted order") or by ascending or descending chronological order. You also have complete control over which fields are displayed. (The bluesheets that explain the databases will show you what information is in which field in each case.)

All of the above applies to offline printouts as well. These are 50¢ per page (two computer screens) in most cases, plus postage. The only VU/TEXT offerings that assess display charges at this writing are ABI/INFORM, PTS PROMT, the Geneva Consultants Registry, and DISCLOSURE. There is no document delivery feature, though of course you are free to contact the non-newspaper databases or an information broker to arrange document delivery on your own.

Online Tip: VU/TEXT offers gateway service to QL Search, one of the leading Canadian database vendors. QL has more than 80 full-text and bibliographic/abstract databases of its own, including The Canadian Press Newstex (the complete Canadian Press News Wire from January 1, 1981, to midnight last night), Federal Court Reports, Standing Orders of the House of Commons, and Arctic Science and Technology.

The cost is $85 an hour for Option I subscribers; $100 an hour for Option II (open rate) customers. And you'll have to contact VU/

TEXT Customer Service to get a special password. But that's all there is to it. For more information on QL Search, contact:

QL Systems Ltd.
112 Kent Street
Suite 1018, Tower B
Ottawa, Ontario K1P 5P2
Canada
(613) 238-3499

NewsNet

NewsNet, Inc.
945 Haverford Road
Bryn Mawr, PA 19010
(800) 345-1301
(215) 527-8030, in Pennsylvania

CUSTOMER SERVICE

9:00 A.M.–8:00 P.M. Eastern

Mon.–Fri.

Hours of Operation: 24 hours a day, every day.

Non-prime time runs from 8:00 P.M. to 8:00 A.M. Eastern time, *not* your local time. Weekends and holidays are billed at non-prime-time rates as well.

Access: Tymnet and Telenet.

Connect rate: Basic rate varies from $18/hour to $72/hour, depending on speed of communications (300, 1200, or 2400), and time of day. Telecommunications costs are included, but there are varying royalty charges for each newsletter on the system.

What's on the System?

Have you ever encountered something so good that you can't wait to share your discovery with a friend? If you have, then you've got an inkling of what it's like to come upon NewsNet for the first time. We suggest, however, that you resist that impulse. NewsNet is too good to share with any but your *closest* friends and business associates, and it is so powerful that under no circumstances should you risk telling a potential competitor about it. Like single-malt Scotch, "A Prairie Home Companion," and any book by John McPhee, NewsNet is one of the good things in life.

There are two reasons why NewsNet deserves such praise, and why it is probably the one online system that virtually all executives, managers, and professionals should subscribe to. The first is the nature of the information its databases contain. Although it has other features, NewsNet is at its heart an electronic vendor of trade, industry, and professional newsletters. These are the types of newsletters whose print editions typically sell for $100 to $500 a year or more for 12 to 24 issues.

Most are produced by seasoned experts or small editorial staffs who have devoted themselves to the intense coverage of a single, relatively narrow field of interest. Typically, newsletters of this sort offer a currency and depth of coverage not found in most trade journals and other industry-specific publications. And, depending on the editor/author, they can provide an insight and perspective available from no other source. In short, reading a good newsletter is like having an expert offer a private consultation concerning matters of great interest to you and your business.

So from the word "Go!" NewsNet starts with top-quality, high-octane information. But the company could easily have screwed it up. Instead, NewsNet presents its information via a powerful but natural system that makes it easy to find what you want. Anyone with a modicum of online experience elsewhere can use NewsNet almost instinctively. And brand new online communicators can get to that stage with very little effort. In essence, all you have to do is pick an industry, type in a keyword or phrase, specify a date range, and choose the articles you want to read from the resulting "menu" of headines the system creates to satisfy your search.

The system began in the spring of 1982 with 17 newsletters. At this writing, more than 300 newsletters covering over 30 industries and professions are available, and more are being added all the time. About 70% of these publications are not available online anywhere else. (NEXIS has about 50 newsletters, some of which are also on NewsNet.) NewsNet is a full-text database, and subscribers have access to most newsletters within *minutes* after their authors have uploaded them to the system.

We will be citing specific NewsNet newsletters in appropriate chapters in Part III. However, to get an idea of what you'll find on the system, consider the following titles: "Defense Industry Report," "Manufactured Housing Newsletter," "Japan Computer Industry Scan," "Environmental Compliance Update," "American Banker," "Tax Notes Today," and "PACs & Lobbies."

Among other things, the system also offers you access to AP Datastream Business News and the UPI, Reuters International, and the PR newswires at the same time that editors in the nation's newsrooms receive them. But it is the TRW credit reports that are likely to be of special interest. The TRW Business Profiles database—actually a gateway to the main TRW system—provides up-to-date payment histories on nearly eight million businesses on a pay-as-you-go basis. The cost is $29 per report, plus connect charges. Heretofore the only way to obtain this kind of information was to sign an annual contract with a credit reporting company, and most contracts start in the $1,000 to $2,000 range. NewsNet was the first, and at this writing the only, system to offer this service.

Online Tip: Want to try NewsNet for free right *now?* Fire up your system and dial your local packet switcher access number. If you don't know the number, you can phone the numbers listed below 24 hours a day for that information.

	Tymnet	Telenet
	(800) 336-0149	(800) 336-0437
Alaska and Hawaii:	(703) 442-0145	(703) 689-6400

Once you are connected, use the following procedure to sign on. (Telenet needs to have you hit <ENTER> twice before it sends you any prompts.) The characters in italics are what you type, and <ENTER> means "hit your <ENTER> or <RETURN> key." The demo is menu-driven, and you have the opportunity to test the system's commands, find out which newsletters are available in your field of interest, review an explanation of NewsNet's pricing, and so on. You may also elect to start your NewsNet subscription by filling out an application online. But you will probably be better off if you call NewsNet Customer Service during regular business hours, since they can give you an ID and password over the phone and have you online in about five minutes.

The demo begins by requesting your name and address, so that NewsNet can send you information. This is *not* a sign-up. Though it may not say so, the system will be satisfied with any random characters you enter if you do not wish to provide this information. You may exit the demo at any point by typing QUIT.

Tymnet	Telenet
1. Type *A*	1. Type *D1* <ENTER>
2. Type *NET* <ENTER>	2. Type *C 21566* <ENTER>
3. *ID FREEDEMO NEWSNET* <ENTER>	

Account-Related Matters

Subscriptions, Manuals, and Costs

A subscription to NewsNet is free. However, there is a $15 per month account maintenance or subscription fee. The minimum subscription period is 30 days. You may also choose to pay all of your monthly fees as an annual lump sum, in which case the cost is $120 (a savings of $60 over the monthly option). Or you can select a six-month subscription for an initial payment of $60 (a savings of $30).

NewsNet sometimes runs special promotions offering a certain amount of free time on the system to new subscribers. However, you should know that it has long been the company's policy to give all new subscribers at least $24 of free time, special offer or no. That's an hour at NewsNet's basic, 300-bit-per-second (bps) prime-time connect rate. However, what it really amounts to is a $24-discount on your first bill.

Four factors determine what you will be charged for using NewsNet: time of day, speed of communications, the particular publications you choose to read, and whether or not you are a subscriber to said publications. NewsNet uses the prime time (8 A.M. to 8 P.M. Eastern time) 300 bps rate of $24 an hour as its base. At 1200 bps that rate is doubled ($48), and at 2400 bps it is tripled ($72). During non-prime time the rates are $18, $36, and $54, respectively. These are the rates that apply when you are searching the system, scanning newsletter headlines, or generally doing anything else but actually reading a newsletter. Telecommunications costs are included.

When you do decide to read a publication, a royalty rate or "read premium" is added to the basic connect rate. These are set by the newsletter publishers themselves. They are always a multiple of 12 and prime and non-prime-time discounts do *not* apply. However, the doubling and tripling of charges due to higher communications speeds *do* apply. The good news is that in many cases, if you already subscribe to the printed version of a newsletter, you will be charged a lower read premium or no premium at all. You are then considered a "validated" subscriber to the newsletter, and it may be available to you at whichever NewsNet basic connect rate applies.

You can find out what any given newsletter will cost to read or obtain a price list covering every newsletter on the system while online. Rates are quoted for validated and non-validated subscribers at 300 bps during prime time. To determine the royalty being charged, subtract $24 from the quoted figure. To get the non-prime-time cost, add the royalty to the non-prime 300 bps rate of $18 an hour, and multiply by two for 1200 bps access and by three for 2400 bps.

Online Tip: This is a real quickie, but can save you so much money that it is worth highlighting. Your status vis-à-vis validation for a particular newsletter is completely in the hands of that newsletter's publisher. Sometimes, if you ask them politely, some newsletter publishers will validate you whether or not you subscribe to the print version of their product. Use the NewsNet feature that lets you send electronic mail to the newsletter's publisher, or get the publisher's name and address online using NewsNet's INFO command.

You may not meet with success. But since validation can save you literally hundreds of dollars annually on a newsletter that you read regularly, it is certainly worth a try.

You can sign up for NewsNet by simply calling the toll-free customer service number during regular East Coast business hours. Your ID and password will be issued on the spot. And you have a range of payment options. You can have your charges billed to your MasterCard or VISA. You can opt for CHECKFREE® (U.S. subscribers only) billing under which your payments are automatically deducted from your checking account. Or you can choose direct billing (for a one-time, non-refundable $25 application fee).

This businesslike approach to the online business is one of the things that makes NewsNet so appealing. Yet another example of this is the Corporate Account option. If your company has more than one News-Net subscriber, you can benefit from grouping them all together into the same account. One subscription costs $15 a month or $120 a year if paid annually. Under NewsNet's Corporate Account Plan, the second through tenth subscriptions cost $100 a year. The 11th through 20th cost $90 each. And so on. Every subscription after the 50th costs only $50 a year. Under this plan, a single bill is issued, but it includes an itemization of charges for each individual account.

The NewsNet manual is included with your subscription. Published in a size designed to fit a man's inside suit pocket, it consists of two separate booklets in a single vinyl folder. The first (about 60 pages) details how to use the system. The second (about 80 pages) provides a complete list of the newsletters on the system, including their access codes and a two- to three-sentence description of what they cover.

The system manual is well laid out and comprehensive. It tells you everything you need to know to use NewsNet effectively, including some advice on selecting search terms. A "quick-start guide" is included as a separate folder, and there is a ready reference card to keep near your machine.

Search-Related Matters

System and Search Language

NewsNet offers a blending of the command-driven and menu-driven approaches that might best be called "prompted-command mode." You can often stack commands in a single line once you know the system, or you can go step-by-step with NewsNet prompting you for the newsletter or industry group code, the date to scan, and so on. And unlike virtually any other system, when NewsNet conducts a search, it lets you know what it's doing. If you are searching a group of ten newsletters, for example, NewsNet will display either a period (no hits) or an exclamation point (signifying at least one hit) as it finishes with each newsletter.

The command language, too, offers a nice compromise between power and ease of use. You can use the Boolean operators AND, OR, and BUT NOT. You can do proximity searching (locate a word within a certain number of other words). You can search for a specific string of characters or words by enclosing the target phrase in quotation marks. A single search statement can be up to 76 characters long.

You can also specify truncation. Significantly, NewsNet never uses the information industry term "truncation." Instead it refers to searching on the basis of a partial keyword as using a "wildcard," a term most personal computer users are familiar with. The wildcard character is an asterisk (*).

NewsNet is obviously designed to allow a computer-using businessperson to sign on, type in a natural keyword or phrase, and retrieve the information relevant to it. There are no fields to worry about. No authors, indexing words or descriptors, or anything else. Just a fast full-text search for relevant keywords and phrases.

Problems with Headlines and Lack of Accession Numbers

There are only two major complaints one might make. The first concerns the descriptiveness of newsletter headlines. NewsNet conducts its search and then gives you the option of displaying the headlines of newsletter articles containing your keywords. Since the headlines are the main criteria you use to decide whether to actually read a portion of a newsletter, they should give you enough information to make that decision. Many of them do. But some of them don't. NewsNet's ANA-LYZE feature, which lists the number of hits in a given newsletter, offers a partial remedy. But the problem won't disappear until the newsletter writers themselves make their headlines and subheads more descriptive.

The second complaint concerns the problem of retrieving a specific hit once you have signed off and signed back on again. NewsNet is designed for immediate information delivery. You enter your search, and NewsNet responds with a menu listing the headlines of each newsletter story containing your keywords. You then read a given hit by entering a number from this ad hoc menu. The problem is that if you are interrupted in the middle of a session, there is no easy way to go back into the system and call up the information you did not get a chance to read earlier. There are no accession numbers for the records. If you have to sign off prematurely, you must either print or download the ad hoc menu before you leave, since it includes enough information to retrieve the articles again, or simply make a note of your search strategy and re-enter it the next time you sign on.

Customer Support

In general, however, NewsNet is a very satisfying system to use. Though there are undoubtedly exceptions, just about any businessperson, regardless of previous online experience, can quickly find useful, relevant information on NewsNet. There is thus small need for customer training or special software, and the company does not offer any. However, there is a LIBRARY function to let you read sample issues of almost any newsletter to get a feeling for what it covers. Time spent here is billed at the basic NewsNet rate, so it offers an economical way to learn to use the system. The NewsNet "Action Letter" is sent to subscribers each month. It contains announcements of new additions to the system, search and use tips, articles by the editors of individual newsletters, and other standard vendor newsletter fare.

Information Delivery

You can easily order a subscription to any newsletter on the system with the built-in ORDER function. And you can send electronic mail to newsletter publishers to request copies of back issues, should you need to see a picture or graph. Publishers' policies vary on what, if anything, they charge for this service. Basically, though, since NewsNet is a full-text database, offline printouts and similar information delivery topics do not apply. The system's default is to scroll continuously, but you can enter the PAGING command to get it to pause. Information is displayed in 80-column lines.

NewsNet does have an SDI service, however, and it is definitely worth looking into. It's called NewsFlash™, and it lets you enter up to ten SDI profiles, each of which can contain up to 70 characters. You can specify which newsletters or groups of newsletters you would like to have the system automatically search. You can use the AND (+) operator, truncation, and string search feature in your profile. There is no charge for storing your profiles on the system, and no charge for running them against every system update.

However, there is a charge of 37¢ for each hit. The system notifies you of your hits each time you sign on. At that point you can either read, erase, or SAVE them. The hits you save will be at the top of your NewsFlash list the next time you sign on. If you read them, you will be charged the applicable read rate for the relevant publication. One final point: The UPI, AP, and Reuters International newswires are available only through NewsFlash. You cannot search or read them as you would a newsletter.

Wilsonline

H. W. Wilson Company
950 University Avenue
(212) 588-8400

CUSTOMER SERVICE

(800) 622-4002
(800) 538-3888, in New York

Mon.–Fri.: 9:00 A.M.–8:00 P.M. Eastern
Sat.: 9:00 A.M.–5:00 P.M. Eastern

Hours of Operation
—All hours are given in Eastern time—

Available

Mon.–Sun.: 5:00 A.M.–3:00 A.M.

Not Available

Mon.–Sun.: 3:00 A.M.–5:00 A.M.

System may or may not be available 7:00 A.M. Sunday to 7:00 A.M. Monday, depending on maintenance requirements.

Access: Telenet and Tymnet. Telecommunications charges are extra, billed at $8 an hour for either packet switcher.

Connect Rate: Varies with the database and the subscription plan. Ranges from $50 to $65 an hour. There is no additional charge for 1200 bps communications, and there is no discount for non-prime time.

What's on the System?

Wilson may be the best-known name in library reference indexes. Indeed, if there are 25 or more journals devoted to a particular topic, Wilson probably publishes a comprehensive index of the topic. What's on the Wilsonline system are the electronic editions of about 15 of Wilson's 30 or more index volumes, as well as the Library of Congress MARC file (Chapter 12). The files include such well-known publications as the *Readers' Guide to Periodical Literature*, *Book Review Digest*, *Social Sciences Index*, and the *Art Index*. (See Figure 11.1.)

But Wilson is not without competition. As Barbara Quint reports in *DataBase End-User* magazine, wary of the reputation of Wilson's publications, many in the database industry simply assumed that the company would take its products online. When it became apparent that this would not happen anytime soon, Information Access Company produced its Magazine Index, a file designed to be directly competitive with the *Readers' Guide* (RG). At one point IAC even promised that its file would cover every publication in RG, plus several hundred more.

IAC has succeeded. Magazine Index (MI) covers over 400 publications. RG covers 182. The comparison would be less lop-sided if the number of journals covered in other Wilsonline databases were added to the RG figure. However, MI goes back a lot further, going back to 1976 in most cases and to 1959 for some journals. The RG database reaches back only to 1983. Other firms have also moved to seize the Wilson franchise.

Other Wilsonline databases begin in October 1984. They aren't useless by any means. But while a database of computer magazines or some other fast-changing topic may not have to offer extensive coverage, since so much of what was written two years ago is irrelevant today, this is definitely not the case with something like the Biography Index database (starts with July 1984) or Index to Legal Periodicals (starts August 1981). It is important to realize that the shallowness of coverage is far from a permanent condition. It can be remedied by creating a "backfile" to cover years an existing database does not include. And since Wilson has been in business since 1898, it could reach back a very long way. It is all but inconceivable that Wilson wouldn't do this at some time in the future.

Meantime, Wilson offers the least expensive way to obtain this kind of information. On DIALOG, for example, the Magazine Index sells for $84 an hour, plus display charges. On Wilsonline, the top rate for *Readers' Guide* is $55 ($25 for large deposit accounts), and there are no display charges.

_____ **Figure 11.1. Databases on Wilsonline** _____

Virtually all of the following databases correspond to index volumes published by the H. W. Wilson Company. More will undoubtedly be added in the future. To get a better idea of what you will find online, take a look at the printed versions in your local library. Be aware, however, that at this writing the electronic versions typically don't go back any further than August 1981, and most begin their coverage in 1983 or 1984.

Applied Science & Technology
   Index
Art Index
Bibliographic Index
Biography Index
Biological & Agricultural Index
Book Review Index
Business Periodicals Index
Cumulative Book Index
Education Index
General Science Index

Humanities Index
Index to Legal Periodicals
Library Literature
Readers' Guide to Periodical
   Literature—Social Sciences
   Index
LC/MARC File
Journal Directory
Publishers Directory
Name Authority File

Account-Related Matters

Subscriptions, System Manuals, and Usage Costs

A basic subscription to Wilsonline is free. There are no up-front payments and no continuing monthly minimums or account maintenance fees. You will, however, need a copy of the Wilson manual ($30). Billing is by direct invoice. This is what Wilson calls its "Section 4" or non-subscriber subscription. Sections 1 through 3 offer differing rates depending on whether you subscribe to the printed version of the index you are searching and whether you "subscribe" to Wilsonline, the company's term for deposit accounts. Altogether there are ten rates for using Wilsonline, reflecting the variety of possible combinations of these criteria. It's not a problem, though, since the rate card is well designed.

You have only to find the column that applies to you and forget about the rest.

As you might infer from the large number of deposit account options, Wilsonline was designed with librarians and corporate information centers in mind. The company's promotional literature is filled with references to "patrons," the name the library industry gives to customers. However, since one application Wilson envisions for its product is having patrons conduct their own searches, the manual and associated documentation couldn't be more complete.

The manual comes in a slipcased three-ring binder. (Your account number and password are shipped separately, usually a week or so later.) Its pages are "IBM/PC documentation size," and there are enough of them that with the tabbed dividers inserted the manual is a good inch and a half thick. It's well-written and well laid out, too, with different typestyles, boldface, and red highlighting for emphasis in certain sections. In addition, there is a 100-page booklet offering a variety of tutorials, a rate card, and a 16-page "Quick Reference Guide." If the documentation package is not a loss-leader, it is certainly a self-liquidating offering. It is difficult to see how Wilson can afford to sell it for $30. It puts most of the $50-manuals available in this industry to shame.

Usage costs are simple. Assuming you are a Section 4 subscriber, you will pay $45, $55, or $65 an hour, depending on the database you access. Add $8 an hour for telecommunications, and you've got it. There are no non-prime-time discounts. No 1200 bps premiums. No display charges of any kind.

Search-Related Matters

Search Language, Software, and Training

The search language is powerful. Wilsonline uses the National Library of Medicine's ELHILL software, a program based on an early version of SDC's ORBIT. The language isn't going to set the world on fire, but it has been "user friendly-ized" and it does have some nice features. You can get both brief summaries and more extensive explanations for virtually any command at anytime while you are online. As on ORBIT, you can rename any existing Wilsonline command to one of your liking. And you can tell the system to print a record with fully typed field labels ("AUTHOR" instead of "AU").

But perhaps the most important feature is Wilsonline's cross-file searching capability. You can run the identical search on up to eight different files simultaneously. You don't have to run it once, display records, move to a different database, run it again, and so on. Of course, you'll be charged the hourly connect-time rate for each database you specify. You can also save search strategies and store them on the system at no additional charge.

Wilson has issued a front-end software package called Wilsearch™, but it is clearly designed for library use. There is an annual licensing fee of $150 per disk, for example, and a special rate structure that charges a library by "searches" (one search is defined as ten hits or references).

Training is available in one-day sessions at $60 per person. If you attend a session and buy the manual, the charge for both is $75. (You save $15.) For more information and schedules, contact Customer Service.

Information Delivery

There is no SDI feature or document delivery. You can, however, request offline printouts. The cost is 20¢ per printout, with a minumum $10 charge for printouts ordered in any one session. Postage is included in the price and printouts are mailed within 24 hours.

Part III

—THE INFORMATION—

Introduction:
How to Evaluate Any Database

The chapters in Part III are designed to give you a hands-on introduction to the databases likely to be of most interest to you. In all, nearly 100 are covered to one degree or another. However, as the database directories cited in Appendix B can attest, these 100 represent only a small fraction of what is available. To aid you in exploring others on your own, here are six questions to ask to bring yourself up-to-speed quickly.

1. Where does the information come from?

This is the first question to ask when encountering a database for the first time, because the information is the essence of the product. But you also need to have some idea of the source of the material to know how to search the database effectively and how to view the validity of your results.

2. How far back does the coverage go?

It's important to pay attention to dates of coverage because it would not make sense to look for something known to have occurred in 1981 if the database starts its coverage in 1983. As noted previously, the version of a database on one vendor's system may not go back as far as the version of the identical database on a different vendor's system.

3. How frequently is the database updated?

Again, this is a crucial means of gauging what information will be in the database and what may not yet have been added. Similarly, it can be important to know the average lag time between the appearance of the printed form of a document and its appearance in the database. Updating frequency and lag time can vary considerably depending on the database producer.

Note that on DIALOG all databases have an "update" field. If you want to see how often a database has *actually* been updated, as opposed to the frequency claimed by the IP, key in EXPAND UD= and look at the results. You'll see the date of each update and the number of records added each time. Similarly, if you want to search just the most recent update SELECT UD = 9999.

4. What fields can you search?

As you know from Chapter 5, it is absolutely crucial to know what fields are available for searching, the kind of information you are likely to find in each field, and whether the field must be searched by phrase [WHITE HOUSE] or by word [WHITE(W)HOUSE]. These vital points of access may vary with the vendor, and the vendor's documentation is your best source of information.

5. Is there a controlled vocabulary or a set of special codes you can use?

Controlled vocabulary words and product, event, SIC, MSA, and other codes can be a pain in the neck. But generally the time spent looking up the proper word or code pays off in much more satisfactory search results. The EXPAND, STEM, and similar commands discussed in Chapter 5 can make the code-selection process much quicker and easier. Learn these commands and use them liberally.

6. What search aids are available?

Ultimately, every piece of information you can obtain about a given database is a search aid. We have provided an address or contact point for virtually every database discussed in the following chapters. Use them. Contact the database producer for brochures, literature, and information on thesauri, manuals, and special search tutorials. Many IPs also conduct regular training sessions.

• • •

The majority of the chapters that follow are organized along the lines of types or sources of information—books, magazines, news media, etc. Obviously, however, when you are on an information quest you will want to tap databases from several or even all of these chapters. A special section in Chapter 15, called "Using the Power," is designed to show you the kinds of things you can do when you use a variety of databases synergistically.

Finally, to save both space and sanity, we have not attempted to produce a rigorous list of all the vendors that carry each database. Nor have we made a distinction in most cases among the databases available on the main DIALOG system, those on DIALOG's Knowledge Index, and those on the DIALOG Business Connection. We have treated the various BRS systems this way as well.

The reason is simple. Database availability is such a fast-moving target that it would be pointless to attempt such a list. The electronic universe is constantly reconfiguring itself, so please do not assume that because a particular vendor is not cited as one of those offering a particular database, the database isn't available on that system. Instead, as we have recommended throughout, call the vendor for the latest information.

...12...

Books:
Any Book, Any Subject, Anywhere in the World

T his chapter has twin goals. It will show you how to find any book you want. But it will also help you make an easy transition from searching for information using traditional paper-based materials to searching for it online.

Books are a good conceptual bridge between the traditional and the electronic because they are a form of information everyone can relate to. And since you undoubtedly had to learn about bibliographic listings and library card catalogs in high school, you already know a lot about how the databases discussed here work, for they are essentially electronic card catalogs.

This kind of familiarity with the source material and with the way it is indexed is a real advantage because it frees you to focus on the unfamiliar, electronic aspects of information retrieval. And that's good, because what you learn here about locating books online can easily be applied to every other database, whether it covers magazines, newspapers, or source material that is *not* familiar to you. Thus, if you've never conducted an online search before, you may want to read this chapter even if you don't plan to look for a book anytime soon.

Why Reinvent the Wheel?

Books are the repositories of the accumulated knowledge of our race. Which is to say that basically books save each of us from having to reinvent the wheel every time we want to accomplish something, whether it's putting together a corporate merger or a crazy-quilt down comforter. Broad statements are hazardous, but at this point in human history it's a pretty safe bet that regardless of what you want to do or the goal you wish to achieve, others have been there and done it before.

And at least one of them has written a book about it, a book that can save you a lot of time and trouble if you can lay your hands on it. In this chapter we'll show you how to do exactly that.

We'll start with some nonelectronic suggestions and then show you how to tap the online power of the Library of Congress and *Books In Print* to locate relevant titles. Included as part of that section is an explanation of how to use DIALOG's EXPAND and ?FIELDn commands to improve your search results. This explanation applies to all DIALOG databases. Next we'll look at a database that covers books dating back to the 1500s. Then we'll show you how to obtain copies of the titles you locate electronically from information brokers and the worldwide network of booksellers. Finally, we'll finish up with a brief section on accessing online book reviews.

A Foundation of Published Knowledge

The first and most important point to be aware of is that old books never die. Thanks to an acid-based paper-making process introduced in the last century, over the years they slowly burn away. Thus it doesn't make a great deal of difference whether the book you need is still on the shelves of your local bookstore or not. Bookstores regularly return books to publishers for credit. The book you want may have been pushed off the shelf and into a book mailer by one of the more than 50,000 titles the American publishing industry turns out each year. At this very moment it may be resting comfortably in the publisher's warehouse waiting for you to order it.

Of course if a given title has gotten *too* comfortable and hasn't moved for a period of time, the publisher may say, "Okay book, get out of my space!" and declare the title out of print. The remaining copies will be sold at Woolworths or sent to the pulping machine to be turned into the latest Judith Krantz masterwork. But even the out-of-print stigma does not present a major problem in most cases. No book, not even the worst, thinly veiled autobiographical first novel, has ever been published that didn't sell at least one copy. And as long as that copy physically exists, there is a chance that you can obtain it.

Certainly some books are much harder to find than others, but there are people who have made a profession out of locating and supplying out-of-print books. As we'll see later, for example, it isn't uncommon for a single out-of-print specialist to have an inventory of over 500,000 books or more. There is also a company that will photocopy, bind, and send you any one of the more than 100,000 books in its permanent inventory. In short, there is a vast foundation of published knowledge out there, available to anyone who knows how to look for it.

Pick Up the Phone

As noted in Chapter 5, the prime directive of information retrieval is "Don't go online unless you have to." This rule is especially applicable when you are looking for a book, since no other category of source material is so thoroughly cataloged and indexed or so widely available. If you want a book on a particular topic, call your local public library first. A relatively easy search of the card catalog will quickly give you an idea of how extensive the library's holdings are in that subject area.

Next, call your local bookseller. Nearly every bookstore in the country (and most libraries) has a copy of R. R. Bowker's *Books in Print* (BIP) series. This is the primary reference work of the bookselling trade. Your local bookseller will be able to search by author, by title, or by subject, since there is a set of BIP volumes for each of these areas.

The advantage of taking these steps first is immediacy. If the library's got the book, you may be able to have it in your hands in hours. If the book is listed in one of the three major BIP sets of volumes, you can order it. Delivery time depends on whether the book is in the book jobber's warehouse or whether it must be ordered directly from the publisher. In either case, your local bookseller can help you locate the titles you want and order them for you.

The Electronic Alternatives

If your needs are confined to information published in the last three or four years, you'll almost certainly find the relevant books in the printed reference works. But of course these volumes contain only a small fraction of what is available. To do a truly comprehensive search, you've got to go online.

The two major book databases in the electronic universe are LC MARC, created and maintained by the Library of Congress, and Books In Print, a product of the R. R. Bowker Company. Between them they cover virtually every book published in America since 1968. A third database, REMARC, covers everything from before 1900 through 1967. Each of the two major databases has its own personality, and each offers information and points of access not found in the other.

Books In Print Online

At this writing, the Books In Print (BIP) database is available on systems operated by DIALOG and BRS. It is the electronic equivalent of the master *Books in Print* volumes mentioned above. But it also includes *Paperbound Books in Print, Books Out-of-Print,* and *Forthcoming Books,* a monthly subject, title, and author guide to books scheduled for publication within the next six months. That's the core of the collection. Bowker likes to say that its database includes all of the information in the most current printed editions of a dozen other book reference volumes, including *Medical Books in Print, Children's Books in Print,* and so on. But in reality these books are just subsets of the core volumes.

BIP online currently contains records for more than one million titles produced by nearly 16,000 U.S. publishers, plus over a quarter of a million titles that have been declared out of print since 1979. Bowker adds anywhere from 75,000 to 95,000 new titles a year through monthly updates. Updates are more frequent during peak periods.

The defining characteristic of the BIP database is the fact that it is derived from publications intended for use by bookpeople. It's a directory for men and women who are "in the biz" as it were and need a quick and easy way to locate the books their customers want to order. Consequently, BIP online contains information on how a book is bound (trade, paperbound, text edition, etc.), what it costs, and whether the book is "Out of Stock" "Out of Print," or an "Active Entry" (available for ordering). Similarly, when it tells you that the publisher of a book is, say, Timescape, it usually does not go on to mention that this is an imprint of Simon & Schuster of New York. Booksellers usually know the imprints of the major publishing houses, and they have separate directories to guide them when they don't.

Regardless of the system you use, the best documentation for using BIP is the 46-page DIALOG database chapter. BIP is File 470 on that system, and you must order from DIALOG. Should you need additional information, the database producer can be reached at:

Electronic Products Division
R. R. Bowker Co.
205 East 42nd Street
New York, NY 10017
(800) 323-3288
(212) 916-1727

LC MARC: Library of Congress MAchine Readable Cataloging
The Library of Congress database, in contrast, is more of a librarian's database. Consequently, as we'll see in a moment, it contains a lot of information likely to be of interest to professional catalogers.

Books enter the catalog of the Library of Congress (LC) by being submitted by their publisher. But since the Register of Copyrights is also part of LC and since LC maintains a cataloging and publications division, books may enter the system through those avenues as well. Usually mass market paperbacks (the type sold at newsstands, airports, and supermarkets, as well as at bookstores) are not included. Nor are paperback reprints of hardcover volumes already in the collection. Trade paperbacks, like the book you are now reading, are included, however.

It is important to remember that LC is first and foremost a library created for the use of Congress. Its librarians are charged with developing collections of books that representatives and senators and their committees are likely to need. Consequently, while it often seems that LC contains every book in the country, that isn't necessarily so.

With over two million records at this writing and monthly updates containing 18,000 records or more (216,000 records a year), LC MARC certainly comes close, however. Available on DIALOG, the database covers two files. File 426 includes books published since 1980. File 427 includes books from 1968 through 1979. The database starts with 1968 for English language books. But it also contains books in every other major language, including titles in "Romanized" Korean and Chinese. The start date for foreign-language books varies, beginning with French in 1973.

The Subject at Hand

Because of its size and influence, it was natural for the Library of Congress, working closely with the American Library Association, to establish and promulgate cataloging standards. Indexing and cataloging information is something most of us never have to think about. But if information is to be retrievable, it is crucial to have rules about how it will be filed.

For example, how should books by Mark Twain by filed? Under Mark Twain or Samuel Clemens? What subject headings should be used and how should each be phrased? "Corporation reports" or "Annual reports, Corporate"? "Animal nutrition" or "Animals, food habits of"? Is "Baby boom" a legitimate subject category? Should "Black History" be cross-referenced under "Afro-Americans" or "blacks?" And so on. Right or wrong, for better or for worse, *somebody* has to decide. And for decades the Library of Congress has assumed that burden.

The LC Cataloging Distribution Service publishes various "authority" volumes offering comprehensive lists of the cataloging terms that have been decided upon. (The system currently followed is called "ACR 2" for "Anglo-American Cataloging Rules, 2nd edition." ACR 2 is also used by the GPO Monthly Catalog database discussed in Chapter 18.) The Name Authorities, for example, contain personal and corporate names, uniform titles, geographic names, and so on in the format used by the Library of Congress. Similarly, the subject authority, two volumes called Library of Congress Subject Headings (LCSH), contains the words, phrases, and formats LC uses in its subject cataloging.

These are the *same* subject headings you will use when searching LC MARC and Books in Print online. R. R. Bowker used to publish a thesaurus of subject and other terms for searching its BIP database. But it no longer does so. The company says it now follows *LCSH*. And they aren't the only ones. All of the Information Access Company databases (Magazine Index, NEWSEARCH, Management Contents, etc.) we will be looking at in succeeding chapters use the LC subject headings as well.

After a six-year hiatus, the tenth edition of this two-volume, 2,600-page reference work covering all headings current through 1984 was published in 1986 for $75. An annual supplement covered terms established in 1985. The eleventh edition, scheduled for 1987, will cover everything through 1986 and signal the end of the annual supplements. To place an order, request a free catalog of other LC offerings, and for more information about the LC MARC database, contact:

> Cataloging Distribution Service
> Library of Congress
> Washington, D.C. 20541
> (202) 287-6100

Online Tip: There is no question but that the *LSCH* volumes are a good value, and the Cataloging Distribution Service has worked hard to hold the price to $75. But the volumes are so huge that you may find they represent subject-heading overkill for your purposes. Consequently, you might want to consider ordering *The Subject Guide to IAC Databases* instead. The cost is $85 ($72.25 if you take IAC training), and at 575 pages it is much more manageable.

The guide isn't as exhaustive as *LSCH* and since IAC must be responsive to the rapidly changing subjects reported by newspapers and magazines, the company has supplemented authorized LC headings with terms of its own. But you may find that it gives you everything you need, and it has the advantage of being able to do double duty as a reference for both book databases and IAC magazine databases. For more information, contact:

> Information Access Company, Inc.
> 11 Davis Drive
> Belmont, CA 94002
> (800) 227-8431
> (415) 591-2333

Using LC Subject Headings

The *LCSH* volumes are useful because they help focus your thinking and suggest words to search on that might not normally occur to you. You might not think to search on "Domicile of corporations," for example, or on "Tort liability of charitable organizations." But those are both authorized LC subject headings, and all you would have to do on DIALOG is enter SELECT followed by one of those phrases without the quotation marks to locate a set of relevant titles.

Unless you plan to do a lot of book searching, however, you can probably get by without buying the *LCSH* volumes. Try a search on the topic you are looking for using your best guess as to how it should be phrased. If your results aren't satisfactory—if you get too many hits or no hits at all—call the database vendor's Customer Service number for assistance. You might also call your local librarian. Even the smallest libraries typically have the *LCSH* volumes, usually over by the card catalog, so someone should be able to help you come up with the correct phrase or phrases.

—— **Figure 12.1. The Fields of the LC MARC Database** ——

As noted in Chapter 5, regardless of the DIALOG database you happen to be in at the moment, you can get a list of all the searchable fields of any database with the ?FIELDn command. Enter the question mark, the word FIELD, and the DIALOG file number for the database. The same information can be found on the file's Bluesheet, but a printout of the online field list makes a convenient quick-reference guide. We've added a line space or two and some underlining to make the list more readable.

?FIELD426

FIELD426,427: LC MARC

Prefix-Coded Fields (EXPAND or SELECT)

Field Name	Example
Author	AU = STANSKY, PETER?
International Standard Book Number	BN = 0691066167
Classification Number	CA = NK1142.S7 1985
Conference Location	CL = (NEW(W)YORK)
	CL = ADDIS ABABA

Corporate Source	CS = (ART(W)GALLERY)
	CS = BABYLON THEATER
Conference Title	CT = (AMERIC?(W)LIT?)
Conference Year	CY = 1976
Document Type	DT = MONOGRAPH
Edition	ED = (BILINGUAL(W)ED)
Geographic Location	GL = (UNITED(W)STATES)
	GL = GREAT PLAINS
Government Docu-	
ment Number	GP = LC 42.2-T 32
Intellectual Level	IL = JUVENILE
Language	LA = GERMAN
LC Card Number	LC = 84042558
Named Person#	NA = MORRIS, WILLIAM
Publisher	PU = (PRINCE?(W)UNIV?)
Publication Year	PY = 1985
Report Number	RN = 003-003-01687-0
Series	SE = (AMERI?(W)CIVIL?)
Summary Language	SL = ENGLISH
Update	UD = 8504

#Also searchable in the Basic Index

Basic Index Fields & (SELECT only)

Field	Example
Descriptor*	DECORA?(W)ARTS—DE
	ART "AND" SOCIETY/DE
Named Person	MORRIS(N)WILLIAM/NA
Note	THEORY(F)CRITIC?/NT
Title +	WILLIAM(W)MORRIS/TI
	RESEARCH METHOD?/TI

&If no suffix is specified all Basic
   Index fields are searched.
*Also /DF
+Also /TF

Sorting in Files 426,427 is also
available online or offline by using
the fields AU, CA, CS, LC, PY, TI.

SORT 5/ALL/CA,D
PRINT 10/5/1-45/AU

LC MARC and BIP: A Model Database Comparison

Throughout this book we have tried to emphasize the fact that every database is a unique product. The subject could be books, marketing statistics, or financial information—it doesn't matter—every database is different. Each has its own strengths and weaknesses and its own personality. This section compares the book listings in LC MARC and BIP. But it is also intended to illustrate how one database can differ from and at the same time complement another. Use it as an example of the kinds of differences to look for when considering any set of databases.

Search One or Both?

As mentioned, the Books In Print database is available on systems run by both BRS and DIALOG. But in addition to being on DIALOG as LC MARC, the LC database is also available on ORBIT as LC LINE, and on Wilsonline as the Library of Congress MARC Book File. As you read this, it may be on other systems as well. (LC makes its main database and several subsets available on nine-track tape at very reasonable prices.)

You don't *have* to search both databases, of course. But it's important for anyone who is looking for a book online to be aware of the different personalities of the two files. As a cataloger's database, for example, LC MARC typically doesn't contain a book's price unless the publisher has printed it on the title page or on the opposite (verso) side of that page with the copyright information. Nor will you find notations on whether the book is out of print. But since both of these pieces of information are important to booksellers, you will almost always find them in the Books in Print database.

To get a feeling for the differences between BIP and LC MARC, compare the following two records downloaded from DIALOG. The first shows how BIP lists *The Citadel of the Autarch*, a science fiction novel by Gene Wolfe. The second shows the listing for the identical book on LC MARC.

From Books In Print:

```
1321912    0472795XX
The Citadel of the Autarch
Wolfe, Gene
Series: The Book of the New Sun Ser.,; Vol. 4
Timescape
PB 01/1983
```

Trade $15.50
ISBN: 0-671-45251-7
Status: Out of print (08-85)

From LC MARC:

1669837   LCCN: 82005964
The citadel of the autarch / Gene Wolfe
Wolfe, Gene.
Series: His Book of the new Sun ; v. 4; Wolfe, Gene.
New York : Timescape Books : Distributed by Simon
and Schuster, c1983   317 p. ; 22 cm.
Publication Date(s): 1983
Place of Publication: New York
ISBN: 0671452517
LC Call No.: PS3573.052C5 1983 Dewey Call No.: 813/.54
Languages: English
Document Type: Monograph

Both listings represent their respective database's "full record" formats, so what you see here is everything there is on this particular edition of this book. How do we know that the two records refer to the identical volume? We compare the ISBN numbers, two fields that both records have in common.

Online Tip: ISBN stands for "International Standard Book Number," a classifying system promoted by the International Standards Organization (ISO) in Geneva. The ISBN is a ten-digit number that serves as sort of a Universal Product Code for books.

The first digit is the group identifier, and it signifies a particular country, nation, or language. All English language books, for example, have ISBNs starting with 0. The next set of numbers is the publisher's identifier. The third set is the unique code number of a given book. The final number is a check digit used in data entry.

Since there can be no more than ten digits, large publishers are usually assigned short publisher ID numbers, leaving room for a larger number of book identifiers. R. R. Bowker is the ISO's appointed representative in the United States and is responsible for administering the ISBN program. It issues each publisher a block of numbers to be used as book identifiers, and in the case of publishers who are not part of the system, Bowker assigns a provisional ISBN to their volumes. The check digit is calculated with a modulus 11 formula and is designed to catch errors when ISBNs are keyed into properly programmed systems.

Notice how much more detailed the LC MARC record is. Indeed, LC MARC records on DIALOG may have as many as 24 fields, as you can see from Figure 12.1. Nor does this particular BIP record include the book's Library of Congress Catalog Number (LCCN), though as you can see from the first line of the LC MARC record, the book obviously has one. At the same time, the LC MARC record makes no mention of price or of the fact that this particular edition is a trade paperback or that it is out of print.

Online Tip: Both of these records were retrieved by searching their respective databases on the "Author" field. However, in one of those inexplicable—and inexcusable—quirks, BIP and LC MARC require a tiny difference in format that can really trip you up if you aren't aware of it. On BIP, you can enter SELECT AU = Wolfe, Gene but on LC MARC you must enter AU = Wolfe, Gene. (same as BIP except for the final period) if you hope to meet with success.

Only the LC MARC author field works this way. And the only way to beat it is to either know the correct format of the author's name and enter it with a final period or use the DIALOG truncation (wildcard) character, the question mark, when searching for an author's name (AU = Wolfe, Gene?).

To be sure, this little item is mentioned in DIALOG's LC MARC database chapter, but it isn't explained very clearly. Sometimes it really does seem as if there's a conspiracy to make it as difficult as possible for a person to retrieve online information. There isn't, of course. It's just another manifestation of the not-invented-here-we'll-do-things-our-own-way-thanks syndrome familiar to any computer software user. But at times you really do want to bop somebody.

The two databases complement each other in other ways as well. Sometimes, for whatever reasons, LC MARC will contain titles not found in BIP and vice versa. When we searched BIP with the command SELECT AU = WOLFE, GENE we got 25 hits. When we did the identical search on LC MARC, we got only 10 hits. But among them was this record displayed here in DIALOG's "tagged" format (Format 4 in this database):

```
FN-   DIALOG LC MARC FILE 426
AN-   9015610
LC-   83156127
```

TI-   Quicks around the zodiac : a farce / by Fritz Leiber ; with an afterword by Gene Wolfe ;
      illustrated by Alicia Austin
AU-   <Main Entry> Leiber, Fritz, 1910-
AU-   <Added Entry> Wolfe, Gene.; Austin, Alicia.
IM-   New Castle, Va (Rte. 2, Box 293, New Castle 24127) :; Cheap Street, cl-983.
PH-   25, [4] p. : ill. ; 23 cm.
PY-   1983
PU-   <Place> Virginia
CA-   <LC> PS3523.E4583Q5 1983
CA-   <Dewey> 818/ .5407
LA-   English
DT-   Monograph
NT-   Wolfe's afterword, dated Oct. 1982, has caption: Vunce around der momma's kitchen /
      by Hans Katzenjammer.; "There were twenty-seven lettered presentation copies
      reserved for private distribution. Ninety-eight ordinary edition copies were handsewn
      into wrappers of Strathmore Rhododendron cover with Japanese silk tissue
      endpapers . . ."--P. [28]

We checked, and this book is not in the Books In Print database in
any edition. The book referenced here is obviously a collector's item
published by a small press in New Castle, Virginia. Significantly, the
LC MARC record gives you the information you need to contact the
publisher.

The notes field (NT) contains a comment by the LC cataloger pointing
out unique features. In other records the notes field will contain the
names of individual book chapters, the titles of the poems or short stories, a one- or two-sentence summary of the work, and other information that can give you a better idea of what the book is all about.

REMARC

When You've Got to Get Back in Time
The MARC format was established and the database begun in 1968 by
what was then called the Card Division of the Library of Congress to
help automate the production of catalog cards for various libraries subscribing to that LC service.

But as everyone knows, there was a whole lot of publishing going on
prior to 1968. Indeed, it is estimated that the Library of Congress contains 5.2 million non-MARC cataloging records. To make *these* records
available in magnetic form, REMARC (REtrospective MARC) was created. This is an ongoing project now supervised by UTLAS International. This is the University of Toronto Library Automation System.
Its American subsidiary is UTLAS USA, Inc. The firm acquired the
Carrollton Press, the original REMARC database producer. The

UTLAS unit responsible for REMARC is in Berkeley, California, and can be reached at (800) 523-0449 or (415) 841-9442.

REMARC is divided into five files on DIALOG, starting with File 421 (pre-1900) through File 425, which starts in 1970. At this writing, these files include more than four million records. The pre-1900 file includes some 836 titles from the sixteenth century, over 17,000 titles from the seventeenth century, and literally millions more from then on.

These facts about REMARC aren't published anywhere, but the information was easy to assemble. Although the DIALOG REMARC database chapter doesn't say so, we knew from a database directory that REMARC included works from the 1500s on. To find out how *many* sixteenth-century books it contains, all that was necessary was to enter a search on the PY (publication year) field and look at the results. For example, keying in SELECT PY = 15? retrieved a set containing 836 hits representing every record of a book with a publication date beginning with "15," which is to say, any date from 1500 through 1599.

Among the earliest records in the database are a Spanish hymnary, a German woodcut pamphlet extolling the virtues of Brazil, and this:

```
0203657    LCCN: 52046851
Coniuratio malignorum spirituum
Uniform Title: Coniuratio malignorum spirituum
[Rome, Eucharius Silber, 1500 [8] 1. 14cm.
Place of Publication: Italy
LC Call No.: DG804.M65 (Rare Bk. Coll.)
Languages: Italian
Document Type: Monograph
Descriptors: Exorcism
```

How to Get Copies of the Books You Locate

The second point illustrated by this REMARC record is that it provides all of the information needed to track down a copy of the actual book. We know the book's title, its author, who published it, where and when, and how many pages it contains. Generally, that's more than enough information for an out-of-print book dealer to go on.

There are lots of ways to obtain copies of the books your searches of LC MARC, BIP, and REMARC turn up. Obviously, if a book is still in print, you can order a copy or borrow it from a library. But if it is out of print, there are a number of other alternatives.

Use an Information Broker

The easiest is to ask an information broker to obtain a copy for you. On DIALOG you can KEEP an individual record and enter the command ORDER followed by the name of the document supplier or information broker you have previously chosen from the DIALOG Yellowsheets. That will automatically transmit the record and your name and account information to the selected supplier. Or you can print out the information and telephone the broker you normally use.

There are a lot of advantages to this approach. The broker will probably contact an out-of-print book dealer. Since these dealers often specialize in a particular kind of book, the broker's knowledge of which one to contact to fill your request could be important. It also frees you to let the broker worry about financial arrangements with the dealer.

Contact an Out-of-Print Book Dealer

The disadvantage, of course, is that using a broker could be one of the more expensive alternatives, since both the broker and the dealer have to make a profit. Thus, you might want to contact an out-of-print book dealer yourself. There are thousands of people in this profession, and it's not too difficult to tap into the informal network they maintain.

Some dealers operate as more or less specialized information brokers. That is, if they don't have the book themselves, they will do their best to track it down for you. Usually these dealers prepare a "want list" containing the title, author, publisher, and date of a book and mail it to their contacts each month. Other dealers maintain a large inventory that they will gladly check against your request, but generally don't do any searching. Still others don't have much stock but specialize in searching. Some will do a single search, while others will search continuously over a period of years. And as you might expect, some dealers specialize in a particular kind of book or books published in a certain time period.

Elliot Ephraim, a dealer who's been in the business since 1957, offers some fascinating insights into the profession. Mr. Ephraim has over 500,000 volumes of all types in stock, but he and his associates will also search for a title for up to five years. His contacts "range from retirees with a couple of boxes of books that they've collected over the years and kept in their garage to people who have 100 books in a carpeted gallery somewhere, each of which is priced at $1,000 or more. If they send us even one book a year, we will continue to send them our want-list."

Interestingly, according to Mr. Ephraim, "Only the people who handle books as a marginal business or hobby are going to be able to take the time to look at the 12-page list we send out. Someone who has a very busy storefront bookshop in New York or Chicago isn't going to have the time to look at it. So unfortunately, we can't always communicate with as many people as we would like to communicate with.

"Some dealers have suggested networking inventories into a large database, but that's never going to work because people who deal in used or out-of-print books are all individualists. They tend to be a bit ornery about safeguarding their privacy, and they don't want anyone to know how they operate or what their acquisition procedures are. It's really a very tight-lipped thing. They'll chat with each other at a convention, but they don't give away their secrets about how they obtain their books or to whom they sell."

The Ideal Customer

We asked Mr. Ephraim to sketch what he considers the ideal customer. "That's easy. It's a large research library who sends us a list of books with a ship-and-bill order good for three to five years. The worst customer is someone who calls up looking for a book he needed yesterday who wants to get it at a used-book price. It is important for people to understand that there is a premium that comes along with a search for an out-of-print book."

Mr. Ephraim says that a typical price would be $10 to $20 for paper copies and $35 to $45 for hardcover books. "But it's an imperfect market. The same book priced at 25¢ at a roadside stand in Arkansas may be in a Madison Avenue bookshop at $300. The price also depends on the quality of the actual volume. If it is missing its cover or if it has been written in, it is obviously going to sell for less than a mint copy."

A search can take anywhere from a few days to several years. Much depends on who published the book and when. A trade book published by a major house within the last 20 to 30 years is generally the easiest to find. Expensive technical books of the sort usually purchased by libraries are among the most difficult, since they don't generally circulate in the out-of-print book market.

Mr. Ephraim says that most dealers require advance payment from individuals. And he suggests preauthorizing the dealer to buy a book if it is within a certain price range. "Preauthorization allows a dealer to capture a book as soon as there is a nibble. If the dealer has to call you and you have to deliberate a week or so or if you are on vacation, the book is usually gone by the time you decide to buy it."

Mr. Ephraim probably has the largest collection of out-of-print books in the nation. You can contact him at:

> Mr. Elliot Ephraim
> Elliot's Books
> P.O. Box 6
> Northford, CT 06472
> (203) 484-2184, weekdays between
> 10 A.M. and 5 P.M., Eastern time

Dealer Directories

There are lots of directories of out-of-print and secondhand book dealers. Two of the best are those issued by Moretus Press and by Sheppard Press, Ltd., of London. You may be able to find them at a library, but in case you can't here are both the titles and publisher contact information:

Directory of Specialized American Bookdealers
Compiled by the staff of *American Book Collector Magazine.*
344 pages. $35. Moretus Press.

Moretus Press, Inc.
274 Madison Avenue
New York, NY 10016
(212) 685-2250

Book Dealers in North America
A Directory of Dealers in Secondhand & Antiquarian Books in Canada
& the United States of America by The Sheppard Press, Ltd.
371 pages. $25. Distributed in the U.S. by Europa.

Online Tip: The Sheppard Press of London specializes in books dealing with books. And in addition to the title cited above, it publishes directories of book dealers in different countries. The publisher's ISBN number is 900661, and you can use this knowledge to download a complete list of the books it has issued.

For example, if you were to sign on to BRS/BRKTHRU and select the Books In Print database (BBIP on that system) you could enter the following command with the following results:

```
S1 → 0-900661$.pr.
A1    23 DOCUMENTS FOUND
```

This tells BRS to search the PR (price) field for an ISBN number beginning with 0-90061 followed by any number of numbers. The BBIP page in the BRKTHRU manual explains that field and what it contains. The response means that there are 23 books published by The Sheppard Press, Ltd., in the Books In Print database. The BRKTHRU menus will prompt you through displaying any and all documents retrieved in the "answer" (A1).

UMI's Books On Demand Service

Finally, you should know about a nifty service offered by University

Microfilms International (UMI). As mentioned in Part I, with over 9,000 copyright-cleared magazine titles in its collection, UMI's Article Clearinghouse is one of the leading document delivery services. But UMI has another division called Books on Demand (BOD). BOD will send you a photocopy of any of the more than 100,000 out-of-print books in its collection.

Books are copied on acid-free paper and delivered within 30 days. The cost is 25¢ per page, including paper binding. Cloth covers are available for $6 extra per book. The minimum charge is $20 and the maximum is $160. (Microform copies are available for some titles at half the price of the photocopy.) Shipping within the United States and Canada is billed at applicable rates. Shipping outside the U.S. and Canada is 15% extra. Prepayment is required for individuals, but you can use your Visa, MasterCard, or American Express card.

You should probably check with a used-book dealer first, since it will always be cheaper to buy a secondhand book than to pay UMI to photocopy it for you. However, to be prepared for all eventualities, you should also contact UMI for more information. We suggest asking for information on *both* the UMI Article Clearinghouse and the Books On Demand service. Here is how to contact them:

University Microfilms International
300 North Zeeb Road
Ann Arbor, MI 48106
From the continental U.S.:
(800) 521-0600, for BOD information
(800) 732-0610, for Article Clearinghouse information

From Canada:
(800) 343-5299 (ask for UMI)

From Michigan and everywhere else: (313) 761-4700

How to Access Book Reviews Online

Just as a lathe operator uses different tools to create different patterns in the shaft of metal or wood he happens to be turning, you can use different databases as tools to achieve your goals. Suppose, for example, that you have searched LC MARC or BIP for books on a particular topic. You've now got a printout of, say, 15 titles dating from 1972 to the present. What you don't have is a ghost of an idea of which books on your list are worth pursuing and which are not likely to serve your needs. What should you do?

The Book Review Index *Database*

If you're on DIALOG it's so easy it's sinful. Simply key in BEGIN 137 to get yourself into the *Book Review Index* database (File 137 on that system) and enter SELECT AU = LNAME, FNAME, where the "names" are the last and first names of the author of the book or books you are curious about. If you want to do it by book title, enter WORD(w)WORD(w)WORD and so on, where each "WORD" is in the title.

What you'll retrieve is a set of hits containing a reference for every review of the target book published in approximately 400 periodicals and newspapers since 1969. For example, if you wanted to locate reviews of Hofstadter's prize-winning book *Godel, Escher, Bach,* you might do the following:

```
?SELECT GODEL(W)ESCHER(W)BACH
        1    40 GODEL(W)ESCHER(W)BACH

? TYPE 1/5/1

1010742
Godel, Escher, Bach
HOFSTADTER, Douglas R
Reviewed in : Village Voice Literary Supplement p16
Oct 1981
```

This means that at the time the search was done there were 40 reviews of the book in the database. What is shown here is just the first one of them in the full-record format (Format 5).

The *Book Review Index* database corresponds to the printed book of the same name. It is produced by Gale Research Company and contains over 1.3 million records dating back to 1969. It is updated three times a year. The publications indexed include *The New Yorker,* the weekday and Sunday *New York Times, The Wall Street Journal,* the *New York Review of Books,* and all the other ones you would expect. But *American Heritage, Crawdaddy, Publishers Weekly,* and *Seventeenth-Century News* are also included. You can order copies of the actual reviews online via DIALORDER or through some other document delivery mechanism. Or you can simply go to the library and locate copies of the publications.

Book Review Digest *on Wilsonline*

If you'd rather not go to the library or wait for a document delivery service to get you the review, you might consider the *Book Review Digest* database on Wilsonline. This database corresponds to the printed publication of the same name and is distinguished by the fact that it not only references the review, but also provides you with a short excerpt.

For example, here is the kind of record you would retrieve if you were to sign on and search for the author of *Godel, Escher, Bach:*

```
FIND Hofstadter, Douglas R.

SEARCH 4 (4 FOUND)

USER: prt fu

1 (BOOK REVIEW DIGEST)
Hofstadter, Douglas R.:1945-
Metamagical themas
questing for the essence of mind and pattern
Basic Bks.:us
1985
LC Card No: 83-46095
Library Journal 110:72 My 15 '85
Review word count: 100
Reviewed by: Burneko, Guy
Review excerpts: Boiling things down to their conceptual skeletons in such areas as quantum
theory, genetic coding, and the logic of self-referential sentences, Hofstadter has given us a
generously illustrated collection of essays . . . to complement the intellectual entertainment of
his earlier Godel, Escher, Bach [BRD 1979, 1980] . . .
```

We have shortened this record considerably in the interests of space and shown only about half of the review excerpt. But as you can see, this Wilsonline database can easily give you enough information about a book to decide whether to pursue it or not. *Book Review Digest* covers about 80 American, British, and Canadian periodicals and it goes back to April 1983. Reviews for approximately 6,000 books are added each year.

It is not a huge database, and these limitations mean you probably won't find a review for every book that interests you. But if the book is in the database, the record and review excerpt are definitely worth retrieving and reading.

...13...

Magazines:
Facts, Figures, Features, and Full-Text Articles Online

Magazines are the all-weather fighter-bombers of online information. Regardless of the mission, you can almost always assemble a squadron to send up against an information target, and they will almost always be successful. You will be using magazine databases constantly, so it's important to think about them and their "infoferous" (information-bearing) properties. Each one is different, aimed at a different audience, and likely to treat a subject in a different way.

Pamphlets, periodicals, and "serials" of one sort or another have been published for centuries, but what we today think of as a magazine is a modern phenomenon dating from the 1920s. *Reader's Digest* and *Better Homes and Gardens* were both founded in 1922, *Time* in 1923, and *Newsweek* in 1933. Since then, the number and variety of magazines has expanded directly with the number and variety of new industries, subjects, and identifiable demographic groups that have emerged.

Today there are literally tens of thousands of magazines. Or, as the R. R. Bowker Company puts it in its description of its *Ulrich's International Periodicals Directory* (DIALOG and BRS), the "database provides you with immediate access to more than 126,200 regularly and irregularly issued serials from 65,000 publishers in 181 countries around the world." (Plus information on more than 16,800 serials that have ceased publication since 1974.)

The reason there are so many publications is that the magazine format fills a need that is especially acute in the midst of an information explosion. At one end of the information continuum are television and radio. After that are daily newspapers. Then come magazines, and finally books.

281

Where on the Continuum?

You have virtually no control over the information the electronic media offer you. The depth of coverage usually is not great, and video and audio cassette recorders notwithstanding, it's ephemeral. Newspapers offer more depth and a wider choice of subjects, but they are still a general interest medium. Books provide maximum depth and maximum choice, but they also demand maximum commitment.

Magazines, on the other hand, come in so many varieties that whether it's *Footware News, Refrigerated Transporter,* or *Pit and Quarry,* you can find one devoted to nearly every subject imaginable. Indeed, one can predict the existence of a magazine the way a physicist predicts the existence of subatomic particles. It is one of the laws of the universe that wherever there is a sufficient number of people united by a common interest, there will be advertisers who want to sell them something, and thus there will be a specialized magazine. As an information searcher you don't actually have to have heard of such a publication to know with certainty that it exists.

Television and radio are constantly raising subjects that may be of interest. Most we simply ignore. But when something does strike a responsive chord, you turn to a newspaper for more information. If you're really interested, though, you turn to a magazine for 2,000 words or so of concentrated, focused information augmented with photographs, charts, diagrams, and tables. You thus move from the most general of information sources to the highly specific. In terms of choice, depth of coverage, and required commitment, much of the time only magazines, like Baby Bear's porridge, are "just right."

Seeing the Forest for the First Time

Think about it: magazines are current, detailed, and illustrated, and most are devoted to one particular subject. Each is in effect a volume in one huge, living encyclopedia of our time. But until recently, that "encyclopedia" has been all but invisible. None but professional researchers have been able to see the forest for the trees. And only professionals and doctoral candidates with access to a good university library have been able to benefit from its richness.

The databases discussed in this chapter have changed all that. Now in one fell swoop you can scan 400 to 500 magazines. When you find something of interest, you can tap a few keys and order a photocopy of the original article. Or in a growing number of instances, you can tap some different keys and summon the full text of the original article to your computer screen.

Three Types of Databases

There are three types of magazine databases. The first might be called an "index" or "reference only" database. The best example is the *Readers' Guide to Periodical Literature* most of us had to learn to use in high school and college. Records in these databases are generally limited to the title of the article, the author, the source publication, and the subject descriptor words of a bibliographic citation.

Next are the databases that include not only the bibcite but also about 200 words of information abstracted from the source article. Databases in which each full record is actually the complete text of the original article make up the third category. On most systems, whatever is in the record is searchable, and as we'll see, that's an important consideration when you go online. There are times when you may not want to search the full text of an article, and others when nothing but a full-text search will do.

In this chapter we'll look at many of the leading magazine databases, dividing them into one of these three categories. We'll also look at three of the real powerhouses in this part of the electronic universe, Information Access Company (IAC), Data Courier (ABI/INFORM), and Predicasts Terminal System (PTS).

What's Where?

But first, there's an important publication you should know about. It's called the *Directory of Periodicals Online*, edited by Catherine Chung and published by Federal Document Retrieval, Inc. (FDR). It took nearly three years to create and it is nothing short of a godsend for anyone who wants to know which databases cover which magazines. Most databases will be happy to send you a list of the publications they cover, so it's not a problem to find out which magazines are on IAC's Trade & Industry Index or any other database. But until FDR published its directory in late 1985, there was no single source one could consult to find out which databases cover *Institutional Investor* or *Newsweek* or any other periodical.

The FDR directory does this and more. It also tells you when coverage begins on each major database vendor's system, the lag time between the publication date and online availability on each system, and the format of the information. *Business Week*, for example, is covered by ABI/INFORM, NEXIS, Management Contents, the Magazine Index, and the Readers' Guide, among others. But coverage can start anywhere from January 1, 1959, to 1966 to '71, '74, '77, to 1984 and so on. The format can vary across all three of the major divisions cited above, and the lag time can vary from one day, to one week, to one month. Thus, if you wanted to search *Business Week* on DIALOG, you would find that you have at least a dozen databases to choose from, many of which offer differing coverage and formats.

The directory represents an enormous amount of labor and, perhaps understandably, it is not priced for the individual consumer. There are three volumes, each of which sells for about $90. They include Volume 1: News, Law, and Business; Volume 2: Medicine and Social Science; and Volume 3: Science and Technology. This includes an update supplement issued each six months. "If after examining the Directory," etc., you may return "the undamaged copy for a full refund" within 30 days. For more information, contact:

> Federal Document Retrieval, Inc.
> Directory of Periodicals Online
> 514 C Street, N.E.
> Washington, D.C. 20002
> (800) 368-1009
> (202) 638-0520

Index-Type Magazine Database

The Readers' Guide to Periodical Literature

Though it was late getting out of the starting blocks in the online field—it didn't appear until 1985—the H. W. Wilson Company's Readers' Guide (RG) is probably the quintessential index-type magazine database. It corresponds almost exactly to the contents of the RG volumes you would find at most libraries. For example, on a whim we searched RG with the command FIND PAPER AIRPLANES, and here is the bibliographical citation for one of the seven articles that turned up:

```
1 (READERS GUIDE)
Fold a far-flying paper airplane
il
National Geographic World 128:22 Ap '86
Feature Article
Language: eng
Subject heading: Airplane models
Special refs: Paper airplanes
BRDG86022745
860509
Article
```

In the best tradition of all index-type databases, this citation tells us everything we need to know to locate the source article. We also found articles on paper airplanes in *Science '85*, *Time*, *Sunset*, *Omni*, *Popular Mechanics*, and *The Mother Earth News*. They dated from July 1983 through September 1985. A number of them mentioned The Great International Paper Airplane Contest, a long-standing competition of some reknown. The total time required was one minute and 29 seconds. The total cost was 98¢.

Perhaps only a writer or a professional researcher can appreciate the speed and economy having RG online provides. But for those who haven't spent much time in the reference room of a library, a brief explanation may be helpful. In the library world, the various H. W. Wilson volumes have long been *the* magazine reference volumes. The information is published in monthly booklets that are cumulated each quarter. At the end of the year, all of the quarterly booklets are integrated and combined into one hardbound volume.

Thus, if you wanted to search for articles about paper airplanes dating from 1983 to the present, you would have to consult a number of volumes. If you did your search in 1986, you would have to check the yearly volumes for 1983 through 1985 (three volumes). Then, depending on when in 1986 you did your search, you would have to check anywhere from one monthly booklet to as many as three quarterly booklets, plus the two monthly booklets issued prior to the end of the fourth quarter.

The bottom line is that doing things by hand, you would have to consult anywhere from four to eight separate reference volumes. And you would have to copy the pertinent information for seven citations onto a piece of paper before heading into the stacks to locate the actual articles.

Now combine that with the fact that Wilsonline, the only system from which RG is available, also includes nearly a dozen other H. W. Wilson magazine databases and add in the fact that you can search up to eight of these databases *simultaneously*, and you've got a research tool of considerable power. (You'll find a complete list of Wilsonline databases in Chapter 11, Figure 11.1.)

Altogether the Wilsonline databases cover nearly 3,000 unique periodical titles, with approximately a 10% overlap among its various databases. The start date on these databases varies from June 1982 through October 1984. The databases are updated at least twice a week, but more frequently when necessary.

RG and other Wilsonline databases are indexed with the same controlled vocabulary subject headings found in the corresponding paper versions. At this writing, there is no printed thesaurus of these terms, but the company is working on one. There is, however, an EXPAND command to help you locate authorized terms online, and the system has been programmed to automatically search on the "preferred subject heading" related to what you enter. In the printed versions, for example, if you were to look up "foreign trade," you would be asked to "See Export-import trade." If you were to enter "foreign trade" online, the system would provide the same notification and proceed to search on the "preferred term."

Perhaps the two biggest faults with Wilsonline are the lack of a list of the journals covered by each database and the lack of a document delivery feature. For example, at this writing, the only way to find out which 182 magazines are covered by RG is to consult the explanatory pages at the front of one of its printed volumes. There is no summary booklet. With so many information brokers so readily available, the lack of an online ordering and document delivery service is not a huge problem. But it is an inconvenience.

Profile: Information Access Company Databases

Information Access Company (IAC) is a subsidiary of the Ziff-Davis publishing concern, and it is among the premier names in online magazine databases. It began in March of 1978 with the introduction of its Magazine Index (MI) database on DIALOG. Since that time IAC has either created or acquired nine additional databases, including Management Contents® and Industry Data Sources™ (formerly "Harfax").

All IAC databases are largely based on periodicals and newspapers. And all of them are available on DIALOG, where they comprise not so much a collection of discrete files as a database *system*. Most are also on BRS and NEXIS as well. IAC offers training, search-aid materials, and software built around this "system." So it's important to understand it if you want to be able to use the IAC's products effectively and economically.

The IAC "System"

Publications enter the system in the NEWSEARCH™ database, File 211 on DIALOG. NEWSEARCH contains bibliographic citations and abstracts prepared from over 1,900 source publications, including the major national newspapers, PR Newswire, over 100 local and regional business publications, and hundreds of magazines. NEWSEARCH is updated *daily*. More than 1,600 new records derived from the previous day's news stories are added to the database every business day.

Every 30 to 45 days, all of the records that have been added during the month are collected and distributed to five other IAC files. The clock is reset, and the process begins again. These other IAC databases are the Magazine Index, the National Newspaper Index (which we'll discuss in the next chapter), and the Legal Resource Index.

The seventh file is Industry Data Sources, the online equivalent of the Harfax printed directories of market and investment research, statistical, financial, and economic reports, and similar information. The eighth is the Computer Database™, which covers over 600 computer magazines.

The last two files are Magazine ASAP™ and Trade and Industry ASAP™. The "ASAP" in this instance stands for "as soon as published." The two parent files, MI and TI, offer bibliographic citations covering more than 400 publications each. The ASAP files offer the full text of the articles in 60 to 80 of those publications. Coverage starts with January 1983.

Full-Text Linkage

Each ASAP record consists of the bibcite found in the parent file plus the full text of the article. All of it is searchable. On BRS, the files are separate. But on DIALOG, both ASAP databases are also linked to their parent bibcite databases, MI and TI.

This linkage creates what might be thought of as an instant document delivery service. MI and TI contain *only* citations, but they cover hundreds of journals. Typically you would search them, develop a list of citations for the articles you would like to see, and use DIALOG's online ordering commands to transmit those citations to your chosen document delivery service. You would still do that in most cases, but in those instances where a journal is covered by an ASAP database, you can order the immediate display of the full text of the document. In other words, while you cannot search the full text of a document in MI or TI, you can take advantage of its existence in an ASAP database.

The cost for searching any of the four files is $84 an hour on DIALOG, plus telecommunications and display charges. The cost of displaying a complete document, where available, is $7, a price that's competitive with most conventional document delivery services. To keep your costs to a minimum, we suggest that you tell the system you want an offline printout VIA DIALMAIL. It's not as fast as an immediate display, but the charges for downloading the article are only $18 an hour on DIALMAIL.

Online Tip: When you are about to display documents in either MI or TI on DIALOG, be careful which format you choose. Format 9 is the "full record including full text" format. Whenever you

Online Tip (cont.)

choose it, you will be charged $7 per record—whether it's a full-text article or just a bibcite. The system isn't smart enough to know the difference.

If you want just the bibcite and abstract, where present, request Format 7. Since all citations for which there is a corresponding full-text article have an "Availability" field, if you want to limit things to just those articles, enter the command SELECT AV =FULL TEXT before issuing a TYPE command.

Here's a quick rundown of IAC's seven magazine databases. This is intended only to give you the flavor of each database. IAC will be happy to send you complete journal lists and other information if you contact them at the toll-free number and address given at the end of this section.

Magazine Index
Bibcites, primarily, though about 5% of records have very brief abstracts. General interest coverage, including some 400 widely read U.S. and Canadian magazines. Originally conceived as a direct competitor to the printed *Readers' Guide*, MI includes all publications RG covers and many, many more besides, including *American Heritage, Canadian Composer, Esquire, Guns and Ammo, The New Yorker, Runner's World, Variety, Writer's Digest, Field & Stream*, and so on. Some coverage goes back as far as 1959, but most indexing starts with January 1977.

Magazine ASAP
Full-text articles from about 60 magazines, starting with January 1983. *Atlantic, Boy's Life, Forbes, Fortune, Life, National Review, PC Magazine, PC Week, Playboy, Scientific American, Technology Review, Working Woman, Yachting*, and so on. As mentioned, the cost per article downloaded is $7, plus telecommunications and connect time.

Trade & Industry Index
Like MI, primarily bibcites with the occasional rogue abstract. Coverage begins in January 1983. Over 300 publications, plus *The Wall Street Journal* and the Business Section of *The New York Times*, plus business-related articles from over 1,100 other publications, including a "subfile" called the Area Business Databank™ that features over 100 local and regional business publications. What leaps out at you as you review the database journal list is the large number of trade publica-

tions: *Advertising Age, Bakery Production & Marketing, Chain Store Age, Iron Age, Personnel Administrator, Rubber World, Vending Times,* and so on. Trade journals, as anyone who has ever subscribed to one knows, are invaluable sources of highly concentrated information on a particular industry.

Trade & Industry ASAP

Full-text of over 80 of the leading trade journals, plus such major magazines as *Forbes, Dun's Business Month, Fortune, Money,* and *Women's Wear Daily.* The cost is $7 per article downloaded.

Management Contents

Most records have *abstracts* as well as bibliographical citations. Covers more than 700 business journals, newsletters, proceedings, books, research reports, and self-study courses, starting in September 1974. Management Contents was originally handled by another Ziff-Davis company, but it was made a part of IAC in the fall of 1984. Perhaps because of its origins, there is more than a little overlap between it and TI. However, as a rough-and-ready comparision, TI tends to be characterized by trade journals of the sort cited above. Management Contents is characterized by publications like *ABA Banking Journal, Barron's, Canadian Labour, Management Japan, Long Range Planning,* and *Venture.*

The Computer Database™

Originally started by Management Contents. Most records have informative *abstracts* as well as bibcites. Coverage begins in 1983. Updated twice a month with an average of 3,000 records per update. Indexes and abstracts from over 600 journals, proceedings, courses, newsletters, and reports, including *A+, Ahoy!, Antic, AT&T Laboratories, Technical Journal, Byte, Call-A.P.P.L.E., IBM Journal of Research & Development, IEEE, Spectrum, InfoWorld, Micro Marketworld, Macworld, MIS Week, PC Tech Journal, Power Play, Rainbow, Run, Syntax, Unix World,* and *VLSI Design.*

Legal Resource Index™

Bibliographical citations from over 730 law reviews, bar association journals, subject-specific journals, and seven legal newspapers. In addition to all the American publications you would expect, it has especially good coverage of publications from Canada and Australia. Coverage starts in January 1980 in most cases, and you can search on the basis of case citation, case name, jurisdiction, statute citation, statute name, in addition to conventional fields.

Online Tip: There is some duplication of coverage among various IAC databases, but the company has provided a way to eliminate it. Most files have an "SF" field that stands for "Subfile." Thus, if you have searched Magazine Index and want to conduct the same search on the Legal Resource Index, you can go into that database and enter NOT SF = MI as part of your search argument. Better still, if you plan to search a number of IAC databases, limit the search in each case to publications covered exclusively by each one. Thus SF = MI would be part of your search argument when in Magazine Index and SF = LRI would be used when in Legal Resource Index. See the appropriate DIALOG database chapters for more details.

Online Tip: At this writing, Trade & Industry Index has a feature that is unique among IAC databases and possibly in the industry as a whole. The database has a subfile called Area Business Databank, which as mentioned above, covers over 100 local, regional, and state business publications. Titles include: *Business Atlanta, Crain's Cleveland Business, Texas Business, San Diego Business Journal, Tidewater Virginian Magazine,* and so on. Thanks to the subfile field, if you want to limit your search to just these publications, you may enter SF = ABD as part of your search argument. Otherwise they will be searched along with the hundreds of other TI journals.

Standard "IAC System" Features

One of the advantages offered by the IAC "database system" is the standardization of features in all files. Every IAC file uses the Library of Congress Subject Headings (LCSH) discussed in the previous chapter as the authority for the words and phrases used in the descriptor fields. However, since magazines bring new subjects to light much faster than books, IAC has augmented the LCSH subject terms with headings of its own. Together they form the IAC controlled vocabulary.

There are many other access points as well. To make retrieval easier, IAC has added vernacular and popular phrases that are mentioned in the source article but are not a part of the firm's controlled vocabulary list. In records prior to April 1984, these "un-controlled" terms are in the "Identifier" field. Reflecting a change in policy, records added after that date contain both types of terms in the "Descriptor" fields, which were formerly reserved for authorized subject headings only.

There are also fields for SIC code, named person, product name, and, where relevant, the geographical location the source article deals with. And when an article's title is ambiguous, IAC augments it with descriptive words in parentheses:

Marriott completes acquisition. (of Service Systems Corp.)
Wall Street Journal p48(W) Feb 26 1985
col6 001 col in.
EDITION: Tue
DESCRIPTORS: Marriott Corp.-mergers and consolidations;
Service Systems Corp.-mergers and consolidations

In addition, each database may have a number of unique fields. In TI, for example, there is a field for stock ticker symbol. In The Computer Database, there are fields for operating system and program language.

All IAC databases let you retrieve citations by "article type" (biography, column, editorial, evaluation, obituary, review, etc.). Articles that are reviews (AT = REVIEW) of books, movies, dramas, TV shows, records, restaurants, and so on have a "Grade" field running from A for "Excellent" to F for "Terrible." The grade reflects the IAC indexer's determination of the review writer's opinion.

Beginning with records entered in March of 1986, you may also specify AT = COMPANY PROFILE to limit the records retrieved to that type of article. The equivalent command on BRS systems is COMPANY PROFILE.AT. and on NEXIS, enter DOCT(COMPANY PROFILE).

Online Tip: The terms used in the article-type field vary with the database. MI, for example, has about 22 types. The Computer Database has about 67. To get a list of the types for any IAC database on DIALOG, do an EXPAND of the AT field.

```
?EXPAND AT =

        Items  Index-term
            0  *AT =
        25823  AT = ANNOUNCEMENT
        13762  AT = APPLICATIONS
           71  AT = BIBLIOGRAPHY
         2382  AT = BUYERS GUIDE
            1  AT = EVALATION
        15514  AT = EVALUATION
            1  AT = EVALUTATION
         6828  AT = HARDWARE REVIEW
        11091  AT = HOW-TO
            1  AT = PRODUCT EVALATION
```

Online Tip (cont.)

```
15134  AT=PRODUCT EVALUATION
    1  AT=PRODUCT EVALATION
15134  AT=PRODUCT EVALUATION
    1  AT=PRODUCT EVALUTATION
14542  AT=SOFTWARE REVIEW
```

Since this is an edited list, we have not shown the E numbers that would normally appear. (See the discussion of the EXPAND command in the previous chapter.) As you can see, this list not only illustrates the kind of article types you can search for, but also offers yet another example of the quality problem that plagues all databases. Someone obviously mistyped *evaluation* on a number of occasions when entering it in the AT field. Computers are literal-minded beasts, and if you were to search solely on the basis of AT=EVALUATION or AT=PRODUCT EVALUA-TION, there are a number of records you would not find because of the data-entry errors.

Crucial Documentation

To make the most of any IAC database, you need at least two things. First, you need the appropriate DIALOG database chapter with its plentiful explanations and examples of what you can search for in each field. The cost is about $6 per chapter, and you must order directly from DIALOG. If you think you might be searching all IAC databases, consider ordering a chapter for each at the same time.

Nearly a year after most of IAC's files went up on the various BRS systems, that vendor has yet to produce descriptive chapters on how to use the files. Hopefully this material will be available as you read this. In the meantime or possibly as a substitute, you might consider IAC's *Access to Access* manual ($100) described below. Like the DIALOG chapters, this publication offers a complete explanation of every field in each database, with command examples customized for BRS, NEXIS, and DIALOG users.

The second thing you need is a list of the journals each database covers. These are available for free from IAC, and we suggest you request *all* of them, including the Area Business Databank list. There is also a list of geographic codes used in IAC databases that is free as well.

If you are in a hurry and you want to see whether a particular magazine is covered by a database, EXPAND the journal field (STEM it or ROOT it on the BRS systems). For example, you might enter: EX-PAND JN=ILLINOIS BANKER on DIALOG. The system would then tell you how many articles it had from that publication. If the publication isn't covered, obviously there will be no articles. (See the previous chapter for details on the DIALOG EXPAND command.)

The IAC Subject Guide

IAC publishes at least two other search aids that may be of interest. The first is its 575-page *Subject Guide to IAC Databases*. This volume contains a majority of the most frequently used Library of Congress Subject Headings, plus all of the terms IAC has created to supplement them. You can use the guide effectively on almost any database that follows the LCSH controlled vocabulary. The guide sells for $85, but if you take an IAC training course you can purchase it for $72.25.

The subject guide is divided into two parts. The massive first part lists the subject words that have either been used at least once in an IAC database or authorized for future use. Part II lists "Standard Subdivisions." In all IAC databases, a main subject heading is *always* accompanied by an authorized subhead (a "standard subdivision") in the descriptor field. Since Management Contents and The Computer Database were done differently in years past, they have a large number of records that do not follow these rules. However, according to IAC, these two will be brought into the fold.

Thus if you wanted to search for articles about mechanical problems with food processors, you would consult Part I to see if "food processors" is an authorized term. (It is.) Then you would look at Part II for some authorized subhead that is conceptually close to mechanical problems. You might then see that "defects" is listed, followed by a list of the kinds of things to which the word is applied in the database. These are called "scope notes," and in this case they include *materials*, *structures*, and *products*.

You could enter SELECT followed by FOOD PROCESSORS AND DEFECTS to search all fields in the file's basic index. Or you could use FOOD PROCESSORS(L)DEFECTS to concentrate on just the subject descriptor field. The "(L)" connector tells DIALOG that both terms must be in the same descriptor phrase, and using it automatically limits the search to the descriptor field, so the /DE suffix is not necessary. The connector is needed because main subjects and subheads are separated by a hyphen in the database, but a hyphen is not searchable. This argument will thus retrieve records with "FOOD PROCESSORS-DEFECTS" in the descriptor (subject) field.

Using The Computer Database's Online Thesaurus

Because Management Contents and The Computer Database were not originally developed by IAC, there is a certain amount of discon-

294 . . . The Information

tinuity between their subject headings and those of the rest of the IAC stable. In older records there are subjects that are not on the IAC list, and main headings are often used without a subhead. There are no plans to correct this retroactively, but all records added since these two databases became a part of IAC will conform to IAC's standard indexing policies.

Separate printed thesauri used to be available for these two, but those publications have been discontinued. The Computer Database, however, is one of the few files on DIALOG to offer an online thesaurus. This lets you EXPAND a term and then "EXPAND the expansion" to get a list of related terms. The first expand list will be alphabetical, whereas the related term expand list will be organized by relationship.

For example, if you did an EXPAND on the word COMPUTERS, you would see a list of words that are alphabetically close to it in the file's basic index. But since this file has an online thesaurus, you would also see that there were 26 related terms (the "RT" column below):

Ref	Items	RT	Index-term
E1	1		COMPUTERRE
E2	3		COMPUTERRIFIC
E3	52498	26	*COMPUTERS
E4	2		COMPUTERS AND DATA PROCESSING

Again, because there is an online thesaurus, you can EXPAND any item for which there are related terms. Thus if you entered EXPAND E3 you would get a list of related terms that starts like this:

Ref	Items	Type	RT	Index-term
R1	52498		26	*COMPUTERS
R2	726	N	10	ACCESSORIES
R3	0	N	3	ANALOG COMPUTERS
R4	49	N	6	COMPUTER AUTHORSHIP
R5	945	N	14	COMPUTER CRIME

These terms can also be EXPANDed to look at terms related to *them*. It is important to note that all "related terms" are of the same rank. That is, they are all main subject headings, not subheads. They are equivalent to "See also" references in a printed thesaurus. Your DIALOG manual explains this technique in general, and IAC publishes a free booklet on the topic.

Access to Access *and Training*

The second major publication is a large notebook called *Access to Access*. This manual is designed for end users, but at $100 a copy ($85 if you take IAC training), it is not for the casual searcher. It includes a list of all the terms IAC has created to supplement LC subject headings, a list of the LC standard subdivisions (subject subheads), a list of all the types of products of products reviewed in publications covered by IAC, the IAC geographic codes, the IAC database journals lists, and lists of IAC fields and the policies applied to them. There are also numerous tutorial pages designed to show you how to find a specific kind of information using a particular IAC file on a particular system. There are versions for DIALOG, BRS, and NEXIS, and the topics treated include company information, product evaluations, and information about people.

IAC conducts training programs in major American cities that include a basic course and one course each for business and computer applications. The cost is $50 per person, and it is assumed that you have had prior DIALOG or BRS experience. Attendees receive free practice time during the seminar and are entitled to special discounts on IAC search materials.

Search Helper™ Software

For libraries, schools, and institutions IAC offers a software package called Search Helper™. This is a BASIC program (in every sense of the word) that prompts the user through the preparation of a search strategy and then automatically logs onto BRS or DIALOG and conducts the search. The program's cachet is that it comes with a serial number rated for either 300 or 700 searches. Each search includes the display of 20 hits.

The idea is to offer searches at a fixed cost. Thus for a 300-search version, the cost is $1,350 ($4.50 a search), and the 700-search version costs $2,450 ($3.50 a search). The software itself normally sells for an additional $200, but when we called, IAC had it "on sale" for free.

There are two final points to make about IAC. First, the company has named Dynamic Information Corporation as its authorized document supplier. That means that while you may order photocopies of documents cited by IAC databases from anyone, Dynamic is probably the one supplier that can deliver *any* IAC-referenced document. They can do this because IAC has turned its collection of source publications over to Dynamic. The company's DIALMAIL and DIALORDER name is DYNAMIC. See Chapter 4 for their land address and phone.

The second point concerns IAC's great customer support. Each business day from 10:00 A.M. to 7:30 P.M., Eastern time, you can call IAC for toll-free assistance in searching any of its databases on any system. The vendor Customer Service people can help as well, but the IAC staff is naturally intimately familiar with the company's databases and the best way to search them. IAC also offers a newsletter ("Online News") for its users. It is issued six times a year and it's free if you ask for it. For more information on IAC and its databases contact:

> Information Access Company
> 11 Davis Drive
> Belmont, CA 94002
> (415) 591-2333
> (800) 227-8431
> (800) 626-9935, in California

Abstract-and-Index Magazine Databases

An abstract is a brief summary of a source document. In its broadest form, it is most similar to the "Executive Summary" you might find on the first page of a long report. In the online world, however, it is often much more than that. For example, here's a complete record downloaded from the ABI/INFORM database on VU/TEXT. We wanted to find out what share of the detergent market Procter & Gamble's Tide holds. The search strategy on VU/TEXT was: TIDE and @8 MARKET-SHARES. (We'll explain later.)

ABI/INFORM

```
*TIDE  *  HASN'T TURNED YET
  Freeman, Laurie
  Advertising Age     v56n90     P: 43     Nov 18, 1985
  CODEN: ADVAAQ     ISSN: 0001-8899     JRNL CODE: ADA
  DOC TYPE: JOURNAL ARTICLE     LANGUAGE: English
  AVAILABILITY: ABI/INFORM
```

Liquid*Tide, *introduced by Procter & Gamble (P&G), captured a 6.8% share of the $1-billion liquid detergent*market*in the first half of 1985, although its growth was slower than many had anticipated. More than half of Liquid*Tide's* share came at the expense of existing P&G brands. A heavy media schedule, including television spots from Saatchi & Saatchi Compton, has promoted the new detergent. Still, it has not ousted Wisk from the number one spot. Use of liquid detergents is approaching 50% in the northeastern and north central US. Colgate-Palmolive is spending millions to introduce its new Fab liquid and its reformulated Dynamo, renamed Dynamo 2. Currently, Lever also is testing a Wisk powder. Lever spends 95% of its $50 million advertising budget on TV spots. Lever also plans to introduce Surf liquid and powder detergents and a liquid under its Sunlight brand.

DESCRIPTORS: Soap-&-detergent-industry; Advertising-campaigns; Procter-&-Gamble-Cincinnati; Advertising-agencies; Lever-Brothers-New-York; *Market-shares;* Product-lines; Colgate-Palmolive-New-York; Market-stragegy; Test-markets; Product-introduction

CLASSIFICATION CODES: 9110 COMPANY SPECIFIC/ CASE STUDIES; 8610 FOOD PROCESSING INDUSTRY, INCLUDES BEVERAGES & LIQUORS; 7200 ADVERTISING; 8300 OTHER SERVICES

As you can see, this abstract does at least two things. First, it gives you a much better idea of what the article is about than would be possible with a bibliographical citation. You can thus more easily decide whether you want to seek an actual copy of the source article. Second, it is so packed with facts that the abstract itself may tell you all you need to know. This abstract is in effect the very essence of the source article, distilled, compressed, and concentrated for magnetic storage and online consumption.

But not *only* consumption. As you can see, there are lots of access points in this record. One could look for it by title, author, subject descriptor, and a variety of classification codes, among other things. The "@8 MARKET-SHARES" in the search strategy we used above told the VU/TEXT system to look for that subject in Field 8, the descriptor field on the VU/TEXT system.

However, since on almost every system the entire abstract of a record is *also* searchable, every word it contains is also an access point. By using "TIDE" in the above search strategy we told the system to find that word anywhere it occurs in the database. As the VU/TEXT highlighting makes clear, there were lots of hits in this abstract.

Online Tip: The existence of a searchable abstract can make it much easier to find the information you want. But it can also lead to some typical "search surprises." Among the records retrieved by the above search was an article from a 1980 issue of *Marketing News* about how U.S. beer producers are more concerned about each other's *market shares* than about stemming "the rising *tide* of imports." No soap.

The Question of Quality

In considering magazine abstracts we're moving into an area where the policies and reputation of the database producer become key factors in what you can expect to find online. The format of a bibliographical citation is fixed, and short of gross negligence in the data-entry department, there's not much an IP can do to screw it up. Abstracts are a different story. The only rules about what an abstract must contain are those set down by the database producer itself. Thus it is important to be aware that the quality and utility of abstracts can vary widely, depending on the database producer.

The leading databases in this area are ABI/INFORM and the various databases created by Predicasts, Inc. Both IPs have a reputation for offering the highest quality, most informative abstracts in the industry.

Interestingly, although there is a lot of overlap in coverage, the two really complement each other more than they compete. ABI/INFORM's editorial policy, for example, tends to emphasize management issues, finance, strategic planning, industry overviews, economic trends, and what might generally be called the "macro" viewpoint. Predicasts databases, on the other hand, tend to focus on specific companies, brand-name products, manufacturing processes, marketing strategies, and other subjects viewed from a "micro" perspective.

How Abstracts Are Created

We'll look at both ABI/INFORM and the PTS databases in a moment. But first, since the abstracts themselves are so important, we contacted ABI/INFORM to ask about how an abstract comes to be. As you might imagine, it's a labor-intensive process.

Selecting the Articles

After the journals arrive at INFORM's offices, editors select the articles that will be put into the database. INFORM has designated about half the publications it covers as "core journals," magazines for which almost everything will be indexed. From other journals it selects just business-related stories. From a law journal, for example, INFORM's editors would select articles dealing with commercial law but not those covering legal issues with no direct bearing on business.

The point is that whether from core journals or other publications, articles are selected by ABI/INFORM editors on the basis of the company's established criteria. This is what gives INFORM, and any other selective database, its "personality." We'll discuss the selection criteria INFORM uses later.

Assigning Codes and Index Terms

ABI/INFORM uses a controlled vocabulary of about 8,000 terms, and the next step is for professional indexers to assign between four and twelve of them to each article. (Typically, each INFORM abstract has seven or eight assigned terms.) The indexers also assign two or three ABI/INFORM classification codes. Like the controlled vocabulary, these are unique to INFORM, and we'll have more to say about them later.

All of this information is placed on a worksheet which, along with the source article, is distributed to an abstracter. The abstracters are typically specialists in one particular field. So the law journals go to practicing attorneys, the data processing journals go to professional DP people, and so on. The abstracter prepares a 200-word summary in accordance with INFORM's guidelines, types it onto the worksheet, and returns it.

Editors then review the results for accuracy, grammar, punctuation, and spelling. But they also verify that the abstract accurately reflects the meaning of the source article. A second review is then conducted by a copyeditor. It is INFORM's policy that every abstract is reviewed twice before moving to the production department.

On its arrival at that department, the abstract is reviewed yet again by a proofreader. The article is then keyboarded, the results checked again, and the resulting tapes are sent to the various database vendors that offer ABI/INFORM.

From Doorstep to Database

ABI/INFORM adds approximately 825 new records to its database each week. The turnaround time from the day the original article arrives at INFORM's offices to when it is available for searching online can vary from four to seven weeks. The lag time depends on the updating policies of the vendor. DIALOG updates its ABI/INFORM file weekly. Others update monthly. INFORM also tries to make sure that certain very popular and widely used journals are available as soon as possible. *Business Week, Computer World, Forbes,* and *Fortune,* for example, are always given priority treatment.

Profile: ABI/INFORM

The ABI/INFORM database was started in 1971 as a consulting project and purchased soon after by Data Courier, Inc., a communications concern formerly owned by Louisville's Bingham family. The database is now part of the same Bell & Howell group that owns the University Microfilm Incorporated (UMI) document delivery service. Since that time a number of other products have been added, including the Business Software Database, Pharmaceutical News Index, and Business Dateline (full text of over 100 regional business publications), but INFORM remains the flagship database and that's what we'll focus on here.

The "ABI" in ABI/INFORM originally stood for "Abstracted Business Information," but the letters have since been adopted as the complete official name. INFORM covers some 680 publications, and each of its records contains a bibcite and a 200-word abstract. The journals list includes all of the business magazines you would expect, plus virtually every publication with *business, economic,* or *management* in its name. If a magazine name begins *Journal of* something and it is in any way related to business, it is sure to be on the list. Among those publications are many Canadian journals, plus more than 180 from Western Europe, Japan, and Australia. Articles from the international publications are translated into English.

For major "core" business publications, ABI/INFORM covers everything *except* news items, letters to the editor, book reviews, and regular columns. It focuses instead on feature articles dealing with methods, techniques, and tactics and strategies of interest to managers, administrators, and professionals. The subjects must be judged to be of lasting value. That means articles dealing with management, general business, strategy, planning, and similar topics will be included. But advice on current stock picks and the "Personal Business" column from *Business Week* would not be included. Articles from non-core journals must meet the same criteria and be at least one page in length.

ABI/INFORM is available from most major database vendors, though start of coverage and frequency of updating varies. One thing that is the same on every system is its method of indexing. INFORM uses two methods: a controlled vocabulary for subject descriptors and a unique subject code number system. It is important to emphasize that you don't have to use either one of them. But it is equally important to be aware of the problem both they and the similar system used by PTS databases were designed to solve, since it may affect you.

The Problem with Business English

The problem is that since business covers so many different areas, the identical word can have completely different meanings in different industries. Consider the word *terminal*, for example, and think about the meanings it has in the computer, trucking, railway, and medical fields. Similarly, the word *promotion* means one thing to a personnel manager and quite another to an advertising account executive. If you were to simply search on "terminal" you would get hits for all of these meanings.

INFORM originally attempted to deal with this ambiguity by creating what it called "field" codes. The "field" here refers to field of business, not to an element in a record. There are 23 field codes, including ACC (accounting), INS (insurance), and LBR (labor). They can best be thought of as similar to what other databases would refer to as "subject subdivisions" or subheads.

Adding field codes took the controlled vocabulary word *terminals* and turned it into two words: terminals(trans) and terminals(dp) to distinguish between transportation-related terminals and data processing-related terminals. INFORM also uses other field codes when necessary to signify the context in which a term is used, for example: arbitrage (currency) and arbitrage (securities). These are all controlled vocabulary terms, so you can't add a field code to a subject word and search on that basis. The subject word must already have a field code attached to it on the controlled list.

The ABI/INFORM Codes

In July 1982, ABI/INFORM began implementing a better solution. The firm created a list of four-digit classification codes covering five major areas: business environment, management functions, industries & markets, article treatment, and organization types. The major areas are subdivided, and like SIC codes, each digit to the right denotes increasing specificity. For example, here is part of the Management Functions area:

```
2000 GENERAL MANAGEMENT
     2100 Administration & management personnel
          2110 Boards of directors
          2120 Chief executive officers
          2130 Executives
     2200 Managerial skills
     2300 Planning & strategy
```

(etc.)

The company then went back and added these codes to all records entered into the database from 1971 on. For technical reasons, the records entered between 1971 and mid-1982 can only be searched to the second level (like the 2100, 2200, and 2300 levels in the above example). But all INFORM records now have a CN (code number) field of some sort.

This means that if you want to search for information on computer terminals you no longer have to search on the term "terminals(DP)." Instead you can use the INFORM code number to quickly segment the database. For example, on BRS/BRKTHRU you might make this part of your first search statement: 8651.CC. to immediately select only records containing 8651, the INFORM code for "computer industry," in the classification code (CC) field. On DIALOG you would enter SELECT CC = 8651.

This search argument will produce a set of hits. If you AND that set with TERMINALS (A1 AND TERMINALS on BRKTHRU; SELECT S1 AND TERMINALS on DIALOG), you will retrieve only articles that mention computer terminals. (Unless, of course, there is an article about Amtrak installing IBM/PCs at every station stop or some other "search surprise.")

INFORM classification codes can also be truncated ("wildcarded") such that entering something like SELECT CC = 21? on DIALOG will retrieve articles on all subjects whose codes begin with 21. You may also use OR and NOT, and you may combine them with controlled vocabulary terms or any other search term you like.

Customer Support and Publications

ABI/INFORM offers excellent customer support, both in print and on the phone. We suggest you contact them at the toll-free numbers listed below and request copies of the Classification Code Chart, the Complete Journals List, and "A Guide to Searching ONTAP ABI/INFORM." ONTAP is the INFORM practice file on DIALOG, but this publication will be enormously helpful to you regardless of the system you use. All of these publications are free.

There is also a free bimonthly newsletter called LOG/ON, and unlike many vendor newsletters it spends more time on search tips and strategies than on self-promotion. Don't sign up for it though until you've had a chance to play with INFORM to see whether it will become one of your "A-list" databases.

There is also a DIALOG database chapter and a large manual called *SearchINFORM*. The manual includes *everything*, all the codes, company names, the complete controlled vocabulary, and search examples and field summaries for all the database vendors. The third edition was issued in 1986 and sells for $65. Good as it is, you probably won't need it unless you plan to really get into precision searching. If you combine the explanations presented here with the free materials and a knowledge of how to use your vendor's EXPAND command, you should be quite successful online.

Here is the necessary contact information. If you are interested in the other INFORM-produced databases mentioned at the beginning of this section, you might request information on them as well:

ABI/INFORM
Data Courier, Inc.
620 South Fifth Street
Louisville, KY 40202
(800) 626-2823 (U.S.)
(800) 626-0307 (Canada)
(502) 482-4111

Profile: Predicasts Terminal System (PTS)

Like ABI/INFORM, PTS PROMT also offers very informative, high-quality abstracts of business periodicals and magazines. But as mentioned earlier, the selection and editorial policies of the two databases tend to complement each other, even when they cover the same journals. If you want to know about the computer industry in general, ABI/INFORM should be your first stop. But if you want to know about IBM, its position in the industry, the market share held by one of its products and those of its competitors, and other company-specific data, you should use PROMT. This is a very rough comparison, but both IPs confirm that it is essentially accurate.

Online Tip: ABI/INFORM, Predicasts, and the producers of the Investext and DISCLOSURE databases conduct joint seminars in major U.S. cities (as well as London, Brussels, and Amsterdam) each year. The sessions are free and typically begin at 8:30 A.M. and run to about 3:00 P.M. They are designed to show businesspeople how to use all four databases to locate information on such topics as market analysis, company analysis, mergers and acquisitions, and business climate. Contact any of the four vendors for the latest scheduling information.

"PROMT" stands for "*P*redicasts *O*verview of *M*arkets and *T*echnology." The "PTS" stands for "*P*redicasts *T*erminal *S*ystem," and it is more than just another acronym. Cleveland-based Predicasts, Inc., began in 1960 as a business and market research consulting firm. It created the PROMT database in 1972, and since that time has added many members to its database family. At this writing, the entire PTS family includes:

PTS Aerospace/Defense Markets & Technology (A/DM&T)
PTS Annual Reports Abstracts (ARA)
PTS Funk & Scott Indexes (F&S)
PTS International Forecasts
PTS International Time Series
PTS Marketing & Advertising Reference Service (MARS)
PTS New Product Announcements (NPA)
PTS PROMT
PTS Regional Business News (RBN)
PTS U.S. Forecasts
PTS U.S. Time Series

All of these databases are available on DIALOG. Most are on BRS. PROMT is on VU/TEXT and other vendors as well. What makes these databases a "system" are the relationships between the files and the fact that they are united by Predicasts' unique set of numerical codes and other access points. In general, if you know how to search one PTS file, you know how to search them all.

Both by history and by design, PROMT is the master PTS database. It covers more than 1,500 trade magazines, business journals, newspapers, and annuals, including over 200 non-U.S. publications. (PROMT abstracts are always in English, with appropriate notations of the language of the source article.) In addition to all of the business publications you would expect, plus most American trade journals, you will also find titles like these: *Annual Report of the World Bank, British Ink Maker, Consumer Reports, Economic News of Bulgaria, Modern Tire Dealer, Norwegian Trade Bulletin, Producer Price Indexes, Sumitomo Bank Review, Venezuela Up-to-Date,* and *Yugoslavia Export.*

According to the on-staff business information specialists at Predicasts, most people should start with PROMT. Then, if ever information is needed about an even more specific topic, searchers should branch out into one of the other PTS databases. PTS NPA, for example, offers the full text of company news releases that focus on new product introductions. (After checking PROMT for IBM, you might check NPA for detailed information on a new printer, chip, or computer the firm had announced or introduced.)

PTS MARS contains its own unique set of journals, most of which are intensely focused on the marketing of specific products and the advertising industry as a whole: *Adweek Eastern Edition* (et al.), *Art Direction, Hispanic Business, Snack Food, Incentive Marketing,* and so on. Most MARS journals are not covered by PROMT, but where journal title coverage overlaps, MARS will contain abstracts of the articles on advertising and marketing, while PROMT will contain the others. (MARS would be the place to go for information on who's handling the IBM account, the campaign they plan to mount, the ad budget and how it will be spent, the slogan that will be used, and so on.)

Online Tip: If you search PROMT and then search MARS, how can you avoid encountering (and paying to download) the same abstract twice? There is some duplication between PROMT and MARS, and the way to deal with it is to use DIALOG's "limit" function. Limit functions are file-specific, but one of the options available on MARS is to limit your search to just those journals unique to MARS. As explained on the MARS Bluesheet, just enter /MARS as part of your search statement.

The "Nums"

PTS abstracts differ from those of INFORM in several ways. They can be longer or shorter than the 200 words INFORM shoots for. Tabular data may also be included. In fact, about 10% of all PTS records include statistical tables, and you can make certain that you retrieve them by searching for the word *table* in the "special feature" field of each record (SELECT SF = TABLE, for example). To see what one of these tables looks like, turn back to the discussion of DIALOG's Business Connection in Chapter 7. The information included also tends to focus more on specific companies and products. And above all, you can always count on a PTS abstract to give you any statistics mentioned in the source document.

Both ABI/INFORM and PTS PROMT cover *Advertising Age*. For purposes of comparison we searched PROMT to see how it treated the same article that served as the source for the abstract at the beginning of this section. When we searched PROMT for that specific article, we had no joy. It isn't in the PROMT database. However, when we used a similar strategy (SELECT TIDE AND MARKET(W)SHARE?) on DIALOG, we got (among other things) a table listing the market share of the top ten detergent brands in the U.S. market in 1985. (Source: Kidder Peabody.)

We did find the article, however. It was on MARS. Apparently, even though it mentions market share, the Predicasts indexers felt that the main thrust of the piece was brand-specific. And, as we discovered when we searched on "market share," PROMT has better, more complete information on that topic. You can see the results in Figure 13.1, and it is worth taking a moment to compare this abstract to the ABI/INFORM abstract of the same article.

─────── **Figure 13.1. The Same Article via PTS MARS** ───────

Here's how PTS MARS treated the same article that was the source for the ABI/INFORM abstract shown earlier. This should not be viewed as a qualitative comparison but merely as a demonstration of the different ways the same article can be abstracted, depending on the editorial policy and intended market of the database producer. To make the comparison easier, we have edited the record so that it contains only information *not* found in the INFORM abstract.

Tide hasn't turned yet.
Advertising Age November 18, 1985 v. 56 no. 90 p. 43
ISSN: 0001-8899
Availability: Predicasts Article Delivery Service

Fig. 13.1 (cont.)

Article type: Industry Profile   Source type: News
Special feature: Picture; Company; Agency

. . . Liquid Tide, via Saatchi & Saatchi Compton, that positions the brand as providing superior cleaning, water softening and buffering and soil suspension agents. The product was introduced in early-1985 with a $50 mil marketing budget . . .

   Lever Bros' Wisk continues to lead the category with an 8.8% market share. The liquid detergent market comprises 30% of the total $3.5bil detergent market. Liquid laundry detergents are more popular in northeastern and North Central US states. New Liquid Bold 3 has been nationally rolled out by P&G and it is positioned as cleaning tough laundry problems plus through-the-wash fabric softening and static control. TV spots use the theme, 'So good, we bottled it.' Grey Advertising handles advertising for both powdered and liquid Bold 3. Colgate-Palmolive . . . with a $13.5mil ad budget. The brand is positioned as a heavy duty cleaner with fabric softener and static control in TV spots, via Foote Cone & Belding . . .

   C-P . . . its reformulated Dynamo 2 . . . $10mil ad campaign, via FC&B. Lever Bros is increasing ad spending for Wisk will introduce liquid and powder Surf brand detergents. Surf liquid will be supported with a $100mil national ad campaign, via Ogilvy & Mather.

TRADE NAME: Liquid Tide; Wisk; Liquid Bold 3; Dynamo 2; Fab; Surf
AD AGENCY: Saatchi & Saatchi Compton Grey Advertising; DUNS NO.: 00-698-4876;
   TICKER: GREY; CUSIP: 397838 Foote Cone & Belding; DUNS NO.: 00-543-7769; TICKER:
   FCB; CUSIP: 344872 Ogilvy & Mather COMPANY: Procter & Gamble; DUNS NO.:
   00-131-6827; TICKER: PG; CUSIP: 742718 Lever Bros Colgate-Palmolive; DUNS NO.:
   00-134-4381; TICKER: CL; CUSIP: 194162

COUNTRY: United States (1USA)
PRODUCT: Liquid Household Organic Detergents (2841230); Dry Household Organic
   Detergents (2841220); TV Advertising (7313200)
EVENT: Marketing Procedures (24); Order & Contracts Received (61); Market Information
   (60)
ADVERTISING CONCEPT: Campaign Launched (74); Television (21); New Products/Services
   (57); Positioning (51); Geographic (82); Account Activity (42); Industry Market Data (85)

The Predicasts Coding System

   Predicasts has done its best to bring mathematical precision to information retrieval. In a word, it has a numerical code for just about everything. The Predicasts coding system is not easy to get used to at first, but once you catch on to how it works you can easily zero in on exactly what you want, often with only a single search statement. (See Figure 13.1 after the abstract for examples.)

   The PTS codes are based on the U.S. government SIC (Standard Industrial Classification Codes) list. But they are far more precise and up-to-date. SIC codes are specific only to four digits. But Predicasts has product codes that go out to seven digits of specificity. There are at least 20 codes for the word *terminals*, for example, ranging from "electronic funds transfer terminals" to "graphics terminals" to "point-of-sale terminals." There are "automobile" codes for station wagon, four-wheel drive, rear-wheel drive, hardtop, sports car, compact, subcompact, manual transmission, and so on.

The company uses the four-digit SIC codes as its base, and there is a high degree of correspondence between the two code sets. However, at this writing, the most recent update of SIC codes is dated 1972, and a lot of new industries and products have come on stream since then. Consequently, Predicasts has had to create its own unique codes to cover these areas. In an unusual role reversal, there are indications that the federal government may eventually incorporate Predicasts-created codes into future revisions of the SIC list. In the meantime, a number of companies have used the Predicasts system for their own internal information retrieval projects.

There is a field in each PTS record for "product code." But there are also fields for "event code" and "country code." For North America, the codes are hierarchical. Code 17 is for the West North Central region, while code 1719 is for Iowa and 1746 is for South Dakota. There are codes for each region and country in the rest of the world as well.

The first digit of Predicasts' two-digit event codes divides events into such major categories as institutional structure, market information, costs and prices, and financial information. The second digit makes things more specific. The code for "government and society" is 9. The code for taxes is 92, for example. Other PTS databases have additional codes as well. There are marketing concept codes in MARS (campaign themes, media personnel, point-of-purchase displays, etc.), and there are "use codes" in NPA that correspond to the product codes in PROMT.

Should You Use the Codes?

At first blush, all this talk about codes for this and codes for that can be very depressing. It seems to be yet one more level of complexity you must deal with. But don't let the codes be a problem. They're there for your convenience, and you don't *have* to use them. As you can see from Figure 13.1, for example, every number in the product code field is accompanied by the controlled vocabulary term to which it corresponds. If you want to, you can forget about the codes and just use the controlled words in your search. And as mentioned, since the abstract is searchable, every word or phrase it contains is a potential access point.

On the other hand, the codes remove any doubt about the proper way to enter a controlled vocabulary term. For example, why concern yourself with whether you need hyphens or commas or just spaces when entering the term "off-highway vehicle air filters" on DIALOG, BRS, or VU/TEXT when on all systems you can simply search for "3531326" in the product code field? It's precise and involves far fewer keystrokes.

Cascading Codes

PTS codes are "cascaded." That's a technical information retrieval term that means if you search on say the first three digits of a seven-digit product code, you'll automatically pick up everything below that number in the hierarchy. Here, for example, is how one series of PTS product code numbers is arranged:

28 Chemicals & Allied Products
  283 Drugs & Pharmaceuticals
    2831 Biological Products
      28312 Vaccines & Antigens for Human Use
      2831231 Polyclonal Antibodies

If you keyed in SELECT PC = 28 on DIALOG, you would automatically retrieve every record with a product code number that starts with those two digits. If you did SELECT PC = 28312, you would pick up everything underneath that code in the hierarchy, but nothing above it. All PTS records have seven digits in their product code fields, and as far as the search system is concerned, those seven digits constitute a whole word. Thus if the codes were not cascaded, searching for PC = 28312 would not turn up any hits, since there are only five digits. Of course you could truncate the number with a wildcard symbol, but PTS advises against this. (ABI/INFORM codes, in contrast, do not cascade and must be truncated when you want to search for more general information.)

Online Tip: If you want to limit your search to both general articles and a general industry or area, select the number of digits needed for the desired level of subject specificity and use zeros to fill it out to seven digits. In other words, SELECT PC = 283 will hit articles of all sorts about the drug and pharmaceutical industry. But SELECT PC = 2830000 will retrieve only those articles dealing with the industry as a whole.

For example, if you wanted articles that focused on the general outlook of the drug and pharmaceutical industry, you might enter:
  SELECT PC = 2830000 AND (FORECASTS OR OUTLOOK OR FUTURE)

Documentation and Customer Support

PTS representatives suggest starting most searches with a product code, an event code, and a country code and then using either free text words or other codes to further narrow the search. That's good advice, but you can easily do a free text search of a PTS database and get very satisfactory results. In fact, for basic searches where you want the latest information on a particular company or brand name product (like Tide) and can limit it to some reasonably specific but common concept (like market share), that's probably the best way to go. You'll get some information you don't want, but you can be in and out of the database and offline in less time than it takes to look up all the proper codes.

For more complex searches, however, you'll need the main *PTS Users Manual*. This sells for $50 and contains the PTS code list, case studies, tutorial chapters on using PTS on DIALOG, BRS, VU/TEXT, and the DATA-STAR systems. It is essential for anyone who wants to use PTS databases to their full potential. Additional users' guides are available for PROMT, MARS, NPA, RBN, and A/DM&T at $40 each. These are designed to supplement the main manual with detailed information, examples, and tips for using the respective databases. (DIALOG also sells database chapters for each PTS offering.) Finally, PTS publishes a company directory listing the proper names to use when searching for information on over 125,000 companies worldwide.

Predicasts operates an extensive training program in the U.S. and Canada. The PTS Training Seminar is designed to introduce new users to PTS databases, how to select them and how to search them. The PTS Update Seminar offers an overview of new PTS files and features. There are also various half-day seminars that focus on combined database search applications (instead of search technique) for such topics as the chemical industry, legal issues, and consumer products marketing. All PTS seminars are free. If you live in a major city and can provide a meeting room with phone access, PTS may be able to arrange holding a seminar for your group or organization. Custom on-site training sessions can also be arranged.

PADS (Predicasts Article Delivery Service) is another feature worth knowing about. The cost per article is $10 ($11.50 for locations other than the U.S. and Canada), plus $1 per page for any article over ten pages. Turnaround time is two days, and availability starts with January 1984. Virtually every publication PTS covers is available, including all of the often hard-to-find regional business newspapers and magazines.

Toll-free customer support is also available weekdays between the hours of 8:00 A.M. to 5:30 P.M., Eastern time. There's also a free newsletter, "PTS Online News." For more information contact:

Predicasts, Inc.
11001 Cedar Avenue
Cleveland, OH 44106
(800) 321-6388
(216) 795-3000
Telex: 985604

Predicasts International
First Floor
Central Court
1B Knoll Rise
Orpington, Kent BR6 OJA
Telephone: 0689 38488
Telex: 89888239

Full-Text Magazine Databases

Full-text magazine databases are among the hot new products in the online world. The trend can be attributed to the falling cost of computer storage and the rising use of word processing equipment on the part of the nation's magazine publishers—though as mentioned in Part I, it is often easier to have full-text articles keyboarded offshore than it is to convert a publisher's typesetting tapes for use in a database. Rising consumer demand is also undoubtedly a factor.

Caveats and Cautions

After all, full-text articles are something everyone can understand. No need to worry about bibcites, abstracts, and all that other stuff, right?

Well, not exactly. Full text is something to be enthusiastic about, but not for the reasons most people assume. The fact is, full-text can be treacherous to search. Consider a word like *steel*, for example. *You* may know that what you want are articles about the steel industry, but the database doesn't. Thus if you were to search, say, the full text of *Fortune* magazine for the words STEEL AND INDUSTRY, you would also get hits on any article containing terms like "nerves of steel," "a mind like a steel trap," "the Man of Steel," and the town of "North Industry, Ohio." Multiply that by the number of other magazines you can search at the same time and the number of other ways those two words can be used in our language, and you've got a real mess. You could have scores of hits, each of which represents a full-text article but only a few of which are likely to be relevant to your topic.

Fortunately, on most systems full-text records are accompanied by the conventional bibliographical citation, indexing terms, and abstract. And as we've seen, these tools can make it much easier to retrieve the precise records you want. You can still search the entire text of an article, though you'll want to pay particular attention to proximity operators. On DIALOG the search term STEEL(W)INDUSTRY, for example, would find only records where the words occurred adjacent to each other and in that order.

Now suppose that you refine your strategy so that it generates only seven or eight hits. You can be reasonably certain that the articles will be relevant. But which ones should you choose? On BRS/SEARCH and BRS/BRKTHRU you can ask to see the individual paragraphs containing your hits. But as discussed in Chapter 9, no one does full text better than Mead. On NEXIS it is particularly easy to page forward and back through a document viewing your keywords in context (KWIC).

But what do you do on a system that doesn't have those features? Short of downloading seven or eight complete articles at a cost of at least $7.50 apiece, the only way to make a selection on most systems is to look at the abstract, just as you would in most other databases.

In fact, when you have easy and instant access to the full text of an article, the abstract becomes more important than ever. Good abstracts can help you quickly determine whether you should read the source article. Without them, you could very well find yourself drowning in downloaded full-text articles, each of which you would have to read yourself.

Though it is great to have the option of searching the full text of an article, the main benefit is really instant document delivery. Unless the word, phrase, name, or other item you are looking for is highly unique, you will generally be better off using the bibcite, abstract, and indexing terms to locate and select an article. Then, if the price is right and if you do not need to see the illustrations found in the source document, download the full text.

The Harvard Business Review Online

Produced by John Wiley & Sons, Inc., The Harvard Business Review Online (HBRO) was one of the first full-text databases. At this writing it is available on BRS, DIALOG, NEXIS, and the European system, DATA-STAR. The database contains every article from 1976 onward, plus summaries for articles published between 1971 and 1975, and about 700 summaries of articles published prior to 1971. About the only thing that isn't included is the "Letters to the Editor" column.

Associated with each full-text article are a bibliographic citation, several indexing fields, and a 100- to 200-word abstract. HBRO uses a controlled vocabulary totaling more than 3,500 terms, plus 4,000 additional terms for the top 800 U.S. companies and the top 500 non-U.S. companies. All of these terms are listed in the *HBR/Online Thesaurus* ($50), and they allow you to search on various fields for subjects ("cost accounting"), corporate functions ("compensation"), products and services ("furniture repair"), and other concepts. There is also a field for Translation Language ("Danish," "Japanese," "German," etc.) signifying the availability of an authorized translation of the original article. (Ordering information for these articles is included in the manual.)

A database chapter is available from DIALOG, and Wiley has a number of free user aids: "Full Text Search Tips," "How to Order Reprints Online," and so on. For more information, contact:

> Wiley Electronic Publishing
> 605 Third Avenue
> New York, NY 10157
> (212) 850-6331

Other Full-Text Magazine Databases

We have already considered the two IAC ASAP full-text databases, and you'll find more information on the many full-text publications available through NEXIS in Chapter 9. The full text of all the Time-Life publications is available on VU/TEXT (Chapter 11).

In April 1986 the McGraw-Hill Business Backgrounder database became available on DIALOG (File 624). This database offers bibliographic citations and the full text (no abstracts) of such McGraw-Hill publications as *Aviation Week and Space Technology, Business Week, Byte, Chemical Engineering, Chemical Week, Data Communications, Electronics, Engineering News-Record, Inside NRC, Nuclear Fuel,* and *Nucleonics Week.* Coverage for most publications begins with 1985. For more information, contact:

> McGraw-Hill Business Backgrounder
> McGraw-Hill Inc.
> 1221 Sixth Avenue
> New York, NY 10020
> (212) 512-2103

...14...

NEWS MEDIA:
Papers, Wire Services, Radio, and Television

Tapping an online database is not the best way in the world to get the latest news. In fact, it's among the worst, ranking right up there with balancing your checkbook by computer or using it to keep track of your recipes as an appropriate application of the technology. A 25¢ newspaper will give you far more information for far less money. And with any number of round-the-clock radio and television news channels to choose from, currency is rarely a problem. Unless you need a special kind of news like stock quotes or late-breaking corporate stories that can affect your investment activities, it simply doesn't make sense to get your news online, despite what some database vendors would have you believe.

News is valuable online only when it's available for retrospective searching. Then it can be quite valuable indeed. If you know where to look, you can get an informative report on anything that has happened anywhere in the world in the last 20 years. In effect, your computer screen becomes a glass-bottomed boat with which you can cruise the ocean of news that's out there, peering into the depths and shallows to look at events that took place last week, last month, or many years ago.

We have repeatedly emphasized how important it is to always "consider the source" when you set out to conduct an online search. Nowhere is that dictum more applicable than here. Every type of news source is designed for a particular audience, and this fact profoundly influences both the kind of news and the amount of detail you can expect from each one.

There's no single source that does it all. By judiciously combining news sources, however, you can make these differences work for you with a kind of synergy that will result in a fuller, rounder picture than

313

would ever be possible with one source alone. In this chapter we'll show you what we mean as we consider the two major types of newspaper databases (index and full text), the major wire services, and, yes, online television and radio sources.

NEWSPAPERS
Index-Type Databases

The National Newspaper Index™ and NEWSEARCH™

The National Newspaper Index™ (NNI) and NEWSEARCH™ are both parts of the Information Access Company (IAC) database "system" described in the previous chapter. NNI is available on DIALOG, BRS, and NEXIS. At this writing, NEWSEARCH is available only on DIALOG. The difference between them is that NEWSEARCH is designed for currency. All IAC records start out there, but after 30 to 45 days the records are transferred to their permanent homes in other IAC databases (Magazine Index, Management Contents, Trade & Industry Index, etc.).

Thus, if you want the latest information from all of the publications IAC handles, you can simply go into NEWSEARCH instead of having to go to each of the IAC databases separately. There's even a "Week Indicator" field to make it easy to retrieve records for a given week. (Keying in WK = nn, where *nn* is the week number, is easier than keying in a range of dates.) And starting with records added in March of 1986, you can specify COMPANY PROFILE in the "article type" field to limit retrieval to just corporate information.

IAC adds over 1,200 records to NEWSEARCH every day, and while the indexing of magazines may take a bit longer, indexes for the newspapers are available 24 hours after publication. As the DIALOG Bluesheet points out, "All articles, news reports, editorials, letters to the editor, obituaries, product evaluations, biographical pieces, poetry, recipes, columns, cartoons, illustrations and reviews are included." The only items not included are things like minor personnel notes, stock market tables, weather charts, and horoscopes.

NEWSEARCH and the National Newspaper Index cover the following newspapers: *The Wall Street Journal* (WSJ), *The New York Times* (NYT), *The Washington Post* (WP), the *Los Angeles Times* (LAT), and the *Christian Science Monitor* (CSM). Coverage in NNI starts with January 1, 1979. Records are bibcites like this one from the version of NNI on BRS/BRKTHRU:

AN   65142.   8509.
DB   NOOZ.
TI   American politicians and the trouble with public-opinion polls; Larry the Lobster's predicament shows how silly surveys can become.
AU   Dillin-John.
SO   Christian Science Monitor (CSMOBF), Dec 6, 1983, Tue edition, p1, col 1.
PD   831206.
CI   COLUMN INCHES: 029.
DE   public-opinion-polls: analysis. election-forecasting: analysis. Gallup-Poll: statistics.

Online Tip: Which *editions* does NNI cover? For WSJ, it covers the Eastern (Princeton) and Western (Palo Alto) editions, but not the West and Southwest editions. For NYT, the National and the Late City editions are indexed. For CSM, the Western edition is covered but the New England, Eastern, Midwestern, and International Editions are not.

Online Tip: There is also a newspaper database called NDEX on the ORBIT Search. Owned by Bell & Howell, it indexes nine major U.S. newspapers including the *Chicago Sun-Times*, *Detroit News*, *Denver Post*, *New Orleans Times Picayune*, and the *San Francisco Chronicle*. It also covers seven Black newspapers, including the *Amsterdam New York News*, *Atlanta Daily*, *Baltimore Afro-American*, *Bilalian News*, *Chicago Defender*, and *New Pittsburgh Courier*. Updates are monthly. Coverage dates from 1976 to the present.

For more information, contact ORBIT (Chapter 10) or call Bell & Howell at (800) 521-3044. At this writing the database is available exclusively on ORBIT, but as Bell & Howell gets more involved in the online industry it may eventually appear elsewhere as well.

Abstract-and-Index Newspaper Databases

The Information Bank

The Information Bank was started by the New York Times Information Service in 1968, largely as an outgrowth of the computerization of that firm's widely used printed publication, *The New York Times Index*. From the beginning, however, the "InfoBank" covered more than just the *Times*. Most of the 10 papers and 40 magazines and other publications it includes are now covered elsewhere, though no other system goes back as far. At least a few of its offerings have remained exclusives. At this writing, for example, the InfoBank remains the only online index of the *Atlanta Constitution* or the *Houston Chronicle*, going back to 1976 in both cases.

The Information Bank has been through a lot of changes since those early days. When the parent company decided to get out of the database vending business in 1983, the operation was purchased by Mead Data Central. The InfoBank, along with the full text of *The New York Times*, is now available exclusively on Mead's LEXIS/NEXIS system.

At the system level it is not what one would call a perfect fit. NEXIS is designed as a full-text system, and it works exceptionally well with the full text of *The New York Times*. But the InfoBank is a database of bibliographic citations with searchable fields and abstracts, a format better suited to DIALOG, BRS, or ORBIT. Still, after a little mental adjustment, anyone familiar with those systems can successfully search the InfoBank on NEXIS (or LEXIS). The "abstracts" will not be what you are used to, however. It's not unusual to encounter an "abstract" that is only one or two sentences long, regardless of the length of the source article, and bereft of statistics. For example:

SOURCE: <SEATTLE TIMES> (ST)

DATE: April 14, 1986, Monday

SECTION: Section 3; Page 3, Column 1

BYLINE: BY LISA LEVITT RYCKMAN

ABSTRACT:

Lummi Indians of Washington State are fighting IRS for insisting that tribe's fisherman pay federal income tax on commercial <salmon> sales, as do others who fish in Pacific Northwest; are arguing that their catch is reservation resource protected and exempt from taxation by treaty and by years of case law; photo (M)

SUBJECT: LUMMI INDIANS; INCOME TAX; <SALMON;> FISHING, COMMERCIAL

We searched for the word *salmon* in the *Seattle Times* and, not surprisingly, got about 230 hits. The angle brackets highlighting the keywords in the source, abstract, and the subject fields are automatically inserted by Mead's software.

Instead of narrowing things down with additional search statements, we browsed through the first dozen or so looking for something interesting. The abstract above is the second one we encountered. You could obtain a copy of the source article from a document delivery house. But as we'll see in a moment, thanks to a little news media synergy, you may be able to find all the details you want elsewhere on NEXIS and on other systems.

Full-Text Newspapers

The New York Times and PAPERS
The full text of the final New York City edition of *The New York Times* is online and available for searching on NEXIS within 24 hours of its publication date. The file dates from June 1, 1980, and with the exception of ads, shipping announcements, stock quotes, and other ephemerals, everything is there, including any corrections to previously published articles. You can search the entire paper, or you can limit your search to one or more "desks" that signify the group within the *Times* organization that prepared the story. Included are desks for cultural, editorial, national, sports, foreign, and financial. There are also "special" desks that correspond to the weekday special sections of the *Times* (Living, Home, Science, and Weekend) and there are "Sunday desks" (magazine, book review, regional weeklies, travel, and so on).

It is also possible to specify the "type" of article you want. Options here include editorial, analysis, chronology (articles containing a list of a sequence of events), review (the arts, television, movies, etc.), obituary, and text (the complete transcript of verbatim excerpts from a speech). Best of all, Mead's Version 1.4 communications software package makes it easy to search for articles and to page forward and backward or jump from one article to another once you've found them. It offers the best electronic emulation of the act of reading a newspaper we've ever seen. (See Chapter 9 for more details.)

There are 17 other files in the NEXIS grouping called PAPERS, though not all of them are dailies, and some aren't really newspapers. The *American Banker* is there, however, dating from January 2, 1979, and normally available online within 48 hours of publication. *InfoWorld* (July 4, 1983, on; available within six days of publication) and *Computer World* (January 4, 1982, on; available within eight days of publication) are there, and so are *The Washington Post*, CSM, and *The Manchester Guardian Weekly*.

All of these are full-text files, and you can search them individually or as a group. The same pluses and minuses associated with full-text magazine databases apply here as well. Because no one has prepared an abstract and assigned key subject terms, PAPERS is generally not the place to search for broad concepts. However, it's fine if what you're searching for is relatively unique, like a person, corporation, or product name. If there is no name or term associated with the subject that is unique, spend some time thinking up a unique collection of keywords and look for that. As always with a full-text database, mind your positional operators. And don't forget that Mead Customer Service is available to help 24 hours a day.

The Wall Street Journal

By 6:00 A.M. Eastern time each weekday morning, the full text of the day's *Wall Street Journal* is available for searching on the Dow Jones News/Retrieval Service (DJNR). The database is sometimes called "TEXT 1" because it is the first selection on the //TEXT section menu. Full-text coverage starts with January 1984, and every feature and news article is there, including letters to the editor, the cultural page, and the little two-sentence fact fillers used to round out a column. The only things that are not included are advertising, stock quotes, currency rates, and similar ephemeral material, plus any tabular material not attached to an article. A table summarizing current oil prices, for example, would not be included, but a table reporting raw steel production compared to capacity utilization that was part of an article on that topic would be in the database.

Online Tip: Each day's *Wall Street Journal* is assembled at the company's facility in Chicopee, Massachusetts, and then beamed by satellite to 17 printing plants around the country. The first edition of the day is the "two-star edition" and it is the one you receive if you live relatively far away from one of the plants. The "three-star" edition is the final and it includes any corrections or updates to stories in the first edition. (It is rumored that the two or three stars appearing on the masthead of the front page signify how many times WSJ staffers proofread the copy, but sources at Dow Jones deny that this is the case.)

The *Journal* is published in four regional editions (East, West, Western, and Southwestern). This makes it possible for an advertiser to buy space in something other than the national *Wall Street Journal*. It also makes it possible for a given edition to carry stories likely to be of special interest to subscribers in that region. We haven't done a comparison, but according to sources in Chicopee, there is very little difference among the four regional editions. In any case, all four are part of the online version.

The two WSJ editions that are *not* online are the Asian and the European editions.

The //TEXT database also includes the full text of *The Washington Post* since January 1984, available within 48 hours of publication. There are also full-text articles from the *American Banker, Financial World, Forbes,* and the PR Newswire, all dating from January 1985. There is also the Dow Jones News Archive, containing selected articles from *Barron's,* the Dow Jones News Service (the "Broadtape"), and WSJ summaries dating from 1979 to the present. As is always the case with a newswire, there are many reports that never make it into a newspaper's printed edition, so the DJ News Archive can definitely be worth searching. The WSJ and *Barron's* records in the archive database have been edited and "tightened up," and there is normally a one-day delay between publication date and an article's appearance online.

Like BRS/SEARCH, the DJNR //TEXT database uses a modified version of IBM's STAIRS search language. And frankly, it's a little tough to handle. It does offer the unique capability of retrieval by the same DJ industry or government category codes and ticker symbols used elsewhere on the service. And you can now use the word DATE followed by a space and the date in either of two formats (MM/DD/YY or Month DD, YYYY) instead of the inverted "YYMMDD.DD." format required in years past. There is also a keyword highlighting feature (Print the first page with ..P then enter P* to jump ahead to the next page containing your keywords), but overall it's about as friendly as a jealous bull or a hungry bear.

Of course you can master the intricacies of //TEXT if you work at it long enough. Depending you your area of business it may not only be worthwhile, it may be vital to do so. However, WSJ is also covered by NEWSEARCH, NNI, Trade & Industry Index, Advertising & Marketing Intelligence (AMI on NEXIS), and many of the PTS (Predicasts, Inc.) databases discussed in Chapter 13. You may thus find that your time is better spent learning to use one or more of those systems to *locate* WSJ articles and turning to //TEXT only when you need the full text of a specific article.

It all depends on what you're looking for. But you should know that if you decide to do things this way, you can simply call DJNR Customer Service, give the representative the specs on the article you want, and ask what commands you should enter to retrieve it. Also, be aware that like all systems DJNR can be rather sluggish during business hours due to heavy usage. If you can do your searching and downloading during non-peak hours, you may be able to save yourself considerable time and money.

Regional Newspapers on VU/TEXT

Regional newspapers reflect the soul of the communities they serve.

They can also tell you a lot about local political and labor situations, who the power brokers and community leaders are, tax rates, proposed construction and redevelopment projects, and a good place to have lunch the next time you're in town. For example, a search of the *Boston Globe* turned up a lengthy article on artificial intelligence highlighting the activities of firms in the Route 128 (Silicon Valley—East) area. Some of these firms are so small you'd never hear of them in national sources (at least not until one of them introduces the next VisiCalc), but they're run by local people and so are of interest to the *Globe*'s readership. For similar reasons, there was also a long Sunday magazine interview piece featuring Mitchell Kapor, founder of Lotus Development Corporation. There were plenty of stories on An Wang, Ken Olsen (president of Digital Equipment Corporation), and other computer industry luminaries as well.

Stories from 1985 recounted in painful detail the number of layoffs brought about by that year's slump in the computer industry. But a sidebar in one story focused on a "super salesman" who at 28 was earning $80,000 a year. The fellow used to work for Hewlett-Packard but had just joined a start-up specialty computer company in Westboro, Mass. Now suppose you were an executive recruiter in California . . . .

There were also stories like these:

DATE: TUESDAY MARCH 25, 1986
PAGE: 61   EDITION: THIRD
SECTION: BUSINESS   LENGTH: SHORT
SOURCE: By Gregory A. Patterson, Globe Staff

FOSTER GRANT HAS NEW OWNER

There are some different folks behind those Foster Grants.
Yesterday Andlinger & Co., a Tarrytown, N.Y., investment banking and management company, announced it has acquired Foster Grant Co., the world's leading sunglasses company. Leominster-based Foster Grant also announced several management changes . . .

DATE: TUESDAY January 21, 1986
PAGE: 71   EDITION: THIRD
SECTION: BUSINESS   LENGTH: SHORT
SOURCE: By Desiree French, Globe Staff

ZAYRE REORGANIZES EXECUTIVE STRUCTURE

In response to rapid company growth and as part of an overall management development scheme, Zayre Corp. of Framingham yesterday announced it has reorganized its executive ranks and has created two new positions at Zayre Stores and T.J. Maxx, two of its largest divisions . . .

Note the local references. Foster Grant Co. is in Leominster and Zayre Corp. is based in Framingham. Both articles went on to give the names and other information on everyone involved in the acquisition or the restructuring.

Regional newspapers won't make you a native. But from wherever you happen to be on the globe, their electronic availability lets you take a quick, discrete course in "Wichita" or "Allentown" or some other city that is unavailable any other way.

What Papers Are on the System?

The VU/TEXT system is the premier full-text regional newspaper system. You'll find all of the things you need to know about it in Chapter 11 except the papers it covers:

Akron Beacon Journal
Albany Times-Union
(Allentown)*The Morning Call*
Anchorage Daily News
Arizona Republic
Boston Globe
Charlotte Observer
Chicago Tribune
Columbus Dispatch
Detroit Free Press
El Miami Herald (Spanish ed.)
Fresno Bee
Ft. Lauderdale News
Ft. Lauderdale Sun-Sentinel
Gilroy Dispatch
Houston Post
Knickerbocker News
Lexington Herald-Leader
(Los Angeles) *Daily News*
Miami Herald
Orlando Sentinel
Philadelphia Daily News
Philadelphia Inquirer
Phoenix Gazette
Richmond News Leader
Richmond Times-Dispatch
Sacramento Bee
San Jose Mercury News

Washington Post
Wichita Eagle-Beacon

VU/TEXT also offers gateway service to QL Search, a Canadian system that offers access to NEWSTEX, a database of all news wires of *The Canadian Press* dating back to 1981. And it is growing rapidly, so it is very likely that additional papers will have been added as you read this.

Online Tip: There's a corporate intelligence firm in New York that keeps a database of more than 10,000 people who have changed jobs and thus might be good sources of information about their former employers. Corporate headhunters keep similar files, though for different reasons. Either way, online regional newspapers can let you do much the same thing, since most carry announcements of personnel changes.

A search of VU/TEXT newspapers on words like "personnel," "promoted to," or "appointed" will be too broad. You'll get the kind of information you want, but it will be buried among hits on articles covering political, government, theater group, and virtually every other kind of organization. It's more efficient (and economical) to use controlled vocabulary descriptors. Most papers on VU/TEXT have a KEYWORD field, and the VU/TEXT manual provides lists of the controlled words for each paper.

If you do a keyword field search on the words EXECUTIVE, BUSINESS, and APPOINTMENT, or some combination of authorized descriptors, you'll have much better results. Consult the VU/TEXT manual or call Customer Service for more information on the commands to enter.

Regional Newspapers on DataTimes

As noted in Chapter 11, the other main purveyor of regional newspapers is the DataTimes system of Oklahoma City, Oklahoma. According to the company, contracts for online delivery of regional newspapers tend to be exclusive. So with the exception of *The Washington Post* (and the AP newswire), coverage does not overlap. In addition to the papers listed below, DataTimes offers a gateway for coverage of several Australian newspapers. At this writing three Queensland publications are included: *Courier Mail, Sunday Mail,* and *The Telegraph.* More are scheduled for the future. Here are the papers DataTimes covers at this writing:

Arkansas Gazette
Baton Rouge State Times
Chicago Sun-Times
Daily Oklahoman
Daily Texan (Univ. of Texas,
    Austin)
Dallas Morning News
Houston Chronicle
(Louisiana) *Morning Advocate*
Minneapolis Star and Tribune
Oklahoma City Times
(Oklahoma) *Journal Record*
Orange County Register
San Francisco Chronicle
Seattle Times
*St. Petersburg Evening-
    Independent*
St. Petersburg Times
The Washington Post

DataTimes has two subscription options. Under Option A, you pay a connect-time rate of $60 and any applicable display charges. In return, you agree to use one hour's worth of time a month. Under Option B, there is no monthly minimum requirement, but the connect rate is $95 an hour plus applicable display charges. Both options require a $50 one-time start-up fee that includes a user manual, a quarterly newsletter, and system training. For more information, contact:

> DataTimes
> 818 N.W. 63rd Street
> Oklahoma City, OK 73116
> (800) 642-2525
> (405) 843-7323

WIRE SERVICES

The two leading newswires are The Associated Press (AP) and United Press International (UPI). The AP was founded in 1848 by six New York publishers who figured they could save money and offer better service if they split the cost of fielding a staff of reporters. AP established the first permanent leased newswire in 1875 and has always remained a cooperative that is owned, financed, and operated by its publisher/broadcaster members. The company currently has more than

1,600 reporters, stringers (part-time reporters in given locations), photographers, and editors. It serves some 6,000 radio and television stations and more than 1,500 newspapers in the U.S. and over 10,000 outlets overseas.

The United Press was started in 1907 by E. W. Scripps as an independent business venture. In 1958 UP merged with International News Service and became United Press International. It has had serious financial problems in recent years, and it filed for reorganization ("Chapter 11") under the federal bankruptcy code in April 1985. But it has also had its share of "firsts," including the first news service for radio (1935).

There are other wire services as well. But most have a number of things in common. First and foremost, the world's wire services represent a huge Mississippi River of news that gathers features and reports from thousands of tributaries worldwide. Night and day the news flows in a quantity, variety, and depth that would probably turn you to a pillar of salt—or at least numb your cerebral cortex—if you could look at it all at once.

The reason we never see it in its totality is that as the stream flows by, editors at newspapers and television and radio stations dip into it to pull out just those stories they feel their respective audiences will find of interest. Most newswire news ends up in the wastebasket and never makes it into print or on the air. The newswire copy that does appear is often cut to fit the space left over after all the advertising has been slotted in. On days when ad pages are few, the identical newswire story may occupy twice the space it would be allotted on days when the sales department has sold up a storm.

There's nothing wrong with this, of course. In fact we should be thankful that there are editors to filter the news and advertisers willing to subsidize its broadcast or publication. But it represents a terrible waste. After all, an AP or UPI reporter may file a story containing precisely the facts and figures you need, but it might never appear anywhere and thus be beyond the grasp of conventional research techniques.

Online databases can solve this problem, however, and many of them have been motivated to do so in recent years. It's not too difficult to plug a newswire into an online system and offer "instant" news from reputable, recognizable sources like the AP or UPI. What's difficult is to persuade potential online users that there is a good reason to sign on to a system and *pay* to read the same current news one can get for free via television or radio or for a pittance from a newspaper.

But as noted, archival storage is a wholly different matter. Here is the entire river frozen for all time in magnetic form for you to skate over via an online system. You can pull up stories that never appeared in your local or national paper or appeared only in truncated form. You can trace the development of a story from the day it first appeared on the wire to the point of final resolution. And you can come up with contacts and access points to phone for more information. Online, archival newswires are truly a great, though little recognized, resource.

News in the Raw

Considering the source, however, it's important to remember that the wires in their native state represent "news in the raw." They're designed for newspeople and in some versions make no accommodations for people who aren't members of that profession. Thus, you shold be aware that a "slug" or "slugline" is a one- to two-word description of a story we would refer to as a "keyword" or "subject descriptor." (The term dates to the days of the hot-lead letterpresses.) A "take" is a page of a story designed to be pasted together in sequence with other "takes." Some reports, particularly those from abroad, are still sent via old-fashioned telex machines that are incapable of displaying lower-case letters. So you may see nothing but capital letters in a raw "feed" (story transmission), plus lots of numerical codes decipherable only by news professionals.

The A.M., P.M., and BC Cycles

Fortunately, much of the newswire copy you see online these days has been repackaged for computer-user consumption. But many of the conventions of the wire services still apply. The one that has perhaps the greatest significance to online searchers is the repetition of stories. The AP newswire, for example, issues stories in two main "cycles." The A.M. cycle is for morning papers; the P.M. cycle is for evening papers.

If there are new developments between the morning and afternoon cycles, an updated version of the story will appear in the P.M. cycle. (Stories tagged "BC" for "both cycles" are usually not re-edited during the day.) Usually the P.M. story (or the A.M. story the next day) will incorporate most of the same material found in the earlier edition. But *both* will be online.

You may or may not be able to avoid retrieving two or more copies of the same story, though on most systems you can avoid displaying more than the first page of a duplicate story. (Simply enter the command to move onto the next story in the queue.) See your system manual or call customer service for details.

The Associated Press

NEXIS has prepared and offered a "cleaned up" edition of the AP wire for some time. A special "AP Videotex" version has also been available on The Source and CompuServe for several years. But only with the introduction of the AP's in-house retrieval system in the fall of 1985 has the full wire been available for archival search and retrieval on many systems. The AP wire database on VU/TEXT and DataTimes, for example, is the same database the Associated Press uses internally. The typical delay between a story's appearance on the wire and its appearance in the database is 72 hours.

As you may have noticed, the various news media tend to play off (some would say "cannibalize") one another. Thus it is not uncommon to find a network news anchor reporting a story that originated as an article in last week's *Wall Street Journal*. The same thing happens in print, and as a searcher you can take advantage of it.

For example, a local newspaper reporter's story may alert a newswire reporter to an event or happening, and the wire reporter will do his or her version of the story the next day. Similarly, a wire reporter's story about some national trend may prompt a newspaper editor to assign a reporter to go out and "get the local angle."

And, of course, most newspapers carry a lot of wire copy. That turned out to be the case with the "salmon" story we located in the *Seattle Times* via the NEXIS InfoBank database. (You might want to turn back and take a look at the bibcite now.) As we mentioned, you could order a copy of the actual article from a document delivery house. But before doing that, it would be worth checking the AP (or UPI) newswire databases.

We did this on VU/TEXT, though we could have done the same thing on NEXIS. It turns out that even though the bibcite does not identify it as such, the story is taken directly from the AP newswire. At the end of the newswire story the reporter is identified as the AP's correspondent in the area.

Basically, then, we used the InfoBank to locate the article and the AP newswire database to retrieve its full text. That was serendipity. But even if the two stories hadn't been identical, it would still be worth checking the wire since the issue may have been covered by a wire reporter. Shown below is but a brief, heavily edited sample. The full article tells you everything you could possibly want to know about the situation.

THE ASSOCIATED PRESS

DATE: Monday   April 14, 1986
TIME-STAMP: 1038EST   LENGTH: 1244 WORDS
CATEGORY: Domestic News
SLUG: Tribal Taxes   CYCLE: PM
SUMMARY: Fishing Tribe Versus the Taxman

ILLUSTRATION: Laserphoto
BYLINE: By LISA LEVITT RYCKMAN, Associated Press Writer
DATELINE: BELLINGHAM, Wash.

. . . battle plans to save Lummi Indian livelihood . . .
    The IRS says . . . must pay federal income tax on commercial salmon sales . . . The Lummis argue . . . a reservation resource protected and exempt from taxation by treaty . . .
    When the Treaty of Point Elliott was signed in 1855, the Lummi Indians caught salmon in nets of twine fashioned from the nettles that grow on the San Juan Islands, about 90 miles north of Seattle . . .
    Today they fish with 1,800-foot-long synthetic nets, their reservation consists of 17,000 acres of mainland and tidelands, . . . But their 3,000-member tribe, whose 1,000 registered fishermen make it the largest of the region's 20 small fishing tribes, still depends on the salmon for its livelihood . . .
    The reservation's 85 percent unemployment rate drops to 40 percent in salmon season . . .

The UPI Newswire

The main archival UPI databases are on NEXIS and DIALOG. NEXIS coverage starts with September 26, 1980, and DIALOG coverage begins with April 1983. On DIALOG, File 260 contains the most recent three months' worth of stories. File 261 contains everything else. The following fields are available for incorporation in your search statements: lead paragraph, story tag, story text, byline, cycle, dateline (geographic location), publication date, UPI-assigned priority, news category, time of transmission, and word count. NEXIS offers similar fields but includes a field for "correction" as well.

UPI is also available on CompuServe, NewsNet, and GEISCO (General Electric), but not in archival form. On NewsNet, for example, UPI is available only as part of that vendor's NewsFlash current awareness (SDI) service.

Other Wire Services

Although they are the most famous, AP and UPI don't have a lock on the newswire business. There are *lots* of other wires, each of which specializes in some particular kind of news. Of the systems covered in this book, NEXIS has the widest selection. Its WIRES database offers a dozen different newswires, in addition to AP and UPI. NewsNet and Dow Jones also have some newswires. Highlights include:

• Asahi News Service—Global coverage of economic, financial, political, and technological news, with the emphasis on Southeast Asia and Japan.

• Interlink Press Service—An international wire specializing in coverage of Latin America and Third World countries.

- Jiji Press Ticker—Japan's leading economic news agency; covers every significant trading market in Japan—the Tokyo stock exchange to the Yokohama raw silk market.

- Kyodo—Japan's leading domestic general news agency (politics, sports, business, the arts, etc.). "Kyodo" freely translated means "associated press." Kyodo is a non-profit association of some 62 daily newspapers and the public Japan Broadcasting Corporation.

- Reuters—The well-known British-based news service that specializes in international, political, cultural, economic, and sports stories.

- USA Today—A product of Gannett News Media Services. HOTLINES for national, international, money, and weather. DECISIONLINE summaries of news about specific industries and professions. SPECIAL REPORT features designed to provide the background behind the news.

- Xinhua—The New China News Agency, the official news agency of the People's Republic of China.

Special Services

All news media seem to intersect at some point. As mentioned, a newswire does a story that gets picked up by a newspaper; a television or radio news editor sees it in print and does a version of the story in his or her medium; a newspaper reporter notices the comments of one of the story's leading characters on TV and decides to do a follow-up; and so on and on.

That's the essence of a free press, and it is a wonder to behold. But only relatively recently have the online electronic media been brought into the loop. Even now there are only a few examples of a crossover between radio and television and "online." But where those examples exist, there is a tremendous value added.

In terms of validity of content there is no difference between an interview with a U.S. senator published in a magazine and an on-air interview conducted by a television or radio reporter. In fact, the on-air interview may be more valid as it eliminates any possibility of the subject's being misquoted. The only difference is the media. A published magazine or newspaper interview is searchable and retrievable. A radio or TV interview can be taped, but even if you're a whizz with the "fast-forward" button, it cannot be effectively searched.

Transcripts of broadcasts are a different matter. You won't be able to see the sweat on the politician's brow when the interviewer asks a diffi-cult question, but you'll have his or her response in writing. At *this* writing there are only a few such transcripts online, but they are among the best "talking head" programs going. They include the "MacNeil/Lehrer NewsHour" and "Wall $treet Week."

The MacNeil/Lehrer NewsHour

"The MacNeil/Lehrer NewsHour" is Public Broadcasting's answer to the headline and photo caption services the major commercial networks run each evening at the dinner hour. It features news in-depth and the interview/discussion is its métier. Originally a half-hour program, it went to an hour-long format on September 15, 1983.

Available on NEXIS, this database contains the complete transcript of every broadcast since January 1, 1982. Transcripts are usually online about 21 days after the air date, and they can be 50 pages or more in length. Fortunately you can search by field and use all of NEXIS's pow-erful display features to look at exactly what you want. Searchable fields include air date, headline, byline, and body.

The byline field includes all reporters and guests for the entire pro-gram, as well as the titles, organizational affiliations, and geographic locations of the reporters and guests. That means you can easily see if, say, Senator Soaper has ever been on the show or if anyone from Com-mon Cause has appeared.

The body field is the program transcript and it can be searched by separate segment as well. The "focus segments" are the three to five in-depth interviews, reports, or analyses of major news events done in each program. The "intro" segment presents the headlines of the day and offers an overview of what the show will cover. The "news sum-mary" recaps the top news stories of the day. Here's a sample of what you'll find online:

The MacNeil/Lehrer NewsHour

May 7, 1986, Wednesday Transcript #2768

LENGTH: 8611 words

HEADLINE: Intro;
News Summary;
Tax Reform: Winners and Losers;
Damage Control;
Are We Beating Cancer?

BYLINE: In New York: ROBERT MacNEIL, Executive Editor; CHARLAYNE HUNTER-GAULT, Correspondent; In Washington: JIM LEHRER, Associate Editor; JUDY WOODRUFF,

Correspondent; Guests: In Washington: Sen. BOB PACKWOOD, Republican, Oregon;; Chairman, Finance Committee; HENRY AARON, Economist; Dr. PETER GREENWALD, National Cancer Institute; In St. Louis: MURRAY WEIDENBAUM, Economist; In Bonn, West Germany: THOMAS ROSER, German Atomic Forum; In Boston: Dr. JOHN BAILAR, Harvard University;

BODY:

Intro

ROBERT MacNEIL: Good evening. In the news today, the House joined the Senate in rejecting arms sales to Saudi Arabia. Early today the Senate Finance Committee unanimously passed a sweeping tax reform plan. The Soviets asked West Germany for new help in controlling their damaged nuclear reactor. Details of these stories in our news summary, coming up. Jim?

JIM LEHRER: After the news summary, the Packwood tax reform proposal with Senator Packwood and two analyzers, an update on the Soviet nuclear disaster from a West German expert, and a battleground debate over the war on cancer.

Wall $treet Week

Transcripts of the PBS program "Wall $treet Week" have long been available on the Dow Jones News/Retrieval Service. Everything is included: Louis Rukeyser's opening remarks, the panel discussion and viewer question segment, and the guest interview. However, only the most recent four programs are available. The previous week's telecast is added to the system every Thursday morning at 6:30 A.M. Eastern time and the oldest transcript is removed.

You can choose the broadcast by date and then select the segments you want to see, but the database is not searchable. You may also find that DJNS's short pages and all upper-case formatting leaves much to be desired, but the information is there, and that's what counts. Here's a sample on the opposite page.

BBC Summary of World Broadcasts and Monitoring Reports

The Monitoring Service of the British Broadcasting Company systematically monitors radio broadcasts from 120 countries worldwide. It does not cover the U.S., U.K., or Canada. The source material originates in some 50 different languages. The service translates these into English and prepares a written summary. The summary is published daily Monday through Saturday, and that is what is online.

The database is available on NEXIS and it exists in three sections: the Summary of World Broadcasts (SWB), the Monitoring Report, and the SWB Weekly Economic Reports. The main SWB section is further subdivided into sections corresponding to the areas of the world from which the broadcast originated. These are Eastern Europe, Far East,

WALL $TREET WEEK ONLINE

INDEX OF W$W

PRESS   FOR
01   MAY 30 — W$W IN LOS
ANGELES
02   MAY 23 — MURRAY L.
WEIDENBAUM, DIRECTOR,
CENTER FOR THE STUDY OF
AMERICAN BUSINESS
03   MAY 16 — RICHARD SANDOR,
SR. VICE PRESIDENT, DREXEL
BURNHAM LAMBERT INC.
04   MAY 09 — HARRY V.
KEEFE JR., PRESIDENT,
KEEFE, BRUYETTE & WOODS
INC.

(We selected 01.)

PRESS   FOR
A   MR. RUKEYSER'S COMMENTARY
B   PANEL DISCUSSION
C   VIEWER QUESTIONS
D   GUEST INTERVIEW

(We selected D.)

—SPECIAL GUEST—

—MR. RUKEYSER: AND NOW, BEFORE
WE MEET TONIGHT'S SPECIAL GUEST,
LET'S TAKE A QUICK LOOK AT THE
HISTORY OF TELEVISION—THE
PHENOMENON OF OUR TIME. (AUDIO
FROM "THE HOWDY DOODY SHOW.")
"SAY KIDS! WHAT TIME IS IT?"
"IT'S HOWDY DOODY TIME!"
  FROM THE EARLIEST DAYS OF
TELEVISION, AMERICANS HAVE
ARGUED ABOUT WHAT ROLE IT SHOULD
PLAY IN OUR CIVILIZATION. THE
GROUNDWORK FOR THE DEBATE WAS
. . .

Middle East and Africa, and the USSR. The Monitoring Report offers a distillation of the main SWB database and news from Latin America. The SWB Weekly Economic Reports cover specialized economic, scientific, and technical news for each of the four SWB areas.

On NEXIS, coverage starts with January 1, 1979. Information is usually available online within two days of print publication. You can search all segments or you can target your search on any country or any issue. For example: (EASTERN EUROPE AND HUNGARY) or (POLAND AND MEAT PRICES) or (USSR AND NUCLEAR POWER). Here's a sample of an SWB summary of a radio broadcast from Iran:

Summary of World Broadcasts/The Monitoring Report

June 3, 1986, Tuesday

SECTION: Part 4 The Middle East, Africa and Latin America; IV(A) THE MIDDLE EAST

PAGE: ME/8275/i

LENGTH: 138 words

HEADLINE: Iranian war expansion plans announced prior to Jerusalem Day

BODY:
Mohsen Reza'i, Commander of the Islamic Revolution Guards Corps, told reporters at a news conference on 31st May, reported by Tehran radio*, that preparations for a far greater participation by the people in the war, both at the battlefronts and in manufacturing arms, would be announced on Jerusalem Day (6th June). "It has been proved today that the world will not pay attention to any logic other than force . . . The only path left to us today is to turn the resistance war into a great war," he said. The radio also broadcast an announcement calling on all trained volunteers to report to guards corps or mobilisation forces bases immediately, for dispatch (presumably to the front) on Jerusalem Day. The programme for celebrating the day would begin on 2nd June, with a speech by President Khameneh'i, the radio said.

Availability on Other Systems

The British-based system Datasolve, a subsidiary of Thorn EMI, carries SWB on the World Reporter database it introduced June 1, 1986. SWB coverage there starts with January 1982. The World Reporter is available via gateway connection through VU/TEXT ($140/hour, including telecommunications), and VU/TEXT offers a ready reference guide that equates World Reporter commands with its own.

World Reporter is also one of the systems that is part of the EasyNet gateway. As mentioned in Chapter 6, EasyNet can be accessed directly or through the CompuServe and Western Union EasyLink systems. In addition to SWB, the World Reporter database includes the Asahi News Service, the AP (European), the BBC External Services News (major British and international news from the BBC in London), *The Economist, The Financial Times, The Guardian, Keesing's Contemporary Archives, The New Scientist,* and TASS, the Soviet news agency.

Finally, SWB is also a part of the TEXTLINE database owned and operated by Finsbury Data Services (FDS). FDS is also based in the U.K. and it represents Datasolve's main competition. In addition to SWB, TEXTLINE carries a lot of information on U.S. and non-U.S. companies and EEC (Common Market) data. It can be searched via free text or with the U.K.'s equivalent of American SIC codes (UK.HMSO). The U.S. representative for Finsbury is Information Access Company (IAC). To contact IAC for more information, call: (800) 227-8431; (800) 626-9935, in California.

...15...

ACCESS:
Directories of People, Places, and Organizations

T his chapter is going to put the unwrapped end of a 220-volt line into your hands. But there's no need to be concerned about your safety: If you don't feel the power surging through your fingertips by the time we're finished, you were either dead, drugged, or on serious medication to begin with. Actually, the only thing that's shocking is how easy it is to locate the points of access to a company, an organization, or a person, including the major details of his or her life.

We hasten to add that everything is public information. In fact, most of the databases considered in this chapter are based on printed directories available at your local library. But the multiple ways you can get at the information once a directory goes electronic, the computer's speed, and the synergy of using several databases together to assemble a complete profile of a person, place, or organization is a little breathtaking.

We're going to do exactly that at the end of this chapter. But first, here are the databases we're going to look at. Except as noted, each is available only on DIALOG at this writing:

> *People*
> Marquis Who's Who
> Biography Master Index
> Biography Index (Wilsonline)
>
> *Companies and Organizations*
> Thomas Register Online
> Encyclopedia of Associations

Places
Electronic Yellow Pages
Instant Yellow Pages (ABL system)

People

Other Biographical Databases
We've selected the online equivalents of several printed directories because they focus on general biographical information. However, there are other databases with biographical information that you may want to investigate on your own. To find them, you have only to tap the online version of the 735-page *Database Directory* published by Knowledge Industry Publications, Inc. (KIPI). This is available in BRS/SEARCH and BRS/BRKTHRU as KIPD. Sign on, select KIPD, and enter the search word: BIOGRAPH$. The BRS truncation symbol ($) allows for both singular and plural occurrences of the word. You'll discover nearly a score of databases that contain biographical information of some sort. Here are some you may want to consider, starting with those available on the systems discussed in this book:

Standard & Poor's Register—Biographical   **DIALOG**

Personal and professional data on more than 70,000 executives affiliated with public and private companies. Companies must have sales of $1 million or more. U.S. and non-U.S. companies are included.

Federal Judiciary Almanac Database   **LEXIS/NEXIS**

Biographical information on judges; names of court clerks and their telephone numbers. Organized by court, by district, and by circuit.

American Men and Women of Science   **DIALOG and BRS**

Biographies of more than 130,000 scientists and engineers in the biological and physical sciences. Corresponds to the R. R. Bowker publication of the same name.

Forensic Services Directory   **LEXIS/NEXIS**

Biographies, background, and capabilities of "expert witnesses" available to help attorneys, journalists, corporations, etc. Also available on WestLaw. For information on St. Paul-based WestLaw, call: (800) 328-0109.

BRWE

Available only in Australia and New Zealand, this is *Business Review Weekly* online. Contains "biographical material on prominent people of interest to Australia, New Zealand and the Pacific regions." Produced by: Info-Line (Australian Financial Review Information Service), John Fairfax, Ltd., P.O. Box 506, 2001 Sydney, NSW Australia; Telephone: (02) 20944. Telex: AA24851.

BIODOC™

Biographical information (in French) on over 50,000 prominent Europeans in the fields of politics, sports, religion, science, and the arts. Corresponds to *Who's Who in Europe* and *Nouveau Dictionnaire Biographique Europeen* (only France). Contact: G-CAM in France at telephone number: 33-1-538-1010.

Canadian Register of Research and Researchers in the Social Sciences

Biographical and career data on over 8,500 Canadian social scientists in government, industry, and universities. Also lists research projects and publications. Database is not available in the U.S. Contact: Social Science Computing Laboratory (SSCL) at: (519) 679-6378.

Labor Arbitration Information System (LAIS)

Biographical information on more than 3,000 labor arbitrators in the U.S. and Canada. Contact: Labor Relations Press, One Labor Relations Plaza, P.O. Box 579, Ft. Washington, PA 19034. Telephone: (215) 628-3113.

Geneva Series I, II, III

Biographies and resumes of over 25,000 consultants by industry and service. Available on CompuServe's Executive Information Service. Call: (800) 848-8199; (614) 457-0802, in Ohio.

Marquis Who's Who (MWW)
    The *Who's Who* (WW) series is probably the best-known source of biographical information in the world. The online version corresponds to two WW volumes: *Who's Who in America* and *Who's Who in Frontier Science and Technology*. In the future, no one can say just when, other WW volumes may be added as well.
    At this writing the Marquis Who's Who database on DIALOG con-

tains over 105,000 biographies. According to the database producer, 50% of the biographies are business figures. In a survey of businesspeople conducted by the Washington Researchers group, the file was chosen as the top source of business biographical information.

That information is collected from and verified by the biographees themselves through questionnaires sent out by the publisher every two years. According to the DIALOG Bluesheet, "If a reference-worthy individual fails to submit biographical data, Marquis staff members compile the information through independent research. Sketches compiled in this manner are denoted by an asterisk."

MWW records have as many as 40 separate fields. And of course that's what makes the online version so powerful. The fields include occupation, current business and home addresses, company name, schools attended, marriage (and divorce) date, memberships in professional organizations, and creative works. As a searcher, you can look for intersections of any of the 40 fields.

Find me a journalist with a background in both print and electronic media who served in the U.S. Air Force and holds an MBA degree. Find me everyone who worked at Procter & Gamble and currently heads an advertising agency in Illinois, Michigan, or Ohio. Or give me the complete record for "Jamerheimer-Smith, John Jacob." And so on. There is no way you could obtain these kinds of intersections from the printed directory. But online it takes only a few seconds.

The DIALOG database chapter (for File 234) is essential for making full use of MMW, since it explains each of the fields and includes a list of "research codes" and "research interest codes" used for biographies from the science and technology directory. Marquis has had various free quick-reference guides designed to supplement the DIALOG documentation for this database and its Marquis PRO-Files, a database of online professinals that is also on DIALOG. For more information, contact:

> Data Products Department
> Marquis Who's Who, Inc.
> 200 East Ohio Street
> Chicago, IL 60611
> (800) 621-9669
> (312)787-2008
> Telex: 181162

Online Tip: If you're interested in the *Who's Who* record of a specific individual, you probably won't need the additional documentation. Just sign on to DIALOG and BEGIN 234. Then enter

Online Tip (cont.)

EXPAND NA = lname, fname where "lname" is the last name and "fname" is the first name or the first initial of the name. If the person is in the database, you should see his or her name on the expand list.

Key in SELECT En where En is the "expand" number of the name you want. Finally, key in TYPE sn/5/n where "sn" is the set number (probably 1) and "n" is the record number (probably 1). The "5" requests the full-record format.

Biography Master Index (BMI)

BMI is a reference database. That is, it doesn't give you the biographical information itself. It tells you where it can be found. At this writing BMI has references for over 5.5 million people, living and dead, famous or not. It occupies two files (287 and 288) on DIALOG and corresponds to the eight-volume *Biography and Geneology Master Index* (BGMI), the five-volume 1981-1985 cumulation of that work, plus each year's BGMI supplement. These works are published by Gale Research, one of the leading names in the directory field.

Where does the information come from? The short answer is that it comes from more than 1,150 editions and volumes of over 565 source publications. That wasn't enough for us so we asked Gale. The answer can be found in a little booklet called *BioBase 1984 Master Cumulation* and its 1985-86 supplement. (BioBase is the name of the product on microfiche.)

Plunging in at random, we found such sources as *Contemporary Artists* and *Contemporary Architects*, both of which happen to be published by St. Martin's Press. There was also the *McGraw-Hill Encyclopedia of World Biography*, *Minnesota Writers*, *The Directory of Infamy: The Best of the Worst*, and *A Dictionary of Contemporary Latin American Authors*. Every volume with the words "Who's Who" in the title was also included: government, graphic art, hockey, Hollywood, jazz, librarianship, opera, the People's Republic of China, and so on. (Only a few of these are published by Marquis.)

All of which means you'll still need a library or some other way to access these volumes. But you won't have to go in guessing. (Great for a busy parent helping a child with a school assignment.) With BMI you can quickly whip up a list of virtually every book or other source that contains biographical information on your subject. As the DIALOG database chapter points out, the database can be searched by name, source publication, and years of birth or death. For more information and a copy of the free *BioBase* source booklets, contact:

Biography Master Index
Gale Research Company
Book Tower
Detroit, MI 48226
(313) 961-2242

Biography Index (BIO)

Like BMI, the Biography Index on Wilsonline covers both the quick and the dead. Jules Verne, Victor Herbert, Heidi Abramovitz, you name the name and Biography Index will pull up a reference to a biographical article or directory entry. There is some unavoidable overlap between BMI and BIO, but the two files are essentially different. BIO covers books and directories. But as you might expect from a product of the Wilson company, it also covers periodicals and magazines. Altogether BIO covers interviews, obituaries, biographies, and book reviews and other articles with biographical content appearing in some 2,600 periodicals, everything from the "Citibank Monthly Economic Letter" to *People* to the *Yale Review*.

Coverage begins with works published in August 1984 onward, and all fields and all nationalities are included. You can search by subject, name, author, article type (interview, autobiography, etc.), periodical title, book title, publisher, and so on. See Chapter 11 for more details on Wilsonline.

Companies and Organizations

Thomas Register Online™

Thomas Register is sort of a "who's who" of American companies, but it's really designed to be more of a "who makes what?" The database corresponds to the *Thomas Register of American Manufacturers*, a 20-volume set found in many libraries. There are over 135,000 profiles of U.S. companies in every industry *except* food and transportation. Over 50,000 products and services are covered, as are over 104,000 brand names. The information is gathered each year from the companies themselves by questionnaire, telephone interview, and on-site visits by Thomas personnel.

This is not the place to go for company financial information. There is a field for "assets" but it's not searchable and is intended primarily as an indication of the company's size. However, if you want a list of every company that makes a particular kind of product, from self-tapping screws to stainless steel valves or sump pumps, Thomas's promises it will contain something that will interest you.

Each record gives you the company name, address, and phone number, plus the types of products it makes and the trade names for each. You can retrieve records on the company name, city, state, product type, telephone area code, trade name, and ZIP code. And you can sort by company, city, state, area code, and ZIP code. Obviously mailing and telemarketing lists and lists of companies likely to compete with you in a given product line or geographical area are a snap with Thomas Register Online.

There is a free booklet called "Thomas Register Online Mini-Documentation," but it's really more of a series of very short case studies than anything else. The main documentation you need is the DIALOG database chapter (File 535). Still, if you want the free booklet or more information, contact:

> Thomas Publishing Company
> One Penn Plaza
> New York, NY 10001
> (212) 695-0500

The Encyclopedia of Associations

We are a nation of associations, of groups of people banded together for their common good. Whether it's encouraging the consumption of fried food, saving an obscure species of blue-eyed mosquito, or merely advocating moderation in all things, if an industry or an issue is involved chances are that somewhere an association's got it covered. And if there's an association, the chances are good that the multi-volume Gale Research *Encyclopedia of Associations* to which this database corresponds has *it* covered.

Altogether, this database covers some 19,500 national associations, chambers of commerce, labor unions, Greek letter and fraternal, ethnic, and hobby organizations, and more. The information is gathered by annual questionnaire mailings to association executives, and updates are made thrice yearly. Non-U.S. associations are covered as well, if they have a substantial U.S. membership or are deemed to be of special interest to Americans.

The database is searchable by founding year, geographic location, officer, name of the organization, and ZIP code. Perhaps most important of all, you can also gain access by "section heading code." There are 18 of these codes ranging from "02—Agricultural organizations and commodity exchanges" to "14—Athletic and sports organizations." Records can be sorted by organization name, subject heading, and ZIP code. There are no special search aids, but there is a DIALOG database chapter (File 114).

Online Tip: If you ever want to know about an industry, its trade association should be among the first places you call. While the information an association provides is almost always biased (What else would you expect?), it is usually both copious and free.

At this writing BRS does not have an equivalent of the above-mentioned encyclopedia, but it does have a database called Associations' Publications in Print. This is produced by the R. R. Bowker Company, the same people who do *Books In Print* and other volumes. It offers bibliographic information on pamphlets, journals, handbooks, and technical reports published by all manner of associations and trade and special interest groups. It covers over 100,000 documents, including both current items and those declared out of print since November 1981.

The database is searchable by subject (do a BRS "root" or a BRKTHRU "stem" on a subject before searching) and many other fields. It makes a nice complement to the Encyclopedia of Associations database, particularly since it does not include association addresses and contact information.

Places

The Electronic Yellow Pages (EYP)

Produced by Market Data Retrieval (MDR), a mailing list company acquired by Dun & Bradstreet Corporation in June of 1986, the Electronic Yellow Pages database includes listings from the Yellow Pages sections of over 4,800 telephone books nationwide. But while the name offers a good quick handle on the database, it definitely does not say it all. In addition to Yellow Pages listings, MDR includes information from 10K financial reports, census figures, vertical industry directories, annual reports, and a host of other directories. Consequently it can give you a lot more than just a phone number, line of business, and an address.

Available on DIALOG, EYP's ten million listings of businesses and professionals are spread over seven files including: construction, financial services, manufacturers, professionals, retailers, services, wholesalers. An eighth file, the Electronic Yellow Pages Index, can help you determine which other EYP files to search for particular kinds of records. Unless you're familiar with the mailing list business, it is always best to check here first.

EYP offers a good way to track down companies not included by sources like the Dun & Bradstreet's Dun's Market Identifiers database, which covers only businesses with $1 million in revenues and more than ten employees. With EYP, on the other hand, if a company's got a phone and a Yellow Pages listing anywhere in the country, it's in the database.

As a searcher you can gain access to each database by a variety of fields. To increase specificity, Market Data Retrieval has added a fifth character to the standard government SIC codes. MDR reports that users frequently search on the basis of company name (CO=) to track down information on some company they read or heard about. Others use EYP to develop lists of sales prospects, telemarketing lists, and mailing lists. Still others use the system as a market research tool to determine how many businesses of a certain type exist in a given range of ZIP codes or some other area.

A number of EYP fields are standard for every file, but many are database-specific. For example, among the fields you can search on in the financial services file are the following:

Advertising class
Assets (banks, savings and loans,
    and credit unions only)
County
City
State
ZIP code
Two-digit primary SIC code
SIC codes—primary four- and
    modified five-digit codes
Number of employees
Telephone area code
Company name

The EYP professionals directory has fields for the person's name, hospital facilities (plus type, ownership, and number of beds), and medical specialty. In the retailers file you can search on number of stores, number of employees, parent company, and city population as well. Again, this is information you won't find in the printed Yellow Pages.

In short, wherever you are you can rapidly develop a list of companies and professionals anywhere else who meet your criteria. You can tell DIALOG to sort your hits on every important field before displaying them, and/or you can ask that the addresses be printed offline on pressure-sensitive labels. You can also take advantage of DIALOG's

REPORT command to create a report containing whichever data elements you choose.

The cost of displaying a record containing the company name, address, and ZIP code is 15¢ (Format 9). The full record with all the additional information is 20¢ plus connect-time charges of $60 an hour, plus telecommunications charges, of course. Clearly EYP is more expensive than the nickel a name you might pay using a list broker. But it's fast, it's customized, and unlike most commercially available lists, the list is not salted with dummy names to track unauthorized use. You can use it again and again, though it's important to remember that Yellow Pages data changes quickly. A quarter of the database is updated every three months.

Online Tip: Here's a nifty trick you might consider trying. As the DIALOG Bluesheets point out, Format 10 is the mailing label format for all EYP databases. It is the one you would use when requesting an offline printout of a list on pressure-sensitive mailing labels. The cost is 10¢ per record, a nickel less than the online name/address/ZIP format (Format 9).

We checked with DIALOG Customer Service to see if it would be possible to use the PRINT VIA DIALMAIL option. As discussed in Chapter 7, this tells DIALOG to send the material it would normally print out on paper to your electronic mailbox on the DIALMAIL system. Customer Service confirmed that this could indeed be done, and as would be the case with an offline printout of labels, the addresses will be arranged three-across. Best of all, as confirmed by Customer Service, you will be charged the Format 10 "offline printout" rate of 10¢ per name.

So instead of downloading a list in Format 9 at 15¢ a name and $60 per hour in connect charges, you can have the list sent to your DIALMAIL mailbox, pay 10¢ a name, and download it at the DIALMAIL connect rate of $12 an hour. (Telecommunications costs must be added in both cases, of course.)

How to Use EYP

The best way to use the EYP databases is to first BEGIN 500, the master index file. Then SELECT *word*, where *word* is the type of product, business, service, or whatever you want. The system will come back with a set of hits. Next, TYPE sn/5/n where *sn* is the set number, 5 is the full record format, and *n* is the hit number (or range of hit

numbers) you want to see. Each record that is then displayed will give
you the name of the category, the MDR modified SIC code to use, the
EYP file to search, and the number of listings in that file. The cost for
using File 500 is $35 an hour, and 5¢ per record.

When you go into the proper EYP file, it is always a good idea to do
an EXPAND of any brand or proper names. MDR enters information
exactly as it appears in the Yellow Pages, so a name like "McDonald's"
may be in the database under a variety of spellings (Mc Donalds,
McDonald, etc.). Should you search for CHEVY or CHEVROLET?
Only EXPAND can tell you.

Market Data Retrieval sells its *User Guide* for $29.95, and it has a
number of free guides and code listings as well. Sources at the company
asked us to emphasize that users are welcome to call MDR's toll-free
number for search assistance. Customer Service hours are between 8:30
A.M. and 5 P.M., Eastern time. For more information, contact:

> Market Data Retrieval
> 16 Progress Drive
> Shelton, CT 06484
> (800) 624-5669
> (800) 435-3742, in Connecticut
> (203) 926-4800

The Instant Yellow Pages (IYP)

EYP's principal competitor is the Instant Yellow Pages Service
(IYP), a product of American Business Lists, Inc. (ABL) of Omaha,
Nebraska. Like Market Data Retrieval, ABL is also a mailing list broker, and it too covers 4,800 phone books. But it does not include all the
additional data available via EYP. The connect-time charge for both
IYP and EYP is $60 an hour, but ABL charges only 10¢ per online
name and address record versus EYP's charge of 15¢ for the same
thing. Unfortunately, to access IYP, you must dial the computer in
Omaha directly, so your long distance charges will vary.

The Instant Yellow Pages is a direct outgrowth of ABL's mailing label business. According to sources at the company, it is designed for
two things. First, ABL's minimum order for a list on conventional labels
is $75 and such a list will contain 17,000 or more names. IYP was de-
signed for the person who needs much smaller lists, like a wholesaler
who periodically wants to pull up a list of retailers in the state or the
area. It's a way to serve that customer without making him or her place
a minimum $75 order.

Second, it is meant to be very simple to use. IYP is a menu-driven
system, so it's not as flexible as EYP. Still, you can specify many impor-

tant search criteria. These include state, professional specialty, brand name code, standard 4-digit SIC code or one of ABL's modified five-digit SIC codes, and ZIP code. There is also an online thesaurus (like EXPAND) to help you find the right code. You may request downloads of the full record, including phone number and SIC code. Or you may request one-up mailing label format, sorted by ZIP code for easy printing on your own printer.

The company will also generate custom reports and mailing label sets, and it can supply lists on both mainframe tape in ASCII or EBCDIC or on any format or size of personal computer media (8″, MS-DOS, Apple DOS 3.2 or CP/M, Macintosh, etc.). The data on personal computer disks can be formatted for most popular database management programs. (MDR offers capabilities similar to all of these options for EYP, too.)

There is a subscription fee of $95 for the first year and $60 a year after that. The initial subscription fee includes a manual and $100 of free usage good during the first month of your subscription. There is a volume rebate schedule as well, with prices as low as 8¢ a name on usage of more than 5,000 names per month. ABL does not have a toll-free number, but they will be happy to call you back if you leave your name. For more information, contact:

American Business Lists, Inc.
5707 S. 86th Circle
Omaha, NE 68127
(402) 331-7169
Telex: 510-101-0855 AMBLIST

Using the Power

In this section we're going to show you how to use a number of the databases discussed in this and previous chapters to do a detailed work-up of a single individual. We chose a corporate executive because we wanted to demonstrate both company directory and biographical databases. It had to be someone prominent so we could be sure he would be mentioned. But he couldn't be someone so prominent that his background was widely known, or so famous that we'd be overwhelmed with information. We chose Victor Kermit Kiam, II, the man who liked the Remington electric shaver his wife gave him so much that he bought the company.

Mr. Kiam published a book about his experiences and techniques in 1986. But we have not read it. We started the search knowing only that the man in the television ads was Victor Kiam and that he owned the company that made Remington electric shavers. Aside from a minor disagreement about the Lady Remington being "the perfect gift"—a gentleman would never give such a thing to a lady—that was it.

Tapping Thomas

For the purposes of this example we pretended that we did not know who headed Remington. Indeed, unless you happened to read the identification tag that appears briefly at the bottom of the screen during Mr. Kiam's TV commercials, you might not know this name.

In any case, it was easy to find out. We had only to search Thomas Register Online for CO = REMINGTON?. Unfortunately, it turned out that there are seven firms with that word in their name—everything from Remington Aluminum Div., Evans Products Co. to the Abrasive Products Division of the Remington Arms Company.

So we entered a new search term, PN = RAZOR? (for "product name"). Then we combined the two retrieved sets of hits with the command: SELECT S1 AND S2. That produced the same results as if we had entered SELECT CO = REMINGTON? AND PN = RAZOR?. It generated one hit, which had to be the company we were after. As the full record from Thomas shown below confirms, it was indeed:

Remington Products, Inc.
60-T Main St.
Bridgeport, CT 06602

TELEPHONE: 203-367-4400

ASSETS: 1M+ ($1,000,000 -$5,000,000)
OFFICES:
     (General Mgmt.) V.K. Kiam, P.
     (Engineering) W. DiGiovanni, V.P. Mfg.
     (Production) W. DiGiovanni, V.P. Mfg.
     (Purchasing) W. DiGiovanni, V. P. Mfg.
     (Sales Mgmt.) B. Gold, S.N.M.
     (Advertising) G.R. Bell, Prod. Mktg. Mgr.

PRODUCTS:
     RAZORS
     SHAVERS--ELECTRIC

TRADE NAMES:
     Lady Remington (Electric Shavers)
     Remington (Electric Shavers)

Apparently whoever supplied this information to Thomas Register was interested to see if it generated any response. The address is "tagged" with a T following the 60 that doesn't show up in any other database containing the firm's address.

What About Who's Who?

Among other things, we now know the president's name: V. K. Kiam. Interested in finding out more about him, we zipped over to check the Marquis Who's Who database (File 234) by entering BEGIN 234. We entered SELECT NA = KIAM, V? to allow for the possibility of either initials or a first name and initial. And . . . Bingo! There was only one hit on KIAM, V? We've edited it heavily, but the listing included the names of parents, spouse, children, plus major career moves, home and business addresses, club memberships and more.

```
380369 WA42, WA43  BIOG UPDATE: 19830811
    Kiam, Victor Kermit, II
    OCCUPATION(S): diversified manufacturing company executive
    BORN: December 7, 1926 New Orleans, LA US
    .
    .
    .
    DUCATION: BS, BA, Yale U, 1948; student Sorbonne, Paris, 1949; MBA, Harvard U,
    1951
    CAREER: Salesman, dist mgr, product mgr cosmetics div Lever Bros, 1951-1953; supr,
    dist mgr Lever Bros (Pepsodent div), 1954-1955; mktg dir woman's wear div Internat
    Latex Corp, 1955-1958 . . .
    .
    .
    .
    chief exec officer Benrus Corp (watch, jewelry, and indsl products mfg), 1971-present;
    .
    .
    .
    chmn, pres, chief exec officer Remington Products, Inc, Bridgeport, CT, US, 1979-
    present;
    .
    . (Nine other organizations were listed in which Mr. Kiam is an officer.)
    .
    CIVIC/POLITICAL ACTIVITIES:
    Mem adv com Norwalk Community Coll;
    mem corp and found com Colgate U;
    trustee U. Bridgeport;
    trustee Hillside Hosp;
    bd dirs Child Welfare League Am
    MILITARY:
    Served with USNR, 1944-1947
    MEMBERSHIPS:
    Mem Inst Dirs (London);
```

Mem Young Pres's Orgn;
Mem US Tennis Assn

.
.
.

Who's Who turned out to be a gold mine of information, all of it supplied by the biographee himself. There are lots of potential search terms here if you wanted to pursue them in other databases or access points if you wanted to simply pick up the phone and call someone. You could search on Benrus Corp. You could check any local or regional Connecticut newspapers covered by the magazine databases discussed in Chapter 13.

If it were less obvious what the U.S. Tennis Association is and does (the last line in the above listing), you could search tne Encyclopedia of Associations database discussed earlier to find out. If Remington were a large national chain, you could search the Electronic Yellow Pages to come up with a list of every one of its stores or outlets in the country.

Checking Biography Master Index

Of course, not eveyone you may want to know about is listed in Who's Who, so you could just as easily come up empty. But whether listed or not, the logical next step is the Biography Master Index database (File 287, A-M). Following the advice given in the DIALOG chapter for this database, we EXPANDed on the name before searching. And a good thing too. For in addition to turning up three records for one Omar Kiam, there was also this:

E5	2	KIAM, VICTOR K, II
E6	1	KIAM, VICTOR KERMIT
E7	2	KIAM, VICTOR KERMIT, II

The variety in the form of the name is due to the different ways the authors of the various source articles chose to write it. We could have hit all of these references by entering the command SELECT NA = KIAM, V? (to allow for either initials or a first name), but it is reassuring to see the different versions laid out as above. If nothing else, it serves as a reminder to allow for such variations when searching other databases.

We entered SELECT E5:E7 to put that range of the "expand" numbers into our search stream. Then we began to display records. Among other things, we learned that Mr. Kiam is in nine editions of various *Who's Who* directories published from 1974 on. There was also a reference to a listing in *Standard & Poor's Register of Corporations, Directors, and Executives,* Volume 2.

As you know from the list of biographical databases at the beginning of this chapter, this is the same directory that is online as Standard & Poor's Register—Biographical (File 526). So we went over to take a look. The results were disappointing. What information there was was identical to the Marquis Who's Who listing and there was far less of it.

Financial Information from Dun & Bradstreet

We will be considering the various Dun & Bradstreet databases in the next chapter. But it seems appropriate to mention what we learned about Remington Products, Inc., from the D&B Million Dollar Directory®, File 517 on DIALOG. Among other things we learned that the company was started in 1979, and we picked up the names of some officers and top corporate people (corporate secretary, counsel, the heads of personnel and data processing, etc.) not listed in our other information. As you would expect, the record also included the company's DUNS numbers. And it included this:

```
SALES:                          $105,000,000
EMPLOYEES HERE:                 750
EMPLOYEES TOTAL:                900

THIS IS:
    A MANUFACTURING LOCATION
    A SINGLE LOCATION
    AN IMPORTER & EXPORTER

BANK: First Nat Bk, Boston, MA
ACCOUNTING FIRM: Alexander Grant & Co, New York, NY
LAW FIRM: Surrey & Morse, New York, NY
```

There are any number of other databases on DIALOG we could check for additional financial information. The PTS Annual Report database, File 17, revealed that a firm called Windmere was sued by the U.S. branch of North American Phillips (Norelco) for alleged patent infringement in November 1984 and that Windmere sued Phillips, Remington, and Victor Kiam claiming "intentional interference with business relationships and trade libel" that same month. Obviously that would be something we'd want to look into if we were doing a work-up of the company. But we're not, so we'll stick to biography.

NEWSEARCH

From the D&B File, it's a quick nine-character hop over to NEW-SEARCH, one of the IAC databases discussed in the previous chapter. We had only to enter BEGIN 211 and we were there. In NEW-SEARCH we found citations for a *New York Times* piece by Edwin McDowell on Mr. Kiam's unique promotional campaign for his new book, *Going for It*. There were citations for book reviews in *Library Journal* and *The Wall Street Journal*. There was also a bibcite and abstract of an article in *Marketing News* noting that Mr. Kiam set an advertising budget of $4 million for his book and that he is considering using the anticipated success of the book as a springboard to a possible game show and a syndicated news column.

So how do we get copies of this material? Checking the printed *Directory of Periodicals Online* (published by Federal Document Retrieval) that we discussed in Chapter 13, we found that the full text of *Marketing News* isn't available online. But it is one of the publications covered by ABI/INFORM and most of the PTS databases, so we could easily get an abstract. As you know from Chapter 14, you can get the full text of *The Wall Street Journal* from the Dow Jones News/Retrieval Service, and you can get the full text of *The New York Times* from NEXIS. Instant delivery of those articles is not a problem.

The National Newspaper Index

Since NEWSEARCH covers oly the most recent month's stories, for deeper coverage you must move over to the National Newspaper Index (File 111) and the other files in the Information Access Company's "system" on DIALOG. Here we did an EXPAND on KIAM, V and found the same kind of thing encountered earlier in BMI, including an error. The data entry operator left out the period after the middle initial on the record cited as E5:

```
E4    7   KIAM, VICTOR
E5    1   KIAM, VICTOR K
E6    3   KIAM, VICTOR K.
E7    1   KIAM, VICTOR K., II
```

As in BMI we SELECTed a range of "expand" numbers (SELECT E4:E7) to get them into our search stream. Then we began displaying records. Among the dozen citations were:

• An article in *The Washington Post* on corporate executives who write books ("What Iacocca Started" by Mark Shields.)

- An interview with Mr. Kiam by Mary Fifield published in the *Los Angeles Times* ("Victor Kiam in a Lather to Succeed: Remington Shaver Chief Says He Thrives on Challenge").

- An article from *The New York Times* dated January 25, 1985, and titled "Chapter 11 Filing by Wells Benrus." Mr. Kiam is referenced as "NAMED PEOPLE: Kiam, Victor K., II—investment activities."

- A *Christian Science Monitor* piece from 1983 called "Lights, Camera, Action! The Boss is on the Air."

- A *New York Times* article titled "Remington's Suit Challenges Phillips on Electric Shavers," and dated February 9, 1982.

- Two other *New York Times* articles from January and November 1980 on the theme of Remington's making a comeback.

- A *Wall Street Journal* article titled "Colgate-Palmolive again tries to sell its Rubinstein unit," from 1979.

- A 1979 *Wall Street Journal* article titled "Wells Benrus Realigns Executives; Chief Gets Duties of Chairman" and listing Mr. Kiam as "NAMED PEOPLE: Kiam, Victor K.—retirement."

- Finally there was a *New York Times* article called "Sperry Rand Sells Consumer Division" and listed a "biography" type article with "Kiam, Victor, K.—finance" listed as the named person. The date was March 1, 1979.

Searching Biography Index on Wilsonline

We left DIALOG and in less than a minute were connected to Wilsonline for a search of the Biography Index. We entered FIND KIAM, V: (the colon is Wilsonline's "wildcard" or truncation symbol). And here are the results:

SEARCH 1 (3 FOUND)

SEARCH 2 ?
USER: prt indented

---

1 (BIOGRAPHY INDEX)
TITLE (PROPER)   — Meet the presidents: Victor Kiam

PERS NAME MAIN AUTHOR	— Andersen, Chris
SOURCE	— Good Housekeeping 201:74+ N '85

2 (BIOGRAPHY INDEX)	
TITLE (PROPER)	— Would you buy an electric shaver from this man
PERS NAME MAIN AUTHOR	— Ross, Irwin:1919–
SOURCE	— Reader's Digest 126:17–18+ Ja '85

3 (BIOGRAPHY INDEX)	
TITLE (PROPER)	— Victor Kiam's guide to success in a buyout
SOURCE	— Business Week 74 J1 2 '84

Since to our knowledge neither *Good Housekeeping* nor *Reader's Digest* is online in a full-text version anywhere, we could either go to the library or contact an information broker or document delivery service to obtain copies. (Wilsonline doesn't have a document delivery service at this time.) Considering the source, you may not be interested in the kind of biography you know you'd find in these two publications anyway.

The *Business Week* treatment, however, is another story. As you know from Chapter 13, it's easy to get instant full-text articles from it. On NEXIS, full-text *Business Week* articles are available back to January 1975. Magazine ASAP and Trade & Industry ASAP have full-text articles back to 1983.

What Next?

It's hard to say which is more breathtaking: the amount of information we were able to assemble or the speed with which we were able to assemble it. Since the database vendors report the total time you spend in each database, it was easy to track the amount of time required. The costs were more difficult to calculate, but they consist of connect time in the database, display charges, and telecommunications costs. Here's a summary:

	Minutes:Seconds	Approx. Cost
Thomas Register:	1:56.0	$4.83
Who's Who	1:1.2	2.08
Biography Master Index:	0:46.8	4.30
S&P Register—Biography	0:27.0	2.20
D&B Million Dollar Directory	1:8.4	3.84
NEWSEARCH	1:19.0	3.20
National Newspaper Index	3:28.8	7.30

Wilson Biography Index   0:45.0   <u>0.50</u>
    Total Time 10:52.2   28.25
         DIALNET: <u> .66</u>
        Total Cost $28.91

Ten minutes and 52.2 seconds! Skeptics and sourpusses can go suck eggs, that's absolutely incredible. A cost of $29 is less amazing. But whether you feel it's a fair price or not, there's no question that it is far cheaper than paying someone to spend a day in the library and paying someone else to type it all up into a report.

Caveats and Considerations
This was not a difficult search. We used only basic DIALOG commands and simple search logic. Anyone who has read the explanations of these tools and techniques in the preceding chapters can do it. At the same time, however, it's important to point out that not all "people searches" are likely to be this easy. Celebrities, major political figures, presidents of large corporations, and anyone else likely to have been covered by one of the media aren't nearly as challenging as the executive vice president of a small midwestern bank or the chairman of a political party in an Arizona county.

But it can be done. Half the battle is knowing what's available. The other half is making an educated guess at where the subject is likely to show up. Is the person likely to have written a trade journal article? Might he or she have been quoted on some issue in the national media? Could there be a wire service story on the company, or a story in a local or regional newspaper? And so on. Every subject is different, and every search depends on what you know about the individual or what you can surmise. You won't always be successful, and you won't always be able to get everything you need online. But it's so easy to check that you really can't afford not to.

...16...

Investment and Competitive Intelligence:
Industry Profiles, Credit Reports, and Corporate Financials

There's not much difference between investment and competitive intelligence. In both cases you're after information on a company or an industry. And in both cases your goal is to take—or avoid taking—action before someone else does. You won't always be successful. But whether you're buying stock, acquiring companies, or maneuvering for a competitive advantage, you can vastly improve your chances if you've got the information edge.

The databases we'll look at in this chapter have a great deal of the information you need. We'll show you how to put a copy of any public company's balance sheet and income statement on your screen in seconds, and how to obtain surprisingly detailed financial information on millions of privately held businesses as well—from multi-billion-dollar construction companies to your corner grocer and favorite car dealer. We'll also look at the leading sources of corporate news, market quotes, and industry analysis.

Business information is the hottest, most competitive section of the electronic universe right now. *Everybody* wants your connect-time dollar. However, almost everyone starts with the same publicly available information. Any number of databases, for example, include balance sheets, income statements, annual report excerpts, and selected extracts from other public documents on file with the Securities Exchange Commission (SEC).

The challenge for a database producer is to find a way to add value to the material. Some include financial ratios based on the data and thus save you the trouble of calculating them yourself. Some include commentary and analysis. Some concentrate on getting the information

354

online especially fast. And needless to say, some are more successful in adding value than others.

We've chosen some of the very best databases in this category. But even so, anyone who accessed all of these databases on a regular basis would soon die of accelerated information overload. Business information has gotten out of hand. There's too much of it, available from too many different sources, for any single investor or businessperson to comprehend.

In the discussions that follow, we have tried to highlight the unique or especially valuable features of each database. If you can, try to sample all of them at least once. Then choose the two or three you find best suited to your needs. Also, give some thought to the ways you can use the power of the online systems to find companies or industries that meet a collection of criteria. ("All the companies in Oregon with an SIC code of NNNN, annual sales of $X million, etc.")

It is worth remembering that almost any database can be used to gather competitive and investment intelligence. That includes the magazine, newspaper, and directory databases discussed in the previous chapters and the databases in the chapters to come.

Public Companies

Every publicly traded company is required to bare its financial soul four times a year by filing 10-Q and 10-K reports with the Securities Exchange Commission (SEC). The 10-Q reports are quarterly income statements. The 10-K reports are yearly business and financial reports. There are also corporate annual reports, proxy statements, prospectuses, and Registration Statements for new public companies. The amount of paper involved is staggering: 100,000 reports each year totaling more than six million pages.

But it is the second quarter that is the most challenging. Year-end reports are due between January 1 and March 31, and naturally everyone waits until the last minute, generating a crunch of some 5,500 documents near the end of March. Those documents stop arriving just as the annual reports, most of which are issued in the second quarter, begin to come in. All of them must be put onto microfiche for the SEC.

• • •

DISCLOSURE II

Focus/Source: Securities Exchange Commission (SEC) filings.
Companies: Approximately 10,200 publicly traded U.S. and non-U.S. companies. NYSE, AMEX, NASD (OTC), and regional exchanges.

Coverage: Current information and up to five years of historical financial data.

Updates: Weekly; but delay of three to four weeks between date of filing and online availability.

From 1968 until 1985, the Disclosure Information Group had the exclusive contract to do just that. But in return, Disclosure was able to sell the documents to its online and other customers. Sources estimate that the business was worth some $9 million a year. In 1985, however, Disclosure lost the contract to Bechtel Information Systems, a division of the huge U.S.-based heavy construction firm. Reports indicate that Bechtel promised the SEC a three-day turnaround compared to Disclosure's ten-day turnaround time.

Shortly thereafter, Steven Goldspiel, Disclosure's executive vice president, was quoted as saying that only about 1% of his company's online data came from actual SEC filings in any case and that it was easier to put together reports from the New York Stock Exchange (NYSE), the American Stock Exchange (AMEX), the over-the-counter market run by the National Association of Securities Dealers (NASD), and other sources.

At this writing, Bechtel has put up a directory database listing all forms filed with the SEC by nearly 11,000 public companies from 1980 to the present. According to Jack H. Kemeny, Bechtel Information Services marketing manager, information on which documents have been filed with the SEC is online within one hour of the time Bechtel receives the documents from the SEC. The system and associated document delivery services are available through Bechtel. For more information, contact:

> Bechtel Information Services
> 15740 Shady Grove Road
> Gaithersburg, MD 20877
> (301) 258-4300

DISCLOSURE on the Move

Although it remains to be seen whether Bechtel will offer a competing product, the loss of the SEC contract does not seem to have put a crimp in the Disclosure operation. The company's ECFI (Electronic Company Filing Index) is similar to Bechtel's one-hour notification service, and it is considering services similar to its main SEC-document-based product for Japan, Canada, and Europe. It also offers MicroScan, a series of disks containing information on 5,100 companies, updated monthly. It has Compact DISClosure, a CD ROM-based product that works the same way. And it has introduced LaserDisclosure, a product that delivers real-image reproductions of documents via fiber optic cable to the company's best customers. (Cost: $97,000 a year.)

The firm's most important electronic product, however, remains DISCLOSURE II. (The "II" was added to distinguish the online version from the original microfiche product, but it is usually dropped when speaking of the database.) DISCLOSURE offers extracted figures and text from SEC filings, and it has grown from 43 searchable fields in 1980 to 75 fields in 1982 to more than 250 fields in 1986. Today there is virtually no significant piece of information about the finances of a public company that DISCLOSURE does not include.

The database is available on more than a dozen vendors, including CompuServe, NEXIS, Dow Jones, VU/TEXT, BRS, and DIALOG. However, it is important to be aware that while the data may be the same, the number of ways you can get at it varies with the system. On the Dow Jones News/Retrieval service, for example, access is by ticker symbol. You cannot scan for companies whose financials meet a variety of criteria. On BRS and DIALOG, however, screening reports is very easy to do.

DIALOG and BRS Differences

On BRS, the "DSCL" database contains everything. But on DIALOG, the information is divided into two files, DISCLOSURE® Financials (File 100) and DISCLOSURE ® Management (File 541). The Financials database includes quarterly balance sheets (for up to three quarters), annual funds flow, price/earings (P/E) information including dividends paid, and up to five years of historical annual income statements and balance sheets. There are also over 30 pre-calculated financial ratios (Quick, Current, Net Income/Net Sales, Total Liability/Total Assets, and so on). The P/E figures come from Muller Data Corporation and are updated weekly. Latest trade date, shares outstanding, high or low price asked or bid, and close or average price are also included. File 100 also supports the DIALOG REPORT format, so you can easily generate a customized report containing just the information fields you want.

File 541, Management, includes such textual material as the list of officers and their salaries, the list of directors, and the management discussion from a firm's annual report. There is also the president's letter from the annual report.

You can obtain actual copies of the SEC documents using DIALORDER and requesting delivery from the Disclosure Demand

Service (DISCLO) or some other supplier. Or you can contact one of the many Disclosure Demand Service offices (New York, Chicago, Los Angeles, Tokyo, London, Toronto, et al.). Call the main Demand Services office at (800) 638-8241 for numbers and prices. (In Maryland, use the main "301" Disclosure number given below.)

Online Tip: You may also be able to find the full text of the 10-K or 10-Q report you need on NEXIS, though only selected companies are covered and there is a ten-week delay between filing and availability. In addition, although the service is not available at this writing, a company called SEC Online [(212) 686-2650] is expected to offer 10-K, 10-Q, and annual reports pertaining to some 4,000 companies on CompuServe at some time in the future.

There is a DIALOG database chapter and a BRS AidPage, and other vendors' manuals have information on their version of the database. But DISCLOSURE itself has a number of pamphlets, manuals and quick reference guides as well, plus a software package called micro-DISCLOSURE that is designed for use with DIALOG. The cost for using either file on DIALOG is $45 an hour, plus telecommunications, and $7 for each full record displayed online. For more information, contact:

> Disclosure Information Group
> 5161 River Road
> Bethesda, MD 20816
> (800)-638-8076
> (301)-951-1300

Online Tip: For information on "insider trading," be sure to ask about DISCLOSURE/Spectrum Ownership, File 540 on DIALOG. The information here is derived from SEC Form 3 (initial statement of ownership) and Form 4 (statement of change of ownership, such as purchase, sale, gift, etc.) and other documents. Over 5,000 companies are covered, including institutional holders, 5% holders, and corporate insiders. The corresponding printed works are the series of "Spectrum" books published by Computer Directions Advisors, Inc., of Silver Spring, Maryland. The database is updated quarterly.

Insider Trading Monitor™ is a database with similar information. Available on NewsNet and Dow Jones, among other systems, it too is drawn from SEC Forms 3 and 4, though it tends to concentrate more on corporate executives and individuals than on institutions. It corresponds to the *Official Summary of Insider Transactions*, a government publication, and the database producer is FCI/Invest-Net, (305) 652-1721.

Moody's Corporate Profiles

Focus/Search: Concise descriptive and financial overviews "of 3,600 of the most important publicly-held companies."

Companies: Every company on the NYSE and AMEX, plus 1,300 selected companies traded on the NASD over-the-counter market.

Updates: Weekly

Moody's Investor Service, Inc., is owned by Dun & Bradstreet, and it has at least three databases available on DIALOG. As we'll see in a moment, the other two are news-oriented databases that also contain tabular data. This one, File 555 on DIALOG, has 54 searchable fields and includes information drawn not only from SEC filings and annual reports, but also from news releases, stock exchange bulletins and lists, leading newspapers and trade journals, and public information from whatever regulatory agency (ICC, CAB, FERC, etc.) or agencies the subject company must report to.

The financial information is fairly standard: five years of annual earnings and dividends per share, balance sheet, P/E ratios and other statistics, and so on. What makes it interesting is that each of these fields is searchable. If you wanted to find every company with a return on assets of between 10% and 30%, for example you could enter SELECT RA = 10:30. Each record also has concise, exclusive Moody's textual reports summarizing quarterly developments of import and comments on the company's expected short-term future.

Moody's has a free "MiniSearch Guide" on a laminated notebook page to help you get the most out of the CORPORATE PROFILES database and the two news databases considered later. A toll-free customer support hotline is available during regular East Coast business hours as well. The cost for using the file on DIALOG is $60 an hour, plus telecommunications, and $4 per full record displayed online. LABEL and REPORT formats are available. For more information on this database (or the two Moody's news databases discussed below) contact:

Customer Support
Moody's Investor Service, Inc.
99 Church Street
New York, NY 10007
(800) 342-5647
(212) 553-0857, collect from
New York, Alaska, or Hawaii

• • •

S&P Corporate Descriptions and PTS Annual Reports Abstracts
The Standard & Poor's Corporate Descriptions Online database on
DIALOG (File 133) and the PTS Annual Reports Abstracts on DIALOG
(File 17) and BRS are two other databases likely to be of interest to
anyone tracking down information on public companies.

S&P Corporate Descriptions covers 8,000 publicly owned U.S.
corporations. Together with the S&P News files considered later, it
corresponds to the widely used, seven-volume *Standard & Poor's Corporation Records.* The information comes from SEC filings, press releases, wire service reports, leading newspapers, and reports from the
government agencies charged with overseeing the company.

Updates are added twice a month, but each company record is revised
annually on a rotating basis, so the information you encounter could be
quite new or nearly a year old and ready for updating. The database has
a lot of information, including stock data, earnings and finances, and
annual report financials. However, none of these fields is searchable. In
all, File 133 has only nine searchable fields, plus a corporate background
paragraph textual field. This means it cannot be used for the sophisticated kind of screening one might do with DISCLOSURE or some other
databases. But it is a good way to get a quick handle on a company. The
cost is $85 an hour, plus telecommunications, and $3.50 per full record
displayed online.

PTS Annual Reports Abstracts is yet another product of Predicasts,
Inc., the same firm that produces PTS PROMT and the other databases
discussed in Chapter 13. Unlike the S&P database, this one also covers
selected international companies. In all some 3,000 public companies are
covered, the information being drawn primarily from annual reports,
supplemented by 10-K statements where necessary.

The PTS database contains three kinds of record formats: textual abstracts (300-400 words), financial abstracts, and a corporate establishment record presenting location, sales, major product line, and number
of employees. In all there are nearly 30 searchable fields. This is not a
high-powered investor's database, however. (The financial abstracts are

replaced annually; textual abstracts, every three years; and corporate establishment sections, annually.) It is intended primarily to help identify companies by product line or service areas, and to aid in that goal, it uses PTS "event" and product codes (as well as DUNS numbers and ticker symbols.)

Private Companies

The life of a public corporation is an open book, but private companies are a different matter. Since they aren't selling their securities to the public, they aren't required to reveal their financials to anyone but the taxman. There is thus no equivalent to SEC 10-Q and 10-K reports.

So when it comes to getting information on privately held companies you're out of luck, right? Well, not exactly. Virtually every company, whether public or private, has at one time or another applied for credit. And since the Dun & Bradstreet Corporation is the country's largest business credit-rating bureau, there's a good chance that D&B has a file on the firm.

D&B credit reports are available online only through DUNSPRINT, a separate subscription system owned and operated by Dun & Bradstreet. There are indications that D&B credit reports may one day be available on DIALOG, but they aren't online at this writing. What is online is a great deal of information collected in the process of assembling those reports. The information exists in four D&B files on DIALOG, and with the removal of certain DIALOG file-size restrictions, there will be even more of it in the near future. We'll look briefly at each D&B online file and then consider some points that apply to all of them.

Online Tip: D&B credit reports may not be available from the database vendors just yet, but reports from TRW are. The TRW Business Profiles™ database is available via NewsNet, and it is remarkable in that it represents the first time business credit information has been available "on demand." TRW has been offering credit reports online since 1975, but an annual subscription fee of between $1,000 and $2,000 has usually been required.

The cost per report is $29, plus the applicable NewsNet connect-hour rate. Reports typically include 30-, 60-, and 90-day payment histories, public record data (UCC filings, tax liens, judgments, bankruptcies, etc.), and company background and business information supplied by Standard & Poor's, Trinet, and Harris Publishing.

Online Tip (cont.)

Over eight million businesses are covered. The database dates from 1976 to the present. See Chapter 11 for more information on NewsNet.

### D&B—Dun's Market Identifiers® (DMI)	File 516

Focus/Source: D&B credit reports
Companies: More than 2,000,000 companies, over 90% of which are privately owned. Expected to expand to 6,000,000 companies in near future.
Coverage: Address, sales, and directory-type information. Over 30 searchable fields.
Updates: Each record is updated at least every 18 months.

• • •

D&B—Dun's International Market Identifiers® (IDMI) File 518

Focus/Source: Credit reports from D&B international offices
Companies: Over 530,000, but expected to expand to 3,000,000 in near future.
Coverage: Essentially same as DMI, but fewer (19) fields.
Updates: Same as DMI.

• • •

### D&B—Million Dollar Directory® (MDD)	File 517

Focus/Source: Questionnaires sent to companies. Corresponds to three-volume *Million Dollar Directory* series.
Companies: Over 120,000, all of them either headquarters or single-location companies. Must have net worth of $500,000 or more. All types of businesses are covered.
Coverage: Essentially the same as DMI. However, since it is supplied by the company itself, the line of business description tends to be more precise. MDD records also usually include more corporate officers and directors (up to 30), the name of the company's law firm, and its ticker symbol if it is a public company.
Updates: Annual.

• • •

### D&B—Dun's Financial Records® (DFR)	File 519

Focus/Source: Credit Reports.
Companies: Over 700,000 companies, 98% of them privately held.

Coverage: Up to three years of balance sheet and income statements, 14 precalculated ratios on each company, comparison of company's performance with industry norm, operations and background summaries, and more.

Updates: Same as DMI.

• • •

Credit Reports: The Core of the Operation

Although they may contain many of the same types of information, credit reports are not the same as SEC 10-K reports and other public documents. The information is supplied by the subject company in both cases, but if the firm is privately held there is no way to verify its validity. Consquently, the reputation and experience of the credit-reporting company is paramount. The company now called Dun & Bradstreet has been involved in the field since 1840, and until TRW entered the market in 1976, it had things pretty much to itself. The overall reliability of its information and procedures is unquestioned.

Online Tip: Except perhaps by Greenmoss Builders, Inc., of Vermont. In a case that sent wide ripples through the information industry, a 5-4 Supreme Court decision on June 26, 1985, upheld the ruling of a lower court against Dun & Bradstreet and in favor of Greenmoss. At issue was an erroneous report by D&B that Greenmoss was bankrupt. The report was quickly corrected, and apparently no damage was done. But Greenmoss sued and won a $50,000 award for damages presumed to have occurred and $300,000 in punitive damages. D&B appealed this lower court ruling, arguing that it ought to enjoy the same First Amendment protections that apply to a newspaper publisher.

This was the first case of its kind. But as society and the law come to grips with the new information technology, it most certainly will not be the last.

The core of D&B's online offerings is its vast, eight-million-item file of credit reports on U.S. and international companies. That figure represents perhaps 60% of all companies. If you don't count the small "Mom-and-Pop" operations, you can say, as Dun & Bradstreet does, that it represents 80% to 90% of the more active companies in the U.S.

Whenever a D&B Credit Service subscriber requests credit information on a given company, D&B checks its master file. If a report exists and is current within the last 18 months, a copy is sent to the sub-

scriber. But if there is no report or if the one on file is out of date, a
D&B business analyst is dispatched to conduct an on-site interview with
the appropriate person at the subject company. D&B has over 1,700
such analysts worldwide and they count four former U.S. presidents
among their alumni (Lincoln, Grant, Cleveland, and McKinley).

When on-site interviews are not possible, the analyst may conduct the
session on the phone. He or she might also contact the company's bank,
accountant, suppliers, real estate and insurance brokers, or a variety of
public records. (The analyst never tells the subject for whom the report
is being done.)

The analyst will then review the collected data to see if it makes
sense. A report presenting the subject company will then be prepared.
Credit rating, SIC codes, and (where needed) a DUNS number will be
assigned, and the report will be added to the company's in-house database. That database is updated every month, and 500,000 changes and
revisions per update are not uncommon.

Note that, unlike SEC reports for public companies, an online D&B
report for a private company may include any number of fields bearing
the "NA" ("not available") designation. That's because the subject company is free to report whatever information it wants to report. Indeed,
it may choose to report nothing at all, and where that is the case, you
may see a capital *E* next to annual sales and other figures indicating
that the numbers are D&B estimates.

The DUNS Numbers and How to Use Them

Every record contains at least one DUNS (or "D-U-N-S") number.
These are nine-digit numbers that are randomly assigned to each business. They are, in the words of a D&B representative, "like Social Security numbers for companies." The letters stand for "*D*un's *U*niversal
*N*umbering *S*ystem." There is no relationship between the DUNS
number for a subsidiary and the one for its parent. Each will have a
unique number. Most important, the D&B records are set up such that
they *include* the names and numbers of legally related establishments.

For example, a D&B record will at the very least contain a DUNS
number for the business at the physical location specified in the address
fields. But where applicable it will also include DUNS numbers for the
"parent," the "headquarters" location, and the "corporate family."

D&B also refers to this last item as the "ultimate company," by which
it means the top company in the ownership chain. The "parent" company is the firm that owns more than 50% of the voting stock of the
company whose record you are viewing. The "headquarters" is the main
office of a subject firm with branches bearing the same company name.

We'll explain the other fields in a moment. But first, let's use DUNS numbers to quickly climb the beanstalk of corporate ownership. We opened the phonebook and at random picked the name Pearle Vision Center as a subject. We located lots of stores, and among the records pulled up was one for a branch location in Beaumont, Texas. The record included the following DUNS number information:

```
DUNS NUMBER:            13-112-1865
HEADQUARTER DUNS:       02-628-3416    PEARLE VISION CENTER*
CORPORATE FAMILY DUNS:  11-307-1799    GRAND METROPOLITAN USA
                                       HLDNGS*
```

The first DUNS number is the one for the Beaumont, Texas, store. The asterisk after "CENTER" and "HLDNGS" means "Incorporated" and is used as a space-saver when necessary due to fixed-length fields in the record. With this information in hand, we decided to check the head-quarters location. So we keyed in SELECT DN = 02-628-3416. ("DN" is the field for a record's DUNS number.)

We learned that the Beaumont store is a branch of a headquarters location based in Dallas. The Dallas location reported sales of $168,000,000 in 1984. It has a total of 2,500 employees system-wide, 350 of whom work at the Dallas location. It operates out of a 188,000 square-foot rented facility, and its bank is Philadelphia National Bank. The names of the chairman, president, vice president, secretary, and treasurer were also included.

Next we decided to check the "ultimate" company, Grand Metropolitan USA Holdings, Inc. So we keyed in SELECT DN = 11-307-1799. Here is part of the record that was then displayed:

```
1631797                                       Full financials available
GRAND METROPOLITAN USA HLDNGS*
100 PARAGON DRIVE
MONTVALE, NJ 07645

TELEPHONE: 201-573-4000
BERGEN COUNTY       SMSA: 406 (NEW YORK, NEW YORK)

BUSINESS:  HOTEL OPER AND MFRS CIGARETTES, PET FOODS, SOFT
           DRINKS, IMPORTS WHISKEY AND OPER DAY CARE AND
           HEALTH CARE CENTERS

PRIMARY SIC:      7011    HOTELS/INNS/TOURIST C
SECONDARY SIC:    2111    CIGARETTES
SECONDARY SIC:    2047    DOG, CAT & PET FOOD
SECONDARY SIC:    2086    BTL,CAN SOFT DRINKS
SECONDARY SIC:    3949    ATHLETIC,SPRTGDS NEC
SECONDARY SIC:    2131    CHEWG,SMOKG TOBACCO

YEAR STARTED              1980
```

We learned that the company's sales for fiscal 1985 were $1.71 billion, that it has 22,000 employees, the name of its accounting firm, the size of its offices in Montvale, New Jersey, and the names of its principal officers. The firm is a public company.

The phrase "Full financials available" signifies that there is a record for this firm in the D&B Financial Records database, and that the same information is available for viewing here in the DMI database. (More on this in a moment.)

DMI is not cheap. The connect cost is $100 an hour, plus telecommunications. And the cost of displaying each full record is $2. But the process of tracing this corporate ownership chain took less than a minute, and the data displayed was informative and to the point.

D&B Market Identifier Fields

Space doesn't permit a complete treatment of all of the D&B databases, so we'll focus on Dun's Market Identifiers, the largest of the four files, with the understanding that much of what we say applies to the other D&B products as well. DMI contains fields for DUNS numbers and all the standard name and address information you would expect. You can search by telephone area code, county name, primary and secondary SIC codes, and Standard Metropolitan Statistical Area (SMSA). There are fields for business description, legal status (corporation, partnership, proprietorship, etc.), sales territory, and square footage of the facility.

Annual sales and employment figures are given for three years: the base year, the trend year, and the current year. The base year and the trend year are used to calculate two other fields: sales growth and employment growth. The names of the principal company executives are also given. Unfortunately, not all records have figures in the sales and employment fields. According to D&B, this may be because the subject company could not supply them at the time the credit interview took place or because it simply refused.

In any case, there are *lots* of points of access, making it exceptionally easy to create a list of largely privately held companies that meet whatever combination of line of business, sales, and location criteria you have in mind. DMI offers both the DIALOG REPORT and mailing LABEL options, so you can have your information formatted any way you choose.

Personal Applications

For most businesses, the screening capabilities made possible by the D&B record format and DIALOG search software are likely to be of greatest interest. You can easily locate prospects that meet your "best customer" profile, find potential acquisition targets, check your competition in a given sales territory, and so on. However, as the Pearle Vision Center example presented earlier illustrates, it is also easy to get in-depth information on specific companies. In fact, because DMI covers so many millions of firms and because it offers so many points of access, locating specific company information can be easier than netting fish in a barrel. That means you can use D&B-supplied information in your personal life as well.

Dun & Bradstreet promotional literature doesn't talk much about small companies—companies like your local grocer, gas station, or car dealer—but small companies are in the database in quantity. Indeed, approximately 1.88 million of the two million companies in DMI at this writing have a net worth of less than $500,000. A quick check revealed records for nearly 3,000 dentists and nearly 6,000 attorneys. (The search logic was "SS DENTIST?/DE AND ATTORN?/DE," which told the system to look for those words in the description-of-business field.)

We didn't check to see how many car dealers are on the system, but we did pull up records for several Chevy dealers in the area, as well as a favorite stationery store (employees: 15; annual sales: $1.65 million), a hometown swim club (sales: $211,000), and local trucking companies, sporting goods stores, furniture and drapery installers, plant nurseries, and construction firms.

Not every company can be found in the database, and as explained, you can't assume that every record will contain sales figures. However, the uses to which you could put the information are limited only by your own imagination. How about a list of every Ford or Chrysler dealer in the county that has shown a negative sales growth in the previous year? Might those companies be especially anxious to make a sale and therefore be more inclined to give you a good deal? Or a list of every firm in your town that has hired more employees? Could they be good places to contact to get a job? How's that strip shopping center out on the state highway doing? Drop the names of all of the tenant firms into DMI and see what comes up. The information power is yours, the possibilities, endless.

Online Tip: If you are going to look for a firm or a person by name, do an EXPAND on the name first (EXPAND CO = NAME) or use the following search logic: SELECT FNAME(F)LNAME. You may reverse the order of FNAME (first name) and LNAME (last name). The key point is the "F" operator. This tells DIALOG

Online Tip (cont.)

> that the two names must be in the same field of the same record, but that they can occur in any order. It's important because the names may be in the database both ways.

Dun's Financial Records

The information contained in the Dun's Financial Records (DFR) database would be impressive under any circumstances. But since 98% of the companies covered there are privately held, the information is even more valuable. In absolute terms, it is not inexpensive. Depending on the pieces of information you choose to view (company information, operations summary, full financials, etc.), the cost ranges from $18 to $74 per record format displayed. The hourly connect rate is $135, plus telecommunications. However, compared to the quantity of information provided, the effort required to prepare it, and the difficulty of obtaining it from other sources, many users may feel that the prices are quite reasonable.

It is important to point out that DMI is linked to DFR for display purposes. Thus whenever you see "Full financials available" on a DMI record, you can TYPE the record in Formats 4, 7, or 8 and display the same information you would find for that company in those formats if you were in the Dun's Financial Records database. The difference is that in DMI that information is not searchable. In DFR it is.

> **Online Tip:** The *prices* are the same for those formats in DMI as well ($18 to $74). Unfortunately, the DIALOG software isn't smart enough to know whether "full financial information" is available for a given record or not. Consequently, if you mistakenly request format 4, 7, or 8 in DMI, you will be charged the full DFR rate— whether full financial information is available for the record or not. So watch your formats.

What's Doing at Bechtel?

As noted previously, Bechtel, the company that won the SEC contract from the Disclosure Information Group, is one of the largest privately held companies in the world. It thus seemed like an ideal subject to look for in DFR. The results were impressive, and they went on for pages. So many pages, in fact, that it is impractical to present even a heavily edited portion of the record. Instead, to give you an idea of what you can expect, we'll present excerpts and summaries.

The record began with the address of the headquarters of the Bechtel Group, Inc., in San Francisco, and it told us that the firm has 30,000 employees (7,500 at the San Francisco location), fiscal year sales of $8.6 billion, and a worth of nearly $780 million.

The HISTORY field provided the names of the major corporate officers, the date and location of incorporation (Delaware, August 22, 1980), the number of shares of common and preferred stock, and the holder of the stock (Stephen D. Bechtel, Sr., and Stephen D. Bechtel, Jr., as trustees for other members of the family). We also learned the following facts:

BECHTEL JR born 1925. Graduated Purdue University, BS, Civil Engineering; Stanford University Graduate School of Business, MBA; 1972 Purdue, Honorary Doctor Engineering degree. Associated Bechtel interests all his career, is chairman of the Bechtel group of companies. First employed by Bechtel interest in 1941; 1960 president; 1973 chairman. Other business interests include director, The Southern Pacific Company, IBM Corp. He is a Fellow, American Society of Civil Engineers.

Similar information was provided for each of the other officers.

The OPERATION summary described the company and its general activities. It included a summary of contract terms (fixed price, unit price, target price, cost-plus, etc.). It discussed the number of employees and where they are employed. And it offered information on:

FACILITIES: Shares space with affiliates in a 23-story steel reinforced building owned by an affiliate. Subsidiaries also occupy an adjacent 34-story steel reinforced building owned by an affiliate. Premises, well maintained and neat. Space occupied by the group as a whole exceeds 1,000,000 square feet.

LOCATION: Central business section on well traveled street.

A list of the firm's major subsidiaries followed. There are nine of them, almost every one of which has subsidiaries of its own. There are petroleum companies; a variety of heavy construction firms that build everything from dams to nuclear power plants to municipal office buildings; an investment firm; a management services firm; and Bechtel Leasing Services ("Formed 1984, leases equipment, mostly to affiliated interests").

Next were the financials, only a small portion of which are shown below:

12/31/84 INDIVIDUAL FISCAL
(Figures are in THOUSANDS)

FINANCIALS	COMPANY	% CHANGE	COMPANY %	INDST NORM %
Cash	—	—	—	9.9
Accounts Receivable	4,813	—	0.6	28.9
Notes Receivable	—	—	—	0.5
Inventory	—	—	—	3.5
Other Current Assets	131,749	—	15.7	16.7
Total Current Assets	—	—	—	59.5
.				
.				
.				
Accounts Payable	8,509	—	1.0	15.0
Bank Loans	—	—	—	0.9
Notes Payable	—	—	—	2.2
Other Current Liabilities ...	51,975	—	6.2	20.8
.				
.				
.				
Net Worth	779,061	—	92.8	44.4
Total Liabilities & Worth ...	839,545	—	100.0	100.0
Net Sales	8,600,000	—	100.0	100.0
.				
.				
.				
Accounts Receivable	4,813	—	0.6	28.9

The financials were followed by a variety of precalculated ratios for the company and for the industry as a whole, divided by upper, median, and lower quartiles. In this case there were few numbers in the Bechtel columns, though we looked at records for other companies in which all columns were complete. DFR records include the following ratios:

(SOLVENCY)
Quick Ratio
Current Ratio
Curr Liab to Net Worth (%)
Curr Liab to Inventory (%)
Total Liab to Net Worth (%)
Fix Assets to Net Worth (%)

(EFFICIENCY)
Coll Period (days)
Sales to Inventory
Assets to Sales (%)
Sales to Net Working Cap
Acct Pay to Sales (%)

(PROFITABILITY)
Return on Sales (%)
Return on Assets (%)
Return on Net Worth (%)

As with most fields in this database, these fields are searchable. You can thus screen companies by searching for those ratios that meet your requirements. You can also import all tabular data into Lotus 1-2-3®, dBASE III™, or some other program for further analysis. (See Appendix A for guidelines on how to do this.)

Online Tip: Since DFR reports are so expensive, it's important to make sure that you will get what you want before committing to displaying them. One quick and inexpensive way to do this is to search for a report using the firm's DUNS number and then TYPE the result in Format 6, a format that includes the date of the latest statement as well as an indication of whether HISTORY and OPERATIONS texts are available. Here's an example:

```
SELECT DN = NN-NNN-NNNN
S1        1   DN = NN-NNN-NNNN

?TYPE 1/6/1

 1/6/1
0000000
XYZ COMPANY, INCORPORATED

DUNS NUMBER:    NN-NNN-NNNN

HISTORY text available

OPERATION text available

FISCAL: 10/31/86
```

Manuals, Training, and Customer Support

There is a DIALOG database chapter for DMI and the Million Dollar Directory, and there is one for Dun's International Market Identifiers. At this writing one has not been issued for DFR. These are available only from DIALOG.

There is also a notebook-style *Dun's Online User's Guide* for $50, including the first year's updates. This is available only through The Information Store, 140 Second Street, San Francisco, CA 94105 (415) 543-4636. Major credit cards are accepted.

Dun & Bradstreet has a 48-page booklet called "Dun's Guide to Online Codes and Abbreviations." At this writing the booklet is free, though that policy may change. Dun's training classes are also free at this writing, but a small fee may be charged in the future. The fee may cover the cost of the *User's Guide*. There are also plans for a menu-driven, front-end PC software package to make searching D&B files easier. Toll-free customer service and search assistance are available from 8:30 A.M. to 5:00 P.M., Eastern time each business day. For more information, contact:

> Dun's Marketing Services
> Three Century Drive
> Parsippany, NJ 07054
> (800) 223-1026
> (201) 455-0900

Online Tip: Perhaps the most widely used reference work for information on private companies is *Ward's Business Directory*. Volume 1 covers 37,000 private and 8,000 public U.S. companies with sales over $11 million. Volume 2 covers 35,000 private U.S. companies with sales ranging from half a million dollars up to $11 million. Volume 3 covers 15,000 of the largest companies in the world, including emerging nations. Each volume is $350, but you can get the complete set for $900.

What's of special interest, however, is the publisher: Information Access Company (IAC). Since IAC is one of the leading database producers, one can only wonder how long it will be before Ward's too is online. The company is mum on the subject. Meantime, you can get more information on the Ward's directory by calling (800) 227-8431.

Corporate and Business News

As you know from previous chapters, there are lots of places to go online to get news about companies, businesses, and industries. But for intensely focused, fast-breaking news in these areas, you can't beat the four databases cited here. Two of them, Moody's and Standard & Poor's, correspond directly to printed publications long familiar to the denizens of Wall Street. The other two, Dow Jones News and the PR Newswire, have always been electronic and do not directly correspond to any single printed publication. Moody's and Standard & Poor's are available on DIALOG. Dow Jones News is on DJN/R, of course, and the PR Newswire is on a variety of systems.

Moody's® Corporate News—U.S. File 556

Moody's® Corporate News—International File 557

Focus/Source: Equivalent to five printed Moody's "News Reports": *Bank & Finance, Industrial, OTC Industrial, Public Utility,* and *Transportation.* The international file is equivalent to *Moody's International News Reports.*

Source: Annual and quarterly reports, news releases, proxy statements, regulatory reports (SEC, ICC, CAB, etc.), prospectuses, stock exchange bulletins and lists, leading periodicals and newswire services.

Companies: 14,000 publicly held U.S. companies; 4,000 companies in 100 countries.

Coverage: Earnings, merger and acquisition activity of the week, management changes, balance sheets, bankruptcy proceedings, contracts, common stock offered, weekly changes in Moody's bond ratings, and more. Dates from January 1, 1983, to the present.

Updates: Weekly

Two of the most noteworthy points one can make about these two Moody's databases concern the existence of tabular data in many of the records and the unique Moody's "event codes" found in every record. At this writing some 62% of the records include tabular financial information on the subject company. For example, we went into the international database and entered the command to search for "country name" Taiwan (SELECT CN = TAIWAN), which produced "Set 1." We then LIMITed the results to tabular records (SELECT S1/TABLE) and TYPEd a few records. Here is a small fraction of what was displayed:

HUA NAN COMMERCIAL BANK LTD.
Country: TAIWAN
January 13, 1986

Annual Report:
Income Account, years ended June 30 (NT $ millions):

	1985	1984
Int. on loans & disc	14,847	10,162
Fees & commiss	504	500
Int. & div. on secur	1,314	1,305
Inv. & exch. gains	496	304
Other oper. inc	23	33
Total	17,184	12,305

There are more than 100 Moody's event codes, including such topics as management changes, balance sheet, corporate restructuring, lease agreement, spin-off development, warrants offered, orders booked, and airline loading statistics. These codes, used singly or in combination with company access codes, make it easy to track corporate and industry developments. For example, we searched for "event code" 210 (MERGER DEVELOPMENT) and displayed the first record that came up:

```
?SELECT EC = 210

        S1      1642   EC = 210   (MERGER DEVELOPMENT)

?TYPE 1/5/1

 1/5/1
0180168
FORT WAYNE NATIONAL CORP.
May 30, 1986

MERGER DEVELOPMENT: Old-First National Corporation and Co. announced that the two
corporations have reached an agreement in principle to merge Old-First National Corporation
and Co. Under the agreement, the Old-First National Bank would be operated as a separate
bank, retaining its name, board of directors, and officers. The merger is to be accomplished
through an exchange of approximately $14,700,000, for shs. of Old-First National
Corporation. The offer has a value of approximately $73 per sh. of Old-First National
Corporation, less any adjustment in assets after review by the purchaser.

Merger Development   (210)

Source:   Moody's BANK & FINANCE News Reports
COMPANY INFORMATION:
   Moody's Number: 00036908
   DUNS Number: 04-692-0856
   Primary SIC:    6711    HOLDING COMPANIES
   Secondary SIC: 6025    NATIONAL BANKS
```

Moody's, along with the Official Airline Guide, Donnelley Demographics, and the A. C. Nielsen company, is owned by Dun & Bradstreet. There are DIALOG database chapters for all Moody's databases. The cost for using the international file is $96 an hour and $1 per full record displayed. The U.S. file is $75 an hour and 25¢ per full record displayed. For information on Moody's toll-free customer service, and to order your copy of the free laminated Moody's Mini-Search Guide page, see the write up of Moody's Corporate Profiles above.

• • •

Standard & Poor's News Files 132 and 134

Focus/Source: Equivalent to the Daily News section of the seven-volume printed work, *Standard & Poor's Corporation Records*.

Source: Annual and quarterly reports, news releases, proxy statements, regulatory reports (SEC, ICC, CAB, etc.), prospectuses, stock exchange bulletins and lists, leading periodicals, and newswire services.

Companies: 12,000 publicly held U.S. companies "in which there is any degree of public financial interest."

Coverage: Earnings, merger and acquisition activity, management changes, balance sheets, leveraged buyouts, new product announcements, S&P bond ratings, and more.

File 134 is the archival file containing more than 500,000 historical stories on the companies covered by the database dating from June 1979 to June 1985.

File 132 is the current file, dating from July 1985 to the present.

Updates: Approximately 300 to 400 new records are added each day.

If you are an active investor you undoubtedly have your own preferences regarding McGraw-Hill's *Standard & Poor's Corporate Records* and Moody's *News Reports*. In terms of source material and number and type of companies covered, however, they are essentially the same. Their online equivalents are quite similar as well. Both have tabular and textual records and both have "event codes." S&P has 28 searchable event codes. Moody's has more than 100. But in our experience there were a lot of codes in the Moody's databases for which there were no records (You can test this by doing an EXPAND on EC = .), so perhaps the difference is less significant than it appears. Note that this database is updated daily, compared to Moody's weekly updates. Also, we should point out that this is *not* the same S&P database that appears on the Dow Jones News/Retrieval Service.

The cost for using these files is $85 an hour, plus telecommunications, and 15¢ per full record displayed. A DIALOG database chapter is available. For more information on this database, contact:

Corporate Data/Book Services
Standard & Poor's Corporation
25 Broadway
New York, NY 10004
(212) 208-8622 (call collect)

PR Newswire

The PR Newswire was founded in 1954 as a means of quickly and simultaneously distributing the full text of corporate press releases to newspapers, wire service newsrooms, and broadcasters via teleprinter. The wire is produced by the PR Newswire Association, a cooperative with about 10,000 members, nearly 75% of which are either corporations or public relations firms. The remaining members are government agencies, universities, labor unions, political parties, and other nonprofit organizations.

The PR Newswire is available on at least four of the systems covered in this book, though dates of coverage and frequency of updating vary: NewsNet (starts July 10, 1984; hourly); VU/TEXT (January 1, 1985; daily), and NEXIS (January 21, 1980; daily, but a two-day lag between publication and availability). On DIALOG, you'll find the PR Newswire cited in NEWSEARCH, Magazine Index, and Trade & Industry Index. The full text is available in Trade & Industry ASAP.

Typically 150 to 300 news releases will be transmitted each day, and each one carries the name and telephone number of the person to contact for more information. Most releases tend to focus on business and financial matters like earnings, dividends, mergers and acquisitions, tender offers, contracts, management changes, and so on. The rest cover a wide spectrum of news, including sports, labor, medicine, science, features, modern living, and so on.

The full text of each release is searchable on all systems. Shown below are the first few lines of a release downloaded from NewsNet. The entire document went on for the equivalent of two and a half double-spaced pages. The update number refers to the hour of the release. "Update: 14" translates as "update added at 14:00 hours (2:00 P.M.)."

From
PR NEWSWIRE
Tuesday
June 10, 1986
Update: 14

PHILIPS MEDICAL SYSTEMS RECEIVES FDA RECOMMENDATION

TO BUSINESS DESK AND MEDICAL EDITOR:
FDA'S PANEL RECOMMENDS APPROVAL OF PHILIP'S MRI DIAGNOSTIC SYSTEM
    SHELTON, Conn., June 10 /PRNewswire/ —The Radiologic Devices Panel today unanimously recommended to the U.S. Food and Drug Administration that unconditional pre-market approval (PMA) be granted for the Philips Gyroscan, the magnetic resonance imaging (MRI) diagnostic system developed by Philips Medical Systems Inc.
    The recommendation was not contested during the hearing.
    The Philips MRI program has been in clinical use at teaching hospitals and university medical centers . . .

For more information on this database, contact the vendors cited above or:

PR Newswire Association, Inc.
150 East 58th Street
New York, NY 10155
(212) 832-9400

Dow Jones News Service (the "Broadtape")

The Dow Jones News Service is one of the original business wires. The company originally placed two machines in its customers' offices, both of them connected to telegraph lines. The "ticker" printed the latest stock quotes on narrow paper tape. The newswire printed stories filed by Dow Jones reporters on "broad" paper tape. The formatting and all-capitals text in the sample below are direct results of the service's teletype origins.

The "Broadtape" is online via the Dow Jones News/Retrieval Service, and it is without a doubt one of the best sources of corporate and financial information available anywhere. As the DJNR manual states, "When business and financial news breaks, *Wall Street Journal* reporters first send it to our wire service and in 90 seconds it's accessible on News/Retrieval." Stories remain in the Dow Jones News database for 90 days, at which time they are removed. Stories ten days or older can be found in the archive database in the //TEXT section of the service.

Once stories have been transferred into //TEXT, you can use the full power of the DJNR text-searching language to retrieve them. But until then, or whenever you are using the Dow Jones News portion of the service, you can retrieve stories only by entering special codes. There are codes for over 80 news categories (bond market news, dumping, most active stocks, stock splits, etc.) and over 50 industry groups (precious metals, marketing, construction, aerospace, etc.). You can retrieve news on a particular company by entering its ticker symbol. In all, over 6,000 U.S. companies and over 700 Canadian companies listed on the Toronto Stock Exchange are covered.

Here's an example of how one can use the Dow Jones News Service to good advantage. A friend asked for information on a company that has developed a process for repairing buried pipes without digging them out of the ground. "I hear the stock is hot," he said. "I think it's called 'Instituform' or something like that. It's listed on the over-the-counter exchange."

Obviously the way to retrieve information on this firm is to use its stock symbol, which neither of us knew. So we signed on to DJNR and keyed in //SYMBOL to get some help. When prompted to enter the company name, we keyed in INS, the portion of the name we were reasonably sure of. Here's part of what appeared:

SYMBOL   STOCKS   PAGE 1 OF 3

INR   *INSILCO CORP. — NY
INRCW   INSILCO CORP. WT — OT
INEI   *INSITUFORM EAST INC. — OT
IGLSF   *INSITUFORM GROUP LTD. — OT
INGLUF   INSITUFORM GROUP LTD. UN — OT
IGLWF   INSITUFORM GROUP LTD. WT — OT
INSUA   *INSITUFORM OF NORTH AMERICA INC.
              CL A — OT
INSUW   INSITUFORM OF NORTH AMERICA INC.
              WT — OT
IRC   *INSPIRATION RESOURCES CORP. — NY

The asterisks mean that the company has more than one symbol, as is true when there is more than one class of stock. In any case, we found our company, Insituform (from the Latin phrase "in situ"), even though the friend gave us some bum information. From //SYMBOL it was a quick keystroke or two over to Dow Jones News (//DJNEWS). The proper procedure is to enter a period followed by the stock symbol, and that's what we did for several of the symbols. Here is what appeared in one instance, exactly as it came into the computer:

.INEI

N INEI   01/01 AA 1/1
   /INEI
     04/29 INSITUFORM EAST INC. 3RD QTR
   (DW) March 31 NET 8C A SHR VS. 5C
     NET $342,084 VS $210,408.
     SALES $2,771,484 VS $2,284,718.
     AVERAGE SHARES 4,178,000 VS.
   3,975,000.
     9 MOS NET $1,367,115 OR 32C VS
   $966,136 OR 24C.
     SALES $9,134,136 VS $7,301,962.
     AVERAGE SHARES 4,178,000 VS.
   3,975,000.
     YEAR-AGO SHARE FIGURES WERE
   ADJUSTED FOR A THREE-FOR-TWO STOCK
   SPLIT PAID IN OCTOBER 1985.
     1:20 PM

END OF STORY

It's not pretty, and it's difficult to read. But it's a start. The next step on Dow Jones might be to go over to the //TEXT database and check for any *Wall Street Journal, Barron's,* or older Dow Jones News stories on the company. We might also check a database alled Investext to see if there are any investment analyst reports on the company. (There are, as we will see.) One could then sign on to NewsNet to check the PR Newswire, and sign on to DIALOG or some other vendor's system to explore the company further using other databases.

Now that we know the company's proper name, none of this would take a great deal of time. You might want to mull over the information first. But if you had previously established an account with the discount brokers involves, you could sign on to Dow Jones or DIALOG or some other service and enter a buy order for the stock online. Dow Jones offers gateway service to Fidelity Investor's Express. DIALOG offers a gateway to Trade*Plus.

Stock Quotes

Almost every online service can provide you with stock, commodity, and money market quotes. In fact, even if a vendor doesn't offer a specific quote service, you can usually find this information in the AP or UPI newswires that so many vendors carry. However, while much depends on your specific needs, it's tough to beat Dow Jones when it comes to quotes. The Dow Jones News/Retrieval Service is so good at it that one is tempted to ask, "Why fool around with anyone else?" Here, for example, are the major quote sources available from DJNR at this writing:

DNJ/R Quotes & Market Averages Menu Selections

//CQE	Quotes On Stocks & Other Financial Instruments, Delayed 15 Minutes & With A Company News Alert	.I/DJA	Dow Jones Averages Updated Each ½ Hour
//RTQ	Real-Time Stock Quotes With A Company News Alert	.1/ACT	Most Active Stocks & Stock Options, NYSE & AMEX Market Diaries, Closing NASDAQ Most Actives
//QUICK	QuickSearch: Combines Business And Financial Data From Six News/ Retrieval Services	.MARKT	Financial Markets Roundup: Stock,

/ /Futures	Futures Quotes From Major North American Exchanges		Bond, Credit, Gold, Foreign Exchange, And Stock Index Markets
/ /TRACK	Automatic Retrieval Of News & Stock Quotes On Up To 125 Companies	.I/NDX	Stock Indexes: Daily Stock Market Index Futures And Index Options Tables And Related Stories
/ /HQ	Historical Stock Quotes		
/ /DJA	Dow Jones Averages For The Past Year	.I/STK	Morning Market Comment, Filings, Suspensions & Other Stock Market News
/ /SYMBOL	Directory Of Symbols You Will Need To Use Stock Quote Services		

Virtually every quote in existence can be found somewhere on the Dow Jones system. The //CQE database covers every major type of stock on every major American exchange, as well as warrants, options, corporate bonds, U.S. Treasury issues, foreign bonds, mutual funds, and more. For an additional $18.50 per month, virtually all of which goes to the various exchanges, you can receive Real-Time Stock Quotes, without the usual exchange-imposed 15-minute delay.

The "dot" commands in the second column are for use with Dow Jones News. Those shown here pull up the most frequently requested quotes, but DJNEWS has a lot more to offer. Entering .I/REL 01, for example, will give you the headline page (always page 1), for real estate-related news, including quotes on "Fannie Maes," the mortgage-backed bonds issued by the Federal National Mortgage Association (FNMA). Entering .I/MON 01 will generate a page of headlines that includes reports of foreign exchange rates:

```
.I/MON 01

  N  I/MON      01/51
VH 06/11 DOLLAR SLIGHTLY LOWER
   (DJ) IN LATE EUROPEAN TRADING
VG 06/11 TRADE-WEIGHTED DOLLAR CHANGES
   (DJ)
```

VE 06/11 LONDON LATE EURODOLLARS
   (DJ)
VD 06/11 LATE SPOT STERLING RATES AT
   (DJ) LONDON
VC 06/11 SWISS FRANC FOREX RATES AT
   (DJ) ZURICH
VB 06/11 DEUTSCHE MARK FOREX RATES
   (DJ)
UQ 06/11 U.S. DOLLAR OFF 0.0007 AT
   (DJ) TORONTO
UK 06/11 AUSTRALIAN DOLLAR DROPS
   (DJ) FOLLOWING HAWKE'S SPEECH

To read the stories and look at the tables referenced by any of these headlines, you enter the corresponding two-letter code (VH, VB, UQ, etc.). Since there are so many places to find quotes on the system, we suggest that you decide which quotes you want and then call Customer Service and simply ask which keystrokes you should enter. The number is (800) 257-5114; (609) 452-1511, in New Jersey. We have always found DJNR Customer Service staff to be excellent. For more on the Dow Jones system and its other offerings, see Chapter 10.

Online Tip: If you or your computer are into heavy-duty number crunching as a means of identifying good stock investments, the Media General Databank on DIALOG and Dow Jones may be the closest thing to heaven on earth. The database includes price change, moving averages, betas, and weekly high, low, and closing prices covering 53 weeks for over 4,300 public companies. Five years' worth of income statements, revenues and earnings, earnings per share, dividends, P/E ratios, and industry comparisons are also included. There is a lot more as well, including composite data on 180 industry groups.

The cost on DIALOG is $60 an hour, plus telecommunications, and $2 for each full record displayed. The prime time cost on DJNR is $158.40 an hour, at speeds of 1200 or 2400 bits per second. The non-prime cost is $105.60 per hour. DJNR prices include telecommunications and there are no display charges.

Unless you have a favorite program of your own, one of the best ways to take advantage of Media General information is with the Dow Jones Spreadsheet Link or Dow Jones Market Microscope software packages. Market Microscope, in fact, is specifically designed to collect Media General data and assist you in screening it for desirable companies when you are offline. Both packages are available for Apples and IBMs. Contact DJNR for details.

Investment Analysis/Competitive Intelligence

Imagine you're a paper manufacturer and that one of your products is a line of coin rolls that you supply to banks in a three-state area. One day it dawns on you that there are a lot of men out there who hate to carry around loose change and thus routinely empty their pockets into a Mason jar when they come home each evening. But that only postpones the problem. Ultimately someone must still count the change and laboriously pack it into one of your rolls before redeeming it for folding money at the bank.

You sense there's an opportunity here. Why not put automatic coin counting and rolling machines in bank lobbies? They could use your paper rolls, and the bank could offer them as either a free convenience or on a vending machine basis. What about a home coin counting and penny rolling machine? You never know, it could be the next Cuisinart. Does anyone have a product on the drawing board right now? Is there a company you ought to think about acquiring? Has the idea occurred to your competitors?

These are obviously some things you should look into. But whom can you ask? What you need is an expert, someone whose job it is to know everything that's going on in the banking industry and who the major players and products are. A few informed opinions on said players and products and what their prospects are wouldn't come amiss either. Again: Whom can you ask?

The answer is that you can ask a variety of online databases. You might want to start with Investext®, an information product available on DIALOG, Dow Jones, NewsNet, The Source, and through the database producer's system, SI/BRC (Strategic Intelligence/Business Research Corporation). Investext offers you the full text of business research reports prepared by many of the world's leading investment banking firms.

Online Tip: "Investment banking" is a somewhat misleading term. Technically, it refers to the practice of buying a large block of securities and reselling them in smaller blocks in hopes of making a profit. Securities *underwriter* might be a more accurate term, since investment banks are prohibited from accepting banking deposits or doing most of the other things that "real" banks do.

The firms include such well-known names as Bear, Stearns & Co.; Butcher & Singer; Dillon, Read & Co.; Donaldson, Lufkin & Jenrette Securities Corp.; Kidder, Peabody & Co.; Oppenheimer & Co.; Paine

Webber, Inc.; Prudential-Bache Securities; and Smith Barney, Harris Upham & Co. There are also reports from a variety of firms from Amsterdam, Milan, Frankfurt, Brussels, Toronto, London, Winnipeg, Zurich, and Tokyo, as well as transcripts of executive presentations made to the New York Society of Security Analysts.

The reports are generated because these firms, like you, need to know what's really going on in a given industry or with a given company. And the only way to do that is to hire someone to become an expert on a particular industry sector or group of companies. These experts are the folks who interview the company executives, visit the plant sites, scan the trade journals, analyze the financials, and prepare an analytical report of their findings.

The reports contain tabular financial data, explanations of processes, analyses of the company's management, future prospects, place in the industry, the outlook for the industry as a whole, and a lot of other information that would be exceedingly difficult to obtain any other way. Investment banking firms publish the reports for distribution to their sales force of brokers, who may be able to make them available to you, especially if you're a good customer. They also use them when investing for their own accounts.

At least 55 of these firms also turn their reports over to Business Research Corporation (BRC). BRC keys them into its computers to create the Investext database. This is what is available online. Over 5,000 public companies and 50 major industry groups are covered.

As with no other database, the purpose for which you plan to use Investext information dictates the vendor you must choose. Everything depends on how you want to get at the data. On Dow Jones, The Source, and SI/BRC, for example, you can retrieve reports by ticker symbol, industry group code, product term, or report number. On NewsNet you can pick a particular industry group and scan with a free text search. On DIALOG you can do free text searching or use about 20 searchable fields in conjunction with a number of controlled vocabularies.

Costs and coverage vary, too. DIALOG and SI/BRC date back to July 1982 and offer the full file. Dow Jones offers only the current year and only reports from U.S. and Canadian investment banks. NewsNet offers only 22 of the some 60 available industry groups. Coverage on The Source begins with January 1985. Depending on the system, the time of day, and the speed of communications, costs range from $240 an hour and no display charges, to $90 an hour and a charge of $4.50 per page. A company report usually has between two and ten pages. Industry reports are usually about 20 pages, but a few run to 100 or more. Fortunately, you probably won't need to view every page.

Business Research Corporation likes to market its product as a corporate and competitive intelligence tool, and it certainly is that. But that does not change the fact that the source material is prepared for *investors*, most of whom are interested in reports on specific companies or entire industries. Thus the easiest way to use Investext is to search for reports on the same basis, by specific company or industry.

For example, after retrieving the Dow Jones News information cited previously on the company called Insituform East, we keyed in //INVEST to enter the Investext database on DJNR. Prompted to enter a stock symbol or industry group, we keyed in INEI, the same symbol used in the DJNEWS section. Here's what appeared:

```
INVESTEXT                                          PAGE 1 OF 1

                    COMPANY REPORTS

PRESS    FOR
  1     31 MAR 86  Insituform East — Company Report
                   UNLISTED MARKET SERVICE CORP. (THE)
           BY      Purcell, B.J.   15 PAGES

  2     20 FEB 86  Insituform East Inc. — Company Report
                   ADVEST GROUP, INC. (THE)
           BY      Geller, A.   22 pages
```

We selected the first item since it was the most recent, and after the table of contents for the report appeared, chose item 3 to look at the summary.

```
INVESTEXT 03/31/86                                 PAGE 1 OF 1

Insituform East — Company Report
UNLISTED MARKET SERVICE CORP. (THE)

PRESS    FOR
  1     ENTIRE REPORT
  2     Table: Stock Price Data
  3     Summary
  4     Company Products
  5     Equity and Debt Distribution
  6     Corporate Office
  7     Market Makers
  8     Table: Operating Results 1982–86
  9     Table: Balance Sheet 1984–85
 10     In Brief
 11     Business
 12     Results of Operations
 13     Recent Developments
    3
```

SUMMARY:

Insituform East utilizes an innovative patented process of relining underground pipelines using little or no excavation. Revenues for the first half of fiscal 1986 rose 28% to $6.5 million. Net earnings climbed 36% to $1,025,000. In December of 1985, the Company announced the formation of a new partnership, Insituform Mid-South, which has a sublicense from Insituform North America to operate in southern Kentucky, Tennessee and northern Mississippi.

The Unlisted Market Service Corporation, the company that prepared this report, is an independent research firm devoted exclusively to identifying and reporting on little-known, often under-valued stocks on the over-the-counter market. There are over 12,000 OTC stocks, but only a few of the most active issues appear in the newspapers or receive in-depth coverage by traditional Wall Street firms. Consequently, much of the information and analysis in this report would be next to impossible to find elsewhere. But, as you can see, locating it on Dow Jones was a piece of cake.

An Ordeal on DIALOG

Sadly, this was not the case on DIALOG. In fact, Investext as it exists on DIALOG at this writing may be the most difficult, frustrating, and confusing file to use on the entire system. This is not the fault of either DIALOG or BRC. It is due to the uneasy marriage of full-text source material to DIALOG's bibliographic-oriented search software. Each analyst's report has been divided into "pages," for which the display charge is $4.50 apiece. One would normally assume that each investment report would represent a record and that if you searched on a particular term, the number of hits you got would represent the number of reports containing your search terms. But that is not how things work with Investext. In that file the number of hits represents the number of report *pages* that contain your terms.

The pages could be drawn from any number of different reports. You can look at a short-format preview of them without incurring display charges, but there is really no way to know what they contain without looking at the full page. Investment reports are not uniform. You can't count on a market share summary always being on page 5 and a balance sheet always being on page 10. They are thus ill-suited to the "record-ization" process to which they have been subjected on DIALOG.

Furthermore, these reports are written to be read as a whole. Their pages aren't designed to be clipped up and used as a reservoir of raw facts and statistics. For example, here is a portion of a page that was among the hits pulled up by a search for information about competition in the chemical industry. The search logic was: SELECT COMPETITION/DE AND NT = CHEMICALS.

0466303
Specialty Chemicals -Industry Report
PRUDENTIAL BACHE SECURITIES INC.
Pulvirent, S.M.

DATE: 851010
INVESTEXT(tm) REPORT NUMBER: 511554, PAGE 2 OF 5
This is a(n) INDUSTRY report.

SECTION HEADINGS:
  Economics Laboratory -Recommendation
  Products Research & Chemical -Recommendation

TEXT:
    Q. Now that we know your criteria, which are the companies that have met them?

    A. Economics Laboratory, for one, which primarily sells premium dishwashing products to hotels, restaurants, and the like. This may not sound like a high-tech business, but as long as clean dishes and glassware are needed, this company will be able to sell its products. Moreover, because its salesmen have gained access to these hotels . . .

The rest of this "page" seemed to go on forever, and it was packed with great information. Everything except the names and credentials of the person asking the questions and the person answering them. To obtain *that* information you would have to view (and pay for) another page.

How to Use Investext on DIALOG

Learning to use the Investext database (File 545) really is as difficult as it at first seems. But DIALOG's search language is so powerful that it may well be worth the effort. Hours of online testing and conversations with BRC customer support have yielded a workable procedure that you won't find explained in the documentation. The procedure starts with ordering the DIALOG database chapter. You may also want to order the Investext Users Guide from BRC, about which more later. Since File 545 is priced at $96 an hour, plus telecommunications, plus $4.50 per full record/page displayed, you may want to actually read the instructions in the database chapter (all 70 pages of them) before plunging in online.

There are a few points to be aware of before you start. First, there are two types of Investext records, a table-of-contents type and a text type. Each record has a page number, but all table-of-contents records are Page 0. There is no charge, other than connect time, for viewing the table of contents or anything else in the database as long as it isn't information-bearing "text." Each report also has a number, and it is possible to retrieve it with the command SELECT RN = nnnnnn.

Without going into the whys and wherefores, you can use Investext effectively if you view the process as a two-step procedure. The first step is to sign on and conduct your search as you normally would on a DIALOG database. We strongly advise using the file's controlled vocabulary terms to do this. If you try to do a pure free-text search, your results will be unpredictable. The DIALOG database chapter includes many of the controlled terms you need ("company analysis," "competition," "industry overview," "research and development," etc.), and there are even more extensive lists in the appendices to the Investext manual. We also advise making liberal use of the EXPAND command to get lists of search terms while you are online.

When you have narrowed things down to a reasonable number of hits ("pages"), eliminate any table-of-contents pages with the command SELECT Sn/TEXT, where "Sn" is your final set number. Then TYPE the records in the resulting set using Format 3. This will give you a "bibliographic citation" of each page, including the report number. There is no display charge for Format 3.

When you have recorded all of the TYPEs, key in LOGOFF to sign off from DIALOG. Review the download information at your leisure, noting the numbers of the reports that are of interest. Then sign on to DIALOG and BEGIN 545 again. This time, key in SELECT RN = nnn-nnn to retrieve the first of your targeted reports. You will see a number of hits in the resulting set, each of which represents a "page" of the desired report. You can then SELECT either Sn/CONTENTS or Sn AND PAGE = 0 to generate a set containing *only* the table-of-contents page. TYPEing this in Format 2 will give you the complete table of contents of the report. There is no display charge for this either. For example:

```
SELECT RN = 406137

       S1        37  RN = 406137

?SELECT S1/CONTENTS

       S2         1  S1/CONTENTS
?TYPE 2/2/1

 2/2/1
 403879
```

The Industrial Enzyme Market
KIDDER, PEABODY & CO., INC.
Heuer, C., et al.

DATE: 840626
INVESTEXT(tm) REPORT NUMBER: 406137, PAGE 0 OF 36
This is a(n) INDUSTRY report.

SECTION/TABLE HEADINGS:

As you can see from the number of hits for S1, this is a very long report. The table-of-contents page is long as well, so we have truncated it drastically. The final step is "searcher's choice." You can either view the pages you want while online or sign off, print out the contents, make your selections, and sign on again for a third session. Either way, you must make allowances for "Page 0," since it throws off the numbering system, making "Page 1" shown above record number 2, "Page 5," record number 6, and so on.

The easiest way to solve this problem is to limit the set of report pages to text pages. Thus, if you wanted to view "Page 3" to see "How Are Enzymes Manufactured?" you would wait until the entire contents had been displayed and then enter the command SELECT S1/TEXT. That produces another set ("S3 36 S1/TEXT") that eliminates the table-of-contents page and brings the page numbers into alignment with the record numbers. Once you've entered that command, keying in TYPE 3/5/3 will give you the full text (Format 5) of Page 3 of the report.

Search Aids, Training, and Customer Support

There are a number of BRC publications and services you should know about, though if you search by company or industry group on The Source, Dow Jones, or NewsNet, you may not need them. As mentioned, there is a DIALOG database chapter. The BRC-produced manual ($50, plus $5 for shipping and handling) contains the complete list of BRC controlled vocabulary terms and lot of sample searches. It is updated twice a year as new terms are added. If you are going to use this database on DIALOG frequently, it is something you should have.

Business Research Corporation also has free pocket-sized "Smart-Search Guides" that summarize the commands and procedures on various systems. There is a free newsletter called "Investext News." For a subscription fee of $45 a year, BRC will send you a publication it calls "New Research Reports." This is a 30- to 40-page booklet listing all of the new reports that have been added to the database. It is published every two weeks. The company also has a notification service under which it will tell you of reports received and entered on particular industries or companies. The cost is $25 a month. Training is also available in major U.S. cities.

Toll-free Customer Service is available between the hours of 8:30 A.M. and 6:30 P.M., Eastern time, to help you with your search strategies on various systems. Finally, you should know about the firm's "in-house" system, SI/BRC. This is a menu-driven system, accessible via Tymnet or Uninet. The cost is $95 an hour, *including* telecommunications, plus $4.50 per page. That makes it among the least expensive ways to use Investext. Billing is by direct invoice and you can set up an account instantly over the phone. For more information, contact:

> Business Research Corporation
> 12 Farnsworth Street
> Boston, MA 02210
> (800) 662-7878
> (617) 350-4044

NEXIS/The Exchange™, the Wall Street Transcript, and CIRR

The Exchange™ service on NEXIS also contains investment banking reports and transcripts of the New York Society of Security Analysts presentation sessions. Altogether there are approximately 30 participating investment banking firms. These include 19 that are also covered by Investext and firms like Merrill Lynch, Midland Doherty Limited, Sutro & Company, Bain & Company, and seven others that Investext does not cover at this writing. As with the BRC product, coverage in most files starts in 1982 or 1983, though the lag time between publication and online availability may be somewhat greater.

Another good source of investment analysis and corporate intelligence is the Wall Street Transcript database on VU/TEXT. This file corresponds to the weekly print publication of the same name. It covers roundtable discussions by security analysts specializing in various industries, interviews with corporate executives, verbatim transcripts of speeches by CEOs before the New York Society of Security Analysts (NYSSA), and a variety of other top-quality information. The cost is a connect rate of between $250 and $295 an hour, depending on your VU/TEXT subscription option. There are no display charges.

Still another source of investment banking reports is the CIRR database. That stands for "Corporate and Industry Research Reports," and it is available on the BRS system and as a subfile in the PTS PROMT database on DIALOG. CIRR is an *index only* service covering reports from more than 60 investment houses in the U.S., Canada, and Japan. These include most of the firms that are also covered by Investext and The Exchange. Transcripts of NYSSA meetings are also covered.

CIRR coverage starts with January 1982 and updates of 1,000 to 2,000 records are added each month. The full text of most reports is available from JA Micropublishing, Inc., the database producer. Unfortunately, with the exception of NYSSA documents, which are available in paper form, most reports are available only on microfiche. Typical costs are $8 for 15 pages; $35 for 50 pages; and $50 for reports over 50 pages. You can place an order for fiche with CIRR while you are online or call their toll-free number. Customer Service and search assistance is available from 8:30 A.M. to 6:00 P.M., Eastern time. For more information contact:

> JA Micropublishing, Inc.
> 271 Main Street
> Box 218
> Eastchester, NY 10707
> (800) 227-2477
> (914) 793-2130

Online Tip: Downloading a ten-page report from the Investext database will cost you more than $45. But that's the price of immediate delivery. If you're not in a hurry, you can obtain the identical report for $1, or about a dime a page. The key point to know is that CIRR was started in 1983 with the original goal of marketing its fiche collection and printed indexes to public and university libraries. It now sells to anyone, but many large libraries do subscribe to the service.

We made some calls and discovered that the New York Public Library, the Library of Congress, the Cincinnati Public Library, and the UCLA library all have the CIRR collection. And those are just a few of the company's microfiche service subscribers. To find one in your area, contact the reference librarian at your nearest library. He or she may be able to check OCLC or one of the other computer systems that track "who's got what" around the country.

You can then place an interlibrary loan request to obtain a copy of the report you want. There may be a small fee for photocopying. If you live near a library that has the collection, you will be able to obtain full-text copies of the reports you locate on Investext, The Exchange, and CIRR for about 10¢ a page, or whatever the library charges for photocopies of microform documents.

A NewsNet Intelligence Sampler

If investment banking reports are like round-the-clock, on-call experts, industry newsletters are like personal advisors. It's not an analogy one should push too far, but it is a fact that in many cases a single individual *is* the newsletter. He or she may have a staff of assistants, but much of the time what you're buying when you subscribe to a newsletter is access to the opinions, analysis, and expertise of a respected authority in a given field. Since newsletter writers are not constrained by the pin-striped propriety required of an employee of a major investment banking firm, they often have a more personal tone and are not averse to including a little insider's gossip and other "good stuff" now and then.

Of course you pay handsomely for that access. Annual subscription fees of $200 to $500 or more are not uncommon. Deductible or not, those fees are not to be taken lightly, particularly if you need to subscribe to several publications. However, as you know from Chapter 11, NewsNet makes hundreds of these publications available online. The information they contain can be so good that it is a source no investor or corporate intelligence officer can afford to overlook.

Space does not permit individual profiles of all the relevant newsletters on that system. So we have tried to do the next best thing. Listed below are 36 newsletters chosen because they deal with investment and intelligence topics and because they have generally descriptive names. If you read the titles on this list, you'll have an excellent idea of the kind of information you can expect to find on the NewsNet system:

American Banker	Consumer Electronics
Asian Intelligence	Credit Market Analysis
Biotechnology Investment Opportunities	Engelsman's Construction Cost Indexes
Cable & Satellite Express News	Fiber Optics News
Central America Update	Forex Commentary
China Express Contracts	German Business Weekly
Common Carrier Week	Iron and Steel Technology Insights
Computer Market Observer	

Japan Semiconductor Quarterly
Manufactured Housing
  Newsletter
Mobile Phone News
Mutual Fund Monitor
Optical Information Systems
  Update
Outlook on IBM
Prescription Drug Update
Radiology & Imaging
Real Estate & Venture Funding
  Directory
Report on AT&T

Robot News
Satellite Week
Semiconductor Industry &
  Business Survey
Seybold Report on Office
  Systems, The
Star Wars Intelligence Report
Telecommunications Counselor
U.S. Rail News
Utility Reporter—Fuels,
  Energy & Power
Video Week
Wall Street S.O.S. Options Alert

You can generate a complete list of all newsletters on the system by keying in PRICES at the command prompt. The list takes about two minutes to display at 1200 bps. You can look at a description of each newsletter by keying in INFO followed by a space and the newsletter code. Sample issues of each publication on the system are available in the LIBRARY for reading, searching, or scanning at the basic connect rate (no read charges).

Online Tip: What would you say to a 50% discount the next time you stay at a Marriott hotel? How about $5 off the next time you eat at a Red Lobster restaurant and 30% off the Care Bear books of your choosing, courtesy of General Mills? Would 25% off your next cruise up the Mississippi on the *Delta Queen* set your stern-wheeler paddling? Well, if so, then you've got to tap into a fun little database called Shareholder Freebies.

Prepared by Eamon Fingleton of Buttonwood Press/Wall Street Response in New York, the database is available on CompuServe and The Source. It focuses exclusively on the goodies and discounts many companies make available to their stockholders. Each write-up contains an informative description of the benefit, how it is distributed, any minimum number of shares one must own, and a company phone number or address to contact for more information.

Admittedly, a lot of the freebies are nickel-and-dime items—a free product here, a $5-discount coupon there—but some of the benefits can add up to real money. British and Canadian firms are included as well. Bass, the large brewer and hotel operator, offers discounts of about 30% at the company's 100 Crest Hotels in the U.K., Germany, Holland, and Italy. Grand Metropolitan offers 25% off at some of its Intercontinental hotels. And The House of Fraser gives discounts to shareholders at many of its stores, including Harrods.

Hard-copy printouts of the information are available for $10. The database is updated quarterly. For more information, contact:

Wall Street Response
41 Park Avenue, Suite D
New York, NY 10016
(212) 689-4643

...17...

Sales and Marketing:
Advertising, Demographics, and Opportunities

Someone once said that ultimately everything comes down to sales. Whether that's universally true or not, it certainly applies in the electronic universe. There is virtually no database that can't in some way be used to help with a sales effort, whatever that effort may be. In this chapter, however, we're going to focus on a number of databases that directly address sales and marketing topics. We'll show you how to extend your reach across the country or around the world to uncover and profit from hundreds of sales opportunities you would never locate any other way.

We'll look at trademarks, demographics, a database that tracks magazine ads placed by computer and software manufacturers, a database of commercially available market research reports, and a variety of newsletter databases that are especially relevant to sales and marketing issues. There's no doubt about it: If you're in a position to take advantage of it, online databases can make or save you a lot of money.

SALES OPPORTUNITIES
Domestic

Commerce Business Daily

If you're a businessperson, entrepreneur, consultant, or professional—if you've *anything* to sell, anything at all—you have absolutely got to know about the Commerce Business Daily database on DIALOG. At least three factors are responsible for this enthusiasm. First, *Commerce Business Daily* (CBD) is a print publication that summarizes a huge percentage of the procurements planned by thousands of U.S. Government agencies. Second, the publication itself is all but unreadable without a magnifying glass. And third, virtually no one knows about this wealth of opportunities. Compared to the millions of businesses in this country, the 54,000 organizations who subscribe to the printed edition of CBD are a mere drop in the bucket.

There are about 4,500 federal agencies that do procurement around the world. They buy everything from battleships to shoelaces. When they have a "procurement action" totaling $10,000 or more, they are required by law to submit a standardized 200- to 300-word synopsis of their needs to the Commerce Department for publication. These submissions include descriptions of the goods or services, the name and address of the project officer one should contact for more information, an identifying number characterizing the planned procurement, and so on.

Every business day these summaries flow into the main CBD editorial offices in Chicago, where they are edited and keyed into magnetic form. Altogether about one million characters—or about 140,000 words—are entered each day. The computer tapes are sent to a photocomposition contractor (typesetter) each morning. By roughly 2 P.M., the compositor has finished with the tapes, stripped out the typesetting codes, and made duplicates for DIALOG and the three other systems that have a license to offer the information online. The tapes are air-expressed to the online systems, where they are added to the CBD database and become available for searching within hours.

In the meantime, the paper edition is printed on Government Printing Office (GPO) presses and mailed via first- or second-class mail. (Both mailing options are offered to subscribers.) The CBD editorial offices, the GPO press, and the post office are all located in the same Chicago building.

The Commerce Department deserves high marks for this not inconsiderable accomplishment. But of necessity, the 32 to 96 pages of the print publication contain so much information that an exceedingly small typesize has been used. If you can imagine all of the fine print in all of the contracts you've ever signed published on thin, European-style newspaper stock, you'll have a pretty good idea of what CBD is like. As one person we spoke with said, "In spite of all the upgrades and changes that have taken place over the years, CBD is still a typical government 'Listerine' type of publication. It's 'the taste you hate once a day,' but you read it because someone pays you to do so."

The reduction in eyestrain alone would be reason enough to use CBD online. But there's an even more important benefit: scannability. With CBD on DIALOG, you can instantly scan any number of CBD issues for exactly those announced procurement actions relevant to your line of business. The database is formatted with a variety of special codes that make this relatively easy. For example, suppose you own a home furnishings store in Aurora, Illinois. What's the government buying that you might be able to supply? Let's take a look:

?BEGIN 195

File 195:Commerce Business Daily — 860401-860613

Set   Items   Description

SS SC=72 AND SP=IL

      S1   134 SC=72 (HOUSEHOLD/COMMERCIAL FURNISH. AND)
      S2 2369 SP=IL
      S3   3 SC=72 AND SP=IL

?TYPE 3/5/1

3/5/1
1403019
  BLINDS, MINI VENETIAN, LEVELOR, RIVIERA CUSTOM OR
EQUAL, alum slats, torque tilt wand, compact railhead
1-1/2″ deep #110 white, installation is required by
vendor. Reqs for quotes must be submitted in writing
to Contracting Div, Attn: L Camellino, Bldg 142, Ft
Sheridan, IL 60037-5000. Include self-addressed label
for quote pkg. RFQ will be issued 15 days after date of
CBD publ. Closing o/a 23 Jul 86. (143)
  SPONSOR: Contracting Div, Attn: L Camellino, Bldg 142,
Ft Sheridan, IL 60037-5000
  SUBFILE: PSU (U.S. GOVERNMENT PROCUREMENTS, SUPPLIES)
  SECTION HEADING: 72 Household and Commercial
Furnishings and Appliances
  LEGEND: 1
  CBD DATE: MAY 29, 1986   ISSUE: PSA-9099

?T

7/5/2
1391994
  PLANTERS w/artificial plants. F1160286T4959. Due 17
Jun 86. POC Susan Raup, 217/495-3733. See Notes 32, 88,
95. (135)
  SPONSOR: CTTC/LGCS/Base Contrs Office, Bldg 270, Stop
23, Chanute AFB IL 61868-5320
  SUBFILE: PSU (U.S. GOVERNMENT PROCUREMENTS, SUPPLIES)
  SECTION HEADING: 72 Household and Commercial
Furnishings and Appliances
  CBD DATE: MAY 19, 1986   ISSUE: PSA-9092

This file uses "the commodity groups in the Federal Supply Classification system." A complete list of these codes is supplied with the DIALOG database chapter. We searched the supply classification field (SC) for code 72, Household and Commercial Furnishings and Appliances. The SP field is the field for "sponsor," and since it always contains the address of the requesting agency, we searched it for the state code for Illinois (IL). The SS is DIALOG's "select sets" command, and as you can see, it creates a set for each of the elements of the search argument.

There were three procurement requests for household furnishings in Illinois (Set S3, above), so we TYPEd the first one in Format 5, the full-record format (TYPE 3/5/1 means type Set 3 using Format 5, and display Record 1). This took only seconds of online time. The cost for this database is $54 an hour (plus telecommunications), and 25¢ for each record TYPEd.

All of the codes and abbreviations are explained in the DIALOG database chapter. The sentence "See Notes 32, 88, 95" in the second record refers to a list of 100 standard Notes. Note 32, for example, reads, "When requesting bid set(s), provide information as to whether your organization (together with its affiliates) is a large or small business." The line in the first record reading LEGEND: 1 means that "the procurement item is 100% set aside for small business concerns."

You'll have to spend some time learning to use this database. It's not overly complicated, and you can do free text searches. But for best results, you really should use the government codes. Also, you may not want to limit your search to your own state. By law, the file also contains reports of contract awards of $25,000 or more, listing the amount of the contract and the winning firm. We saw lots of contracts let by government installations in one state that were filled by companies in distant states. Since in most cases government agencies are required to award the contract to the low bidder, you don't have to be a local firm to get the business. Here's an example of a contract award report that illustrates this quite nicely:

XEROGRAPHIC PAPER Contr GS-02F40366, 17 Jan 86 (RFP 86-F-0239), $40,608. Alco Standard Corp, 3825 Dacoma, Houston TX.
SPONSOR: U.S. Army Tank Automotive Material Readiness Command, Warren, MI 48397-5000 313/574-6802 or 6807
SUBFILE: CSU (CONTRACT AWARDS, SUPPLIES)
SECTION HEADING: 75 Office Supplies and Devices
CBD DATE: APRIL 2, 1986   ISSUE: PSA-9059

This brings up another important point. The current file on DIALOG is File 195. This contains up to three months' worth of records. On the first weekend of each month, however, the oldest month's records are transferred to File 194, and File 194 goes back to October 1982. Since contract awards are included in both databases, public interest groups and government watchdog organizations can easily track who got which contract and for how much. Corporate intelligence personnel can just as easily pull up a list of contracts awarded to competing companies from October 1982 to the present.

If you are searching for potential sources of new business, however, you may find it convenient to eliminate the records of awarded contracts from your search universe. You can do this by keying in NOT SF = CS? as part of your search statement. The "SF" stands for "subfile," and the "CS?" can stand for "Contract Awards—Services" (Code CSE) or "Contract Awards—Supplies, Equipment, and Material" (Code CSU).

The place to start is with a DIALOG subscription and a copy of the DIALOG database chapter for Files 194, 195. The cost is $6. There are no special search aids or training classes, though the Commerce Department does publish several brochures. Annual subscriptions to the printed edition of CBD are $160 for first-class delivery, $81 for second-class mail. Six-month subscriptions are $88 and $45, respectively. Contact the Superintendent of Documents at the Government Printing Office at (202) 783-3238 to subscribe (Visa and MasterCard accepted).

The database is also available on the SOFTSHARE, Data Resources, and United Communications Group systems. Contact CBD for details:

> Director
> Commerce Business Daily
> U.S. Dept. of Commerce
> Room 1833
> Herbert C. Hoover Building
> Washington, D.C. 20230
> (202) 377-4878 and -0632

Online Tip: If you're too busy to sign on to DIALOG and conduct as often as you would like, consider setting up an SDI profile. Read the supplemental DIALOG database documentation chapter and try some searches. Then call DIALOG Customer Service for help in refining your search strategy. Finally, store the strategy you have developed on the system as an SDI profile. For $5.95 a week, DIALOG will automatically run your SDI search strategy against CBD updates and notify you of the results.

The Herb Ireland Sales Prospector®

Prospector Research Services, Inc., of Waltham, Massachusetts, publishes a monthly newsletter designed to alert subscribers to industrial, commercial, and institutional expansion and relocation activity. The newsletter is available in about 16 editions, one for each major region of the United States and an edition for Canada. The print versions typically run seven to ten pages an issue, and each carries a subscription rate of $125 a year.

Each edition is also available on NewsNet at a rate of $24/hour for validated print subscribers and $60/hour (300 bps) for all others. We read the sample issue in the NewsNet online LIBRARY to get a feeling for the kinds of things the publication covers and, equally important, the kinds of keywords that might be most productive. Then we signed back on and did a simple search.

We decided to see who had announced planned renovations in Tennessee. So we searched the edition of the Sales Prospector that covers Louisiana, Mississippi, Arkansas, Oklahoma, Kentucky, and Tennessee. The code for that edition on NewsNet is GB15. Here's what the start of the search looked like:

```
Enter command or <RETURN>
—>SEARCH GB15

Enter LATEST for the latest issue, or other date options
—>LATEST

Enter Keyword(s)
—>RENOVATION* and (TENN* or TN)
!
      2 Occurrences

Enter HEAD for headlines, TEXT for full text, ANALYZE for occurrences in each service,
BACK for new keyword(s)
—>HEAD
```

We used the asterisk (*), NewsNet's wildcard/truncation symbol, to allow for singulars, plurals, and abbreviations of the keywords. The exclamation point appeared when the NewsNet computer had finished searching the edition we requested. If there had been no hits on our search statement, a period would have appeared instead. Since we were searching only a single issue (LATEST), this search doesn't really demonstrate NewsNet's notification feature. But it is especially nice when you are searching several issues, as would be the case if we had specified a range of dates, or when you are searching an entire category, as would be the case had we specified just "GB" instead of GB15.

By sending you a period or an exclamation point each time it finishes searching a newsletter issue, the system reassures you that it is working on your request. And by noting the number of punctuation marks, you can tell how far it has gotten at any time. Finally, if you see a lot of dots and no exclamation points, it may be a sign that your search terms need to be redefined. You may want to issue a <BREAK> to stop the current search and enter a new strategy.

It's always wise to look at the headlines first on NewsNet. Headlines usualy (though not always) give you a better idea of where the hit occurred, and you can view them at the basic NewsNet connect rate. The "read" rates don't kick in until you actually read the text of a newsletter. Here are the headlines for the two hits, followed by the text for headine Number 2:

```
1) 5/1/86  GB15  SALES PROSPECTOR/LA MS AR OK KY TN
   T.A. Lupton, Chattanooga TN
   RENOVATION, Mixed-Use Complex

2) 5/1/86  GB15  SALES PROSPECTORS/LA MS AR OK KY TN
   Franklin L. Haney, Chattanooga TN
   FUTURE, Office Renovation

Enter Headline numbers to read, PREVIEW, AGAIN, BACK, STOP,
QUIT, or HELP
—>2


Copyright
SALES PROSPECTOR/LA MA AR OK KY TN
       May 1986


2)
Franklin L. Haney, Chattanooga TN
FUTURE, Office Renovation

CHATTANOOGA, Tenn. — Developer Franklin L. Haney, Commerce
Union Tower, Suite 1700, Chattanooga, Tenn. (615/265-0537),
has received city approval for $29 million in bond financing
to refinance and renovate two office tower and three parking
garages on Chestnut St. in downtown Chattanooga. According
to Mr. Haney, $11.8 million will be used to renovate the
Commerce Union Bank Building, in which he will relocate his
Arkansas Coca-Cola bottling company headquarters, and three
nearby parking garages. Also planned for restoration is the
Chestnut Street Tower. The developer is a limited partner in
the partnerships that own the structures.
```

If you were in the construction or building supplies business and you lived in Chattanooga, you would almost certainly know about this planned office tower/parking garage renovation. But suppose you lived on the other side of the state, or in Alabama or Georgia. Suppose you're an office furniture manufacturer in Philadelphia, a Houston financial consultant who specializes in floating successful bond issues, or a plumber in Minnesota who is fed up with long, cold winters and would like to head south.

The Sales Prospector newsletters on NewsNet date back to September of 1984. As you can see, the items they contain are not as specific as those in *Commerce Business Daily*. You'll have to use your imagination to perceive all of the opportunities. But there are plenty to be had. For more information on the print publication, you can contact:

> Sales Prospector
> Prospector Research Services, Inc.
> 751 Main Street
> Waltham, MA 02154

Online Tip: There are at least four other newsletters on NewsNet that do a good job of using information technology to help buyers and sellers make contact. The first two are the "Real Estate Buyers Directory" and the "Real Estate & Venture Funding Directory." Aimed at real estate sellers, the first offers the names, addresses, and telephone numbers of individuals and companies who buy real estate for investment purposes or commercial uses. The second is aimed at buyers and offers directory information on real estate lenders, the types of deals they prefer, their geographical preferences, and so on. Both publications exist in electronic form only. Updates are added once a month. For more information, contact:

> Coert Engelsman Intl. Ltd.
> P.O. Box 112
> Coudersport, PA 16915

The other publications worthy of special note are Rohn Engh's "Photoletter" and "PhotoMarket." Both exist in print form as well and both focus on matching photo sellers with photo buyers (advertising and government agencies, corporations, magazines and other publications, etc.). "Photoletter," however, comes out monthly and is positioned as more of a professional photographer's trade journal. "PhotoMarket" comes out twice a month (the first and third Thursday), and is more of a quick notification service of photo buyer

Online Tip (cont.)

needs. For more information on these and other photo-related publications, contact:

> PhotoSource International
> Pine Lake Farm
> Osceola, WI 54020
> (715) 248-3800

International

Trade Opportunities and Foreign Traders Index

Both Trade Opportunities (TO) and Foreign Traders Index (FTI) are
produced by the U.S. Department of Commerce. Both are available on
DIALOG.

The Trade Opportunities database (Files 106 and 107) is a lot like the
Commerce Business Daily database. Both include announcements of
purchase plans or requests for bids or proposals dealing with specific
items or services. The difference is that TO items all pertain to requests
from non-U.S. companies and governments.

The information is gathered by Foreign Service officers stationed in
more than 130 countries around the globe. Records contain the name of
the company or government agency, a description of the desired product or service, information on how to enter a bid or whom to contact for
more information, as well as the date, deadlines, and SIC, country,
business name, and type of opportunity codes.

One can do a free text search of the parargraph describing the product as well. But we decided to see if there were any opportunities in
India for products covered by SIC code 3545, "machine tool accessories
and measuring devices." The "PC" (product code) filed is based on the
SIC codes. Figure 17.1 shows what we found.

—— **Figure 17.1. Machine Tool Sales Opportunities in India** ——

Shown below is a complete DIALOG session, the goal of which was to
investigate opportunities for selling machine tools in India. Had we
wanted to, we could have been much more precise. (See the DIALOG
Bluesheet for the searchable fields at your disposal or key in
?FIELD107 when online.) We have greatly shortened the descriptive
paragraph in the interests of space.

? BEGIN 107

File 107:Trade Opportufnities — 8501-8624

Set Items Description

?SELECT PC = 3545

    S1   122   PC = 3545   ←——— There are 122 items in the database that fall under the "3545" SIC code.

?SS S1 and CN = INDIA   ←——— "Select Sets" (SS) for all of the above for which the country name (CN) is given as India.

        122   S1
    S2   511   CN = INDIA (CC = 533)
    S3   11   S1 AND CN = INDIA   ←——— Eleven hits or items.

?TYPE 3/5/1   ←——— Type the first item in Set 3, using Format 5.

 3/5/1
256472 DATE: 860117 INDIA DIRECT SALES TO END-USER
  SURFACE TEXTURE MEASURING MACHINE USED FOR RA VALVES, FOR HIGH
PRECISION QUALITY CONTROL ON PRODUCTS INCL. COLD DRAWN ERW TUBE,
SHOCK OBSERVER TUBE, ETC. SPEC: (A) TYPE: TAYLOR HOBSON SURFACE
ROUGHNESS MEASURING MACHINE; (B) MODEL: SURTONIC-3 HAND-HELD
SURFACE TESTER WHICH IS CONSIDERED HIGHLY SUPERIOR FOR RA . . .
. . . QUOTE BOTH FOB & C&F-CALCUTTA PRICES, WITH EARLIEST
DELIVERY. TERMS L/C. TISCO IS THE 2ND LARGEST INDIAN CO. IN TERMS
OF ITS TOTAL ASSETS & TURNOVER. TATA GROUP OF INDUS. IS
CONSIDERED ONE OF THE MOST PROGRESSIVE & PROF. MANAGED BUSINESS
CONGLOMERATES IN INDIA.
  REPLY TO—
S.B. SARKAR, PURCHASE OFFICER
THE TATA IRON & STEEL CO. LTD. (TISCO)
TUBES DIV., TATA CENTER, 43 CHOWRINGHEE
RD., CALCUTTA 700071, INDIA
CABLE: ITEECEE-CALCUTTA
PHONE: 44-2311 (10 LINES)
TELEX: 021-7511 & 021-2768
PLEASE SEND COPY OF YOUR RESPONSE TO
AMERICAN CONSULATE GENERAL (COM-TOP)
CALCUTTA, INDIA
DEPT. OF STATE
WASHINGTON, D.C. 20520

```
PRODUCTS (SIC): 35452 ; 38321
BUSINESS CODES : M (BN = MANUFACTURER);
COUNTRY CODE : 533
TYPE OF OPPORTUNITY CODE : 101
NOTICE NUMBER : 043528
```

The database corresponds to the *TOP Bulletin* ("Trade Opportunities Program"), a joint activity of the Departments of State and Commerce. File 107 is the current file and it is updated weekly. File 106 is the historical file. Updated quarterly, it contains information that originally appeared in File 107. The historical file is particularly valuable to anyone who wants to scan for potential sales leads, company information, or market analysis-type information. Use of either file is restricted to U.S. DIALOG password holders only.

The Foreign Traders Index database is, as its name implies, a directory. It includes manufacturers, service organizations, agent representatives, retailers, wholesalers, distributors, and others who either already import from the U.S. or are interested in doing so. As with TO, the information in FTI is collected by U.S. Foreign Service officers at 200 U.S. embassies and consular posts around the world. The information comes through direct contacts with firms involved.

The database always includes the latest four years of information. It is updated thrice yearly. Records include the nature of the business's activity and its products or services, the name, phone and telex numbers of the company's chief executive, the relative size of the firm (small, medium, large, very large, unknown), the number of employees, and whether or not the firm is an East-West Trader and/or a member of the American Chamber of Commerce. There are DIALOG database chapters for both TO and FTI, and they are essential.

Related Information and Services

In the category of "Your Tax Dollars at Work," most businesspeople don't know it, but the Department of Commerce has a wealth of information that can help you sell your products abroad. The Export Promotion Services section of the Office of Information Product Development & Distribution (OIPDD) has scores of market research reports, for example, covering everything from agricultural machinery in Venezuela to food processing and packaging equipment in Spain. (Typical report price: $10 to $60.)

For a very reasonable fee, the Office of Trade Information Services will prepare a customized report to help you evaluate potential foreign markets and competitors. "World Traders Data Report" will give you information on a foreign firm's reputation and payment history, as well as its sales figures and trade and credit references. The Agent/Distributor Service will help you find the right overseas sales agent or distributor ("Let our embassy officials worldwide assist you in locating the best representative for your needs").

This only scratches the surface of what's available—if you ask for it. In the course of researching the databases cited above, we spoke with many Commerce Department people, and we were always pleasantly surprised to find that they were more businessperson than bureaucrat. They want to help. And they even take MasterCard, Visa, Carte Blanche, and Diners Club, to make it easy to place an order over the phone.

The entry point, whether for more information on TO and FTI or the other services, is the address and number given below. But please note that the department has offices in at least 70 U.S. cities that can also be of service. The Washington Customer Service desk is staffed weekdays from 9 A.M. to 5 P.M. Eastern time. We suggest that you ask for a summary of everything the Office of Trade Information Services can provide.

> Export Promotion Services
> OIPDD
> U.S. Department of Commerce
> P.O. Box 14207
> Washington, D.C. 20044
> (202) 377-2432 (Customer Service)

Online Tip: A lot of newsletters cover international trade and exporting, and a number of them are available for search and retrieval on NewsNet. Those listed below are specifically designed to aid American businesspeople in taking advantage of foreign trade opportunities. "China Express," for example, focuses on opportunities in "the rapidly opening People's Republic of China." "German Business Weekly" provides a "broad overview on Europe's leading economy and its link with the U.S. Each week this newsletter of the German American Chamber of Commerce, Inc., summarizes trends and conditions in the German business world." Descriptions of these and other publications are available with the INFO command, and sample issues are available for low-cost reading in the NewsNet LIBRARY:

Asia Cable: Report of Asia/Pacific Business Opportunities
China Express Contracts
Frost & Sullivan Political Risk Newsletter

MARKETING
Advertising, Demographics, and Market Research

FIND/SVP

FIND/SVP (the "SVP" stands for "s'il vous plait"—"please" in French) is one of the largest information brokers in the country. With offices in 16 countries and correspondents in 13 more, it may well be the largest in the world. As one company brochure puts it, "Finding information is a full time job. Ours. Not yours."

The company could be on to something. Apparently you can sign an agreement with FIND (the "SVP" is often dropped), pay them about $350 a month, and turn over all of your information needs to them. We haven't tried the service, but Bristol-Myers, Campbell Soup, Samsung, Matsushita, Citicorp, IBM, ITT, Squibb, and the Ford Motor Company have and have been satisfied.

The FIND/SVP database on DIALOG corresponds to the *Findex* directory of market research reports, studies, and surveys, a printed volume that sells for $255. The word *directory* is the key, since this database will tell you who has done a market study on a particular product or service, but it will not summarize the results and findings. In all, over 11,000 studies done by more than 500 U.S. and foreign research firms are covered. FIND/SVP can supply copies of reports from 70 of those publishers. For the others, you must contact the publisher yourself.

For example, we wondered about the seltzer water market. Since seltzer water has as much carbonated zip as club soda without the sodium, and since sodium intake has been a major nutritional topic in recent years, it seemed worth exploring. We signed on to DIALOG and keyed in BEGIN 196 to get into the FIND/SVP database. Then we simply SELECTed "seltzer." Here are the results:

```
?SELECT SELTZER

      S1        1 SELTZER
?TYPE 1/5/1
```

1/5/1
019325
   THE BOTTLED WATER MARKET
   MAY 1986 200 P. $1250 ONE-TIME
   Publ: FIND/SVP,   NEW YORK, NY
   Availability: PUBLISHER OR DIALORDER FINDIT
   Report No.: AA125
   Document Type: MARKET/INDUSTRY STUDY
    This study analyzes sparkling and still mineral water, club soda, seltzer water, and bulk water market segments. It covers market shares, distribution, advertising and promotion strategies, mergers and acquisitions, new products and flavors, new packaging, and provides projected growth rates through 1990. Topics discussed include Perrier's introduction of flavored water and the sales of bulk water driven by health consciousness and concerns about the safety of municipal water supplies.
   Descriptors: BEVERAGES ; BOTTLED WATER

There is a DIALOG database chapter, and FIND/SVP publishes a manual ($25) that contains all of the controlled vocabulary terms (descriptors) used in the database as well as the names and addresses of the report publishers from whom you can order the studies. For more information, contact:

> FIND/SVP
> 500 Fifth Avenue
> New York, NY 10110
> (212) 354-2424
> Telex: 148358

ACT I and ACT II

In the past, these two DIALOG databases have been produced by Data Courier, Inc., though at this writing their status is uncertain. The "ACT" stands for "Advertised Computer Technologies." ACT I is a directory database that contains information on more than 32,000 computer-related products advertised by nearly 11,000 companies. The database dates from 1983 to the present. There is one record for each company, and approximately 4,000 records are added each year, or at least they were at the height of the computer boom.

You can use the database to get a list of all computer products made (and advertised) by a particular firm. Or you can use it to locate the firm that makes a particular product. That's what we did with Chart-Master:

?SELECT CHARTMASTER OR CHART(W)MASTER

     0 CHARTMASTER
   63 CHART
  227 MASTER

```
                 2   CHART(W)MASTER
         S1      2   CHARTMASTER OR CHART(W)MASTER
?TYPE 1/5/1


  1/5/1
  0009204


    Decision Resources Inc
    25 Sylvan Road South
    Westport, CT 06880


    201-222-1974


  Company ID: DCSNRS
  Organization Type: 1000  (ON = Manufacturer)


  Trade name:      Chart-Master 6.1
  Trade name code: CMAS61
  Classification:  S2240 (CN = Graphics)
  Description:     Graphics software featuring network
                   compatibility support for over 90 plotters
                   and printers, and on-screen instructions.
```

If you deal with a lot of software or hardware, it is sometimes difficult to remember who makes what, let alone how to contact them. ACT I offers an easy solution. The response was instantaneous, well worth the 75¢ charged to display the full record, only part of which is shown here. (The connect-time rate is $96, plus communications.) We also learned that Decision Resources makes programs called Diagram-Master, Map-Master, and Sign-Master. The second hit was due to the use of the phrase "compatible with Chart-Master" in the record of another software company.

Now let's go over to ACT II and see how Decision Resources has been supporting its Chart-Master product in print. ACT II draws its material from the same 100 magazines used by ACT I, but the information each record provides is different. There were 154 hits on the search term CO = DECISION RESOURCES?. Since the database dates from 1984 to the present, and since each hit represents one magazine ad, we can tell that Decision Resources has been fairly active. At the time the search was done, that worked out to over five ads a month.

When we combined the first set (S1 154 CO = DECISION RESOURCES?) with the product name [S1 AND CHART(W)MASTER], we got 80 hits, one of which is shown below. Note that the price of the ad is given as well. By displaying all of the hits in one format or another, one could come up with a pretty good estimate of what kind of budget Decision Resources has been putting against Chart-Master for the past few years:

228942　　　　86027125

Trade name(s):　Chart-Master (TC = CHRTMS)
Classification:　S2240 (CN = Graphics)

Ad description:　Business graphics software for use with
　　　　　　　　the IBM PC and compatibles. Menu-driven.
　　　　　　　　Produces presentation quality graphics on
　　　　　　　　transparencies, paper, or 35mm slides.

Availability:　　Photocopy available from Dialorder vendor
　　　　　　　　INFORM

Journal:　　　　　　Lotus (JC = LOT)
Publication date:　860200
Page number:　　　26-27 (PG = J)

Journal trim size:	8 by 10 3/4
Total pages in issue:	145
Editorial pages in issue:	75
Ad pages in issue:	70
Ad size (pages):	2 (SZ = F)
Ad type:	Spread
Ad color:	2C4C
Ad category:	Product
Quadrant:	Lower left
Ad shape:	Horizontal
Ad cost:	$19,750
Manufacturer:	Decision Resources Inc (CI = DCSNRS)
	25 Sylvan Road South
	Westport, CT 06880
	203-222-1974
Organization type:	1000 (ON = Manufacturer)

Data Courier sells a manual called *SEARCH ACT* for $57.50. In addition to sample searches and all the codes you'll need, it contains tips on using ACT together with D&B—Dun's Market Identifiers, PTS PROMT, DISCLOSURE II, and ABI/INFORM to work up a complete report on a given company or product. See Chapter 13 for contact information.

Online Tip: There is another worthwhile database that, as far as we know, originated the idea of collecting print ad information. The database is called AdTrack™, but unfortunately it is considerably less useful than in years past. In fact, at this writing it appears to be among the database dead.

The concept behind AdTrack is to index every advertisement of a quarter page or larger in 150 U.S. magazines. According to

Online Tip (cont.)

AdTrack literature, those 150 publications account for over 98% of consumer magazine advertising revenues in most major categories. The file dates from October 1980 and is supposedly updated monthly with "approximately 13,000 records per month."

Unfortunately, that has not happened recently, and this is the real reason we've mentioned the database. There's a trick you can use on DIALOG to discover the date of the most recent update for any database. You have only to get into the database and EX-PAND the UD (update) field. After sampling AdTrack in mid-1986 and noticing that none of the records we looked at was dated later than 1984, we did the following:

Ref	Items	Index-term
E1	11136	UD=8312
E2	29306	UD=8409
E3	0	*UD=86
E4	29306	UD=9999

That let us check for any updates entered in 1986. But as you can see, the most recent update was made in September 1984 (UD=8409). The reason the number of items is the same for UD=9999 is that "9999" always references the most recent update. Apparently something is wrong with AdTrack. We made repeated attempts to reach the database producer to no avail.

Donnelley Demographics

Donnelley Demographics is File 575 on DIALOG. It offers selected demographic information drawn from the 1980 census, enhanced by Donnelley's proprietary techniques for developing current-year estimates and five-year projections. You can search by such demographic characteristics as mobility,, housing, education, occupation, income, race, age, population, and households. You may also search by geographic level, including city, county, state, MSA (SMSA), ZIP code, and more. You can also search using A. C. Nielsen's Designated Marketing Areas (DMAs), Arbitron's Areas of Dominant Influence (ADIs), and the SAMI designation from Selling Areas Marketing Inc.

Here are the results of a very simple search to find out what's what in Laramie, Wyoming. The search logic was: SELECT LARAMIE AND ST=W and LV=COUNTY.

```
4/2/1
0003177
LARAMIE CO WY
```

Level:	County
State:	WY
County:	LARAMIE CO WY
ADI:	CHEYENNE
DMA:	CHEYENNE-SCOTTSBLUFF-STERLING
SAMI:	DENVER

	1980 Census	1985 Estimate	% Change 80 TO 85	1990 Projection
Total Population	68,649	74,684	8.8%	81,037
Total Households	25,292	27,702	9.5%	29,958
Household Population	67,454	73,489	8.9%	79,842
Average Household Size	2.7	2.7	−.4%	2.7
Median Household Income	$17,913	$23,631	31.9%	$30,722

The database is updated during the third quarter of the year to replace the current-year estimates and projections and to add projections for the fifth year ahead. You can sort output seven ways from sundown and the DIALOG REPORT format is so thoroughly supported that there is a special Technical Note (TN7) to show you how to do it. The DIALOG database chapter is 96 pages long and it is the only search aid available at this time. The connect cost is $60 an hour plus communications. Display charges range from 25¢ to $10. Format 2, the one shown above, is $2. For more information, contact:

> Client Services Representative
> Donnelley Marketing Information Services
> 1351 Washington Blvd., Fourth Floor
> Stamford, CT 06902
> (203) 965-5454

TRADEMARKSCAN™

Produced by Thomson & Thomson, the oldest trademark search firm in the United States, TRADEMARKSCAN™ is File 226 on DIALOG. It contains all active registered and pending trademarks on file with the U.S. Patent and Trademark Office (PTO). At this writing it contains over 700,000 records, and it's updated every week. The "marks" date from 1884 to the present.

Each record contains the trademark and its U.S. class number, the name of the owner and a description of the goods or services to which the mark applies, as well as information about the status of the mark (pending, registered, etc.). Conducting a trademark search is a serious business, and Thomson & Thomson strongly advises using a search of the database as a preliminary step only. Before you can feel reasonably safe in using a given mark, state registrations, phone books, industry and trade association directories, and other sources of Common Law trademark and tradename information have to be checked.

However, as a spokesperson points out, when you are trying to come up with a new product name, it can be enormously helpful to run a quick check in the database to see if the name has already been used. When you consider that the alternative is to blindly submit a name or list of names that you like to a full-dress (and often expensive) trademark search, a preliminary check makes a lot of sense.

On a lark, we decided to see if the word "Klingon" had been trademarked. We simply entered SELECT KLINGON and got three hits. Interestingly, the actual names were KLING-ONS (non-adhesive decorative decals), KLING-ON (plastic auto sidemolding), and KLINGONS (dolls and toy figures). None of these marks matches the search statement. The reason we got hits on them is that TRADEMARKSCAN has made special provisions for retrieving a string of characters, regardless of where it occurs in a word. Here's the full record of the KLINGONS (as in evil intergalactic empire) trademark:

```
        0215568
KLINGONS
        WORD COUNT: 01
        US CLASS: 022 (Games, Toys, and Sporting Goods)
        INTL CLASS: 028 (Toys and Sporting Goods)
        GOODS/SERVICES: DOLLS & TOY FIGURES
        SERIES CODE: 3   SERIAL NO.: 026200   REG. NO.: 1011089
        STATUS: Registered
        STATUS DATE: May 20, 1975   REG. DATE: May 20, 1975
        PUB. DATE: February 25, 1975      DATE OF USE: April 15, 1974
        OWNER: MEGO CORP NEW YORK NY
```

There are nearly a dozen search aids to help you use this database, but you should probably start with the 70-page DIALOG database chapter. See the DIALOG "Search Aids" list for details on the other items. You should also definitely contact Thomson & Thomson, as they will be able to explain things in more detail. Contact:

> TRADEMARKSCAN
> Thomson & Thomson
> One Monarch Drive
> North Quincy, MA 02171-2126
> (617) 479-1600
> Telex: 6971430

NewsNet Newsletters

NewsNet is also a good source of advertising, marketing, and product information. The Market Research Review, for example, is a newsletter that analyzes and evaluates commercially available market research and technology assessment reports. It's updated every two weeks.

The World Food & Drink Report concentrates on just that. Sample headlines include: "Coors Candy Bar a Bust," "British Coffee Consumption Up," and "Heineken Shopping in Greece." The database is particularly strong in marketing statistics. Issues go back to August 26, 1985.

The Manufactured Housing Newsletter focuses on news of marketing and regulation in the mobile home, modular, panelized, pre-cut, and component housing industries. Computer Market Observer, Computing Today!, Consumer Electronics, and several other newsletters track marketing and financial developments in the personal computer and electronics fields. Video Week covers the sales and distribution of video cassettes, pay TV, and "allied new electronic media."

Financial Services Week concentrates on news and analysis of the financial services industry, "including networking, cross-selling, profitable market segmenting, regulation, deregulation, new technology, and customer trends." IMS Weekly Marketeer does the same thing for the insurance industry.

Many other newsletters carry advertising, marketing, and product information as well. These may or may not be of interest, but as always, NewsNet is worth a look.

...18...

Washington Watch:
Publications, Periodicals, and Statistics

Professional critics and politicians who are between jobs are fond of railing about government waste. But none of them ever touches upon one of the biggest wastes of all: the waste of huge quantities of top-quality information. Every day men and women all over the country sit down at their desks in federal office buildings and collect, analyze, and publish information. Every week a federal agency somewhere commissions a private consultant to prepare a detailed report. Every month university professors and graduate students win grants to study some macro or micro phenomenon.

The amount of information prepared and produced each year as a result of federal government activities is staggering. Equally impressive is the breadth and depth of the topics covered. Since government is in some way involved in virtually every aspect of our business and personal lives, there is scarcely a topic you can name that isn't covered in one way or another. There are books, booklets, maps, charts, computer programs, filmstrips, videotapes, reports, and magazines. The number of individual items is in the scores of thousands. Even the government doesn't know for sure how many items it publishes.

The information is usually quite good and quite reasonably priced. In fact, a lot of it is either free or downright cheap because you've already paid for it with your taxes. Many agencies have done the best that their budgets will allow in letting citizens know what they offer. But that isn't much compared to what a commercial magazine or book publishing firm can do. As a result, most of us have no concept at all of the vast amount of material that is available, let alone how to find that one crucial publication on the "Molluscan Record from a mid-Cretaceous Borehole in Weston County, Wyoming." (At least not when we need it.)

Because of this, a great deal of government information is vastly under-utilized each year.

Fortunately, a lot of government information and a lot of information about where to *find* government information is now available online. As you know, that changes everything. At the very least, it makes the information itself enormously powerful.

We are blessed with a government and a society that are committed both by inclination and by law to public information. (The depth of this commitment is something you will sense if you spend much time with the databases in this chapter.) But in the past it has been difficult to pull together all the bits and pieces and correlate them into a coherent whole. No one who isn't being paid for it wants to spend every spare moment plowing through the thin paper and fine print of committee hearings, floor debates, and congressional documents to see what Senator Soaper had to say about the effect of gamma rays on marigolds or some other issue.

But now you don't have to. Indeed, even though the information has been public all along, the same representatives and senators who are so happy to have television broadcast speeches from their respective chambers might not be so pleased if they knew how easy it is for "the folks back home" to monitor their other activities with a personal computer. As we'll see, with a few keystrokes you can find out exactly how many times your representative has appeared on the floor of the House and what he or she has done in committee.

With similar ease you can follow the actions, both proposed and implemented, of regulatory and other agencies in the executive branch. You can search through and download the full text of news conferences, radio addresses, executive orders, and other presidential papers. You can scan through literally hundreds of thousands of items published by the Government Printing Office to locate the one document containing the information you need. And you can display the latest Census Bureau or Consumer Price Index statistic on your screen or locate the source document for any statistic published by the U.S. government.

It isn't difficult, and since many of these are government-produced databases, it usually isn't expensive. It's not difficult to obtain copies of the desired government documents either, once you know how to go about it. Since this is such an important part of "Washington Watch" information, that's where we'll start.

How to Order Copies of Any Government Publication

There are at least three ways to obtain copies of virtually any non-classified document published by the United States Government. You can order copies through an information broker or document delivery service. You can order directly from the Government Printing Office (GPO). Or you can contact one of the many official U.S. Government Depository Libraries across the country.

Federal Document Retrieval

Federal Document Retrieval (FDR) is an information broker and search service based in Washington, D.C. But the company has associates in major cities across the country. The FDR brochure is headlined: "Name a Document. Name a City. Name a Deadline." The subhead reads: "Get any publicly available document from any place in the U.S. And get it fast."

For $15, plus 38¢ per page for photocopying (or the actual document cost) and applicable delivery charges, FDR provides any publication from Congress, the White House, executive departments and federal agencies, the courts ("decisions, briefs, pleadings from any court in the U.S."), the GPO, the National Technical Information Service, the General Accounting Office, and more. Photocopies of out-of-print publications are available as well.

For more information and a free brochure and price list, contact:

> Federal Document Retrieval
> 514 C Street, N.E.
> Washington, D.C. 20002
> (202) 628-2229

Free GPO Catalogs

If you'd rather not pay an information broker or document delivery service, the easiest way to lay your hands on a government document is to simply phone the GPO order desk in Laurel, Maryland. The desk is staffed Monday through Friday, 8 A.M. to 4 P.M., Eastern time. You may use Visa, Choice, or MasterCard, or you can establish a deposit account with the Superintendent of Documents. You can also order by mail using these options or a check or money order.

If you do not know a publication's stock number, you can order up to six items per phone call, including subscriptions to most government periodicals. If you *do* know the stock numbers, you can order up to ten items per call. Prices are very reasonable. The cost of a single issue of the *Congressional Record* is $1 domestic, $1.25 foreign. The cost of a single issue of the *Federal Register* is $1.50 domestic, $1.88 foreign. Postage is included in all GPO price quotes.

The first items you should order, possibly even before continuing with this chapter, are these FREE publications:

- "Consumer's Guide to Federal Publications"

  Published four times a year, this 20-page guide lists booklets from nearly 30 government agencies, approximately 40% of which are available free of charge. The rest are in the 50-cent-to-$2.75 range. The guide also describes the GPO Sales Program, tells you how to order, and suggests other sources of federal publications.

- "Government Periodicals and Subscription Services, Price List 36"

  Published in each of the four seasons, "Price List 36" (as it is known) lists over 500 subscription services operated by more than 40 federal agencies. It tells you how to order subscriptions or single copies, where available. Generally, anything published on a regular basis, like the *Congressional Record*, will be listed here.

  The booklet also lists the 24 bookstores the GPO operates in 21 cities around the country. If you live near one of these bookstores, you will probably be able to obtain your documents faster than if you order from Washington. Understandably, however, GPO bookstores cannot stock everything, though of course they can order any item for you. The exact list of items they have in stock varies with the interests of the surrounding population.

- "The NEW CATALOG"

  This quarterly illustrated catalogue represents a selection of 1,000 books drawn from more than 16,000 in-stock GPO publications. The items represent the most popular books in the GPO inventory and include titles like *Infant Care, National Park Guide and Map*, and *The Back-Yard Mechanic*.

- "New Books"

  Printed on newsprint, this is a bimonthly listing of all the new publications added to the GPO Sales Program in the intervening two-month period. According to the GPO, it is "designed primarily for use by people in professional and technical fields, announcing publication information in a timely manner."

Here's the address to contact and the number of the GPO order desk:

Superintendent of Documents
U.S. Government Printing Office
Washington, D.C. 20402

Order Desk:
Mon.–Fri., 8 A.M.–4 P.M.
(202) 783-3238

GPO Publications Reference File

Most of the items listed in the free booklets, and many other items as well, can also be found in the GPO Publications Reference File, a database on DIALOG (File 166) that is usually referred to as "PRF." With PRF, you can create a customized list of every item for sale by the GPO that bears on your subject area. The cost is $35 an hour, plus telecommunications, and 10¢ per full record displayed. You can order any publication found in PRF directly from the GPO via DIALORDER. Details are on the GPOPRF DIALOG Yellowsheet.

The GPO itself distributes only a portion of all that it publishes. Distributions are handled by the GPO Sales Program, a group whose funds come primarily from income generated by document sales, as opposed to budgetary appropriations. PRF is the GPO Sales Program's catalog of available items.

The coverage concentrates on the legislative and executive branches and includes books, pamphlets, periodicals, maps, posters, and other documents from over 60 major federal departments and agencies and from smaller federal bureaus. Between 17,000 to 25,000 titles are in stock at any one time. Most were issued in the last five years, but forthcoming and recently out-of-print publications are included as well. The file corresponds to a microfiche product of the same name and it dates back to 1971. Updates are every other week.

Online Tip: The *GPO Monthly Catalog* database we will be considering later is an exhaustive list of *all* federal publications. Only about 16% of these publications are available from the GPO. The rest must be gotten from the organizations that sponsored them or found in a depository library. PRF is thus a subset of the *GPO Monthly Catalog.*

A free "PRF User's Manual" is available. Contact the Records Branch of the Sales Management Division of the GPO or simply call the above order desk number. Though aimed at users of the microfiche product, the booklet does a good job of explaining the file and telling you whom to contact if you need more help. The best documentation, however, is the DIALOG database chapter.

Sampling PRF

We had a good time playing with PRF. The connect and display charges aren't too expensive, and the prices of the documents themselves are low. We simply began keying in search terms as they occurred and waited to see what would come up. It's cheaper than a video game and more fun than Trivial Pursuit®.

SELECTing GYPSY(W)MOTH yielded a hit on a publication called "Homeowner and the Gypsy Moth: Guidelines for Control." Prepared by the Agriculture Department, this 34-page illustrated booklet sells for $2. The word TIRES brought up a Labor Department report called "Technology and Its Impact on Labor in Four Industries: Tires and Inner Tubes; Aluminum; Aerospace; Commercial Banking." A strange combination of topics, to be sure, and while it was not the guide to buying car tires we had hoped for, at 10¢ a record who cares?

The term GRAND(W)CANYON yielded hits on a booklet prepared by the National Park Service. There was also a Geological Survey presenting a study of "the environment and history of four red bed foundations, partly marine and partly continental, that comprise the Supai Group of Grand Canyon, Arizona." Uh-huh. Then the term HAMMERED(W)DULCIMER produced this:

```
8203472
    Hammered Dulcimer in America
    Groce, Nancy
    Smithsonian Institution
    1983: 99 p.; ill.
    047-001-00152-4 UNIT: 5 DOLC. 04-01-85
    Each  $6.00  DOMESTIC  $7.50 FOREIGN Discount
    PRICE-ESTABLISHED: 111483
    RELATED-DATA: Paper Cover, Sew; Paper. Weight: 8 oz.
——————— >  OUT OF PRINT-GPO STATUS CODE: 15 STATUS DATE: 04-01-85,
    NB025U4 QC024N4 QC031Y5 QC032V5
    Smithsonian Studies in History and Technology, No. 44
    Study of the role of the hammered dulcimer in the musical
    history of the United States. Explains what the hammer
    dulcimer is and how it differs from other dulcimers,
    describes the physical structure of this instrument, tells
    of its early history in the ancient world and in Europe,
    describes how the dulcimer was introduced into the United
    States, its role in music and in American social life, its
    decline and survival in the 20th Century, and the history of
    dulcimer manufacture. Contains copyright material. L.C.
    card 82-600259.
        SERIES: 221    252BS
    Smithsonian Studies in History and Technology    44
    Dulcimer in America
    Music
```

This sounded very interesting, but as you can see, it is "out of print." The GPO leaves out-of-print records in the file to be used as a "research tool . . . in tracing the history of sales titles and in identifying old titles once a part of the Sales Program." The GPO Status Code of 15, according to the documentation, means that the GPO has no plans to reprint, but "often a limited number of copies may be obtained by writing to the issuing agency."

Not in this case. We phoned the main Smithsonian number and, after being bounced to no fewer than five different extensions, came away no wiser, and one phone bill poorer. The last person we spoke with said, "Yeah, there were some copies around here someplace. But you know, we send a lot of stuff to someplace in Michigan to be microfilmed."

"You mean University Microfilms Inc.—UMI?"

"Yeah, I think that's the place."

We called UMI's Books On Demand service. Unfortunately, no one there was able to tell us whether Books On Demand includes any out-of-print government publications, let alone those of the Smithsonian Institution. So we gave up. Such are the trials of an information searcher. As we have said before, you won't always be successful. Either that, or you will find that success isn't worth the time and effort required to achieve it. Besides, why would we ever want to give up the accordion?

U.S. Government Depository Libraries

The U.S. Government Depository Library program is based on three principles. First, that with certain specified exceptions, all government publications shall be made available to depository libraries. Second, that such libraries shall be located in each state and congressional district to make government publications widely available. And third, that these government publications shall be available for the free use of the general public.

The outline of the current program was drawn up in 1857, and documents have been accumulating ever since. By law there are two libraries per congressional district and one for each senator, plus assorted state libraries, libraries of the land-grant colleges, and so on. The total is now close to 1,390 in the U.S. and its protectorates.

Basically, the libraries are permitted to select and obtain any government publication free of charge in return for allowing the public to have free access to it. As one librarian we spoke with put it, "The materials are *on deposit* with us. We don't own them, the government does."

Not every depository library has all government publications, though the larger the library, generally the larger the collection. Libraries are presented with a list of government publications and are free to choose the ones they want to have. There is a free 46-page booklet called "Federal Depository Libraries (1985 CONG 590P)." This contains the text of the law that established the program, a state-by-state list of depository libraries, and a list of GPO regional bookstores. Send your order to:

Free Publications
Consumer Information Center
P.O. Box 100
Pueblo, CO 81002

Use the Technology!

How do you find out which library has which publications? The simplest way is to look up the name of the library nearest you in the free directory and give them a call. But there is also an annual directory called "GPO Depository Union List of Item Selections." Unfortunately, it's available only on microfiche, so unless you've got a fiche reader next to your PC, you'll have to contact a library.

We learned about this publication from a librarian who said that something like a Union List for these libraries existed, but he could not remember the exact title. So rather than call Washington, we did a little practicing of what we've been preaching. We signed on to DIALOG and checked the GPO Publications Reference file:

```
        Set    Items    Description
?SELECT DEPOSITORY(W)UNION(W)LIST

               37    DEPOSITORY
              164    UNION
              228    LIST
        S1      5    DEPOSITORY(W)UNION(W)LIST

?TYPE 1/5/1

  1/5/1
8602384
GPO Depository Union List of Item Selections, Jan. 15, 1986
Government Printing Office, Superintendent of Documents
1986: 35 microfiche, 48X.
021-000-00135-0   UNIT: 7   DOLC: 05-30-86
Each  $3.25  DOMESTIC  $4.10 FOREIGN Discount
RELATED-DATA: Specialty Iterm; Microfiche; Envel.  Wt.: 5 oz.
IN STOCK — WAREHOUSE & RETAIL (PRICED) STATUS CODE: 04
Describes over 5000 item number categories which represent
United States government documents distributed through
the Federal Depository Program. Lists depository libraries
that select each of the items. Item 0551.
```

GOVERNMENT PUBLICATIONS
Congress

CIS: Congressional Information Service, Inc.

CIS gives you complete access to the working papers of the United States Congress. (Note that CompuServe Information Service is also referred to by the same three letters, but of course it's quite a different service.) CIS identifies, collects, indexes, and prepares abstracts for the publication of nearly 300 House, Senate, and joint committees and subcommittees. That covers a lot of territory and it includes hearings, "prints," reports, documents, and special publications. Collectively, according to one CIS brochure, these sources "contain among the best (and sometimes the only) information available on a given subject."

There are many ways to get at the data, not the least of which is a free text search of the abstracts and controlled vocabulary descriptors CIS has assigned to each record. But since each congressional committee has been given a code (H18 is the House Appropriations Committee, S25 is the Senate Budget Committee, etc.), you can zero in even further. You can also search by congressional session, publication year, document type, GPO (Government Printing Office) accession number, witness name, and other fields.

Government is an industry like any other, so it's not surprising that it has developed its own jargon. Fortunately the CIS documentation does a good job of explaining what the major codes and abbreviations mean. However, you may not have to worry with these. It all depends on what you're after. If you want to find out what your congressional representative has been up to lately, for example, you can simply search on his or her name. At random we picked a name of Hal Daub, a representative from Nebraska, out of a directory of the 99th Congress. Then we keyed it into DIALOG. (CIS is also available on ORBIT.) Here's what came up:

```
          Set    Items   Description

?SELECT DAUB

          S1      17     DAUB

?TYPE 1/5/10

 1/5/10
455506     85-H141-21     2
   Energy Assistance and Home Health Care for the Elderly.
   June 8, 1984     98-2     iv + 78 p   +
```

FICHE: 3   ITEM NO: 1009-B-2; 1009-C-2
Y4.Ag4/2:En2/8
85-601497
DOC TYPE: HEARING
JOURNAL ANNOUNCEMENT: 8507
Committee Publication No. 98-480. Hearings before the
Subcom on Housing and Consumer Interests to examine home
energy assistance and home health care needs and programs
for the elderly in Michigan.
Full Committee Member Tom Lantos (D-Calif) chairs
hearings. Full Committee Member Hal Daub (R-Nebr)
presents statements (p. 11-12, 36-37) and participates in
questioning witnesses.
Hearings were held in Niles, Mich., in the morning and in
Holland, Mich., in the afternoon.
Includes submitted statement and correspondence (p.
77-78)
DESCRIPTORS: Subcom on Housing and Consumer Interests.
House; Aged and aging ; Energy assistance programs ; Home
health services ; Geriatrics and gerontology ; Lantos,
Tom; Daub, Hal; Michigan; Niles, Mich.; Holland, Mich.;

If a representative or a senator has been active on a committee his or
her name will be in the database. Similarly, if you wanted to get a list of
all the reports and other publications issued by, say, the Senate Public
Works Committee (committee codes: S64) in 1986, you could key in:
SELECT CC = S64 AND PY = 1986. Whether you're a competing politician, a public interest group, or simply a concerned citizen, this kind of
access is invaluable.

Online Tip: If you're interested in politics, there are at least two
other databases you should look into. One is called CANTRACK,
for "Candidate Tracking." Produced by PAC Researchers, Ltd.,
this database is the electronic version of *Candidate Reports*. CAN-
TRACK includes the financial status of all nonpresidential campaigns, as well as summaries of candidate filings with the Federal
Election Commission. CANTRACK is available on the Public Affairs Information system [(916) 444-0840] at $120 an hour.

The second database is PACs & Lobbies, a file on NewsNet that
corresponds to a printed newsletter of the same name. The newsletter covers developments regarding campaign financing and lob-
bying at the federal level. The latest lobbyist and foreign agent
registrations are also included, as are the newest political action
committees (PACs). For more information on these two databases,
contact:

Online Tip (cont.)

CANTRACK
PAC Researchers, Ltd.
1925 N. Lynn Street, Suite 903
Arlington, VA 22209
(703) 247-3930

PACs & Lobbies
Amward Publications, Inc.
2004 Twelfth Floor
National Press Building
Washington, D.C. 20045
(202) 544-1141

BART, Tooth Decay, and Aspirin

It's important to realize, though, that this database has uses that go far beyond the political. Congress prepares or commissions all manner of special reports on virtually any subject you can name, and it frequently summons expert witnesses. CIS indexes all of this material. And once you find what you want, you can order copies directly from CIS, from the government, or from some other document delivery service.

As a quick test of the breadth of information CIS contains, we did separate searches on the Bay Area Rapid Transit system (BART) in San Francisco, tooth decay, and aspirin. We learned that Congress has not issued a report on BART since 1982. But we located a publication from 1974 containing a comparison of BART train failure rates with those of other systems. That is probably too dated to be of much current value, but anyone writing a history of the BART project would certainly want to see it.

On the tooth decay issue, we encountered a lot of material on the banning of saccharin in 1977, and a 46-page report from the Robert Wood Johnson Foundation entitled "Preventing Tooth Decay: Results from a Four-Year National Study" (December 1983). The report is one of the documents issued by a committee hearing.

From February and March of 1985 there was a report on a hearing to investigate whether aspirin labels and advertising should carry a warning about "the purported association between aspirin use and Reye syndrome, a rare disease affecting children." We conducted the search more than a year and a half later, but that was still the most recent record. However, when we keyed in SELECT REYE?(W)SYN-

DROME we got 16 hits. If we'd wanted to, we could have looked at all of those hits and thus traced the history of the issue in Congress.

If you were an aspirin manufacturer, you could create a DIALOG SDI ("current awareness") profile containing those search terms. Then when CIS is updated each month, the system would automatically notify you of any new hits on those terms.

For the Small Businessperson

Actually, an aspirin manufacturer would probably have other ways of monitoring the status of this proposed act. But a small businessperson or investor wouldn't, particularly someone interested in expanding into a new field with which he or she may not be familiar. The cost of searching CIS on DIALOG is $90 an hour, plus telecommunications, plus 25¢ for each full record displayed. The hourly cost is the same on ORBIT, but displaying a record costs just a nickel. Under some circumstances, you may not be able to afford *not* to check CIS.

There is a DIALOG database chapter, and CIS sells its online *User Guide & Thesaurus of Index Terms* (covering both DIALOG and OR-BIT) for $75. There is also a toll-free customer support number and a variety of inexpensive search aids, code lists, and booklets. Be sure to ask about the company's document delivery services. And, since the company also produces the ASI (American Statistics Index) database considered later in this chapter, you may want to get information on it as well. Contact:

> Congressional Information Service, Inc.
> 4520 East-West Highway
> Bethesda, MD 20814
> (800) 638-8380
> (301) 654-1550

Congressional Record Abstracts

As we've seen, the CIS database covers what goes on in congressional committees. Congressional Record Abstracts covers debates and other activities taking place in the floor of the two houses. The *Congressional Record* is published every day that either the House or the Senate is in session. It contains bill and resolution introductions, floor debates, roll call votes, and much more, including an "Extension of Remarks" section that allows senators and representatives to insert just about any kind of material they please, whether it was presented on the floor or not.

Congressional Record Abstracts is produced by Capitol Services, Inc., which gives us a "CSI" to go with the "CIS" just considered. (No one ever said dealing with things Washingtonian would be easy.) CSI is

a division of the National Standards Association, Inc., and this database
is available on DIALOG, ORBIT, and BRS. Though the word *abstracts*
is part of its name, "annotated index" might be more accurate. For example, we decided to see what Representative Hal Daub, the same gentleman we scanned for in the CIS database, has been doing on the floor
of the House. Here's a small portion of what we found:

```
?SELECT SF = HOUSE PROCEEDINGS AND DAUB


          87140    SF = HOUSE PROCEEDINGS
            565    DAUB
     S1     441    SF = HOUSE PROCEEDINGS AND DAUB
?TYPE 4/5/100

 4/5/100
1978793
   MEYERS leads colloquy on House rules reform; pro
H.Res. 220, consider H.Res. 164, amend House rules to
improve legislative process. Addtl stmts by VUCANOVICH
H6241; MICHEL, WHITTAKER H6244; J.LEWIS H6245; RIDGE H6246;
DAUB, LOTT H6248; MCKERNAN, C.MILLER H6249.
   Source: 99-100    Page: H6240
   JULY 24, 1985
   Subfile: HOUSE PROCEEDINGS
   Descriptors: POLITICAL-LEGISLATIVE AFFAIRS (3914)


 4/5/104
1974930
   DAUB notes dedication of Roman Hruska Law Center in
Lincoln NE; former NE Sen Hruska speech, remarks.
   Source: 99-086    Page: H4924
   JUNE 25, 1985
   Subfile: HOUSE PROCEEDINGS
   Descriptors: TRIBUTES TO MEMBERS (6101)
```

To limit things to just activities on the floor of the House, we selected
the subfile (SF =) for House proceedings. The other subfiles are the
Senate proceedings, extension of remarks, and the digest. Because representatives and senators are referred to in the *Congressional Record*
(CR) by their last names, that was the only name we used. (When there
is a possibility of confusion, the first initial is used as well.)

The above records give us all the information we need to obtain the
correct document. The line "Source: 99-100" means 99th Congress,
100th session, for example. And of course the date and starting page
number are given as well. When asked about supplying copies of CR
pages, a Capitol Services spokesman said, "I suppose we could. But

most people just send a messenger down to the Senate Office Building or get it from the GPO."

We asked him what he was taking for it.

"For what?"

"Potomac Fever."

Print Edition and Other Services

Congressional Register Abstracts corresponds to a series of daily print publications of the same name. In addition to the Master Edition covering all topics, there are editions covering just defense, foreign affairs, energy, and other topics. CSI also has a special custom report service. Subscribers choose from a list of nearly 40 subject categories (Agriculture, Law Enforcement, Labor, etc.) and 325 topics (General, Grand Juries, Strikes & Meditation, etc.). The company then prepares customized daily reports on CR contents that pertain to the selected areas of interest. The minimum price is $400 for one to eight topics. The price goes down as the number of requested topics goes up.

There is a DIALOG database chapter. For more information on the database, contact:

> Capitol Services, Inc.
> 5161 River Road
> Bethesda, MD 20816
> (800) 638-8094
> (301) 951-1389

Federal Agencies

Federal Register Abstracts

The databases we've considered so far cover Congress. Federal Register Abstracts (FedReg) covers the executive branch. The *Federal Register* is published every official U.S. federal working day. It contains presidential documents, summaries of agency rules and regulations, and documents that must be published by law. The database contains many types of records: rules, proposed rules, presidential documents, executive orders, notices, meetings, hearings, and public law notices. For example:

```
Set    Items   Description

?SS DT=PROPOSE? AND AGRICULTURE

    S1    28748   DT=PROPOSE?
```

```
        S2    13973   AGRICULTURE
        S3     2742   DT = PROPOSE? AND AGRICULTURE

?TYPE 3/5/1

258544
   Proposed: 7 CFR Parts 907 & 908
   Agric Marketing Service to hold hearing on proposed
amdt to marketing orders for navel oranges grown in AZ &
certain parts of CA; June 10 1986, Visalia CA; text,
tables thru p.20671. Doc.No. AO-245-A9 & AO-250-A7.
CONTACT: Ronald Cioffi (209) 487-5837.
   Source: 51   109   Page: 20664
   JUNE 6, 1986
   Descriptors: AGRICULTURE-DOMESTIC MARKETING  (1012)
```

Here we searched for a proposed rule using the "document type" (DT) prefix. The DIALOG database chapter for FedReg suggests truncating document type terms to allow for variable punctuation and format. "Agriculture" is one of the controlled vocabulary descriptors, a list of which is also in the DIALOG database chapter. We simply wanted to look at the first record, so we didn't get any more specific. But since you can search the abstract as well, you would have gotten a hit on this record if you were looking for, say, NAVEL(W)ORANGES, AZ OR CA, or MARKETING(W)ORDER, or any other word above.

FedReg is available on DIALOG, BRS, and ORBIT. The Federal Index, another database handled by CSI, is also on DIALOG as File 20. This contains similar information, but it is a closed file, covering only October 1976 through November 1980. FedReg starts in March 1977. As with its *Congressional Record* product, CSI offers special editions of its Federal Register Abstracts publication (Master, Business, etc.). The company also offers the same type of customized report service used for CR. As mentioned, there is a DIALOG database chapter.

Full Text on NEXIS

Among other things, NEXIS carries the full text of the *Federal Register* dating from July 1, 1980, to the present. Issues are available for searching usually within 72 hours of publication. NEXIS also carries the *Code of Federal Regulations*, an annual revised codification of the general and permanent rules published in the *Federal Register*. A third file, Presidential Documents, is published by the Office of the Federal Register and contains the full text of the weekly compilation of presidential documents and the annually produced Public Papers of the Presidents. These are the official series of presidential writings, addresses, news conferences, press releases, executive orders, proclamations, transcripts of radio addresses, remarks by the president at various functions, and so on.

Internal Revenue Service Taxpayer Information

The Internal Revenue Service is probably the one federal agency with which all citizens have contact, and it too is online. DIALOG, BRS, and NEXIS are just a few of the many vendors who make some portion of the IRS Taxpayer Information (TAXINFO) database available. The complete database, at this writing, consists of the full text of 71 of the booklets and guides the IRS publishes each year to provide information on how to file individual income tax returns. Titles include Filing Status; Travel, Entertainment, and Gift Expenses; Depreciation; Earned Income Credit; and Taxpayer's Guide to IRS Information, Assistance, and Publications. Several chapters of *Your Federal Income Tax* are also included. The only thing that is not included are the actual forms you need for filing.

The IRS has been very forward-thinking in making this material available. The text for these publications is prepared on word processors and computers and then coded with the Standard Generalized Markup Language (SGML). SGML contains codes for headlines, subheads, boldface, italics, and various other printing elements. What is of interest is that SGML is device-independent. With the proper software, the identical IRS data tape can be fed to a typesetting machine, a braille printer, or a database system, without the need to go through the documents and recode them for each application.

The database is updated each year and it covers the current tax year. The connect cost on DIALOG is $18 an hour, plus telecommunications, and 10¢ per full record displayed. The cost on BRS/BRKTHRU is $45, prime time; $21.50, non-prime. There are no display charges on BRKTHRU. NEXIS charges $10 per search query, plus connect time, plus an extra $1.50 to display items. We recommend the DIALOG database chapter ($6) regardless of the system you will be using.

The Government as a Whole

The GPO Monthly Catalog

The Government Printing Office issues a hefty (about 400 pages) paperback volume that lists the publications printed, processed, or issued each month. Its official name is *The Monthly Catalog of United States Government Publications*, but is usually called the "GPO Monthly Catalog." The catalog includes items sold by the Superintendent of Documents, items available from the issuing agencies and other bodies, items for official use, and items sent to depository libraries. The items can be anything from computer programs to maps to microfiche to the standard books, pamphlets, brochures, and folders. Each catalog contains between 1,500 and 3,000 items. That works out to close to 30,000 publications a year, more than enough to keep the many GPO printing plants and thousands of printing contractors busy day in and day out.

It will keep you busy too if you're trying to locate something using the paper catalog. Although a cumulated index is issued twice a year and an annual *Serials Supplement* is published, you'll still have *lots* of volumes to check to find the publication you need. As with the *Readers' Guide to Periodical Literature* discussed in Chapter 13, putting the GPO Monthly Catalog Online adds immeasurably to its usefulness and value.

The database is available on DIALOG for $35 an hour, plus telecommunications, and 10¢ per full record displayed. It's available on BRS/BRKTHRU for $35 an hour and 6¢ per display, prime time, and $17.50 with no display charge during non-prime time. In both cases, it dates from July 1976 and includes literally hundreds of thousands of records. But DIALOG gives you about ten more searchable fields. That makes things easier, so that's the system we will focus on for the remainder of this discussion.

The file uses the Library of Congress Subject Headings (LCSH) and the Anglo-American Cataloguing Rules, Second edition (AACR 2) discussed in Chapter 12 as its controlled vocabulary. You can also retrieve records using the correct International Standard Book Number (ISBN) or serial number (ISSN). But you'll probably find the named person field (NA=JEFFERSON, THOMAS) and the geographic location field (GL=PACIFIC OCEAN) to be the most useful.

The subjects covered by the GPO Monthly Catalog are as varied as life itself. When we searched on GL=ONTARIO, for example, we hit a study by the University of California called "The Impact of Changing Women's Roles on Transportation Needs and Usage" (32 pages, 1984). Apparently the study was conducted in Toronto, Ontario. We also hit a study by the U.S. Army Corps of Engineers called "The Effectiveness and Influence of the Navigation Ice Booms on the St. Marys River" (12 pages). When we looked for GL=IDAHO AND POTATO?, we found "Treatment and Disposal of Potato Processing Waste Water by Irrigation," a research report done by the Science and Education Administration (37 pages, $1.40, "for sale by the Supt. of Docs., U.S. Govt. Print. Off.") Then we did the following:

?EXPAND GL = maine

Ref	Items	Index-term
E1	720	GL = LUXEMBOURG
E2	8	GL = MACAO
E3	411	*GL = MAINE
E5	15	GL = MALAGASI REPUBLIC
E6	13	GL = MALAWI
E7	38	GL = MALAYSIA
E9	6	GL = MALDIVE ISLANDS
E11	15	GL = MALTA
E12	6	GL = MANITOBA

The State of Maine looked promising, so we entered a new command:

?SELECT GL = MAINE AND LOBSTER?

	411	GL = MAINE
	12	LOBSTER?
S3	1	GL = MAINE AND LOBSTER?

?TYPE 3/5/1

3/5/1
0172048   C 55.13-NMFS SSRF-747
   Movement, growth, and mortality of American lobsters,
   Homarus americanus, tagged along the coast of Maine/
   Krouse, Jay S.
   Corporate Source: United States. National Marine
   Fisheries Service.
   Series: NOAA technical report NMFS SSRF ; 747
   Seattle, Wash. : U.S. Dept. of Commerce, National Oceanic
   and Atmospheric Administration, National Marine
   Fisheries Service, [1981] iii, 12 p. : ill., maps ;
   Publication Date(s): 1981
   LCCN: gp 83004451
   Place of Publication: Washington   GPO Item No.: 208-C-4
   (microfiche)
   Local Call No.: SH11.A335 no.747
   Languages: English
   Document Type: Monograph
   Geographic Location: Maine
   "September 1981." Bibliography: p. 12.
   Descriptors: Lobster fisheries-Maine; American lobster

The GPO Monthly Catalog covers only a portion of all of the publications issued by the U.S. Government each year. And of those covered only about 17,000 titles can be ordered directly from the GPO. These items are tagged with a "for sale by" line and the price. If that line does not appear, the chances are you will have to obtain the document from the sponsoring agency, a document delivery service, or a depository library. Nevertheless, the database is still an incredible resource for anyone who needs information on virtually any topic.

There is a DIALOG database chapter available, but it must be faulted for not adequately explaining the contents of the file and how it is indexed. The chapter current at this writing is dated July 1980, so perhaps a new edition will be issued before too long. You can search this database using nothing but the Bluesheet or BRS AidPage, however. If you think you might be using the GPO Monthly Catalog regularly, we recommend buying a single issue ($18 from the GPO), since it contains most of the agency addresses you'll need to order items not a part of the GPO Sales Program.

More on the Dulcimer

Yes, we officially gave up on trying to locate a copy of the out-of-print Smithsonian Institution publication called "The Hammered Dulcimer in America." But it was so easy and inexpensive to check the GPO Monthly Catalog database that we couldn't resist. We got two hits on SELECT HAMMER?(W)DULCIMER. The first was a bibliography of "The Hammered Dulcimer and Related Instruments" done by the Archive of Folk Song (U.S.), whatever that is. The second was:

The hammered dulcimer in America
Groce, Nancy.
Corporate Source: Smithsonian Institution. Press.
Series: Smithsonian studies in history and technology
Washington : Smithsonian Institution Press : For sale by the
Supt. of Docs., U.S. G.P.O., c1983. 93 p.: ill.
Publication Date(s): 1983
Price: $6.00
Place of Publication: District of Columbia GPO Item
   No.: 910-F (microfiche)
Stock No.: 047-001-00152-4; GPO
Distributed to depository libraries in microfiche.
Bibliography: p. 91-93. Discography: p. 84-86.
Descriptors: Dulcimer.

We've edited the record for reasons of space but left the key information intact. The most important points are the fact that this record refers to a *microfiche* copy of the publication and that the fiche has been distributed to depository libraries. If the library charges a nickel a page for microfiche photocopies, we can obtain this 93-page document for $4.65. Every now and then you win one.

Index to U.S. Government Periodicals

The federal government publishes an estimated 1,000 magazines, newsletters, serial publications, and other periodicals. Infordata International Incorporated of Chicago, Illinois, the same firm responsible for the Index to Reader's Digest database discussed in Chapter 13, has produced an index to 185 of them. The periodicals are chosen by a blue-ribbon review board on the basis of their lasting reference and research value. No other database covers so many of them, nor does the government do this kind of "Readers' Guide" style magazine indexing.

The database corresponds to a quarterly, printed volume of the same name. It is available online from BRS/SEARCH, BRS/BRKTHRU, and Wilsonline at this writing, but you may find it on other systems in the future. The cost on BRKTHRU is $75 per hour and 32¢ for each item displayed during prime time, $27.50 per hour with no display charges, non-prime.

The file dates back to 1980 and is updated with about 1,100 new items each month. Often the lag time between publications and online availability is one month or less. The periodicals covered include titles like *Agricultural Research, Alcohol Health and Research World, Military Chaplain's Review, Navy Civil Engineer, Recombinant DNA Bulletin,* and *Spotlight on Affirmative Employment Programs.*

"GOVT," as this database is called on BRKTHRU, is as much fun to use as the GPO databases, and for the same reason: almost every topic imaginable is covered. When we searched on SNAPPING WITH TURTLE, for example, we found an article called "Finding on Alligator Snapping Turtle Petition" published in the March 1984 *Endangered Species Technical Bulletin.* The search logic STRESS WITH PERFORMANCE$ yielded two articles. One was called "Stress-Train: Training for High Performance," published in the February 1985 issue of *Military Review.* The other was called "Psychology of Performance Under Stress" and was published in the June 1984 issue of *FBI Law Enforcement Bulletin.*

Then we searched for articles on superconductivity with the term SUPERCONDUC$ and found 80 records, one of which is displayed below:

AN ACCESSION NUMBER: 07118575002601. 8500.
TI TITLE: Another kind of conductivity.
AU AUTHORS: Edelson-Edward.
SO Source: Mosaic, 15:5, 1984. 26-33.
SF SPECIAL FEATURES: Illus. Graphs. Portrait.
DE DESCRIPTORS: Electricity. Conductivity. Superconductivity. Electrons. Molecules. Materials-research. Electronics. Physics: Research. Metals. Waves. Ions. Temperature. Cryogenics. Resistivity. Polymers. Salts. Electrical-resistivity. Electronic-density-of-states. Crystals-and-crystallization: Structures. Niobium. Selenium-and-selenium-

compounds. Electric-fields. Frequencies. Quantum-mechanics. Alloys. Electromagnetic-radiation. Sulfur-and-sulfur-compounds. Tantalum. Molybdenum. Research-methods.

As you can see from the above example, there are no abstracts associated with GOVT records. But the descriptors can give you a fairly good idea of what the article contains and whether it is worth tracking down. Infordata has created its own list of some 25,000 controlled vocabulary descriptor terms and proper names. According to the firm, this was necessary because the Library of Congress Subject Headings and other widely used controlled vocabularies are not updated frequently enough to keep up with new terms, particularly those used in research and development and scientific areas. The company sells its 150-page thesaurus for $50. A BRS AidPage is also available from BRS, and an explanatory database chapter is in the works.

Depository and other libraries carry many of these periodicals. But Infordata International can also handle document delivery. If you want a photocopy of an entire issue, the cost is 20¢ per page with a minimum charge of $20. The per article cost is $15, regardless of the number of pages. Additional copies of the same article are available for $3.50 each. Payment is by check or purchase order. For more information, contact:

> Infordata International Incorporated
> 175 East Delaware Place, Suite 4602
> Chicago, IL 60622
> (312) 266-0260

Online Tip: As you might imagine, the activities of Congress, the president, various regulatory agencies, court decisions, and the Washington bureaucracy are prime material for newsletter writers. Among the newsletters on NewsNet dealing with these topics are the following 25 titles:

Access Reports/Freedom of
  Information
Air/Water Pollution Report
BNA Congressional/
  Presidential Calendar
BNA Executive Day
BNA Tax Updates
BNA's Daily Tax Report
BNA's Private Letter
  Rulings Report

CCH Tax Day: Federal
CCH Tax Day: State
Congressional Activities
Defense Industry Report
Defense R&D Update
FCC Daily Digest
FCC Week
Federal Research Report
Hazardous Waste News
Industrial Health & Hazards
 Update
NASA Software Directory
Nuclear Waste News
PACs & Lobbies
Small Business Tax Review,
 The
Space Commerce Bulletin
Star Wars Intelligence
 Report
State Telephone Regulation
 Report
Toxic Materials News

Statistics

American Statistics Index (ASI)

This database is available on DIALOG and BRS, and it is produced by Congressional Information Service (CIS), the same firm that produces the CIS database discussed earlier. ASI is a guide to "all statistical publications of the U.S. Government." It includes periodicals, annual and biennial reports, irregular series publications, and one-time reports. Altogether, ASI indexes the output of over 500 federal offices and 7,500 titles, including over 800 periodicals, each year. The database dates back to 1973 and is updated monthly.

The important thing to remember about ASI is that it is an index and guide to publications containing statistics—its records do not contain those statistics themselves. However, although tabular statistical data is the main focus, ASI also covers maps, charts, and narrative material it judges appropriate. "Generally excluded from the database are publications of highly technical data, clinical medical studies, contact studies, classified data, or any Congressional appropriations hearings that are indexed in CIS."

A database chapter is available from DIALOG, and there are a number of user-guide publications available from CIS. Paper copies of the referenced statistical material are available from CIS as well. Prices start at 24¢ a page for orders totaling between one and 450 pages. See the previous discussion of CIS for the address to contact.

BLS Consumer Price Index

The Consumer Price Index (CPI) produced by the U.S. Bureau of Labor Statistics (BLS) is familiar to most people from news reports. The CPI measures the average changes in prices over time in a fixed "market basket" of goods and services. The information is collected by the BLS in 85 urban areas across the country using primarily personal visits to grocery stores and the like. "Mail-in questionnaires are used to obtain public utility rates, some fuel prices, and certain other items."

Available on DIALOG as File 175, the database is updated monthly with new data. "When available, monthly, quarterly, and annual data are given for each record." You can use File 175 to check the CPI for various geographic regions and population categories, including selected urban areas and various U.S. cities. You can also check on the CPI for various products and services (steak, white bread, fuel oil, appliance and furniture repair, etc.) in various geographical areas.

This is a heavy-duty statistical database in which most records are primarily tabular matter. Since a variety of special codes are used for searching, the DIALOG database chapter is a must. The government also produces a variety of free booklets and other explanatory material, including the BLS Handbook of Methods (Volumes I and II), "Relative Importance of Components of the Consumer Price Indexes," and more. Start with the DIALOG chapter, then contact the address below for more information:

> BLS Consumer Price Index
> U.S. Department of Labor
> Bureau of Labor Statistics
> Division of Consumer Prices and Price Indexes
> Washington, D.C. 20212

BLS Producer Price Index

Much of the discussion of the CPI applies here as well. This is File 176 on DIALOG, and there is a database chapter to explain how the file is organized and how to search it. The Producer Price Index (PPI) used to be called the "wholesale price index." It is based on the more than

10,000 price quotes the BLS receives each month, primarily via mail-in questionnaires sent to producing companies. Some prices are taken from trade publications, however, or from other U.S. government agencies. Prices are usually reported for the Tuesday of the week containing the 13th day of the month. The database is updated monthly.

CENDATA™—The U.S. Census Bureau Online

We've saved the most innovative statistical database for last. It's called CENDATA and it is produced by some very forward-thinking people at the U.S. Department of Commerce, Bureau of the Census. It contains selected summary statistics from all Census Bureau programs, as well as news releases and product ordering information. Geographically, it offers statistics for the nation as a whole, for individual states, counties, and metropolitan areas and large cities. Subjects covered include agriculture, business, construction and housing, foreign trade, international data on 200 countries, manufacturing data, and population data.

The information is equivalent to what can be found in hundreds of traditional paper-based Census Bureau reports, including such best-sellers as "Market Absorption of Apartments," "Advance Monthly Retail Sales," "Flour Milling Products," and "Projections of the Population of the United States by Age, Sex, and Race: 1983 to 2080." What makes CENDATA so special is that the Bureau has taken some imaginative steps to make the data as easily accessible as possible. CENDATA is a *menu-driven* system. When you sign on to DIALOG and enter BEGIN CENDATA, you are presented with a greeting screen and main menu like that shown in Figure 18.1.

——— **Figure 18.1. The CENDATA Main Menu on DIALOG** ———

?BEGIN CENDATA

    Welcome to . . .
                    CENDATA

          The Online Information Utility
          of the U.S. Bureau of the Census
               on DIALOG

A very small portion of the Census Bureau's vast data holdings
has been included in this "information utility." In addition to
limited amounts of current and historical data, also included is
information on products released during the past month and press

Fig. 18.1 (cont.)

releases issued during the past week. If you have any questions about census data or products, see our "For Further Information" section of the "Introduction to Census Bureau Products and Services", the first item on the CENDATA main menu.

— CENDATA MAIN MENU

1 Introduction to Census Bureau Products and Services
2 What's New in CENDATA (Including Economic Survey Release Dates)
3 U.S. Statistics at a Glance (Including Economic Time Series Data)
4 Press Releases
5 Census User News
6 Product Information
7 CENDATA User Feedback
8 General Data
9 Agriculture Data
10 Business Data
11 Construction and Housing Data
12 Foreign Trade Data
13 Governments Data
14 International Data
15 Manufacturing Data
16 Population Data

> If you're a new or infrequent user of the CENDATA menu system, key HELP <cr> to learn of the available short cuts in using the system.

For a listing and a location key of all Census Bureau reports contained in CENDATA in whole or in part, key M1.2 <cr>

Enter item number, or ? for help

If you choose the HELP option while viewing the Main Menu, a brief explanation of the commands at your disposal appears. Keying M, for example, always returns you to the main menu. Keying Mn, where n is a submenu number, will take you to that submenu. If you choose the first option on the Main Menu, you will be taken to a submenu that includes a selection for "Telephone Contact List for Census Bureau Data Users." This list contains scores of names and phone numbers to call for each particular kind of statistic (Apportionment; Birth expectations and child care; Birth number, race, and place; Citizenship; etc.). If you have ever tried to find the right person to talk to at a government agency, you know that this kind of information is pure gold.

We decided to look at the Construction and Housing Data, selection 11 on the Main Menu. The following submenu then appeared:

11.5 — PRICE INDEX OF NEW ONE-FAMILY HOUSES, 1ST QUARTER 1986

1   Price Index of New One-Family Houses: Text
2   Price Index of New One-Family Houses: Tables

We selected the first option (text) and were presented with a report-style explanation of the current price index figures for single-family homes. Here's just the first portion of the report:

11.5.1,2 -May 2, 1986
PRICE INDEX OF NEW ONE-FAMILY HOUSES SOLD
FIRST QUARTER 1986

The price index of new one-family houses sold was 180.1 (1977 = 100.0) during the first quarter of 1986 as compared to 179.2 for the fourth quarter of 1985 according to estimates reported today by the U.S. Department of Commerce's Bureau of the Census. Compared to the same quarter a year ago, the index is 2.5 percent higher. The price index is designed to measure changes in the sales price of new houses sold which are . . .

Source:
Construction Report, Series C27, Price Index of New One-Family Houses Sold. The C27 Report is available from the U.S. Government Printing Office. Annual subscription: $10.00.

Questions regarding these data may be directed to Steven Berman, Construction Starts Branch, telephone (301) 763-7842.

This is obviously a report issued to accompany the "tables" listed as the second option on the "11.5" menu. But at least three things are significant about it. The first is the phrase "estimates reported *today.*" CENDATA is updated at least once a day so that time-sensitive data like housing starts or advance retail sales are available within an hour of their official release time. Second, the source of the data is given at the end of the report, as well as information on availability (GPO) and price. Third, a contact person and phone number are provided if you have any questions. Whoever designed this system deserves high marks for thoughtfulness.

Finally, we decided to look at a few numbers. After all, what's a statistical database without columns and columns of numerical tables? We went back to Menu 11.5 and selected the second option. Here's a small, drastically truncated part of what appeared:

11.5.2–May 2, 1986
PRICE INDEX AND AVERAGE SALES PRICE OF NEW ONE-FAMILY HOUSES
SOLD FIRST QUARTER 1986

Price index (1977 = 100.0	Average sales price of kinds of houses sold in 1977 (estimated from the price index)	Average sales price of houses actually sold(1)

PERIOD		Price (dollars)	Period to period Percent change(2)	Price (dollars)	Period to period Percent change(3)
QUARTERLY DATA					
United States					
1984:					
1st Quarter	167.8	91,000	0.8	94,700	4.3
2nd Quarter	172.3	93,400	2.7	99,200	4.8
3rd Quarter	175.4	95,100	1.8	98,500	−0.7
4th Quarter	175.6	95,200	0.1	97,800	−0.7
1985:					
1st Quarter	175.7	95,200	—	98,500	0.7
2nd Quarter	175.5	95,100	−0.1	100,500	2.0
3rd Quarter	175.5	95,100	—	100,500	—
4th Quarter	179.2	97,100	2.1	103,800	3.3
1986:					
1st Quarter(p)	180.1	97,600	0.5	107,500	3.6
2nd Quarter					
3rd Quarter					

CENDATA is also available as File 580. Both File 580 and the menu system contain the identical information, but File 580 can be searched with DIALOG's standard command language. The other main difference is that File 580 is updated overnight instead of within the hour of a document release, as the menu system is. The cost for using either file is $36 an hour, plus telecommunications. There is no charge for displaying information online.

At this writing the Bluesheets for the two files are the only DIALOG documentation. However, as noted in the list of DIALOG search aids, the Census Bureau sells a number of publications designed to explain census data. For more information, contact:

Data Access and Use Staff
Data User Services Division
U.S. Bureau of the Census
Washington, D.C. 20233
(301) 763-2074

...Appendix A...

Importing Information:
How to Import Downloaded Data into Lotus 1-2-3™, dBASE™, Chart-Master™, and Other Programs

Downloaded information can be a powerful tool all by itself, but in many cases you can make it even more powerful by feeding it to one of your computer's applications programs. For example, as you know from Chapter 15, you can use the Electronic Yellow Pages (EYP) database on DIALOG or the Instant Yellow Pages system to create a customized mailing list. With a bit of word processing to clean up the downloaded file, you could easily use the file to print pages of mailing labels.

But imagine how much more useful the information would be if you could put it into a database management program like Ashton-Tate's dBASE III. If you could do that, you could sort the addresses by state or ZIP code, create a list of just names and telephone numbers for your telemarketing operation, search for and find a given company name instantly, and much, much more.

Similarly, imagine you're responsible for preparing a report for your manager on the fast-food market. You access PTS PROMT or the DIALOG Business Connection and generate a list starting with McDonald's at 7.6 and ending with Big Boy at 0.8, as shown in Chapter 7. Wouldn't those figures have more impact if you could display them as a pie chart? If you could just "clip out" the table and get it into Lotus 1-2-3 or Symphony or a dedicated graph-drawing program, you'd be in business. What about historical stock quotes on Dow Jones or the corporate financial data available from the Dun & Bradstreet databases? Wouldn't it be helpful to be able to put them into a spreadsheet for further processing—without having to rekey all the data?

All of these things can be accomplished with relative ease, if you have the right software and if you have a basic understanding of the prob-

lems that must be overcome. We'll start with a brief explanation of the
problems and close with some suggestions on the kind of software that
can make solving them a veritable snap.

A Question of Format

The main consideration when "importing" downloaded data into a personal computer program is getting the data into a format that the target
program can accept. For example, like most database management systems (DBMS), dBASE III organizes information into records, each of
which contains one or more fields. A single record might be the complete address of someone on your mailing list, and it might consist of a
field for the person's first name, one for his last name, as well as separate fields for the company name, the street address, the city, the state,
and the ZIP code.

When you create a dBASE database, you must first tell the program
how many spaces to reserve for each field and how many fields each
record will have. That's called defining the record structure, and it
causes dBASE to create a template containing your specifications. You
then key in your information, filling in the fields for each record, and
store the results on disk as a file. Later, you can boot dBASE, load in
the database you have created, and edit existing records, add new ones,
or do something else with the data.

Now, how does dBASE know where one record in the disk file ends
and the next one begins and which characters in a given record go into
which field? The answer is that when dBASE sees the ASCII character
for a carriage return paired with a line feed character in the file, it
knows that one record has ended and another has begun. That is simply
the way the program is set up.

To determine the boundaries of the fields in each record, the program
counts characters. If you told dBASE to reserve ten characters for the
first-name field in the database when you defined your record format,
and if the first name is the first field in the record, dBASE would suck
up the first ten characters in a record and shove them into the first
name field when it loads the database file. It doesn't matter if the first
name of any given person in your file occupies fewer than ten characters. The program knows that you have reserved ten characters for that
field and it will have padded out any unfilled slots with the ASCII character for a blank space when the database was created. The program
thus "sees" each address record as one long string of characters ending
with a carriage return/line feed combination.

In other words, dBASE doesn't see John Smith's address like this:

John Smith
1414 Park Drive
Anytown, CA 12345

It sees this and every other address in the file like this:

John	Smith	1414 Park Drive	Anytown,	CA 12345
Elmira	Beebops	4782 Maple Street	Othertown,	ME 78910

If you can get your downloaded addresses into this format, you will have no problem fooling dBASE into thinking that the file is one of its own data files, and it will gladly welcome it to its bosom.

Let DIALOG Do It for You

The easy way to do this is to download your addresses in the required format in the first place by taking advantage of DIALOG's REPORT option. This feature lets you specify a columnar output of exactly the sort dBASE needs to see. It also lets you tell DIALOG which fields you want to have displayed and in what order. You'll find a detailed explanation of the REPORT option in DIALOG Technical Note 7 in the old DIALOG manual (or in the new one that should be available as you read this). At this writing the DIALOG databases for which REPORT is available include DISCLOSURE II, EYP, and several of the D&B databases. Hopefully more will be added in the future. (Note that because REPORT makes more than normal demands on the DIALOG mainframes, you will obtain your results faster and at a lower connect-time cost if you wait until 9 P.M. or so Eastern time to do the deed.)

Once you have downloaded a file in REPORT format, the next step is to make a backup copy of it. Then use your word processing program to remove all non-data material. (If you are using WordStar, be sure you set it for "non-document" mode to prevent the insertion of any strange control characters.) Then, go into dBASE and create a database whose specifications match those of the DIALOG report. Finally, use the APPEND FROM command in dBASE to tell the program to read in the data from your downloaded file. (The files are in the SDF format, something that dBASE will need to know while APPENDing.)

Preparing Records Semi-Automatically

REPORT makes it easy. But even when this feature is not available, you still aren't out of luck. As long as all of the downloaded records have the same number of lines, it would be relatively simple to write a little BASIC program to perform the conversion from mailing-label format to columnar format.

Easier still perhaps is the alternative of using a word processing program in combination with a program like SmartKey, ProKey, or New-Key. Each of these programs can record a series of keystrokes that you can then reproduce by hitting a single key. If you developed a procedure for reformatting your records with your word processing software, you could record the keystrokes and from then on convert an entire record by hitting a single key. SmartKey and ProKey are commercial programs. NewKey 3.0, including a printed manual, is available for $24.95 from FAB Software. An earlier but quite powerful version (NewKey 2.4) is available as shareware (voluntary contribution requested) from many user groups or for $7.50 from FAB. Contact:

> FAB Software
> P.O. Box 336
> Wayland, MA 01778

CSV, DIF, and Other Data Formats

The data format we have just described—fixed-length records ending with a carriage return and a line feed—is known as SDF or "system data format," and it was first popularized by Digital Research, Inc., creator of the CP/M operating system. Other formats exist as well, most commonly the "comma separated value" or CSV format. Here, fields are separated by commas like this: John,Smith,1414 Park Drive,Anytown,CA,12345. As your dBASE manual points out, you can use this format to import data as well.

There are also a variety of spreadsheet data formats. These include DIF (Data Interchange Format), SYLK (Symbolic Link), SDI (Super Data Interchange), and the native worksheet formats of VisiCalc, Lotus, and Symphony. A number of these are explained in *How to Buy Software*, but for the purposes of importing downloaded data there are only a few things you need to know.

First, most leading spreadsheet programs, like Lotus, have the ability to import and export data in several different formats, including pure ASCII text files. However, if you import a file into Lotus as text, you will not be able to calculate with any of the numbers in the file because Lotus will see them as text. Lotus does permit you to import a text file as "numbers," but there are complications here as well. Any text must be set off with quotation marks, for example, and you can't use any commas in your numbers. The number 123,456 would be seen as two separate numbers due to the presence of the comma.

The OneShot™ Solution

The easiest solution here is to use a program called OneShot™ from

Dataviz, Inc. The program can quickly convert downloaded text file data into any one of seven different formats: WKS (Lotus), WRK (Symphony), CSV (for dBASE, BASIC, etc.), space-delimited DIF (VisiCalc and others), SYLK (Multiplan and others), and tab-spaced (WordStar and others).

OneShot is designed to work with columnar or tabular data such as the financial statements you might download from DISCLOSURE or one of the D&B databases, the industry data you might find in PTS PROMT or PTS MARS, or the tables of statistics you might obtain from CENDATA, the U.S. Census Bureau database.

The program lets you bring the file into the screen exactly as you downloaded it. There is no need to clean it up with a word processing program. It then lets you in effect "clip out" the columns and rows you want it to use in creating a new file. That in itself is a nice bit of legerdemain. But it only hints at the program's power.

OneShot does not require you to physically select each row and column you wish to have converted. Instead it lets you "teach" it what you want by selecting a few representative samples. It then *automatically* runs through the file, selecting what you want. You can even program it to select rows based on whether a given row's data meets certain conditions. OneShot operators and functions include AND, OR, NOT, IF, TRIM, and more.

Your instructions are automatically saved in a template that can be used to convert a file in the same format containing different data. This feature may or may not be useful to an online searcher, but it really comes into its own for someone who routinely downloads something like a monthly sales report from a corporate mainframe. In addition, once you have defined the template, you can easily create files in any or all of the seven formats. There is no need to reselect the data. You have only to change the "Output" option.

OneShot is both fast and smooth. However, while the 50-page manual is well written, it is not what one would hope for, particularly if you're a novice. There is far too little information on how to bring a file into dBASE, Lotus, or some other applications program after it has been converted. And even experienced users will find the explanation of the OneShot programming language inadequate. According to Dataviz, a new manual is in the works, and as the company points out, the program does include an extensive context-sensitive online help function. (Just hit F1.) There is also a very good disk-based demo/tutorial that requires about 20 minutes to complete, and there is a customer support hotline.

OneShot sells for $195 and is available in retail stores or directly from the company. A demo disk is available for $10. OneShot is designed for

IBM/PCs and compatibles. Dataviz also has a product called MacLink™ that is designed to transfer files (with all special formatting codes intact) from the PC to the Macintosh. The company also specializes in "databridge" consulting and custom programming. For more information, contact:

> Dataviz, Inc.
> 16 Winfield Street
> Norwalk, CT 06855
> (203) 866-4944
> TWX: 5101004900

The Softerm® PC Bundle

If you do not yet have a communications program and you want to save some money, you might consider Softerm® PC. This program sells for $195 and, under a special agreement with Dataviz, it *includes* OneShot. Softerm PC itself is loaded with features. It can precisely emulate over 30 terminals, run in the background, and control up to four serial ports and three parallel ports. The program supports up to 72 user-defined keyboard macros and 10 printer macros, plus a powerful (35 commands) script language. It offers XMODEM, Kermit (with sliding windows), Hayes verification, and Crosstalk (CLINK) protocols as well as its own Softrans™ protocol. For those wishing to use the Softrans protocol when connected to a corporate mainframe, FORTRAN 77 source code is included. Customized versions of the FORTRAN program can be downloaded from the Softronics 24-hour bulletin board system.

There is also a unique feature called the File Agent that can be programmed to dial up or connect with any number of remote systems, each of which it treats as an additional disk drive. The module loads into your system and resides in the background, where it intercepts DOS and application program commands. When you or your applications program tells your system to get a file stored on a "File Agent drive" (Drives H, I, J, etc.), the program handles the job automatically. The company calls this its Seamless File Transfer feature. There are many other features as well, most of which are especially suited for communications in a corporate environment. For more information, contact:

> Softronics
> 7899 Lexington Drive, Suite 210
> Colorado Springs, CO 80198
> (800) 225-8590
> (303) 593-9540

Chart-Master™: From Raw Data to Refined Graphics

Finally, let's consider briefly the matter of converting downloaded data into one or more types of graphs. If you use Lotus, Symphony, or a comparable integrated program, you know that you can produce graphs from spreadsheet data. Lotus 1-2-3, for example, can create five different types of graphs: bar, line, stacked bar, pie chart, and XY (sometimes called a "scatter plot" because it includes data points without connecting lines). Of course, as discussed, you have to get the downloaded data into the spreadsheet before you can graph it.

Whether you have an integrated program or not, however, if you want to produce high-quality graphs with as much flexibility and ease as possible, you should probably consider a dedicated graphics program like Chart-Master™. Produced by Decision Resources, Chart-Master includes a module called The Data-Grabber. The Data-Grabber can read three different file formats: DIF, SYLK, and pure ASCII text files. This makes it ideal for downloaded data.

To use The Data-Grabber, you simply bring your downloaded file into the screen and use your cursor keys to "clip out" the data you want Chart-Master to use. Once this has been done, you can return to the main Chart-Master menu and begin experimenting with different types of graphs. Chart-Master can create eight types: line, clustered bar, stacked bar, scatter plot, pie chart, area chart (a line graph in which the space under the line has been filled in with shading), a mixed chart that combines bar graphs with line graphs, and a high/low/close chart of the sort used to plot stock quotes.

Chart-Master lets you use seven different type styles, including bold, script, Gothic, and Helvetica in 16 different sizes. It can do italics, right-, left-, and center-justification, and underlining. It offers 90 different symbols, including a car, a plane, a sheaf of wheat, mathematical symbols, weather symbols, and a wide variety of arrows. When viewing charts on the screen, you can use either the PC's black-and-white high-resolution mode or one of two user-selected color palettes. You can also output to a wide variety of plotters. The program even includes special features designed for use with the Polaroid Palette Recording System, should you wish to make color prints or 35mm slides of your charts.

In short, Chart-Master has just about every feature one could want in a graphics program. The three-ring, slipcased manual is quite good as well. However, while the program is easy to use once you get the hang of it, there's a lot to learn. In addition, with so many features at your disposal, it is easy to waste time adding unnecessary embellishments to your charts. The program includes an excellent online help function, and the company offers a customer support hotline.

You can buy Chart-Master Version 6.1 at a discount through the mail for about $240. For more information on this and the company's other products (Sign-Master, Diagram-Master, and Map-Master), contact:

> Decision Resources
> 25 Sylvan Road South
> Westport, CT 06880
> (203) 222-1974

Using Chart-Master with the CPI

As an experiment, we signed on to DIALOG and entered File 175, the Bureau of Labor Statistics (BLS) Consumer Price Index (CPI) database. Using the information on the Bluesheet and in the DIALOG database chapter for File 175, we entered a search strategy designed to retrieve a table of consolidated CPI figures for all U.S. urban consumers (SS SF = CU AND IC = 0 AND GC = 0000). Here's the full record that we then displayed:

CUU0400000 CONSUMER PRICE INDEX FOR ALL URBAN CONSUMERS SUBFILE
ALL ITEMS;
U.S. CITY AVERAGE;
UNADJUSTED DATA

INDEX(1967 = 100)

1983	NA	1982	289.1	1981	272.4
1980	246.8	1979	217.4	1978	195.4
1977	181.5	1976	170.5	1975	161.2
1974	147.7	1973	133.1	1972	125.3
1971	121.3	1970	116.3	1969	109.8
1968	104.2	1967	100.0	1966	97.2

SOURCE: U.S. BUREAU OF LABOR STATISTICS   DIALOG FILE 175
DATES AVAILABLE:(1966–JUNE 1983)

Unfortunately, this is not in a format convenient for chart making. So we brought the downloaded file into a word-processing program and rearranged the information into two columns, one for years and one for the corresponding CPI figure. This was a step in the right direction, but the years were arranged in descending order, starting with 1983 and ending with 1966. So the next step was to sort the data into ascending order. We removed all of the text so that the file consisted of just two columns of numbers. Then we used the SORT filter supplied with DOS to rearrange things. (See the DOS manual for details.) The result looked like this:

1966	97.2
1967	100.0
1968	104.2
1969	109.8
1970	116.3
1971	121.3
1972	125.3
1973	133.1
1974	147.7
1975	161.2
1976	170.5
1977	181.5
1978	195.4
1979	217.4
1980	246.8
1981	272.4
1982	289.1
1983	NA

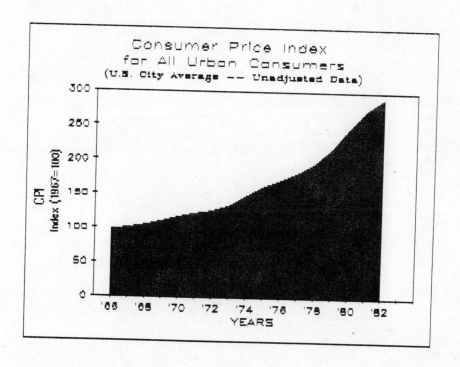

We then loaded ChartMaster and selected The Data-Grabber module.
We used the cursor keys to tell Data-Grabber to put the years column
on the X axis and the CPI figures on the Y axis. Then we went back to
ChartMaster's main menu. Since the program holds the data in memory

and operates very fast, it is easy to experiment with different graphs and different type styles for graph titles and data labels. However, for this kind of data a line graph was the obvious choice, and as you can see in Figure A.1, that's what we told ChartMaster to produce.

...Appendix B...

Reference and Resource:
How to Locate Other Databases

Is There a Database on. . . ?

The eight vendors considered in Part II give you access to perhaps 1,000 (net) of the most valuable and widely used databases in the electronic universe. As noted elsewhere, however, this represents only about a third of all that are available. To find the other 2,000, many of which are single-subject databases on small, independent systems, you'll have to do some digging.

Perhaps the best place to start is with an information broker or professional searcher who specializes in the subject you are interested in. (See Chapter 6.) These men and women are experts, and as long as your request doesn't take too much of their time, most would be happy to point you in the right direction. You might also want to contact one of the users groups that are part of the National Online Circuit (NOC) or consult one or more of the magazines that specialize in the online field. (More on the NOC and magazines in a moment.)

The quickest solution, however, is to check several database directories. There are nearly a dozen such publications, but most of them are expensive. Prices of $100 or more are typical. Thus, unless you are stocking a corporate information center, you will probably prefer to pay a visit to your local library rather than pay for one of these volumes.

Indeed, even if you've got a large budget you should *still* try to examine a directory before buying it. Directories vary widely in quality and depth of coverage. Some offer scant three-line database descriptions, while others provide three or four paragraphs or more. And none of them is 100% comprehensive. Directory A may include databases that Directory B leaves out, and vice versa. Directory C's coverage of a

451

given database may include important details not found in the write-ups of the identical database offered by A and B.

Fortunately, three of the best database directories are also available online, making it easy to quickly consult all three without paying for the printed edition of any of them. The Cuadra directory is on Westlaw, a system that competes with Mead Data Central's LEXIS. More importantly for our purposes, it is also on Data-Star, one of the systems you can access through EasyNet. As explained in Chapter 6, EasyNet is also available to CompuServe subscribers as IQuest and to Western Union EasyLink subscribers as InfoMaster. The directory published by Knowledge Industry Publications, Inc., is on BRS/SEARCH, BRKTHRU, and After Dark as KIPD. And Martha Williams' *Computer-Readable Databases* is on DIALOG as File 230, Database of Databases.

Unrefined Subject Indexing

Additional information on all three of these directories is provided below. But before charging off to consult either the printed or online versions, bear in mind that database directories in general do not offer truly extensive subject indexes. Most directory publishers rely on questionnaires and promotional literature supplied to them by the database producers. The publishers distill this information into two- or three-paragraph write-ups of the database, and then they have the directory indexed.

The people who prepare the indexes base their subject classifications on the database's major focus, but they don't get any more detailed than that. Thus if you were to look up "Movies" or "Films" in most directories, you would definitely be referred to CINEMAN, a database consisting almost exclusively of movie reviews. You would also find a reference to the Boston On-Line magazine database. This is not because movie reviews are its primary focus but because, on the basis of information supplied by the database producer, one of the subject headings assigned to Boston On-Line is "Entertainment Guides and Reviews."

What you will *not* find, however, are references to the *Boston Globe* database (or any other newspaper) on VU/TEXT. The *Globe* includes movie reviews, but the database as a whole is classified as "News." Nor will you find references to the *Time* magazine full-text database on NEXIS, the full text of *Playboy* in Magazine ASAP, or any of the other databases that *also* contain movie reviews.

The point is that when you are looking for a database that includes information on a particular topic, you cannot rely on the subject indexes of database directories to be comprehensive or detailed. When using a printed directory, the broader the subject term, the greater your chances of success. For example, look for "Geology," not for "Earthquakes" or "Plate tectonics."

The Online Alternative

An online search of a directory helps to solve this problem. Because all three of the directories currently online are full-text databases, you can search not only the equivalent of their printed subject indexes, but the *descriptions* of each database as well. For example, suppose you were interested in databases containing information on nylon. If you were to check the printed subject index for the KIPD directory, you would find no listings. The closest you could come would be "Textile Industry." At this writing, you would find four databases under that heading: Man-Made Fiber Producers' Data Base, Textile Technology Digest, Titus-E, and World Textiles.

If you were to sign on to BRS/BRKTHRU and search KIPD online, the results would be somewhat different. As the search results reproduced in Figure B.1 show, three records (database write-ups) in the database contain the word *nylon*. Significantly, only one of them (Man-Made Fiber Producers' Data Base) is included under the heading "Textile Industry" in the printed directory. The reason, say, the World Textiles database was not retrieved by the online search is that the word *nylon* does not appear in its write-up. Whoever prepared the database description used the term "fiber-forming polymers" instead.

The lesson then is this. Searching a database directory online can give you hits on highly specific terms (like "nylon"), and it can thus turn up databases you might have missed had you relied solely on the rather unrefined subject index alone. However, it does not eliminate the need also to search on broad, general terms. After all, it is largely a matter of chance that the write-up for the World Textiles database used "fiber-forming polymers" instead of "nylon." So cut down the odds and use *both* general and specific terms when searching a directory online.

─────── **Figure B.1. Searching KIPD on BRS/BRKTHRU** ───────

Shown below is part of an online session searching the Knowledge Industry Publications database directory (KIPD) on BRS/BRKTHRU. Intervening menus and other clutter have been edited out for clarity and space.

The database was searched for the word *nylon*, and the system responded with three hits. These included the Man-Made Fiber Producers' Database, which is also listed in the print edition's subject index under "Textile Industry." Interestingly, the search also turned up the

SPI/SAGE Plastics Data Base and the database described below, neither of which was among the databases listed under "Textile Industry" in the print edition.

The reason we got hits on all three of these databases is that the word *nylon* was in the descriptive write-up for each of them. Note that the elements in the SUBJECTS field below correspond to the subject headings used in the printed directory's subject index.

```
* WELCOME TO DATA BASE DIRECTORY SERVICES, AN ONLINE PRODUCT OF
* KNOWLEDGE INDUSTRY PUBLICATIONS, INC. IN COOPERATION WITH THE
* AMERICAN SOCIETY FOR INFORMATION SCIENCE.
* COPYRIGHT 1986 KNOWLEDGE INDUSTRY PUBLICATIONS, INC. *

BRS /KIPD MMM YYYY

S1 -->NYLON

A1          3 DOCUMENTS FOUND
```

AN 1796. 8511.
DB DATABASE NAME: CHEMICAL MARKET ASSOCIATES PETROCHEMICAL MARKET
REPORTS. (CMAI).
SU SUBJECTS: Energy. Petrochemicals. Plastics. Gasoline.
AB SUMMARY: Three analytical petrochemical reports issued each month. Each focuses
upon a critical dimension of the petrochemical marketplace and provides textual
commentary on current developments and future prospects, as well as numeric forecasts
of emerging trends. Reports vary in length, averaging 5 to 7 pages of text plus 2 to 4
pages of tables. The C4 Market Report concentrates primarily upon butadiene, butylenes,
and their derivatives. The Fiber Intermediates Market Report focuses on polyester, nylon,
and acrylic fiber intermediates.
PR PRODUCER INFO: I.P. Sharp Associates, Ltd., 2 First Canadian Place, Suite 1900,
Toronto, Ontario, Canada M5X 1E3; Tel: 800-387-1588; Telex: 0622259; also Chemical
Market Associates, 11757 Katy Freeway, Suite 750, Houston, TX 77079; Tel:
713-531-4660; contact Tom Beasley. database available online from producer.
TC TIME COVERAGE
UPDATE FREQUENCY: monthly or semi-monthly.
HISTORICAL TIME SERIES: two latest issues of each report are available. This is not a
time series database.
TY DATABASE TYPE: textual and numeric.
UR UNIT RECORD: statistical data.
VI VENDOR/PRICE INFO: I.P. Sharp Associates, INFOMAGIC cost/connect hour $90 (300
baud), $190 (1200 baud); no monthly minimum. Subscription to Chemical Market
Associates, Inc. Petrochemical Reports, $3000-$5000 per report per year.
OD ORIGINAL DATA SOURCE: Chemical Market Associates, Inc.
LG LANGUAGE: English.
RC RESTRICTIONS/CONDITIONS: subscription required.
AC ACCESS: IPSANET, Telenet, Tymnet, Datapac, Datex-P, PSS, Transpac
NT NOTES: subject coding/classification scheme, MMR, C4MR.

Three Leading Database Directories

Here are more details on the three database directories discussed above. As noted, they are not the only directories available, but in our opinion they are among the very best. Most medium-sized libraries should have a copy of at least one of them. However, if that is not the case in your area, you might contact the publishers for a descriptive brochure.

Directory of Online Databases (Cuadra)

Prepared by Cuadra Associates, Inc., and published and distributed by Elsevier Science Publishing, Inc., the "Cuadra directory," as it is known, has long been considered the most authoritative directory in the field. Certainly no one else monitors the field more closely or is more assiduous in following database changes, demises, and new arrivals.

An annual subscription to the Cuadra directory is $95 and it includes two complete reissues of the 500-page main directory, plus two issues of an update supplement. As noted above, the directory is available for online searching on WESTLAW, Data-Star, and Telesystemes-Questel, and hence via EasyNet, CompuServe, and Western Union's EasyLink.

For more information, contact:

> Cuadra/Elsevier
> P.O. Box 1672
> Grand Central Station
> New York, NY 10163-1672
> (212) 916-1180
> (212) 916-1010

Database Directory (KIPD)

Published by Knowledge Industry Publications, Inc. (KIPI) in co-operation with The American Society for Information Sciences (ASIS), this directory is sold as a subscription package. One year's subscription includes two editions (Fall and Spring) of the 750+ page directory and 12 monthly issues of "Database Alert," KIPI's newsletter. The cost is $215. A six-month subscription (one printed volume and six newsletters) is available for $120. As noted, the directory is available for online searching via BRS. At this writing, the "Database Alert" newsletter is scheduled to go up on NewsNet.

The format of the printed directory is particularly convenient. Databases are listed alphabetically, and as you can see from Figure B.1, each write-up includes names, phone numbers, and other contact information as well as pricing. The Cuadra directory, in contrast, offers one master list of database and vendor addresses to which one must refer *after* looking up the database itself. Both directories cover about the same number of databases.

KIPI is also a publisher of books dealing with library science and online information. So be sure to ask for the firm's catalog. For more information, contact:

>Knowledge Industry Publications, Inc.
>701 Westchester Avenue
>White Plains, NY 10604
>(800) 248-5474
>(914) 328-9157, in New York State

Computer-Readable Databases (Williams)

This directory is produced by M. E. Williams, Inc., in collaboration with the Information Retrieval Research Lab at the University of Illinois (Urbana-Champaign). Professor Martha Williams has been editor of the directory since its first edition in 1976. (That edition covered 301 databases; the current one covers over 3,000.)

The directory consists of two volumes. Volume I is subtitled "A Directory and Data Sourcebook—Science, Technology, Medicine." Volume II is subtitled "A Directory and Data Sourcebook—Business, Law, Social Science, Humanities." The price for the set is $160.

As noted, the entire directory is on DIALOG as File 230, where it is known as the Database of Databases. The directory is published in Europe by Elsevier Science Publishers and in North America by the American Library Association. For more information, contact:

>American Library Association
>50 East Huron Street
>Chicago, IL 60611
>(312) 944-6780

Magazines and Journals

There is no better way to place your fingers on the pulse of an industry than to subscribe to the magazines and journals devoted to covering it. At this writing there are at least seven publications that do just that. Within their pages you'll find discussions of issues that affect the online world, announcements of new information products, and in-depth database reviews and comparisons.

You may also find a sense of community of the sort that existed in the microcomputer world before the arrival of Big Money and Big Markets. Many of the people who started the information industry are still involved, often still at the helm of their original companies. And while the field certainly isn't small, it is still small enough for most members of the community to at least know who these leading figures are and what they have accomplished over the years. In short, while there are large organizations, the industry is still characterized by personalities, not faceless corporations.

The seven magazines likely to be of greatest interest to someone interested in the information industry can be roughly classified into three groups. At one end of the spectrum are *Online*, *Database*, and *Online Review*. These magazines are the field's scholarly journals. Most articles are written by librarians, searchers, and other information professionals, and most include a healthy helping of illustrative "tables" and "figures." These are the magazines to turn to if you want a professional's analysis of a new or existing database.

The next two publications might be considered the industry's trade journals. They are *Information Today* and *Database End-User*. *Information Today* is published in a tabloid-sized newspaper format. Issued monthly, it includes new product announcements, software reviews, and pieces on topics like CD-ROM, copyright, expert systems, and so on, written from a business perspective. In some respects, it fills the same role that *InfoWorld* fills in the microworld.

Edited by Barbara Quint, *Database Searcher* is one of the family of magazines produced by Meckler Publishing. (Other Meckler titles include "Bulletin Board Systems," "Videodisk and Optical Disk," "Small Computers in Libraries," and more.) Ms. Quint, a professional searcher of long experience, has confected a publication of news, reviews, commentary, and advice that is aimed at "the professional searcher and the searching professional." Articles about individual databases or vendors tend to be meaty without telling you more than you really want to know.

Finally, there are two magazines that are more or less aimed at the general public and at managers and professionals who do not have much search experience. These are *Link-Up* and *Online Access Guide*. Although it is published in tabloid format, *Link-Up* is printed on much better paper than a newspaper. This not only makes it more pleasant to handle, it also lets the publisher use color photos and four-color illustrations. The magazine covers the entire online field, including not only information retrieval but also bulletin boards, conferencing, electronic mail, and other topics. Perhaps the best quick handle on *Link-Up* is that it is to the online field what *Personal Computing* (and *Popular Computing*, before it folded) is to the microworld.

Online Access Guide covers similar material. However, it considers its audience to be made up largely of managers and professionals, and its coverage is more focused in that direction. Perhaps not surprisingly, in layout, tone, and illustration, *Online Access Guide* "feels" a lot like *Lotus*, a magazine aimed at the same group of readers.

Contact and subscription information for all seven magazines is listed below. As you will undoubtedly note, the subscription prices for some of them are rather high by commercial magazine standards. On the other hand, most carry very few ads and offer lots of information. Most of the publishers have brochures or sales literature they can send you if you need more information.

Database and *Online*

The publisher bills *Database* as "the online searcher's how-to-journal that specializes in in-depth coverage of selecting, using and creating databases." *Online* is "the practical journal that covers everything from new databases . . . to videodisks and CD-ROMs." However, it has been our experience that, while there is no overlap in coverage, it is hard to tell the two publications apart. Consequently, to make sure you don't miss anything, we suggest subscribing to both of them and taking advantage of the 20% discount offered for this choice.

Each is issued six times a year, and each carries a subscription price of $85 from the U.S. and Canada. A joint subscription is $136. Those are institutional rates. If you subscribe as a private individual, pay by check, and have issues mailed to your home; the cost is $42.50 per subscription ($85 for both). Online, Inc., will mail subscriptions virtually anywhere in the world, but rates vary with postage costs.

Note that Online, Inc., sponsors one of the two major industry conferences and exhibitions held each year. It's called ONLINE '87 (or whatever year is appropriate), and you may wish to ask for details. Contact:

Online, Inc.
11 Tannery Lane
Weston, CT 06883
(800) 824-7888, from the continental U.S.
(800) 824-7919, from Alaska or Hawaii; ask for operator 982
(203) 227-8466
Major credit cards accepted.

Database Searcher

Published monthly, a year's subscription is $37. However, if you are subscribing for personal use, pay by check and have issues sent to your home; the price is $24.50

> Meckler Publishing
> 11 Ferry Lane West
> Westport, CT 06880
> (203) 226-6967
> Major credit cards accepted.

Information Today and *Link-Up*

Both of these magazines are published by Learned Information, Inc. Both are monthlies, and both cost $22 a year for subscriptions in the U.S. and Canada. Prices for other countries vary with postage costs.

Learned Information, Inc., is also a publisher and distributor of books about information technology and the online field, and it sponsors the National Online Meeting, one of two major industry conferences and exhibitions held each year. You also might want to request a copy of the firm's free book catalog and more information on the conference. Contact:

> Learned Information, Inc.
> 143 Old Marlton Pike
> Medford, NJ 08055
> (609) 654-6266

> Learned Information Ltd.
> Besselsleigh Road
> Abingdon, Oxford OX13 6LG
> England

Online Access Guide

This is the newest kid on the block. So new that at this writing, the first issue has yet to be published. Based on the company's promotional materials, however, the magazine appears to have the potential to become a leader among the more popularly oriented publications in the field. *Online Access Guide* is scheduled to appear six times a year with a subscription price of between $19 and $25. For more information, contact:

Online Access Publishing Group, Inc.
53 West Jackson Blvd., Suite 1750
Chicago, IL 60604
(800) 922-9232
(312) 922-9292
Visa and MasterCard accepted

Online Review

This magazine began publication in March 1977. It's a bimonthly (six issues a year), and subscriptions are $78. Edited by Martha E. Williams, *Online Review* is probably the ultimate scholarly journal in the field. Also, it tends to devote more space to the international scene than the other publications. For more information, contact Learned Information, Inc., at the addresses given above.

ASIS and the National Online Circuit

There are many associations, societies, and users groups in the electronic universe, and as is the case in the microworld, they represent an invaluable resource. If you're new to the field and want to tap in, the American Society for Information Science (ASIS) and the National Online Circuit offer two of the best gateways.

ASIS is a nonprofit national and professional association "organized for scientific, literary, and educational purposes and dedicated to the creation, organization, dissemination, and application of knowledge concerning information and its transfer." Among its more than 4,000 members are managers, administrators, information science specialists, system analysts, professional searchers and information brokers, librarians, and students.

Membership includes the ASIS *Handbook and Directory* of members, subscriptions to the bimonthly "ASIS Bulletin," the bimonthly *ASIS Journal*, and the monthly "ASIS News." There are also member discounts on all ASIS publications (such as the above-mentioned KIPD database directory), reduced registration fees at the ASIS Annual and Mid-Year Meetings, free career counseling and career placement services, group insurance options, and more.

ASIS has about 25 local chapters in the U.S. and Canada, plus one in North Europe and one in Taipei, Taiwan. It also has some 23 special-interest groups devoted to topics like "Arts and Humanities," "International Information Issues," "Office Information Systems," and "Storage and Retrieval Technology."

A full year's membership is $75. A half-year membership is $50. Student memberships start at $20. For more information, contact:

ASIS
Suite 204
1424 16th Street, N.W.
Washington, D.C. 20036
(202) 462-1000
Visa and MasterCard accepted.

As in the personal computer world, online users groups tend to be largely volunteer organizations made up of people who have come together to exchange information, tips, and discoveries, to discuss issues and ideas, and to help solve each other's problems. Meetings are typically held once a month at a school, college, or company facility. A given group may also publish a newsletter.

Since a large percentage of user group members do online searching for a living, they are a vendor's or database producer's prime customers, and most of these companies manage to pay a visit to the leading user groups on a fairly regular basis, especially when they have a new product or service to introduce. This, too, closely parallels the personal computer world. Where the online groups part company with PC users groups is in the establishment of a national organization, the National Online Circuit (NOC).

The NOC is an umbrella organization that serves as a clearinghouse for user group information and as a focal point for groups across the country. A directory of member organizations is available for $10. To order a copy or to obtain more information, contact:

Mr. Bill Richardson
Santa Barbara Public Library
P.O. Box 1019
Santa Barbara, CA 93102

Index

Colbert, Antoinette W., 74–75
Columbus Dispatch, 321
Command Chart, 110
Commands. *See also under specific
    vendors and databases*
  chart of, 110
  eight crucial, 111–12
Commerce, Department of, 395, 404–5
Commerce Business Daily, 394–98
Commitment discounts, 44
"Common Carrier Week," 391
Communications costs, 44–46
Communications port (RS-232C), 17
Communications software, 16, 18–19,
    64, 129–30
  DIALOGLINK, 178–79, 188
  for NEXIS, 217–19
Compact DISClosure, 357
Companies, 339–45. *See also*
    Investment and competitive
    intelligence
*Complete Handbook of Personal
    Computer Communications,
    The* (Glossbrenner), 9, 16
CompuServe, 9, 53, 134, 326
  Work-at-Home Special Interest
    Group (SIG), 147
Comp-U-Store, 233
Computer Database, The, 287, 289
  online thesaurus for, 293–94
Computer Directions Advisors, 358
"Computer Market Observer," 391,
    413
Computer-Readable Databases
    (Williams), 456
Computer resource charge, 46–47
Computer Shopper, The, 17
Computer World, 299, 317
"Computing Today!," 413
"Congressional Activities," 435
Congressional Record, 416, 425–27
Congressional Record Abstracts,
    425–27
Connect-hour charges, 45, 47–48
Consultants. *See also* Information
    brokers
  biographies and resumes of, 336
"Consumer Electronics," 391, 413
Consumer Price Index (CPI), 26, 436,
    448–50
Consumer Reports, 304

"Consumer's Guide to Federal
    Publications," 417
Contemporary Architects, 338–40
Contemporary Artists, 338–40
Controlled vocabulary (thesaurus),
    28–29, 100, 260. *See also*
    Subject headings for The
    Computer Database, 293–94
Copyright Act of 1976, 77
Copyright Clearance Center (CCC),
    77–78
Copyright fees, 77–78
Corcoran, Maureen, 146
CORPORATE PROFILES, 359
Cost centers, billing by, 52
Costs. *See also* Discounts; *and under
    specific vendors*
  of database vendors, 44–45
  of manuals, 43, 44
  of subscriptions, 43, 44
  usage
    computer resource charge, 46–47
    connect-hour charges, 45, 47–48
    display charges, 46, 49–51
    downloading issue and, 54, 56
    for EasyNet, 136–37
    high-speed surcharge, 45, 47
    Key Question Checklist for, 82–83
    per search charges, 46
    prediction concerning, 53–54
    prime-time premium, 45–46
    print or offline print charges, 46
    as too high, 52–53
Coverage of databases, 24–25, 39–41,
    259
Cox Enterprises, 56
CPI (Consumer Price Index), 448–50
CPU time charge, 46–47
Crain's Cleveland Business, 290
Crawdaddy, 279
Credit information. *See also* Credit
    reports on privately held
    companies, 93
"Credit Market Analysis," 391
Credit reports, 247
  Dun & Bradstreet, 361–64
  TRW, 361
CROSS, 63, 94
Cross-file searching
  on NEXIS, 220–22
  on Wilsonline, 255–56

Index

About the Author

Alfred Glossbrenner is president of FireCrystal Communications, a worldwide producer of computer documentation, films, and corporate communications for industry and science. Based in Bucks County, Pennsylvania, FireCrystal and Mr. Glossbrenner make extensive use of personal computers, word processors, and a wide range of online electronic databases to pursue their goal of making today's high technology accessible, understandable, and above all, useful to everyone. Mr. Glossbrenner has written ten other books.

J. T. Miller

The author welcomes comments and suggestions about this book. They should be mailed to Alfred Glossbrenner, c/o St. Martin's Press, 175 Fifth Avenue, New York, NY 10010. Reader comments can also be sent to the author, via communicating computer, at the following electronic addresses:

Source: TCS772
CIS: 70065,745

670 Appendices, Glossary, Software Buyer's Quick Reference Checklists, Index.

$14.95 paperback

- A Main Selection of the Small Computer Book Club
- A Book-of-the-Month Club/Science Alternate Selection

"How to Buy Software is truly awesome. "I'm sure it will set the standard for some time to come. The whole concept and execution is just what is needed in the field."

—Tom Beeston
co-author of *Hooking In*

"If there was ever a computer book that will return its price many times over, this book is the one. . . . *How to Buy Software* brings together the latest information that every computer owner needs."

—*Interface Age*

"This book gets a rave review. It's an easy-to-grasp introduction to software, a fine buying guide for beginning users, and an excellent reference book for experienced users."

—*List* magazine

"The best book for finding out what personal computers can do for you and for tracking down the right software. I can affirm—not just hope—that this is the definitive software shopper's guide. For intelligence and thoroughness, no one else comes close."

—*Whole Earth Software Review*

Other Bestsellers by Alfred Glossbrenner . . .

546 pages, Resources, Glossary, Index.
$14.95 paperback

- A Main Selection of the Macmillan Small
  Computer Book Club
- A Book-of-the-Month Club/Science and Quality
  Paperback Book Club Alternate Selection

"An enjoyable book. Invaluable."
— Bert I. Helfinstein, president and C.E.O.,
Source Telecomputing Coporation (The Source)

"Alfred Glossbrenner is a master explainer. He really *does* deliver 'Everything You Need to Go Online with the World.'"
— Ardell Taylor Fleeson,
Graphnet, Inc.

"Fills an enormous void. Personal computer users are really hungry for this kind of information."
— Thomas B. Cross, director,
Cross Information Company

"Clear, well-written, packed with useful information—it's an absolute must for computer owners everywhere."
— Gary G. Reibsamen,
vice-president and general manager,
NewsNet, Inc.

"Not only is Glossbrenner's the best book to use with a personal computer, it may be the best reason to *buy* one."

—Davis Elias, Inc.,
newsletter to investors

"Unequivocally the most informative and best-written I have ever seen."

—Norman Burnell, president,
Electronic Safety Products, Inc.

To order these books, please use the coupon below.

Books are available in quantity for promotional or premium use. Write to Director of Special Sales, Patti Hughes, St. Martin's Press, 175 Fifth Avenue, New York, NY 10010, for information on discounts and terms, or call toll-free (800) 221-7945. In New York, call (212) 674-5151.

St. Martin's Press, Inc./Cash Sales Department/175 Fifth Avenue/ New York, NY 10010

Please send me____copy(ies) of THE COMPLETE HANDBOOK OF PERSONAL COMPUTER COMMUNICATIONS @ $14.95 each*

____copy(ies) of HOW TO BUY SOFTWARE @ $14.95 each*

____copy(ies) of HOW TO GET *FREE* SOFTWARE @ $14.95 each*

*Plus $1.50 postage and handling for the first book and 50¢ per copy for each additional book

I enclose a check or money order for $_____

_____

Name

_____

Address

_____

City   State   Zip

Return coupon with check to:
St. Martin's Press, Inc./Cash Sales Dept./175 Fifth Avenue/New York, NY 10010